G000279017

MORE
LIVES
THAN
ONE

THE EXTRAORDINARY LIFE OF

FELIX DENNIS

FERGUS
BYRNE

EBURY
PRESS

1 3 5 7 9 10 8 6 4 2

Ebury Press, an imprint of Ebury Publishing
20 Vauxhall Bridge Road
London SW1V 2SA

Ebury Press is part of the Penguin Random House group of companies
whose addresses can be found at global.penguinrandomhouse.com

Penguin
Random House
UK

First published by Ebury Press in 2015

www.eburypublishing.co.uk

A CIP catalogue record for this book is available from the British Library

ISBN 9780091959685

Printed and bound in Great Britain by Clays Ltd, St Ives PLC

Penguin Random House is committed to a sustainable future
for our business, our readers and our planet. This book is made
from Forest Stewardship Council® certified paper.

To the five girls in my life:
Victoria, Ismay, Tara, Isla and Hebe.

CONTENTS

PART THREE: TAKEN AT THE FLOOD

FOREWORD

On 28 June 2013, I answered the phone in my office in Dorset and a voice said, 'This is Catherine from Felix Dennis's office in Dorsington. Felix would like to speak to you, if you have a moment.' I had recently written an article about him and desperately racked my brain to figure out whether I had said anything that might have bothered him or, God forbid, incurred his wrath.

'Of course I'd be delighted to speak to Felix,' I said, my voice an octave higher than normal. Thankfully, nobody noticed when I followed that up with a breathless and cheery 'Hi, Felix' to what turned out to be a recording of him reading his poetry. As Lord Heseltine was to tell me many months later, Felix was a master of the art of self-promotion and time spent on hold was simply a sales opportunity.

My first real introduction to Felix Dennis had been through poetry when I read his poetry book *A Glass Half Full* in 2002, so both watching him perform and listening to him recite his poems was not a hardship. As the on-hold recording thundered, 'I remember we did it again and again, and we screamed...' the voice of his long-time PA, Caroline Rush, cut in to tell me that he was just finishing something up and would be with me shortly.

Small talk was never Felix Dennis's forte, so when he came on the line he quickly got to the point. 'I enjoyed your article,' he said. 'How would you feel about writing my biography?' I knew him well enough to know this wasn't a time for procrastination but one question did leap into my head. 'I'd love to,' I said, 'but you have always said you wouldn't do a biography whilst your mother was alive.' With little hesitation he replied sharply, 'Well, she doesn't really know what's going on these days.' It was a statement imbued with an edgy sadness, along with what I later learned was more than a hint of frustration.

From that moment on, my life was to change dramatically, though not quite so dramatically as his. A little less than a year later, I found myself gazing down at a hole in the ground in the middle of a peaceful wood that he had planted near his home in Warwickshire. Carefully lowered by friends and colleagues, his wicker coffin was already spotted by lumps of earth and flowers dropped by those offering a final memento of their affection. A carefully folded handwritten note had slid to one side of the casket and, as the group of friends and colleagues began to walk away, it was hard not to wonder which of the many, many people whose lives he had touched had left him that particular final message – and what it may have said.

Shortly after we had begun talking about his extraordinary life, Felix was diagnosed with inoperable lung cancer and what started out as a ramble through the peaks and valleys of a life lived with gusto and zeal quickly changed and took a new direction. Prior to his diagnosis, we had joked about the fact that one book could never really tell the full story of his life. It turned out that, many years before, he had thought about producing an autobiography and had even toyed with names for different volumes. They were to be what he called a 'Shakespearean trilogy' and would be named *A Green-Backed Penguin*, *The Glory Years* and *Taken at the Flood*. However, on learning that his time was limited, he had decided to do what he did best; he elected to focus on the people and the legacy that would be left behind, while adding to that with an intensity that was as fierce as it was forensic.

Nobody close to him, he explained, would be happy with any description of his life, whether written by him or anyone else. But the purpose of telling his story was not to make anyone happy, he saw it simply as social history and a chance to leave a mark on the world that readers might learn from. What they might conclude and learn would be up to them, he said: 'A man's life is simply that – a life, nothing more, nothing less.' We could only learn from our own interpretation of how a life was lived and what it achieved. He had therefore decided to concentrate on distilling his own final thoughts into lines of verse.

Reflections during a time of impending death bring an honesty and introspection that isn't available to everyone, but watching Felix Dennis go through a process of raw, yet calculated analysis for the purposes of recording his findings in verse was as bewildering and at times astonishing as the life he had led. What made that life even more extraordinary was the fact that it shouldn't have been so, for his background wasn't one of privilege. His grandmother, Gladys Coller, the illegitimate daughter of a young girl in service, helped instil a fighting spirit into Felix's mother Dorothy, while his father, Reg Dennis, descended from a steel-cutter, who was himself descended from a man who had spent 47 years of his life in a mental asylum, left Felix with few memories, but it left him with a strong sense that he could and must do better – and he did.

To say he lived more than one life is not an exaggeration. Eventually owning estates in England and Mustique, as well as property in New York and Connecticut, he inhabited a lifestyle that, on the surface, looked charmed. But few lives painted by the broad brush strokes of a press hungry for bare skin and torn morals are what they seem. Felix shouldered notoriety first as a defendant in the 1971 *Oz* trial, when in the longest conspiracy trial in British history he was accused of conspiring to corrupt public morals by publishing an issue of the underground magazine *Oz* that was deemed obscene, and then later as a crack cocaine addict, whose excesses surpassed those of many more notorious than he. He often described his life as a sustained series of unlikely events. These included recording a chart single with John Lennon, co-authoring a biography of Muhammad Ali and becoming one of the most successful entrepreneurs of his generation.

Endlessly crossing the Atlantic, over 250 of those trips on Concorde, he created two distinct business lives in two very different commercial climates. His vision and fearlessness changed the face of the publishing industry in both the UK and North America. He quickly became known as a maverick, bringing a hint of sixties idealism to a suited world of hard-nosed commerce. When offered the starring role in the BBC's *The Apprentice*, he turned it down on the basis that he didn't like the idea of having to fire people all the time but he never hid his veneer of steel when it came to closing a deal.

None of those close to him saw a difference in his character from one life to the next, even during the almost 20 years that he took on a somewhat Godfatherly role as the go-to man on the island of Mustique in the Caribbean. He had bought David Bowie's house and gradually turned it into a lavish estate, eventually becoming close friends with the Prime Minister of St Vincent and the Grenadines, Dr The Honourable Ralph E. Gonsalves. Nor was there any noticeable change when he wrote an international bestseller for entrepreneurs, or even when he decided to found a new charity to plant the largest native broadleaf forest in the heart of England.

Perhaps most surprisingly, there wasn't one person close to him who saw a change in his personality when he was suddenly overcome by a compulsion to write poetry – despite entreaties from friends and colleagues not to. To most of those who knew him, every avenue and every turn of his life was simply 'Felixness'.

As I sat across the table from him in a cottage on his estate in Mustique in January 2014, I saw one man, not the multiple personalities that some observers had reported over the years. However, it was a man still driven and focused yet also tortured by a burden of wisdom and the frustration of helplessness.

He laughed. Behind him the sun slowly edged its way around to Britannia Bay and a hummingbird darted between the wildflowers. A red-footed tortoise ambled across a well-tended lawn. Surrounded by such an earthly spectacle of beauty and tranquillity, Felix was remarkably cheerful for a man aware that, for him, time was fast running out. He asked me to photograph him beside a sign on his door advising visitors to 'Please Go Away' and chuckled as he recited the opening verse of a poem he had written a few weeks before. It was about the slow deterioration of his body. 'Masturbation,' he said, presented 'no problems', and with a bellow of laughter he went on to recite, 'although I have little call or energy to work the thing at all'. The poem was called 'Many Parts are Functioning Normally' and offered a classic mixture of his wit and hard-won sensibility but mostly represented a man still searching, wondering and learning. It finished with a line that he admitted had a touch more bravado than he was comfortable with, suggesting that, thanks to the genes from his mother's family, he would fight for life 'though armed with just a feather, a quill to spill my guts from deep within'.

Although he had written those lines, there was still a part of him that didn't really accept or believe in his fate. Felix was a great believer in chance and at the back of his mind there was always one more spin of the wheel.

The remarkable truth about the many lives of Felix Dennis is the fact that he inhabited each and every one of them with a focus, a vision and a gung-ho verve that left little room for down time or negativity – it was filled with opportunity. His philosophy was to go forward at full tilt, to just do it and apologise later. As John Lagana, his good friend and chairman of his US company, put it, 'Felix was never afraid to roll the dice.'

Fergus Byrne, 2015

PART ONE

A GREEN-BACKED PENGUIN

CHAPTER 1

DADDY WE MISS YOU

Despite giving many hundreds of TV, radio and print interviews, there was one story that Felix Dennis simply couldn't be completely honest about – at least not while his mother was alive. In later years, he occasionally hinted at the truth about his father, but when it came to talking about him, he usually presented a story that wasn't entirely accurate. Felix was doggedly unsentimental about him and was also adamant that there were few similarities between them. But how much of that lack of sentimentality was because his dad left the family home and emigrated to Australia when Felix was just four years old, or whether it was the result of loyalty to his mother is hard to determine. Some believed the lack of affection was a natural trait in Felix's character. It would be very much later in his life before he was to admit that the story that he had trotted out for so many people simply wasn't true. And although there certainly were similarities between the two, Felix was never to admit it.

His father, Reginald Dennis, never returned to England, and Felix, despite having discovered his whereabouts, never visited Australia to see him. They did not communicate and, as befits a tragic story, Reginald died young in 1980. His death was attributed to a fall in hospital while being treated for alcoholic dementia. It was at a time when his son was on his way to becoming hugely successful. It's probably fair to say that, although Felix was surrounded by Australians, some of whom had returned to Australia and even offered him work there, the period of his life between 1970 and 1980 was one of highs and lows, both on a business and personal level.

With his signature attitude, he claimed that he simply had no interest whatsoever in seeing his father.

Born at the end of the First World War in south London, Reginald Claude Albert Dennis was the eldest of four children born over a spread of 15 years. Reg was admired and loved by his younger siblings but, in the way that only immediate family can really appreciate, he was also fondly remembered for being a bit of a tearaway.

His youngest brother Tony, a national hunt jockey for 40 years, remembered a wild, brave and fearless older brother. However, Tony was 15 years younger than Reg, who was away at war and then left for Australia when his younger sibling was just 16 years old. Many of Tony's memories are vague but one incident was not only firmly imprinted in his memory but also left quite a few physical marks at the time.

Reg had taken Tony out for the day, and they set off to play by a railway line. The age difference meant that Reg was really playing a babysitting role, letting his mother have a bit of down time from dealing with a growing family. At one point, the boys had climbed onto a bridge and found themselves trapped as a train suddenly appeared around the corner. There wasn't time to run to safety, so Reg ordered Tony to jump into the river. It was a 40-foot drop and Tony froze. Assuming his little brother would jump with him, Reg took the dive to safety only to find Tony hadn't done so. The train, spewing steam and sounding its whistle, thundered past and for a moment, coming up for air and splashing about in the river, Reg was convinced his brother had perished. Tony had survived but had taken one hell of a pounding as the locomotive steamed past. His cuts and bruises were only discovered by his mother days later when he was heard moaning in the bath. He was just as afraid of telling his mother and getting a telling-off as he was of getting his big brother into trouble.

Another family legend describes how Reg fell foul of one of the great fairground attractions of the time, the boxing booth. The booth usually consisted of a brightly coloured hoarding with photographs and colourful drawings of boxers. Behind the hoarding was a tent containing a makeshift boxing ring, with a semi-professional boxer ready to take on all comers.

Successful challengers might get a piece of the takings or even a bit of the gambling money, but pride was the main currency at stake. Being 'handy' with his fists, Reg fancied his chances. The story goes that he didn't necessarily do as well as he had hoped, but kept coming back to try his luck again and again. In the end, after he arrived home with a thundering black eye, his mother stormed down to the fairground to pay off the promoter and make sure her son wasn't allowed to fight any more. Reg's mother Hilda was a formidable woman, who was not to be crossed.

This may have curtailed his boxing-booth antics, but it didn't stop Reg from proving himself with his fists. He was a scrapper, who was unafraid to make his point of view clear, regardless of the consequences. Although fisticuffs may not have been Felix's style, he was certainly to take on aspects of his father's forcefulness. Felix's uncle Tony also remembers how Reg, and his future brother-in-law, Cecil 'Sonny' Coller, would go out for a night on the town, often with the sole intent of getting into a fight – something Reg's poor younger brother Gordon, a mild-mannered hairdresser – found difficult when he was caught up on the periphery.

Another aspect of Reg's character that Felix inherited was a love of music. Initially a drummer – which Felix was later to become – Reg was also a highly regarded piano player, much in demand. Growing up listening to jazz and swing, Reg would have been just as likely to play Count Basie, boogie woogie or even 'Let's Gather Round the Old Piano' with principal singer Betty Driver, as he was to play classical pieces. Whatever the music, Reg could always be relied on to get the party going. Generally he made a beeline for the piano wherever he went and there were times when his popularity on a night out caused friction with his wife, Dorothy.

'You have 'im all week, let us have 'im for one night at least,' his brother-in-law, Cecil, would say.

Reg's second wife, Pam Allery, suggested that he got a fondness for alcohol in those early days when he was encouraged to jolly up the party with a few tunes and was rewarded with free drink.

Just 19 years old when Germany invaded Poland to start the Second World War, Reg experienced the horror of the sight of German bombers in the skies over London in 1940. On a beautiful sunny September afternoon, with thousands of Londoners enjoying the late summer heat, Hitler sent 348 bombers supported by 617 fighter planes to begin an intense bombing campaign that went on for nearly nine months.

Ernie Pyle, one of Britain's most popular war correspondents, remembered the thrill that he and a couple of the other young boys experienced after the attack had begun.

'Half an hour after the firing started, I gathered a couple of friends and went to a high, darkened balcony that gave us a view of a third of the entire circle of London. As we stepped out onto the balcony, a vast inner excitement came over all of us – an excitement that had neither fear nor horror in it, because it was all too full of awe.'

London was burning and for young boys, like Reg's brother Gordon, who was 16 during the Blitz, it was full of exciting noises: explosions, the crackle of guns and burning debris, screaming fire engines and air raid sirens. Adrenaline was high and people rushed for shelter beneath railway arches, warehouses and the London Underground. Fire crews came from as far as Oxford to help fight the raging blazes, passing hundreds of people fleeing to the suburbs to escape the chaos. Identifying sounds became a pastime as people tried to determine whether a bomb was headed directly towards them or would hopefully land in another street. Youngsters quickly learned to tell the difference between the sound of a German Messerschmitt and an RAF Spitfire. Those on the cusp of manhood excitedly talked of joining the services, eager to get into the scrap, and in many cases driven by a need to fight an invisible enemy that was turning their lives to carnage.

By the middle of the summer of 1941, Reg had signed up for the RAF and was shipped to Blackpool, where he quickly qualified as a wireless operator and air gunner with the rank of second-class aircraftman. Although he finished the war with the rank of warrant officer, his time was mostly spent in exotic places, far from his family and the rapidly deteriorating morale in London.

He was first stationed in Ceylon and his service record shows a busy time in search-and-rescue, as well as supply missions. However, during that period, and probably in between time spent in various Operational Training Units, Reg had one particularly important mission – a proposal of marriage to Dorothy Coller, also from his hometown of Surbiton.

Dorothy Grace Coller was born in Queen Charlotte's Hospital in Marylebone on 15 September 1919. She was the daughter of William Sidney Coller, a mechanical engineer who worked at Surbiton Waterworks. Like her grandfather, Alfred Coller, who received a medal for his involvement in the New Zealand 'Maori' wars, Dorothy's father also joined the services. He had served in the First World War as a private in Her Majesty's Army. Dorothy's mother, Gladys Carpenter, was the illegitimate daughter of Louisa Charlotte Carpenter, a domestic servant born in Warminster. On her marriage certificate, Gladys had named John Foley, a traveller, as her father.

Reg and Dorothy had met at the local fairground when he became friends with her brother Cecil. Both he and Cecil had their fair share of adventures and scrapes while Dorothy tagged along. She and Reg married in 1942 when they were both 22, Reg describing himself as a wireless operator and Dorothy as a spinster. The wedding was at St Matthew's parish church, Surbiton and the reception for family and friends was at a nearby pub, the Toby Jug. Tony Dennis remembered being a page boy and his sister Grace was a bridesmaid. Grace had fond memories of her brother proudly wearing his uniform.

After their wedding, the couple lived in Grove Close, Kingston upon Thames. Reg returned from war and was given an honourable discharge in 1946.

Their first son, Felix, was born just after midnight in Queen's Road nursing home on 27 May 1947. Soon afterwards, Reg and Dorothy moved to Hampton Road in Twickenham, where they opened a grocery and general provisions shop. To buy the shop they had been helped financially by Reg's parents and Tony fondly remembered early morning trips to Covent Garden to buy fresh produce. The shop was a long, corridor-style room with goods on shelves opposite a long counter. Reg's sister Grace remembers its mustard and coffee smell. The family lived above the shop and there were rooms at the back, where the children would play. Dorothy was always 'immaculately dressed' and 'very proper'.

For shop owners like Reg it was a long day – collecting stock, stacking shelves, greeting customers and running the shop. Grace remembered how impressed she was by his ability to tot up the figures in the accounts book he kept on the long counter. It was 'brain power' he would say to her. She also remembered Felix in the background as an 'affectionate' and 'bubbly kid'.

Combining two quick minds and a shared accounting ability, Reg and Dorothy should surely have been expected to grow a successful business in what were initially hopeful post-war years. However, the reality of their lives was an atmosphere of austerity, with rationing still part of daily life, and the shop did not prosper.

On 30 July 1949, Dorothy gave birth to her second son, Julian, at Twickenham Road, Isleworth. By then, Reg gave his profession as master grocer.

By the time Julian was born, Reg and Dorothy had fallen out with the rest of the Dennis family over the money needed to keep their shop afloat, and consequently neither Felix nor Julian had any memories of their Dennis grandparents, Albert and Hilda. Reg's sister, Grace, who was actually an adopted niece, remembered how devastated her mother was at never seeing her grandchildren. Grace blamed the whole affair for the stroke that her mother suffered at the time and also claimed that the 'family trouble' contributed to the death of her father Albert, who died around the same time.

Working in the shop and dealing with financial difficulties that had ripped the family apart, Reg became increasingly despondent. He had returned to England a war hero. For six years before he had lived a life that could not have been more at odds with that of a shopkeeper: flying countless adrenaline-filled missions over enemy lines, more often than not swooping dangerously low in search of drop zones. He had been hospitalised twice, shot down and captured; he also spent seven days in the sea, and, like many of his colleagues, he had contracted malaria. After the excitement of battle and the camaraderie brought about by shared danger, life in suburban England was very hard to cope with. Against a backdrop of the launch of the Festival of Britain, a colourful national exhibition organised by the British Government to cheer up the country in the aftermath of war, Reg made plans to leave and seek a better life for his family. As Winston Churchill prepared for a general election that would put him back in power after six years in opposition, Reg said goodbye to his wife and two boys and sailed to Australia on the RMS *Oronsay*, arriving in Melbourne in September 1951.

The Australian immigration scheme at the time was such that, to get work there, one had to be sponsored by another family, and, as it happened, the Dennises' old next-door neighbours, the Allerys, had already emigrated and offered to sponsor Reg to come to Australia to make a new start. In a letter thanking them for sponsoring him, Reg explained that life in England was pretty miserable and that many people were finding it tough. A recent budget, he told them, had increased taxes, and the constant rain was likely to devastate future crops. He explained that he and Dorothy were very busy, what with bringing up the two boys and running a business full time. They were on the go about 14 hours a day, he said, but he was looking forward to new beginnings.

'I can't tell you how happy I shall be to get a fresh start out there and how much I want to get Dorothy away from this endless slaving day after day,' he wrote.

Sadly, his dream of a new start for himself and his family in Australia never came to fruition as Dorothy and the children did not follow him. Instead, while Reg struggled to build a new life on the other side of the world, Dorothy sold the business in Twickenham, and after 11 years of her raising the two boys on her own, the pair divorced and she eventually married an old friend named David Sawyer in December 1962.

Reg also married again, to Pam Allery (the daughter of the family who had sponsored his move to Australia), but he never really overcame the trauma of trying to cope after the war. He had fallen out with his parents and siblings and was then cut off from his wife and children. Slowly, he descended into an alcoholic oblivion, which his new wife Pam was helpless to prevent or to treat. Theirs was a turbulent marriage, with good times and bad. At one point Reg was holding down a full-time job and they ran an import business on the side. When that failed, his drinking coincided with Pam having psychiatric problems. She was admitted to hospital and, when

Reg came to take her out, he himself was admitted instead. At one point he moved out of the family home to live in a hotel where, as Pam put it, drink was 'on tap'. A voracious reader, a habit that his son Felix was to inherit, Reg was told by one hospital that he was going blind and would never be able to read again. Pam proceeded to get him some new glasses and gave him a copy of the Bible, along with some Enid Blyton books.

Reg died on 17 November 1980, and, although they had separated, Pam nursed him to the end. She returned to England to fulfil Reg's wish to have his ashes scattered on British soil. After scattering most of them in a cemetery she took the rest (what she had determined were his hands) and sat at a table in the Palm Court in what she remembered as the Regent Hotel in London, where before the war Reg had played the piano. She ordered lobster thermidor and, while no one was looking, deposited the last of Reginald Claude Albert Dennis into a potted palm next to the table.

For Pamela Allery that was the end of an unsettled journey and a fitting finale to her life with the jazz-playing father of the future chairman of Dennis Publishing.

Remembering that he 'used to play the piano divinely', she said, 'How do I know they were his hands? How do you know they weren't?'

Felix insisted that his and Julian's upbringing was happy and normal and claimed they weren't really affected by the sudden disappearance of their father. Later in life he was to receive a copy of a note he had sent to Australia saying, 'Daddy we miss you', but he dismissed this as something that would have been expected of any child in that situation.

Doris Dench had played the role of nanny to young Felix and baby Julian while Dorothy helped Reg in the shop. Many years later, sitting in an apartment in New York, Felix wrote to Mrs Dench to thank her for the kindness she had shown to the two boys at what was obviously a difficult stage of their lives. He enclosed a cheque begging her not to think of it as charity but as a gift in thanks for her kindness. In family photographs, she had been referred to as 'Auntie Dench'. Felix could remember playing for hours with her husband's peaked railway cap and whistle, and listening to

Children's Hour and *Listen with Mother* on her radio. He told Mrs Dench that he believed he had inherited 'the strong resolution' of his mother and grandmother, together with some of the 'creative (and slightly unstable) characteristics' of his father. For the rest of his life he was to interpret his mother's indifference towards his father as anger at his leaving the family.

Julian's early memories simply highlight for him how different the two boys were. However, he also remembered Felix occasionally playing the role of big brother and trying to look after him. They quickly found friends of their own but would sometimes play together at a local playground, and Julian remembered at least two occasions when Felix had to come to his rescue after nasty accidents. Once, when Julian went headfirst down a slide with particularly bloody consequences, Felix rushed to the door of a nearby house and pleaded with an elderly lady for help. Another time, when Felix had been the cause of the accident – a swing hitting Julian square on the chin and nearly knocking him out – with a maturity beyond his years, Felix managed to flag down a passing taxi and, with an early indication of his persuasive abilities, convince the driver to take the two boys home free of charge.

Like many small boys they argued constantly, or so it seemed to their mother. They also wrestled, with Felix usually getting the upper hand. However, Julian remembered this coming to an abrupt end when he decided to punch Felix on the nose.

'I'd just joined the school boxing team,' he remembered. 'I was very small and I was being bullied a lot, but always used to fight back. I was always taught to fight back. And I remember he put me in this wrestling hold and I got out of it and punched him on the nose. And he immediately ran to the mirror and said, "What have you done? You've broken my nose" because there was blood pouring out of it. Fortunately I didn't break it but he never, ever came near me again.'

Felix was later to claim that Julian 'used to beat the shit out of me'. When it came to size, his younger brother had outgrown him, though not by much.

Born with a lazy eye, or 'boss-eyed' as he later described it, Felix was prescribed glasses at an early age. Because one eye had a slight squint he was also given a patch, which according to Julian helped straighten the eye. His big spectacles with thick lenses were often the cause of teasing and bullying in school. In later life, Julian worked as a lens maker and the powerful prescription for his brother's glasses was never forgotten. He also remembered how his big brother had an unusual habit of knocking things over, such as ink on carpets or milk on the kitchen table, usually eliciting shrieks from his fraught mother.

Despite their battles, Felix and Julian had a family bond and later in life Felix was to bring him closer to his business and other projects. But although he said they weren't close as kids, Julian was always aware that his brother was different.

'It was almost like from day one he was on a mission,' he recalled. 'He'd have a faraway look in his eye and always be skirting the edges, looking for something that was completely different, that other people wouldn't do or wouldn't say or wouldn't see.'

CHAPTER 2

SNOGGING THE BRIDE

The transition from little boy to teenager and then to young man was adventurous for Felix as the fifties moved into the sixties, and for his mother that meant many challenges. Having gone back to work after selling the shop, Dorothy was not only busy looking after naturally boisterous boys as well as trying to hold down a job, but she was also dealing with an older son whose individuality and strength of character were becoming very apparent. While still quite young, Felix's dominant and abrasive nature clashed with his mother's similar attributes. He also showed unusual and wayward traits that, had he been born 30 years later, might have had him hauled to a paediatrician for assessment and educational intervention. But life was different then. Intervention from the school more often than not took the form of a caning, and parents were rarely included in disciplinary action.

Working as a bookkeeper for a local builder and studying to become a chartered accountant, Dorothy had to find a way to keep the children busy in the summer holidays and so she sent them to board with a lady named Mrs Monk, who lived in a small three-bedroom terraced house in Siverst Close in Northolt. It was a perfect arrangement for Mrs Monk: suffering from arthritis and unable to work, she would take in lodgers to help pay the rent.

Maureen Hadley, whose garden backed onto the close, remembered the first time she met Felix and Julian. Siverst Close was a cul-de-sac with a small patch of grass in the middle, where the local children would congregate and play. She remembered one day looking out of her window and seeing two boys she hadn't seen before. They were particularly noisy, with grubby knees and excited faces, she recalled. Seeing her looking out of her window, one of them motioned and shouted for her to come out and join them. As she had finished the chores set by her mother, off she went. In what was to become a trademark ability to attract women to him, by the end of that morning Felix had made one of his first conquests. Although it wasn't sexual ('My balls hadn't dropped by then,' he later admitted), the relationship was an early marker of his burgeoning interest and eventual fascination, if not obsession, with the opposite sex.

Maureen remembered how, when the other children from nearby houses had joined them, they played the usual games such as hopscotch, tennis and kiss chase, during which 'Felix gave me my first kiss, which I have never forgotten,' she said. As Felix was 11 years old and Maureen only nine, it was a pretty innocent relationship and Maureen remembered him as more of a big brother, great friend and boyfriend all rolled into one. However, over the years their bond grew, and, although it remained platonic, their friendship revealed a young man with a strong morality, loyalty and respect for his friends. Later in his life there were to be times when Felix would get a reputation for having a travelling harem, but initially, and for the most part, he showed a deep respect and enjoyment of female companionship.

Maureen also remembered how she would have tantrums that Felix would put up with and he would always be able to tease her out of them. Occasionally he would be the cause of the hurt, as when he called her 'Charlie's sister' because she was so thin – Charlie was the nickname they had given the school skeleton. Either way, regardless of where the insult or unhappiness came from, Felix was always able to make her laugh and would gently extract the source of the pain. He was an attentive boyfriend and even more than half a century later, sitting in his study at the Old Manor in Dorsington, he could remember what really mattered to a young boy.

'She was a wonderful girl,' he said of Maureen, 'very pretty, very bubbly and vivacious. And I was at an age where you didn't care if they had never heard of Hemingway.'

While it may be that these were idyllic summers, for Felix's mother Dorothy there were difficulties. Julian remembered Felix acting older than his years and showing off his knowledge of how things worked. Felix also remembered taking on the role of the alpha male. Growing up without a man in the house had helped shape his personality and no doubt ensured that he matured more quickly than many of his contemporaries. He would be the one to take spiders out of the bath, fetch coal for the fire or change a light bulb, when necessary. It was a process that, coupled with his natural intellect and growing confidence, inevitably gave rise to occasional conflict, even if at times on a relatively innocuous level.

Maureen recalled an occasion when one neighbour, whose husband worked nights, complained of the noise the children made in the street. Felix eloquently and rather aggressively for a boy of his age argued the case for the children's right to be there as much as anyone else. As Maureen remembered Felix 'not rudely' stuck to his guns and the argument went on for some time. In those days he did, however, always appear to show great respect for his mother – remembered by Maureen as a 'cultured lady' with a 'quiet authority'.

In 1958, after receiving extra tuition at the Surbiton house of a Professor Goddard, to his own great surprise Felix passed his 11 Plus and began attending Surbiton County Grammar School, where he remembered going to rugby practice by bus. He hated his time there, especially the Latin, and was expelled for non-attendance. Maureen recalled the move well as it affected the amount of time Felix spent with her. He would come to visit every Sunday, buying a return ticket from West Ruislip to Northolt. While Maureen and her sister practised their piano, Felix waited patiently in the sitting room. They would play chess or go for long walks and Maureen sweetly kept the chess pieces all through her later life. She only remembered beating him once and was so excited she jumped around the room, to the great consternation of her mother, even though she admitted that he had probably let her win. Sometimes the family would picnic at Hampton Court or Richmond and Felix would always be invited. The Isabella Plantation, another favoured picnic location, was an early influence on Felix's future love of trees.

As Felix moved into his teens there was a new person in his and Julian's lives – someone whom Julian accepted happily, but Felix did not. Dorothy had started a relationship with a man named David Sawyer. A gentle giant, 14 years older than she, Sawyer was an engineer who lived in West Molesey. He had been a friend of the family for many years, appearing in family outings as far back as 1952, just after Reg had gone to Australia. Unaware that his father had recently remarried and insisting afterwards that it was irrelevant anyway, Felix naturally didn't take to David's new status and the possible upheaval it might cause. As he remembered it, he was the man around the house and so he showed his displeasure mostly through rows with his mother. On one memorable occasion Felix huffed and puffed and stormed out the door, saying he was leaving home forever.

'Yes, of course you can, dear,' said his mother. 'But not in those clothes.'

'What do you mean?' stuttered Felix, momentarily distracted from his tantrum.

'I paid for them,' she replied. 'You can leave but you're not taking any of the clothes.'

Dorothy was one of the few people who could completely snooker Felix.

After moving to West Ruislip and leaving Surbiton Grammar School, Felix started at St Nicholas Grammar School in Northwood Hills. If Dorothy had hoped a fresh start would help her wayward son to settle down, she was to be disappointed. Felix immediately fell foul of whatever authority was thrust upon him.

'I don't think the transfer did me any good,' he would later say. 'I was an idle student. I didn't want to learn from teachers, I wasn't interested. I was truly an independent spirit and always in trouble, just endless trouble – couldn't be bothered. If I had to get myself out of trouble, I'd use my wits and I could learn very quickly and then the teacher would forget about me because I'd obviously reformed, and it was all complete bullshit.'

He was later to describe his teachers from those years as 'terrifically damaged goods'. From his point of view there were many that came back from the war who should not have been allowed in contact with the public, let alone children. As far as he could see, 'Every guy that came back from the war that wasn't an outright murderer just became a teacher. Anyone that behaved the way that those teachers behaved, anyone that behaved like that today, would go straight to prison,' he insisted.

As is often the case there were individual teachers who stood out. Felix would later write a poem about his English teacher, whom they called 'Abdul Rowe', mainly because he had a beard. Rowe was, he recalled, the first one to tell him that he had a natural gift for writing. Many years later, after he had made a substantial sum as well as having successfully published a few books, Felix wrote to one of his classmates to see if he could track down the teacher, whom he heard had become blind. He wanted to see if he could help him. Sadly he never was able to find him.

Another early influence on Felix's life, head of tutor and popular art teacher Brian Tilbrook remembered keeping an eye on him during what he called 'three mildly troubled years'. Felix was not popular with the head teacher, Mr Watson, and was quickly in danger of being expelled.

'At the end of each year, at a review meeting with the staff, I would defend Felix's right to his place at the school, dismiss his apparent slacking and gain for him another year of assessment and hope,' Tilbrook remembered. However, at the end of that third year, having taken the whole form, all 30 boys, to the cinema for a treat, Brian Tilbrook left to visit Malaysia on a two-year secondment. When he returned, Felix was gone.

'Waiting until I was away, the headmaster had sorted out those he saw wasting time, and in his opinion, Felix was a prime candidate,' he explained.

Brian remembered Felix as being helpful and enthusiastic, especially when it came to organising the school fair. No doubt most boys would be eager to help with this sort of activity instead of schoolwork, but Felix apparently attacked it with gusto. Brian remembered borrowing a life-sized knight on horseback from a nearby art school and carefully placing it on a trailer to tow around the local area, hoping to draw attention to the upcoming fair. Felix sat in the passenger seat, pretending to be a racing driver, and, according to Brian, gave the impression that he was going much faster than the actual driver. As it happened he may have learned of some of the dangers of being in charge of a motor vehicle during that promotional trip, when Brian, misjudging the height of a bridge, decapitated the knight on the trailer and sheared off his proudly held stave.

David Wallbank, who was to become part of a band that Felix first got involved with in St Nicholas Grammar School, remembered that, apart from being very literate and the twist champion at the local youth club where they used to hang out, Felix was already quite the ladies' man.

'Felix always had the best-looking girlfriends,' he said. 'He never had a problem getting girlfriends at all. Most of the people at the youth club had what you might call long-term relationships. Not Felix. He always had lots of different girlfriends and probably more than one at a time, running three or four girls at a time. Sexually precocious, I think.'

One of the things that Felix became known for later in life was his ability to keep in touch with many of those he met along the way and St Nicholas Grammar School cultivated a few strong friendships that endured and produced more than a few adventures. Peter Quesnel was one of those with whom Felix tussled in the early days. Peter remembered that Felix very quickly showed a 'powerful personality' and had to stick up for himself because he was smaller than many of his peers. He also remembered that Felix often got into scrapes because of his argumentative nature. In Peter's case, a game of chess started a disagreement that was to become a foundation stone of their friendship.

'I don't remember who was the accuser and who was the accused,' Peter said. 'Suffice it to say, a row developed, and it turned physical and the two of us started fighting. We fought, not punching each other but wrestling and trying to get supremacy, and we fought our way out of that classroom, down the corridor and in and out of some other classrooms. It was a real needle match, you know, we really meant it, and nobody was getting the better of it. We ended up at the end of the corridor in the boys' cloakroom and I have this vision of the line of basins and the toilet cubicles and we were still fighting! Suddenly we stopped, realised we were both completely knackered and that nobody was actually going to give in or win and we started laughing.'

Their friendship sealed, they were to spend many happy hours in each other's company over the coming years.

Peter also remembered some of Felix's mother's efforts to humour and treat her son.

'Whenever there were picnics or packed lunches Felix's were a bit special,' he recalled. 'I think I saw my first baguette coming out of his packed lunch. She would work the fillings from one end to the other so he would be able to munch his way through egg mayo, into cheese and tomato and finish up with a bit of ham salad. Then she made the most wonderful devil's food cake. I remember Dorothy for her cakes.'

Peter suggested that perhaps one of the reasons why they got on so well was that they both came from broken homes. His father had walked out when he was three years old and he thought that was quite unusual in those days. He remembered how he was always interested in other people's fathers, something that made him acutely aware of David Sawyer when he began to be associated with Dorothy. Felix also pointed out later that there were very few kids in school whose parents had separated.

In October 1962, the Western world held its breath. Felix was just 15 and the Cuban Missile Crisis was threatening to plunge the United States and Russia into a nuclear conflict, something veterans of the previous world war simply couldn't comprehend. Ron Komatsu, a Japanese native who was head of chemistry at St Nicholas Grammar, had more of an interest than most and was glued to his radio. Students remembered he had a car standing by, ready to leave at the first sign of the conflict escalating. Felix remembered it with some amusement.

'We lived next to Northolt! How far did he think he was gonna get in his car?' he boomed.

Inevitably most youngsters were fairly unaware of the impending disaster and were more interested in football or the cultural changes happening around them. Music was beginning to offer a way into an exciting new world and there were the beginnings of a beat revolution in some quarters, though not anywhere near St Nicholas Grammar.

Felix's interest in rock and roll had come from a slightly different quarter to that of his friends. Across the main road from the quiet, leafy, triangular estate his mother had moved them to stood a Ministry of Defence site called RAF West Ruislip. It had been leased to the US Air Force in 1955 and, following the war, was being used for the repair of vehicles, coaches, aircraft engines and radar. A squadron of the 7500th Air Base Group had also been transferred there. For youngsters like Felix and Julian, it was an exciting place to visit. They weren't supposed to be in there, but as Felix remembered, this wasn't a problem.

'You duck underneath the big red pole and you start running,' he laughed. 'What is a soldier going to do? Look like an idiot and chase after you. What is he going to do, shoot you?'

He maintained that the US military wanted to have the locals on board so needed to win their hearts and minds. Julian remembered visiting it many times and had vivid memories of tough servicemen getting horribly drunk and falling foul of the military police. Later on, he even came to their canteen to watch Felix play in a band there.

It was one such serviceman, a deep-voiced southern black man called Anthony, who opened Felix's eyes and ears to the blues.

'Before I met Anthony,' he recalled, 'the only black music I listened to was Nat King Cole, Fats Domino, Chubby Checker and Little Richard, and thanks to his kindness I became a blues fanatic, not to mention a blues snob.'

As a trade-off he promised to introduce Anthony to classical music.

'I knew nothing about classical music, but I knew more than he did!' he laughed.

Many years later Felix wrote a poem about Anthony. 'The Janitor's Offer', written from the serviceman's point of view, included the line: 'Maybe if we took turns t'choose, You c'd play me this cat Mendelssohn, And I c'd introduce ya to the blues'.

'I never got around to playing him Mendelssohn because he wasn't remotely interested in listening to it,' he said. 'I only had probably two albums that my parents had somehow managed to get hold of, and so I had just been bluffing.'

A practice at which he would later become very adept.

Felix's introduction to the world of playing in a rock and roll band began with the back of a biscuit tin in 1962. He and Peter Quesnel and a group of other friends from St Nicholas had started what they called a Tape Club on a Friday evening after school. They would write short sketches, bits of music and jokes, record them and then play them back for their own amusement. Because it was a single-sex school and therefore essentially a male-only club, most of the parents of the kids involved were happy to leave them alone in the house while they went out to the pub. As far as they were concerned, with no girls involved they couldn't get up to any mischief. Peter Quesnel remembers how they changed the venue each week so as not to outstay their welcome. Parents would sometimes leave out sandwiches, biscuits and cake, and if the boys were lucky, soft drinks as well. David Wallbank brought his guitar and Felix would drum on the back of a biscuit tin. In time he upgraded to a set of bongos that he purchased on a school holiday to Greece and afterwards a drum kit bought on hire purchase.

'A proper Premier kit,' he remembers. 'But I was appalled to figure out that I was going to have to use my feet as well, which came as a terrifying shock. Of course I knew, because I had been watching bands all my life, but I had never thought about it.'

The Tape Club led to the formation of a band called the Flamingos, which variously consisted of Bruce Sawford on rhythm guitar, Peter Quesnel on vocals and harmonica, David Wallbank and Martin Jones on lead guitar, Terry 'Spud' Murphy on bass and Felix on drums. In the early days, one of Bruce's specialities was strumming his steel guitar so hard that he lacerated his fingers, spraying blood all over himself and anybody who happened to be nearby. In a later incarnation, Ken Daughters joined, playing a Phillips organ. John Brooks, who hung out with the band, helping lug equipment, occasionally stood in for musicians who might be late for a gig. He remembered them being one of the best bands in the area, although he insisted they were not quite as good as Ronnie Wood's band, the Thunderbirds, who played the circuit at the same time. He also recalled that Felix stood out as the leader, with thick long hair, sporting a full-length military-style overcoat, even in hot weather; he also had a habit of wearing a cape.

The Flamingos had a fairly eclectic repertoire, not least because they had a drummer who was determined to stamp his own developing personality onto live performances as well as rehearsals. By this time Felix had created a name for himself as something of a live wire, the one most likely to rise above the crowd, and the opportunity to take that personality out in front of an audience, and a paying audience to boot, was just too good to miss.

With a nod to the great drummers who led from behind, Felix not only produced enthusiastic drum solos – at times jumping out of a pub window in mid-solo only to appear again through another window, drumsticks in hand, to tap on punters' bottles and glasses before reaching the stage again to continue – but he also swapped places with singer Peter Quesnel for three or four numbers. He would produce raucous renditions of blues classics such as Bo Diddley's 'I'm a Man' and Willie Mabon's 'I'm Mad'. Peter remembered that his performances were so full of showmanship that they created a bit of a cult following for the group – even though the rest of the band had to keep on their toes to avoid the swinging microphone that accompanied the performance. That same showmanship would be put to good use later in his life, not only in business, but also when taking a turn at the annual Mustique Blues Festival.

Felix's ability and penchant for attracting and entertaining a crowd didn't end on the stage, though. Many people remembered his antics outside a pub called the Fisheries in Harefield, where the Flamingos played regularly. Now a quiet countrified bar and restaurant named the Coy Carp, in the sixties the Fisheries played host to many bands, and a garage next door was also occasionally used for rehearsals. It is situated on the canal, close to a weir and a drainpipe spans the canal next to a bridge. The pipe is about 18 inches in diameter with large spikes at either end to stop people from walking on it.

With night falling, and not much light to go by, Felix would bet drinkers from the pub that he could run across the canal along the drainpipe without falling in. Nowadays it would be a Health and Safety nightmare but in those days the potential for amusement, had he failed, was too great a temptation for many. Felix's beer money was easily won.

He remembered it well and talked about it often, citing his natural balance as a real money earner. Another bet winner was his ability to turn his feet in such a way as to look like he could walk backwards. It became known as his penguin walk.

The Flamingos was Felix's entry into the heady world of rock and roll and all that it brought. 'All you could drink and all you could shag,' as he remembered it.

Leftover cheese sandwiches produced by a landlady after a gig would be demolished in seconds and, on those nights when no food was produced, the band might pile into a Chinese restaurant or a Wimpy, where you could 'fill your boots for half-a-crown'. However, this was also a period where his natural entrepreneurial spirit and need to take control began to affect those around him. Peter Quesnel remembered Felix's efforts to make the band more professional. He began to coach Peter on how to present himself on stage, telling him to rehearse in front of a mirror but eventually deciding that, as a front man, his best option was just to stay in one place.

'I wanted to be a showman but I wasn't a natural,' remembered Peter. 'I looked ridiculous because I would leap about like Freddie Garrity of Freddie and the Dreamers.'

Eventually, in the days after they had left school, David Wallbank, who at the time worked for a bank, got hold of an old-fashioned, 'solid as a rock' bank stool and Felix said to Peter, 'Right, sit on that and don't move!' The result actually worked in their favour as it gave the band a rather unusual look.

One evening, on the way home after a gig, they picked up a hitchhiker who turned out to be a photography student. Never one to miss a trick, Felix managed to extract a promise from the student to take photographs of the band in return for the lift. The photos were done in the style of the cover of the Fab Four's *With the Beatles* album, a popular style at the time, where the boys' faces were shot partly in shadow. Felix set up the photographs on an easel outside each venue, complete with short biographies of each band member. At one point he and Bruce Sawford had 100 silkscreen Flamingos' posters made with the words 'Flam Fans Breed Fast'. He also made stage sets from his bedsit. Later, in another band, Felix created giant-sized cardboard cutouts of characters from Marvel comics and placed them around the stage. It was an early sign of the promotional and marketing talent, as well as the unusual attention to detail that Felix brought to every initiative he was involved in, from his early days in music and business through to his successful poetry tours in later life.

Throughout his late teens, residencies at the Fisheries and the Witches' Cauldron in Belsize Park helped the band to gain quite a following and Felix was all for making a go of it and seeking fame and fortune. They recorded a demo and even spent a day at the BBC to help soundmen test their recording studio. Peter Quesnel also remembered a support gig for Gino Washington and the Ram Jam Band, one of the hottest groups around at the time, during which they cheekily covered one of Washington's own numbers in their set.

'I maintain we did it better than they did, except that we didn't have the brass,' he said.

David Wallbank remembered gigs at the Fisheries 'being packed' and Bruce Sawford recalled punters dancing on the towpath outside the pub.

But the road to pop superstardom wasn't what everyone wanted. Unfortunately, according to Peter, the rest of the band found Felix's enthusiasm, aggression and need to run the group more than they could cope with and eventually decided to get a new drummer. Both Bruce Sawford and Felix understood the split had more to do with Peter needing to settle down rather than Felix's first steps towards world domination, but the reasons that were given varied. In the case of the Flamingos, it never really mattered. The one most likely to succeed was going to do it, no matter what path he chose.

In an ironic parallel with another successful band, the Beatles, the Flamingos later landed an opportunity to try the German circuit after Felix had left. But when they got there, they discovered that their replacement drummer was only 15 and therefore too young to be allowed to play in the clubs. A similar problem had occurred with the Beatles in 1960 when the authorities sent George Harrison home from Hamburg for being too young. However, this was where the comparison ended.

After he left the Flamingos, Felix began depping in various bands around the area. He would stand in for drummers in other bands, pocketing what he remembered as good money for doing something that was all about having a good time and pulling more girls than anyone else. He and Bruce even played in a band called Wham! long before George Michael and Andrew Ridgeley graced the eighties with their sparkling smiles and coiffured hairstyles. Felix still believed that he could carve out a future in the career that was giving him so much fun.

'I was certain that music was going to be it,' he said, many years later. 'I was going to be able to write. I knew I could write songs – I mean, I could write hits. I could have done it. I should have done it. I should have kept at it, but I didn't – and there you go.'

Throughout his teenage years and his time spent living day-to-day playing in rock and roll bands, Felix made a pretty memorable impression on almost everybody he met. This included teachers, friends and parents of friends but, most importantly, women. He already possessed a remarkable enthusiasm and capacity for sex, which left most of his friends and acquaintances scratching their heads in wonderment at how he managed not only to attract so many girlfriends, but to juggle them without getting into hot water. He had no interest in having just one girlfriend and his honesty that he simply didn't believe in monogamous relationships, coupled with a powerful intellect and an ability to charm when necessary, seemed to yield results.

He was young, not bad-looking, energetic and lippy but he also had a way with words. One telling comment by an early girlfriend, Sanchia Pearse, who went on to become a teacher, highlighted his intelligence. Sanchia enjoyed his skill in arguing with focus and conviction but was also amazed at how well he wrote at such a young age. She pointed out that looking back on Felix's letters and comparing them to the SATs papers she later marked as a teacher, there was no comparison. For someone she remembered didn't do well in school and was constantly in detention, he showed serious literary ability.

Her explanation of how difficult it was for Felix to remain monogamous says as much about why he was attracted to her as it does about Felix's waywardness. She said that accepting his need for an open relationship was an interesting stage to work through.

'It makes 100 per cent sense when you have got so many different aspects to your personality,' she explained. 'No one person could possibly satisfy you in that sense. I wouldn't like to postulate why, but it has to do with your whole upbringing and background. I have got a lot of sympathy with that idea that you don't ever want to tie yourself down and always want to explore new things. And when you are bright, you want to be intellectually stimulated as well as physically stimulated, and you are always exploring new avenues. It is unusual to find. I don't think I know anybody else who has had so many different relationships and managed to keep them all bubbling along.'

Sue Walls, who saw Felix off and on for a year or so, remembered the best times as those when he and Bruce would come around to her house in Pinner and sit in the front room playing guitars, sometimes until four in the morning. They had first met when he and a couple of friends turned up, uninvited, to a party at her house. Although they had initially thought about throwing them out or even chucking them into a nearby pond, Sue was intrigued by Felix's strong character. Though opinionated, he was also focused and exciting, she felt. She remembered him as a perfect gentleman with impeccable manners, except perhaps for the time when he was caught snogging the bride-to-be at the end of her own engagement party!

Sue got the impression that Felix enjoyed the homely feel of her home – hers was a close-knit family. However, she also remembered Felix's need to spread his wings.

'He would turn up and then he would disappear again for a while,' she said. 'That was Felix, he could not be tied down.'

It would be easy to suggest that Felix was typical of most teenagers whose physical growth outpaces their intellectual maturity but he was a little more than the average teenager. The fire in his belly was more like a nuclear-fuelled vat of bubbling oil that never cooled from his mid-teens through to his days writing poetry and taking business calls at his desk in Mustique. His own description of how he handled difficulties during his school days shows much of what was to be remembered by those who knew him.

Talking about the stigma of being from a divorced family, he said, 'You carried it on your back. You just shrugged it off, you know, you took no notice. There wasn't any other way of dealing with it. And I think that did hone my mouth, my wit. So, if you had a bully and guys that were getting into you, you could make them look like a fucking idiot because you could speak faster than them and make people laugh.'

He remembered that if you were a smallish lad you had to develop a ready wit. However, it was a talent that he used as much on teachers as he did on bullies. He never responded well to authority and simply wasn't going to do what they wanted.

'I couldn't give a shit. I wasn't going to do what they told me,' he recalled.

His lack of respect for authority also brought him into conflict with his mother. Determined to afford Felix every possible opportunity to better himself, Dorothy had worked hard to give her family a good life, and for each school that he was expelled from she redoubled her efforts to get him extra tuition or a chance at another establishment. As every parent with difficult teenagers knows, there is little one can do other than point them in the right direction and hope they don't fall down too many black holes, but that didn't stop Dorothy from pushing herself beyond limits to help her sons. For her partner David Sawyer it was mindboggling. He had no experience of bringing up children, yet carried a strong traditional sense of right and wrong and had to stand by watching the woman he loved attempting to control an errant teenager. As his niece Gerry Ashworth was to point out many years later, 'David was the kindest, softest man you could ever meet. How he ever got married to Dorothy I'll never know. He was always in the doghouse.'

Although moving out of home can be both an exciting and a traumatic time, for Felix it was as much to do with finding his own feet as it was to do with the change brought about by his mother remarrying in 1962. He had the greatest respect for his stepdad, but was not about to allow him to be a replacement for his own father. Many years later, with a romantic loyalty to his father that he had rarely spoken of, he said, 'I do think they were in love with each other. I'm quite sure that my mother never loved David Sawyer in the way she loved my father.'

Much as he respected Sawyer, Felix couldn't cope with his simpering politeness and was especially irritated by his habit of standing up whenever a woman came into a room. It seemed to Felix that David was like a jack-in-the-box, jumping from his seat every time Dorothy popped her head around the door. A towering man and a successful engineer, who at one point had to sign the Official Secrets Act when working at Marconi, David also worked on Concorde, and would spend his Sundays outside, washing and shining his Rover. In many ways he represented much of the traditional culture that young people like Felix were keen to rebel against and break away from.

Against a backdrop of political turmoil, with Harold Macmillan's Conservative government reeling from the public outcry at the Profumo affair, Felix had moved out of the family home in the summer of 1963 to a bedsit at 13 St Kilda's Road in Harrow on the Hill. Promised a place at Harrow Technical College and School of Art, he had somehow convinced his mother that he could look after himself and would benefit from learning in an art institution. It was the year the Beatles had recorded 'Please Please Me' and Felix was unknowingly following a similar path to John Lennon, who, after failing his O-levels six years previously, had gone on to Liverpool College of Art. Felix and Lennon's lives shared many parallels but their paths would not cross until a few years later.

It was a totally alien world to Felix's mother Dorothy, but the fact that she helped him find a bedsit, even supplying pots and pans, crockery and a few bits of furniture, showed that she had by now either completely lost any parental control over him, or believed he could go it alone. As both he and his mother were particularly strong and remarkably similar characters, it's likely to have been a combination of both.

'My mother was not easygoing,' he said later. 'She was a very strict woman.'

It was also another attempt to channel Felix's obvious intelligence. For those without a vocational, engineering or academic leaning, Britain's art schools were a last attempt at staying in education. They were also beginning to play an integral part in shaping the pop landscape. Not far away in Ealing, Pete Townshend and future Rolling Stones guitarist Ronnie Wood were already reaping the benefits of studying at Ealing Art College. Pete claimed he was inspired to smash his guitar on stage by lectures given by auto-destructive art pioneer Gustav Metzger. He took the opportunity to try it out at the Railway Hotel in Harrow in 1964. In a dingy basement room, the High Numbers would play to a motley group of mods perched on a stage made from beer crates. First accidentally poking a hole through the ceiling where he kept banging his guitar, Townshend progressed to smashing up a Rickenbacker to the amusement of a growing band of followers. By the time they became the Who, the stunt was an expected part of the act.

Art college had already been a hotbed of ideas and home to burgeoning beat-era protesters and poets who eventually played a role in the counter-culture revolution. However, despite its potential for education and new adventures, including the opportunity to meet a clutch of trendy and potentially liberal-minded women, it simply didn't work out for Felix. Bruce Sawford remembered meeting him walking down the road in Harrow on the day he had decided to quit. Felix was angry and gave his explanation in words that left no room for any other interpretation.

'Why should I go to fucking Harrow Art School,' he fumed, 'and learn how to fucking well draw fucking noughts when I can fucking well buy the Letraset?'

At the same time he had been making posters for his band and explained that all he wanted from art school was to learn how to make better posters to promote the Flamingos. In an interview with author Jonathon Green many years later, he suggested that part of his problem with Harrow School of Art was the fact that he had played a prank involving 16 pairs of girls' knickers and was expelled for it. It was just one more institution that he had been expelled from. As it happened, it was the same year that another drummer and ex-Harrow School of Art student, Charlie Watts, was to join a new band called the Rolling Stones.

Thankfully, his love affair with art didn't die with his exit from art school. Later on, he was to hound Jon Goodchild, designer of *Oz* magazine, until he let him help on the design of the magazine. In the meantime, though, he had to make a living, and, although his band was beginning to tighten up enough to play more paying gigs, he needed a day job. He was employed by the local council to mow lawns as well as do a bit of grave digging and spent time working as a window dresser for the department store Sopers, which was down the road from Harrow School of Art. Calling itself 'Harrow's Own Great Store', Sopers offered fashions, drapery and furnishings as well as a food section and restaurant. Today it is a Debenhams store. He also worked at Waring & Gillow on Oxford Street and even had a spell helping out at Liberty. Coincidentally, he would later appear as one of their VIP customers in a TV show about the store in 2013. His one remaining memory of Waring & Gillow and Liberty is of being the only one there who wasn't gay. He remembered it as an odd sort of sexism. As he was different, he was always the butt of all the jokes.

'They'd try it on a couple of times and you just smack them in the gob and they leave you alone,' he later claimed.

Felix's bedsit in St Kilda's Road was his first official 'shag pad'. Not necessarily just for his own amusement – he later claimed that to help pay the rent he would hire it out to friends who had nowhere to go with their own girlfriends. Like many young people first escaping the clutches of a demanding mother, he was to remember the joy of that initial feeling of independence and privacy in a poem called 'A Room of my Own' – 'Linoleum nailed to the planks on the floor, and to top it all off, a lock on the door!'

Working in the design department at Sopers allowed him to decorate his bedsit in the kind of style that nobody his age could possibly have afforded. Peter Quesnel described it as 'a very interesting flat' full of 'accessories' procured from his place of work. He felt it was an opportunity for Felix to express his personality; however, sometime later his landlady was to take a completely different view. Felix painted every surface in the flat including the furniture and covered the walls and ceiling with his artwork. His landlady hit the roof and told him in no uncertain terms to find a new home.

One girlfriend named Jane, who spent time at his bedsit in St Kilda's Road, had made quite an impression on Felix. However, he hadn't made quite such a good impression on her parents. Hoping to keep her away from Felix's amorous attentions, they decided to take her on a summer holiday to Wales. This of course didn't stop Felix and in some ways had the effect of a red rag to a bull. Fortunately, she had managed to get a note to him with the address of where she and her parents were planning to stay. He decided to go to Wales to see her and, as he didn't drive and neither did he have the money to pay for travel, his journey was full of adventure.

He rode a bicycle out towards Slough, got lost in Maidenhead, slept in Newbury and eventually found a train heading west, only to wake in Torquay. Finally, he arrived at Jane's door, dishevelled and weary. Her parents took him in and explained that Jane had become engaged to someone else. As Felix remembered it, her father drove him all the way back to London in his Mercedes.

'My first drive in a posh car,' he would later quip.

Jane had many fond memories of Felix and recalled being besotted with him at the time. She would sit around while the Flamingos rehearsed and remembered how the band seemed to argue a lot.

From the day he left home, Felix was on a mission to sleep with as many girls as he possibly could. He kept a list of those he met along the way and later explained that he had developed a coded system to remind him of how much his amorous advances had succeeded with each one. Although he couldn't remember too much detail, he said that by the early seventies there were hundreds on his list. Most, but not all, had been successful conquests. Talking about the years after leaving home, Felix explained that his life was wayward and directionless. He described it as a 'kind of blur because you're living from day to day. Literally one minute you'd have £15 in your pocket and then you'd have nothing.'

That blurred existence, living on his wits, picking up money and girls in a gypsy-like existence fuelled by a tenuous wish to be a successful rock and roll musician, filled Felix's early years until one day a colourfully designed magazine front cover caught his attention.

CHAPTER 3

REEL TO REEL

For the best part of a month in 1971, Britain's flamboyant counter-culture, along with much of the rest of the country, was swallowed into the belly of an obscenity trial that was to be the longest in the country's history – it dug deep into the massive divide that had opened up between the traditional post-war establishment and a relatively small but vocal section of the country's youth.

In retrospect, the *Oz* magazine trial was seen by many as a case that was the pinnacle of a revolution with personal freedom at its core. British writer and barrister John Mortimer (creator of *Rumpole of the Bailey*), who represented the defence at the trial, said that he saw the case as 'standing at the crossroads of our liberty, at the boundaries of our freedom to think and say and draw and write what we please'. At the time it was also the somewhat inevitable reaction to what Britain's conventional society saw as the downright cheek and bad behaviour of a section of the youth of the day, who had for half a decade been parading their sexual and chemical excesses like naughty schoolchildren. In some respects, it was akin to a schoolboy pushing his teacher's patience as far as he could to gain kudos from the rest of the class, and then glorying in his triumph after a caning. Or perhaps a more fitting legacy might be that it was the tipping point that began the process of rooting out serious corruption and a catalyst for change of out-dated attitudes.

The first issue of *London Oz* magazine, which had been published in February 1967, included Richard Neville, Paul Lawson, Jon Goodchild, Martin

Sharp, Peter Ledeboer and Martin Robertson on the masthead for editorial, design and photography. It also included contributions from Andrew Fisher, David Widgery, Terry Bunton and 'the lovely Louise' amongst others.

The magazine had originated in Australia, as a satirical underground magazine started by Richard Neville, along with Martin Sharp and Richard Walsh. After falling foul of the Australian establishment for lampooning public figures and publishing articles questioning the handling of contentious issues, the editors found themselves on the wrong end of an obscenity trial, where they were found guilty and sentenced to three to six months in prison with hard labour. Thankfully, they were released on appeal, and Neville and Sharp made their way to London where they founded *London Oz*. Hoping to recreate their original satirical magazine, they had quickly pulled together a motley crew of contributors.

Already buzzing with its own enthusiasm, the opening page also ran a piece calling for contributions, setting the tone for what it hoped to receive: 'Will Malcolm Muggeridge write for *Oz*?' it asked. 'Let's hope not. He already dominates contemporary media. Here's your chance to break into print. Contributions are encouraged and will be paid for. Rush hard core satire, soft core pornography, articles, off-beat news cartoons.' The address given was that of Richard's sister Jill, where he was then living. The rest of the magazine, mostly black-and-white except for some of Martin Sharp's cartoons, was indeed very like the *Private Eye* that it hoped to emulate and it teased readers with the promise of an interview with Malcolm Muggeridge in the next issue. It also launched its Martin Sharp 'Playmate of the Month' cartoon with a darkly forbidding image of Lyndon Baines Johnson entitled 'The Madonna of the Napalm'. The stage was set: *London Oz* was out to get noticed and to cause a stir if at all possible.

London Oz 2 did contain the promised interview with Malcolm Muggeridge and his 'struggle against the 20th century', again complete with brilliant Martin Sharp cartoon. It also contained a feature article on British breasts signed by 'Germaine'. Bemoaning the fact that the British breast was being ignored by fashion trends, Germaine said that the British manufacturer was convinced 'possibly rightly, that the British breast is either meagre and knobbly or big and floppy. It has either to be built up by gay deceivers and "foam" and cushions or hoisted as far up and out as it will go.' It seemed that *Oz* magazine's call for contributors had already snared a great writer, who would, in time, help to expand both its reach and tone. Alongside the article was the launch of 'The *London Oz* Beautiful Breasts Competition', where readers were invited to send in two photos of their breasts to win £20 and 'have your bust immortalised over a double-page *Oz* pin-up'. However, Martin Sharp's Playmate of the Month in that issue was 'The Toad of White Hall', described in the text as 'Toad Wilson of Whitehall. Toad's twice the size of last month's inaugural Playmate LBJ – but then twice as conceited'. *Oz* was continuing to goad those in high places.

As it happened, the promised double-page spread immortalising a reader's breasts wasn't printed in the following issue, but the soft-porn look, the hardcore satire and the promotion of everything alternative, from drugs to contraception and pirate radio to abortion, was enough to at least gain the notice of a growing readership, including Felix Dennis.

The path from school expulsion through art school and rock and roll was a well-trodden trajectory for many of those who found themselves at home in the hippie world of the sixties, a path that Felix followed with relative ease.

How Felix went from being a gravedigger in Pinner to a member of the *Oz* Three has been well documented over the years, often with varying degrees of accuracy, and indeed no shortage of contradiction. Like all good tales, the story expands, contracts and is embellished over time but, in most of the telling, it seems to begin with an abortion.

In an interview with the author Jonathon Green, whose books *Days in the Life* and *All Dressed Up* give a fascinating insight into the world of the sixties, Felix claimed his first contact with Richard Neville, the editor and founder of *Oz* magazine, was via a reel-to-reel tape made on a machine that he was about to sell to pay for a girlfriend's abortion. Having already sold his precious Premier drum kit and found it wasn't enough to settle the Harley Street fees, he decided to sell his trusty Grundig tape player too.

However, the night before selling it he made a recording about a copy of *Oz* magazine he had picked up at a nearby tube station.

'It was a very amusing tape,' he declared, 'cos it was done very late at night and I was a bit smashed.'

Felix passed on words of wisdom, along with hints and tips about what was wrong and what was right with the magazine, as well as a bit about his own life, including the fact that he was about to sell his tape recorder to pay for an abortion.

'Anyway,' he said later, 'I thought no more about it and just put it in the mail. I knew that if you just get a tape with nothing else attached to it, there's one thing for sure as hell you've got to do – you've got to listen to it.'

As it happened, one of the issues that *Oz* magazine had recently covered was the need to change the law on abortion, and when Richard Neville received the tape he reacted in exactly the way Felix had expected and put it on his own reel-to-reel. Furthermore, he played it to his girlfriend, Louise Ferrier.

'It was quite moving,' Richard said later. However, he played down Felix's subsequent claims that his comments were very negative about *Oz* and instead remembered the tape as being 'of worshipful praise of the magazine'. He said he was flattered, and when the BBC came to film a short piece about *Oz* magazine, he immediately gave them the tape. Feeling that the producer was trying to show that *Oz* was making an impact on society, he handed it over 'without even thinking of the rights of the person who had sent it in, particularly'. As he later pointed out in his book, *Hippie Hippie Shake*, any media attention was welcome as at the time they didn't have enough money to promote the magazine.

Not long afterwards, the piece was shown on the BBC with Felix's voice from the reel-to-reel tape as the sound track to film of an issue of *Oz* magazine being pasted up. Felix remembered how one of the girls from a flat he was living in after leaving his over-decorated bedsit in Harrow suddenly shrieked that he was on television. In another room at the time, Felix immediately assumed it would be footage of his band and came rushing in, but couldn't understand what she meant until he heard his voice in the background. He immediately telephoned Richard Neville and went round to his basement flat in Palace Gardens Terrace in Notting Hill, thinking he might be able to get some money for the use of his voice. According to Neville, Felix was crestfallen when told that it was just the same as publishing a reader's letter and, besides, *Oz* was a fledgling publisher and there was no money.

'Anyway, he gave me a couple of bales of magazines,' Felix recalled. He was instructed to 'go out on the street and sell them'.

Initially reluctant, Felix did his best to look cool and point out that he was a working musician – though currently without a drum kit. In the end, however, he agreed and took the magazines. It was the start of a chapter in the life of Felix Dennis that would not only land him in Wormwood Scrubs, but would also see his mother writing to him in despair. However, it was also the opportunity that led to the development of an entrepreneurial spirit that would ultimately make him a lot of money, as well as allow him to touch many lives. He promptly went back to the flat with his bundles of magazines and persuaded some of his flatmates to don their shortest mini-skirts and come out onto the streets, selling magazines with him.

'I was like a sort of hippie pimp,' he remembered. 'As soon as you'd go up to people and shove them in front of their face they'd give you half-a-crown! It was amazing! We sold about a hundred the first day. A hundred half-crowns was a lot of money in those days.'

The next day he went back to Neville and demanded more bundles of magazines. His appetite for easy money whetted, he also developed a brilliant sales technique. Instead of simply asking people if they would like to buy a magazine, he discovered that if they were approached in more of a conspiratorial fashion, as though part of a special club, they would be even quicker to part with their cash. He would teach the girls to ask punters if they had got their copy of *Oz* yet. 'Oh gosh, no, I haven't got it yet' was often the reply, as people eagerly handed over their money. He also taught them to look out for the men sporting just a hint of longer hair – they were more likely to be wannabe hippies earning money in proper jobs, where they couldn't be seen to let their hair grow too long.

Neville realised that Felix was onto something and making money in a way that they hadn't done before, so he offered him a 50/50 deal on future sales. It was in the days when a hippie uniform was becoming de rigueur, and Felix, having been on the rock and roll circuit for some time by then, had already developed a keen sense of style. He was wearing below-the-knee afghan coats and platform snakeskin boots. At one point, on hearing that Felix's coat was made of rabbit fur, a friend quipped, 'You can't come in here, we've got myxomatosis.' Even the *Notting Hill Post* had snapped and published a picture of him cruising down the King's Road. He had also gone to the hairdresser and spent a fortune on having his hair frizzed, Jimi Hendrix-style. His former school friend Tony Wallcott described it as making him look as though he had a chrysanthemum on his head.

One of many school friends who were to stay in touch, Wallcott was also drafted in to help with magazine sales and remembers what a boon it was at a time when money was tight. He also recalled that there were more ways to generate cash than simply by sales alone.

'Every Saturday we'd go and pick up 20, 30, 40 or 50 copies of *Oz* and we would go down the King's Road. It was just a huge parade of part-time hippies, the beautiful people and the American and Japanese tourists. We were in all our pretty clothes and we used to paint our faces and arms, daffodils and kaftans. We were just flogging these *Oz*s. People would come up and ask to take a picture. Little Jimmy from Arkansas would stand between us and have his picture taken. We used to hustle quite a lot, no such thing as a free picture. It used to cost them half-a-crown, I think.'

Felix soon became a regular face at the home of *Oz* magazine and, as his sales prowess grew and the money he brought in began to make a difference, his confidence also developed. Designer Jon Goodchild remembered him bringing a much-needed energy to the whole operation.

'I became aware of him when he would come zooming down to the basement apartment that we used in Palace Gardens Terrace – rushing in and out, loudly shouting his enthusiasms about this, that and the other, telling people what to do and then rushing off again with armfuls of the magazine. He tried to pump enthusiasm into it, because I think at this point in time it was beginning to fade away. I think the editor was beginning to lose interest and wanted to do something more important. I was getting very bored. Partly because there was a lot of work and I needed money, frankly. Jim Anderson turned up at that point and began to tentatively take over things, but I think without Felix's enthusiasm it would have faded away right there because Richard [Neville] surely didn't have the energy to keep it going. So, Felix came along at just the right moment. The fact that he was able to prove that, if he took it out on the streets, he could sell every one he had really astounded us. I don't think any of us had ever thought of that before. I mean, we weren't having a lot of fun with the normal distributors because they hated it, really. They didn't want to touch it and it was Felix who kind of twisted their arm a little later and forced the distribution issue. None of us would have done that.'

Distribution, along with printing, was a huge issue for the underground press, which at the time also included *IT* magazine. Many traditional outlets wouldn't touch what they regarded as pornographic or even subversive material, and other than using Moore Harness Distribution, a company who would later work with Felix's post-*Oz* business, it was difficult to get magazines into traditional outlets.

This of course had contributed to the value of Felix's street selling, but it also made it difficult for the business to survive, let alone grow. *Oz* had a distribution deal with ECAL (Effective Communications Arts Limited), which was based in Betterton Street in Covent Garden. It had been set up by the owners of *IT* to help distribute their magazine. However, like many enterprises of that era, it suffered from sloppy management and perhaps also from a lack of focus and idealism, combined, of course, with the joys of too much marijuana. ECAL owed *Oz* a lot of money from magazine distribution and advertising, and, as Felix was the one showing the most enthusiasm, Richard Neville asked him to see what he could do about getting them paid.

'I was brought in as a horrible, tough little bastard to try and get the finances sorted out,' he later told Jonathon Green. 'The first thing I did was to try to fire a lot of people, which was very difficult in those days because, as they hadn't joined in the first place, it was very difficult to fire them.' It was probably Felix's first opportunity to put a rocket under people to get them to work harder, a talent he nurtured and used to great effect in future years. Even though he became known for his gruff, no-nonsense and aggressive nature, that wasn't how Richard Neville originally saw him. Richard remembered their first exchange over the BBC tape as being very friendly and he described Felix as a 'scruffy kid' who was 'rather charming and very eager and really energetic'. He added that Felix was quite diplomatic too. Interviewed in 1998, he said, 'Felix is now often bossy and bumptious, that wasn't there in those early stages. That much tougher part of his personality didn't really manifest itself until later on as he became more and more entwined in the workings of *Oz*.'

The ECAL effort proved to be successful and Felix managed to find a way to get them back on track. ECAL had also sold posters for the Big O Poster Company, which had been founded by Peter Ledeboer in partnership with the soon-to-become very well-known music promoter Harvey Goldsmith. Prior to that, Ledeboer had been involved with *Oz* magazine so it was likely that Felix was thrown into a somewhat complex situation. In an interview with Big Vision Publishing, many years later, Ledeboer likened the period to a 'haphazard toboggan ride', saying the only things that ever really worked for Big O were those things that were unplanned. It was the sort of comment that could easily have applied to a number of operations that grew and somehow survived the sixties.

The posters, however, along with the artwork of many of those who designed them, had made a huge impression on Felix and fed his growing interest in graphic design and underground art. They included iconic images of Che Guevara, as well as Australian artist Martin Sharp's seminal Jimi Hendrix and Bob Dylan posters. Bruce Sawford, another member of the Flamingos, remembered being drafted in with his van to help move posters in one of Felix's efforts to recoup some of the *Oz* debts from ECAL. Felix had begun to salvage copies of some of the most memorable images and in time accumulated one of the most comprehensive collections in private hands. At one point he was to scream at Richard Neville's girlfriend Louise Ferrier when he found her tossing old magazines and *Oz* art boards into a skip. Grabbing a step ladder and clambering over boxes to climb in after them, he berated her, shouting that one day she would regret throwing them away.

Felix's social life prior to his early days at *Oz* magazine wasn't necessarily remembered for wild parties and bad behaviour, but, with beautifully delivered understatement, Jonathon Green remembered, 'One was always jealous of his sex life – which was extensive.'

Felix's move from the Harrow bedsit to Walsingham Mansions, where he had heard himself on the BBC documentary, had come about after a party; he went back to the flat in the Fulham Road and found it was shared by five girls. Initially unsuccessful at getting any of them into bed, he showed what was to become an obsession with tidiness in setting about cleaning the entire flat, which at the time endeared him to the occupants. They decided to let him move in and offered him mattress space in a bay window overlooking the road, but only on the basis that he didn't sleep with any of them. That, they pointed out, would have made things too complicated. Somewhat inevitably, things did get complicated. As Felix remembered it, there were girls' knickers lying around all over the place and it would simply have been rude not to try to get into some of them.

Throughout this time the London 'scene' was dominated by hippies, and music events were one of the places friendships were made. Felix was to meet Mick Farren, one of the many characters who loomed large in his life, at an unusual venue. Although the folk revival, headed by Bob Dylan's political and socially conscious ideology, had helped to mobilise the activist element of the growing counter-culture, when it came to the hippie masses the music that was to represent the era was becoming psychedelic, influenced more and more by the use of LSD. And as acid became the drug of choice during the mid- to late sixties, a place to gather for 'happenings' outside of festivals was needed. Two entrepreneurial characters, John 'Hoppy' Hopkins and Joe Boyd, impressed by the success of a launch party for *IT* magazine at the Roundhouse in Chalk Farm in October 1966, in which bands like Soft Machine and Pink Floyd had entertained a disparate group of hippies, decided to rent an Irish dancehall known as the Blarney Club in Tottenham Court Road to put on all-night parties promoting psychedelic bands. The *IT* launch party had been a huge success, attracting not only most of the hippies who were beginning to find each other in London but also a few luminaries such as Paul McCartney, Mick Jagger and Marianne Faithfull.

In retrospect, the use of an Irish dancehall for hippie events sounds faintly ludicrous, especially as it was only a few doors down from the local police station, but Hoppy and Boyd saw an opportunity, and, although this wasn't to be a huge financial success, it certainly played a role in helping promote the music and the social movement of the era. Initially calling it 'UFO Presents Nite Tripper', they finally settled on 'UFO'. Unsurprisingly, regardless of the name change, bewildered Irish drunks would still turn up on a Friday night, wondering what time the ceilidh started.

The Social Deviants' frontman Mick Farren, already complete with a hairstyle most likely to be targeted in a baton charge, said that working the door at the UFO club taught him more about the true nature of the counter-culture than any other job. Not that he'd had that many jobs. He had loosely worked as a journalist and writer, hoping really to make it as a musician. But working the door at UFO was something he did on Friday nights when his band didn't have a gig; which in those days was most Friday nights. In his book, *Give the Anarchist a Cigarette*, he described his role as 'playing psychedelic traffic cop to a multitude of chemically incapable lemmings'. Even though the club owner who had leased the venue to Hoppy and Boyd had been known to drop off a case of Scotch to the police station every Christmas, the possibility of large crowds of hippies congregating on the pavement outside wasn't likely to go unnoticed by either residents or the local constabulary, so Farren's task of getting money from disorientated hippies while at the same time keeping the pavement clear meant that the full entrance fee was rarely paid up as he urged them to 'get inside!' In classic Farren prose he described that particular job as 'attempting to stuff 300 or 400 dithering and recalcitrant white rabbits down a very narrow Lewis Carroll rabbit hole'. Dressed in an Incredible Hulk T-shirt, he got a name for himself for being a bit of a heavy, something he said took years to shake off.

It was at the UFO club in 1967 that Farren and Felix Dennis would first meet. Sharing a love-hate relationship with the hippie movement and a thinly veiled disdain for some of the nonsense that latched itself to the Swinging Sixties, they were to meet up on many occasions in the future during the *Oz* era, as well as when Mick had moved to the States. Written in the seventies, one of his novels, *The Text of Festivals*, cast more than a cynical eye over the excesses of his generation. But many years later, after suffering a massive coronary onstage in London with his band, the no longer 'Social' Deviants, Farren passed away with his cowboy boots on and a microphone in his hand – in a style that most rockers could only dream of. He was buried in the arboretum of Felix's Warwickshire home in September 2013.

Interviewed in 1999, Farren's first recollection of Felix was his 'incredible capacity for picking up women'. But beyond that, when he was working at *IT* magazine he also remembered hearing about this 'mad street seller' called Felix Dennis, who was 'getting Richard organised'. Felix's prowess as the energy and organisation behind *Oz* magazine was growing, even before he was to really become part of the team. After his success at recouping money from ECAL, Richard Neville asked Felix if he would like to be the company's business manager and, although the ECAL money was a huge help, as Felix remembered it, things really were a mess.

'I realised they hadn't negotiated with the printers, they hadn't negotiated with the paper merchants. They hadn't paid bills properly. They were getting charged massive, ridiculous amounts of interest. They weren't paying; the whole thing was just chaos.'

This, of course, meant that he had to find more ways to bring in money, so he began looking at how to increase advertising revenue. Although it wasn't something he had ever done before, as someone who had developed a knack of talking his way into (and occasionally out of) more or less anything, he soon got a handle on how to ingratiate himself with potential clients.

Felix quickly realised that one of the key areas that *Oz* really wasn't covering properly, which he knew could bring in advertising revenue, was music. Having begun to frequent clubs like UFO and later Middle Earth, he was witnessing the effect that bands like Procol Harum, The Incredible String Band, Soft Machine and many others were having on the underground scene. Music was driving the acid-enlightened youth into a happy alliance fuelled more by swirling rhythms, light shows and drugs than by political activism. As a musician he was also able to see where the potential mass market for *Oz* magazine might lie. While Richard Neville was hoping *Oz* could be a rival to *Private Eye* and the *New Statesman*, Felix was seeing a much bigger picture altogether.

By this time he was also getting involved in layout and helping Jon Goodchild to deal with the design of the magazine, as well as contributing occasional bits of copy. *Oz 13*, with the 'Wheel of Fire' foldout, a cover that opened out to reveal a poster drawing of a naked woman chained to a wheel, added his name to the contributors list, saying design was 'assisted by Felix Dennis'. Previously he had been credited only as 'Pusher', which, unlike the American reference to purveyors of illegal substances, was a term used to describe someone who sold the magazine on the street. Felix was, of course, still the 'Pusher', credited alongside Louise Ferrier in that particular issue.

Interviewed in 1998, a year before he died of cancer, Jon Goodchild remembered that it was Felix's persistence that eventually got him involved in helping with design.

'He was like an irritation,' he said, 'but he learned very fast. He just turned up and he just did it. It was he too who did a lot of liaison with the printers – the direct contact – and got to find out exactly how far to push it, or how far to push them technically, and I began to rely on him to gather that information, particularly as we had to keep changing printers because they kept getting nervous.'

Goodchild claimed that Felix became indispensable. Unfortunately, in 1969, Jon had already decided to leave to go and work for publishing entrepreneur Jann Wenner, who, with the backing of Mick Jagger, was by then launching *Rolling Stone* magazine in London.

Jon later regretted his decision to leave, pointing out that nobody really understood that Felix was the only one who wanted to make *Oz* a proper magazine. According to him, although Felix was initially attracted to *Oz*'s irreverence and the fact that it was satirical as well as anarchic, he quickly saw that it could become something more. Apart from realising the value of music to the magazine, he introduced the 'Mozic' section – having already contributed interviews with musicians and album reviews. At the time Jon believed that working for *Rolling Stone* looked the better opportunity, but as he later admitted, 'Actually it was the other way around.' He thought that Felix wasn't being taken seriously, partly because of his upbringing: 'There were guys from Sydney who, I think, looked down on Felix initially. There was definitely a class thing going on, so Felix had to overcome all that too.'

Marsha Rowe, who worked at *Oz* magazine before setting up the feminist *Spare Rib* magazine with Rosie Boycott in 1972, suggested that Felix also suffered from being younger than his colleagues at *Oz*. In the early days he was very much seen as the junior around the office.

Jon Goodchild and Felix were to work together again in the future and Jon was designing a reference book on English trees called *Silva: The Tree in Britain* for Felix when he died in 1999. A year before that he paid tribute to one of the qualities that Felix became known for over many years in business: 'He is extremely loyal,' he said, 'out of all proportion, I think, even to people who treated him like shit.' This was a truth that was to prove itself over and over as Felix's generosity and care for others grew, along with his own success.

Felix's grasp of the bigger picture and his growing knowledge of the production process may have contributed to a certain amount of friction between him and Richard Neville but in the main, even though they did come from very different backgrounds, a grudging mutual respect had begun to develop. Most people associated with the magazine remembered they fought on numerous occasions, but they were both ambitious and bright, and with Felix's natural aggression even a minor disagreement may have looked worse than it was. A comment by Neville in his book, *Hippie Hippie Shake*, is an early pointer to the thick-skinned attitude that was to become a hallmark of Felix Dennis's character.

Richard remembered one issue where he really didn't have the time to look at all of the pages as they were being pasted up and was irked by the headline 'Heavy Shit' on Felix's music spread. He says he shouted at Jim Anderson 'who burst into tears' and yelled at Felix too, 'but he just yelled right back at me – even louder!'

As Jon Goodchild also remembered, when it came to conflict Felix had no problem giving as much as, if not more than, he got.

'Felix was quite prepared to be heavy,' he explained. 'He was quite prepared to go after people and challenge and get really quite nasty with them; I don't think any of us would have dared. He had no problem with that at all.'

By the sort of 'jammy' coincidence that Felix was later to allude to as being one of the main reasons for his success in business, Neville was given reason to take his eye off the ball with *Oz* magazine. In 1969 he had been commissioned to write a book about the sixties and was becoming increasingly distracted by the task. Knowing he had taken on more than he could cope with, he began looking for editorial help, initially with the book, but also with *Oz*. That was when he enlisted the assistance of Jim Anderson. When the book was finished, he was then busy promoting it and honing his skills as a chat show guest.

Jim Anderson had escaped a career in law in his native Australia and came to England in that same year in search of a different direction. Although initially there was some circling as they got to know each other, the pair were to become a strong team, between them holding the whole magazine together at a time when everybody was living on pretty slim pickings. Jim later described it: 'Richard had no money. I lived with Richard and Louise, and we cooked together and we ate together and existed on very, very little.' He did begin to draw a wage from *Oz*, but it was extremely minimal.

'I don't know how we got by,' he admitted, 'but it was easy to get by in the sixties. Living was easy. Because we were so interested in the magazine we sacrificed everything because we loved what we were doing, it didn't matter. The magazine itself was the main excitement in our lives.' *Oz* gave them certain perks, like tickets to rock concerts and free LPs, but as Jim pointed out the role that Felix played was vital: 'If it hadn't been for Felix the magazine would probably have folded. It went very, very close.'

CHAPTER 4

POISONING JIMMY PAGE

Never one to be particularly worried about how he appeared in public, Felix was the ideal fall guy for a wacky spectacle at an *Oz* fundraiser held at Middle Earth, the hippie nightclub in Covent Garden, in 1969. Advertised in *Oz 12*, the *Oz* Benefit Concert promised 'incredible big name groups' and 'incredible small name groups' as well as 'happenings' and a 'Sexy Barney Bubbles Light Show'. According to Richard Neville, it also included Pink Floyd, the Pretty Things and Soft Machine. With all kinds of quirky and wild sideshows the whole event was designed with psychedelic hippie appeal. Ironically, the hope was that the event, guaranteed to include much drug-taking and therefore law-breaking on a large scale, would raise money for *Oz* to pay their HM Customs and Excise bill. This was still the peak of Flower Power after all and even Andrew Lloyd Webber and Tim Rice had joined in the fun, recently releasing their new show, *Joseph and the Amazing Technicolor Dreamcoat*. Acid heads were finding Jesus everywhere.

Political activism had hit the headlines the month before when an anti-Vietnam war demonstration had turned nasty and police had charged the demonstrators on horseback. There were many casualties and more than 200 demonstrators were arrested. So when the night-long event at Middle Earth began to ease its way into first light, the sound of shots being fired sent hippies flying in all directions. A group of uniformed men charged into the crowd, brandishing what looked like guns. As they menacingly circled one particular member of the audience, anyone not already having a bad trip was about to have one. The person targeted was Felix Dennis, who put up a typically loud, aggressive and energetic defence before being carried away from his friends. Dragged to a stage area, he was stripped of all his clothes and tied to a cross. The protagonists then raised a sign that read 'Freedom of speech is against the law'. Fear and paranoia turned to confusion and bemusement and talk of 'bad acid' rumbled through the groups of hippies. Richard Neville quickly took to the microphone to calm the crowd, explaining that the whole spectacle was just an 'absurdist' comment on rebellions in Africa.

As Felix bounced from one sexual adventure to the next, sometimes requiring a change of address, his life became far more varied than it had been in the suburbs. He was in Swinging London and as his role in *Oz* developed, so too did his social life. After he was asked to move out of his bay window space upstairs in Walsingham Mansions, he moved downstairs in the same building with his school friend John Leaver – but not before a memorable run-in with one of the girls during a late Sunday lunch. Tony Woollcott remembered staying on occasional Saturday nights at Walsingham Mansions. When they would eventually wake on Sunday, usually somewhere around 4pm according to him, the girls would cook a meal. On one occasion there were about eight to 10 people in the flat and they had all found somewhere to sit and eat. 'Everybody was always very vocal,' he said. Most of the people there had a bit of money, were doing well, and, as he remembered, were highly opinionated, but none more so than 'young Felix Dennis'.

On this particular afternoon, Felix, never one to hold back, 'got a bit spiky' with flatmate Tessa Seddons, saying something that she wasn't too pleased with.

'She picked up this jug of gravy,' said Tony, 'and poured it all over his Afro.' The sight of the thick gravy being slowly drizzled into Felix's Afro is one that would forever remain crystal-clear in Tony's memory.

'And everybody just wet themselves,' he went on. People were rolling around with laughter while Felix was horrified. As Tony said, 'He didn't see the funny side of it at all. He had just had the goddamn thing done and it had probably cost him £20, which was a lot of money and suddenly it was gravy.'

At half-a-crown a pop he would have had to sell 160 copies of *Oz* to recoup that investment, and that's assuming he wasn't splitting the revenue with Richard Neville.

Walsingham Mansions was an imposing six-storey Victorian block not far from Fulham Broadway. Living downstairs in the basement with John Leaver, who also helped out at *Oz* selling ad space and doing a bit of writing, probably wasn't ideal for Felix. Girlfriend Denise Blackie, who worked in Harrods at the time, remembered it as a 'ghastly' flat next door to Chelsea Football ground. There were six people sharing two bedrooms, and as she recalled, nobody was very good at cleaning up. On one occasion, when they were broken into, the only things stolen were John Leaver's condoms. 'That was all they could find of any value!' she said later.

Quick-witted and full of charm, Felix was often able to win over a girl-friend's parents, but in the case of Denise he didn't really impress her mother. When they first met, he was helping Denise to extract herself from a difficult relationship and her mother was not happy with him as the replacement. Denise remembered that her relationship with her mother wasn't too good at the time and there was talk of making her a Ward of Court, something that Felix bravely argued against. When his name started to become prominent during the coverage of the *Oz* trial in 1971, she rang her daughter to say, 'I told you so. No good would come of that one.' She wasn't the only one to swallow her words when he later began to feature on the *Sunday Times* Rich List.

But sometimes it is only those inside a relationship that can see the good. Even in the early days, Felix's generosity and kindness was apparent. Denise remembered how, after they moved from Walsingham Mansions, he would walk her home to Parsons Green. There was a tramp living on Eel Brook Common and Felix would bring him flasks of soup, food and even clothing to help keep him warm at night. The tramp seemed to stay in that park for a long time and she remembered how, when police radio signals were picked up, saying they were going to clear the park, she and Felix would pick up this tramp in her Volkswagen Beetle and take him to another park.

On one occasion, when watching the film *Yellow Submarine*, Denise became very paranoid and appeared to be having a bad acid trip. They concluded that the box of Cadbury's Roses chocolates that Felix had bought her had been spiked with acid. Felix was furious and threatened to write to the company and complain. It of course transpired that the whole thing was mentally rather than chemically triggered and Cadbury was therefore spared the fury of Felix Dennis. Denise remembered that, although she had heard of Felix's reputation long before she met him, it was his relentless energy that was the attraction.

By the time Felix had a letter published in *Oz* the cover price had risen from half-a-crown to three shillings. The same issue, *Oz 17*, featured a photograph of a naked Louise Ferrier and fashion designer and textile artist Jenny Kee, which set pulses racing and sales rocketing. The image was credited to photographer Robert Whittaker, who at the time shared a flat at The Pheasantry in the King's Road with Martin Sharp and Eric Clapton.

Born in England to Australian and English parents, Bob Whittaker had lived in Australia when Richard Neville first started *Oz* Down Under. He had photographed many artists at the time, including Martin Sharp, and was tempted back to the UK by Beatles' manager Brian Epstein, who asked him to be the Fab Four's official photographer. Later, having gone on tour around the UK photographing the rock group Cream, he was shocked when Sharp cut up the prints, made a collage and painted Day-Glo colours over it to produce the iconic *Disraeli Gears* album cover. Barry Miles, whose name was to become synonymous with everything there was to write about the beat era, the sixties and the seventies, recalled Sharp doing something similar at the Indica bookshop in Mason's Yard, Mayfair in the early days.

'He came in and bought this beautiful, rather expensive, book of golf photographs,' said Miles, 'and then proceeded to tear it apart, right there in the shop! I was horrified and wondered what he was doing. He had no interest in the book or the individual images – he just wanted to use them for a collage.' A confirmed bibliophile, Miles saw this as a sacrilege, especially as the book would have set him back a week's wages had he wanted to buy it for himself.

As well as a wacky letter, Felix was also credited in this issue with the launch of the Poverty Cooking column, a new addition to the magazine and perhaps the first to take a broke hippie angle on food. It offered two recipes: one for a Cracked Egg Omelette, which, as cracked eggs were then sold off cheaply, should only cost about 9½p, and the other for a Beggar Stew, which recommended going to the butcher and buying a 'shilling's worth of mutton neck'. Felix had concluded that there were an awful lot of hungry hippies out there who could use a little advice on how to feed themselves cheaply. Richard Neville also thought it a great idea. Poverty Cooking featured again in the following issue, though with less space. It featured a recipe for Ballsed Up Bolognese that, although sounded disgusting, offered to feed up to four people for 4 shillings and 8p. Unsurprisingly, Felix never became famous for his cooking prowess. The smaller Poverty Cooking space was more than compensated for by his *Buddy Miles Express* LP review, which ended with the classic line 'Buddy Miles Express is a great band, all it basically lacks is someone who can tell Buddy Miles when to button his fat pussy and make with the machine gun he uses as a left hand.' He also contributed an interview with British guitarist Terry Reid.

Another photographer he had met around that time was able to vouch for just how hard Felix was working on *Oz* magazine. David Macintosh, originally from the Outer Hebrides, off the northwest coast of Scotland, had been living in a flat on the Wandsworth Bridge Road when Felix and Denise decided that living separately would be a better arrangement than sharing with four others. He remembered how Felix, knowing that David had a spare room, turned up one day and simply asked if he could move in for a while. At the time David was supplementing his income from photography by working as an engineer at Fulham Power Station and a little bit of extra money was helpful. For David it turned out to be particularly fortuitous as, thanks to Felix meeting a couple of girls at a cigarette machine down the road, he would meet the woman with whom he would spend the rest of his life.

Felix and David fell into what David remembered as a 'very agreeable' living arrangement. David would work during the day while Felix worked mostly at night. Setting up his typewriter in the living room at about 10 or 11pm, Felix would work into the small hours, bashing out copy for the magazine, mostly record reviews and music-related stuff. Taxis would turn up bearing gifts from record companies and, as Felix's record collection grew, so too did his knowledge and enthusiasm for the bands around at the time. *Oz 19* in 1969, as well as crediting Felix as the advertising man, also put him on the masthead for his Mozic section.

Opening the section was a wacky interview by the acclaimed feminist Germaine Greer, who was now *Oz*'s own sex therapist. It featured a groupie named Dr G, who claimed to have moved on from being a jazz groupie to rock and roll when she first heard the Rolling Stones singing, 'I can't get no satisfaction'. The eloquence of the groupie, her title of Dr G and Keith Morris's photographs of Germaine posing with Viv Stanshall from the Bonzo Dog Doo-Dah Band left readers in no doubt where their rock and roll fantasies should lie. Greer became a powerful force, both feeding those rock and roll fantasies, as well as being an icon for female sexuality and eventually for women's liberation. As they were both strong characters, she and Felix would often butt heads and argued constantly. Felix later claimed she eventually slept with him just to shut him up.

That particular issue had much to be proud of with an interview with 'Dylanologist' A. J. Weberman. The interview had been culled from another magazine but that didn't matter – *Oz* was part of the underground press syndicate and using material from other sources was not unusual. A review of John and Yoko's experimental album *Two Virgins* would later elicit a thank-you letter from Lennon, but for Felix and many readers, the highlight of the issue was his review of Led Zeppelin's debut album, which they had simply titled *Led Zeppelin*. The first ever published review of the album, it was to get Jimmy Page rushing around to Wandsworth Bridge Road to thank Felix. Its opening line foresaw what hundreds of music critics were to repeat for decades afterwards:

Very occasionally a long-playing record is released that defies immediate classification or description, simply because it's so obviously a turning point in rock music that only time proves capable of shifting it into eventual perspective.

The review went on to praise everything about the album, referring to Page as 'Jim' and pointing out that, 'Few rock musicians in the world could hope to parallel the degree of technical assurance and gutsy emotion he displays throughout these nine tracks.'

Denise Blackie remembered Jimmy Page first bringing the record round to Wandsworth Bridge Road to try to get Felix to review it. 'I didn't even know who he was then,' she admitted.

Photographer David Macintosh remembered Page visiting the flat on a number of occasions but one evening particularly stood out. David had decided to make a fish stew and produced a massive pot when Jimmy turned up. After a vicious attack of the munchies the whole stew was demolished and afterwards Page was to complain that it had ruined Led Zeppelin's next gig, claiming he had stuffed himself with so much stew that he was too ill to really get into the music that night. In David and Felix's personal history, it was to be remembered as the night they poisoned Jimmy Page!

While Felix contributed to the look and feel of the magazine, his concentration on attracting advertising from the music industry caused a bit of consternation when he sold the front and back cover of *Oz 21* to Elektra Records. They were promoting what they called, 'An outrageous collection of exotic, erotic, electric, eccentric phono-graphic albums falling into the much-publicised but barely understood category Underground'. He remembered that Richard Neville 'went fucking berserk', telling Felix he couldn't sell the front cover. Unperturbed, Felix pointed out that it paid the bills – which it did, though only for a while.

By this time *Oz* had moved out of Louise Ferrier and Richard Neville's flat in Palace Gardens Terrace but occasionally work would still be done there. One day Felix was to drive a bulldozer through his already shaky relationship with Neville. After an especially difficult week, he and Jim had come over to help do some paste-up and they had all worked late, eventually calling it a day at about 3am. Felix slept on the floor. When Richard left early the next morning to deliver artwork to a printer on the other side of London, all was quiet. He crept out the door, lugging the art boards, and tramped through drizzly streets to a dreary industrial zone. Later, when Felix eventually awoke, finding that he was alone in the flat with Louise presented an opportunity that they couldn't resist.

When Richard returned later that day, he found the flat empty, with clothes strewn about the room and no sign of Louise or her things.

'The whole house just looked like Dresden,' he said later.

Exhausted from the late night and early morning start, he flopped onto the bed as the phone rang. In his book, *Hippie Hippie Shake*, he repeats Felix's first words of the telephone conversation: 'I reckon I should tell you that this morning I fucked Louise,' he said.

Even in the era of free love it was a bombshell, and Richard was later to admit that, although he tried to play it cool, having just written a book that advocated free love, he was devastated. Amongst the hippie glitterati he and Louise were seen as the coolest of couples and, although neither had been totally faithful, there was a bond that was thoroughly shaken by what had happened.

Richard and Felix met and Felix tried to offer an apology. It was a shuffling, uncomfortable moment, with Richard trying to be gracious. Felix was genuinely sorry, although more from a position of regret than an empathetic understanding of the pain he may have caused. He was also concerned that his position at *Oz* could be in jeopardy. Later he was to say that he thought Richard might never forgive him. In time he did, but it stung for many years afterwards.

When *Oz* eventually fully moved out of Richard Neville's flat in 1968 it was to two addresses in Princedale Road in Notting Hill. The first was described by designer and illustrator Richard Adams as a dingy 'rats' nest', where an Icelandic dope dealer kept his grocery scales. He was known for building huge five-skin spliffs and parading down the street, handing them out to any passing hippies to help build up his custom. The second address, a few doors down, sounded more like a cross between *The Hitchhiker's Guide to the Galaxy* and *One Flew Over the Cuckoo's Nest*. Richard explained that Release, the organisation set up by Caroline Coon to help people deal with drug busts and other legal problems, had moved into an office in the same building as *Oz*, and consequently the place became home to a rich array of colourful characters. This was further enhanced by the fact that the downstairs office housed a gay model agency, run, as Richard recalled, by a couple of queens with tiny Yorkshire Terriers.

'It wasn't exactly a padded cell,' said Adams, 'but if I use the expression "the padded cell", that was where all the fucked-up visitors that were coming round to Release for some help or other would congregate.' He remembered how Little Nell, an Australian tap dancer who appeared in *The Rocky Horror Picture Show*, would 'entertain all these junkies with tap dancing routines'. He also recalled how putting the magazine together downstairs in the studio was a very theatrical affair. All sorts of people would come by.

'Writers with their copy, photographers with their pictures, illustrators with their drawings, cartoonists with their cartoons and just people with dope, records to sell – buyers, sellers, wheelers, dealers, concert tickets, freebies, all the perks. Everything used to just accumulate in this little space at that time. Tramps, dossers, runaway kids, army deserters – any and every freak you can possibly imagine used to come in there.'

If the *Oz* office was like a scene from *The Hitchhiker's Guide to the Galaxy*, 44 Wandsworth Bridge Road, though developing its own rich history, proved a haven for Felix to escape to after endless hours at the office. Louise Ferrier remembered the unsociable hours he would keep.

'He would work for days,' she said, 'days and days and days, without any sleep.' He would then go back to Wandsworth Bridge Road and effectively become a hermit. 'He'd take the phone off and he'd be incommunicado for a week. Then sometimes people would be frantically needing him and pounding on his door and he just wouldn't answer it.'

The fact was that, although in the days coming up to a print deadline the work was relentless, the social round of parties, events and concerts, all fuelled by whatever came to hand, though intoxicating, was also exhausting but it was also an early indicator of the recluse-like behaviour that Felix was often to display in later years.

In June 1969, a month before the Rolling Stones were to give a free concert in Hyde Park, Blind Faith played their own concert in the same venue to an audience of over 100,000 people. A supergroup consisting of Eric Clapton, Steve Winwood, Ginger Baker and Ric Grech, their kit consisted of drums, keyboard, a couple of guitars and a few Marshall amps. It was a far cry from the spectacle that would be required to satisfy an audience some 30 years later, and, as it happened, a very different affair to the Stones' poignant performance the following month, just three days after the untimely death of founding guitarist Brian Jones, who had drowned in his swimming pool.

Blind Faith showcased songs from their album of the same name, the cover of which was to become a bone of contention between Jim Anderson and Felix Dennis. Depicting a topless 11-year-old pubescent girl, it caused much controversy, and the album was released in the States with an alternative cover. Seeing an opportunity to use what he saw as a powerful image and at the same time ingratiate himself with the record label, Felix wanted to use the original image as the cover of *Oz 23* in August 1969, but Anderson had other ideas. *Oz 23* was to be the Gay Issue and, as Jim was gay, he was very much leading the editorial decisions.

'I had a real quarrel with Felix,' remembered Jim, who had already arranged for two gay friends, one black and one white, to be photographed in a naked embrace for the cover shot. It was a multicultural, homosexual statement that represented the liberal and inclusive stance taken by *Oz* on sexual and racial issues. But showing his commercial sense, Felix didn't think it was good enough to sell magazines. Jim remembered the episode as about the only time that they ever really seriously disagreed.

He said later, 'It was really very, very difficult. Felix fought so hard – wouldn't give way until the last minute.' Felix was eventually outvoted and the Blind Faith album cover image appeared on the inside of the magazine on page 33, with just a quote from the *Daily Mirror*, suggesting record dealers should not stock the album as it was 'in outrageous bad taste'. A few pages later the album received a short but positive review from John Leaver but the image and the *Mirror* headline would have been perfect advertising. The gay cover was a huge success, although it did draw the attention of the Obscene Publications Squad, who visited the *Oz* offices to seize back issues. At that time, no charges were brought.

CHAPTER 5

THE FREAK WITH
THE BRIEFCASE

As it happened, the ad that kickstarted the furore of the *Oz* obscenity trial was published in the same issue as Felix's offending headline 'Heavy Shit...' a chatty selection of short music stories tantalisingly given completely irrelevant headings, supposedly from newspapers like the *Daily Express*, the *News Chronicle* and the *Surrey Comet & South Middlesex News*. Had they been condensed stories from different newspapers, he may even have had a jump on *The Week* and made his first fortune many years earlier but there was much excitement to be had before the real money started rolling in.

The ad, on page 46 of *Oz 26*, published in February 1970, read as follows:

Some of us in *Oz* are feeling old and boring, so we invite any of our readers who are under eighteen to come and edit the April issue. Apply at the *Oz* office in Princedale Road, W11 anytime from 10am to 7pm on Friday, 13 March. We will choose one person, several, or accept collective applications from a group of friends. You will receive no money, except expenses. You will enjoy almost complete editorial freedom. *Oz* staff will assist in purely an administrative capacity. If you like, write before 13 March and tell us who you are and [what you] would like to do with a 2 colour 48 page magazine ... *Oz* belongs to you.

David Wills, who also worked on the magazine's design, said that his recollection of how the *Schoolkids' Oz* issue came about was during a conversation with Richard Neville and Jim Anderson in a London cafe. He remembered a discussion about all three of them being about to turn 30 and he thought that it was he who had suggested they give the next issue over to schoolchildren to edit. In *Hippie Hippie Shake*, Richard Neville remembered the inspiration a little differently. He recalled that, at an editorial meeting on New Year's Eve, it was Felix who suggested that Richard was, at nearly 30, too old, and that his article ideas, being too intellectual, were going over the heads of most of the readership.

Felix had claimed that they could triple their circulation with a bit of common sense. As far as he was concerned, the magazine was somewhat elitist and there was a potentially much bigger market out there.

Jim Anderson remembered that on many occasions the authorities would visit printers to warn them not to get involved with underground magazines – the *Schoolkids' Oz* issue was an opportunity for the newly created Obscene Publications Squad to really go after them and close them down. Jon Goodchild maintained that one of the reasons for getting the schoolkids involved was the fact that, at the time, neither Felix nor Jim had enough experience or contacts to put together an issue on their own so getting a bunch of kids in was a way of avoiding pulling together all the necessary pieces that would normally make up the magazine.

Richard went on to say that afterwards, when he and Louise Ferrier were celebrating New Year's Eve at his sister Jill's house, he was reeling from LCD, alcohol and cannabis. In fact, he was so incapable of speaking that he could only grin at his sister when she asked him if he was on drugs. Somehow he managed to remember that, apart from her telling him that drugs made him silly, at the same time he came up with the bright idea of getting a bunch of schoolkids in to produce an issue of *Oz* that would reach a younger audience.

'A collective guest-editorship,' he recalled. 'As the idea dawned,' he added, 'so did a new decade.'

In true underground magazine style, those putting together the small boxed lineage ad had even made their own typesetting errors, leaving out two words. Although the ad called for applications to Princedale Road, one schoolboy, who later admitted that at the time he was actually no longer a schoolboy and in fact already beyond the 'under 18 rule', remembered his first meeting being at the Palace Gardens Terrace flat of Richard Neville. Charles Shaar Murray, who had hitch-hiked down from Reading, described the flat as 'dimly lit and exotically furnished'. Neville and Ferrier were renting a small basement flat for £7 a week and, by the time the schoolkids arrived, it had already become, at least for Louise, far too small to be a happy home as well as a business address. She remembered feeling claustrophobic when it would fill up with *Oz* paraphernalia and assorted hangers-on, and would simply make herself scarce.

About to set off on a course in journalism, Murray was a cut above the others, both in age and maturity. Already he had an acerbic outlook on the current state of the press and underground literature, and later told the *Sunday Times* that, at the time, he felt like he had been searching in the dark for a light switch and '*Oz* was it'.

One of his first memories of Felix Dennis is of a hippie in a suit, or as he put it later, 'the freak with a briefcase'. After accepting the role of business manager at *Oz* magazine, Felix had taken it upon himself to look the part and had abandoned his Afghan coat for more business-like attire. That didn't mean losing the hair or the beard, it took a prison officer to achieve that, but it did mean looking like someone who wouldn't be thrown out of a business foyer. It didn't necessarily endear him to the hardcore hippies but then Felix never cared about being called a bread head. As he would often say later, 'It is what it is'. Charles Shaar Murray was struck by the brown pinstripe suit over Felix's denim shirt and snakeskin cowboy boots but he did remember that, on first sight, Felix did look rather 'wild and unkempt', although he put that down to the possibility that he had just tumbled out of someone's bed, an impression that Murray thought Felix liked to cultivate anyway. As it happened, regardless of whether it was a cultivated look, it was usually true.

Of the first meeting between the editors and the schoolkids, he remembered that Jim Anderson, Richard Neville and Felix were at least as interested in the children as the children were in them. They initially discussed education, politics and society, as well as sex, drugs and rock and roll, and asked the kids what they would like to see in the magazine. It was without doubt a sincere effort to find out how they could add a new level to *Oz* magazine while giving some impetus to their own flagging enthusiasm. *Oz* had been slowly going through a metamorphosis, partly through the influence of Felix, who wanted it all to be humorous, sexy and most of all legible, but also partly because life and the society that they were living in were changing at a fast pace. In retrospect, it appears that the authorities, who behind the scenes in government were plotting to find a way to put a giant gobstopper into what they saw as the mouthpiece of the underground movement, may not have needed to wait that long for a natural decomposition to set in. Instead, their actions may have galvanised disparate groups, causing riots and bringing what was essentially a fairly localised, though quite extended orgy of fun and colour into the mainstream media spotlight – albeit for a short time.

By the time the schoolkids had come along, the magazine had already strayed off its hardcore satirical course, though not without achieving the same effect as shaking a sockful of plutonium at what, for the most part, was still a very dowdy society.

The 27 issues produced before the offending *Schoolkids' Oz* had ruffled a lot of feathers and, although Charles Shaar Murray later said that the cover was 'probably the worst decision in the whole history of the magazine', whatever the schoolkids did was always likely to provoke disapproval. The hounds were circling and the scent of naive hippie meat was wafting tantalisingly through the air.

The smell from the glue used in pasting up the magazine had much to compete with in both Jim Anderson's and Richard and Louise's flats in Palace Gardens Terrace. Whether it was Afghan Gold, Thai Stick or the sweet smell of Moroccan hash, there was often something more than patchouli oil and joss sticks doing battle for the airspace around the *Oz* editors' heads. More often than not though, it was the atmosphere created by chaos that pervaded the rooms.

Jim remembers that none of them was particularly tidy. 'Richard's place was a pigsty and so was mine,' he said. 'We were both very hippie – clothes everywhere and dust in every room.' His rare visits to Felix's conspicuously clean flat on the Wandsworth Bridge Road only reinforced the fact that Palace Gardens Terrace was a tip. However, his and Richard's flats were to be the base from which the *Schoolkids' Oz* issue was to be produced, and Jim's recollection of the whole process is one of bedlam.

'It was a bit like being a teacher,' he explained. The kids were all over the place and having a great time. They obviously had no idea about how to put a magazine together but were enthusiastic, and Jim and Felix, determined to let their creative juices flow, were quite happy to accept any bits of copy they supplied.

Andrew Fisher, an Australian lawyer who had been involved in *London Oz* magazine with Richard Neville in its early days – both writing and helping with the day-to-day running of the business, had always kept an eye on whether the magazine was coming too close to breaking the law. As he had already been involved in an obscenity trial with the Australian *Oz* magazine – ironically reported in the *Spectator* in 1964 as containing 'run-of-the-mill student vulgarity which would excite only local comment in Britain' – they would spend many hours discussing what might and might not come to the notice of the authorities. He remembered having battles with Germaine Greer about what could and couldn't go in.

However, by the time Felix and Jim Anderson were taking over production, Andrew Fisher was also getting restless and looking for a new role. That opportunity came with an offer from Granada for him to present a TV show called *Octopus*, which was to be based in Manchester. This also coincided with Richard Neville taking a long holiday after the publication of his book, which left Jim and Felix to put the *Schoolkids' Oz* issue together with little or no input from the original editors. Jim remembered the kids' contributions and the rest of the content being a little haphazard.

'They didn't contribute that much really,' he said, 'certainly not enough to fill up an issue. But whatever they did contribute, whether it was good or bad, I don't think we checked anything they contributed, in it went.'

Oz had traditionally been a mixture of commissioned work, alongside whatever happened to be available to put in at the time. Although there were themed issues, like the Hells Angels or gay issues, the theme was never the whole magazine. Jim saw the schoolkids' contributions as a few cartoons, mostly sexual, and one or two critiques of the school system, but really not nearly enough to make a complete issue. In fact, *Oz 28* only had about 12 pages that could be attributed to the 'guest editors'.

Indeed, apart from a Rupert Bear cartoon, the cover was to become one of the prosecution's favoured bugbears when the whole thing eventually went to court in June 1971. It came about because of a book that had been hanging around the office for many months. Produced by a mysterious French artist named Raymond Bertrand, it contained a selection of extraordinary drawings. Bertrand's work had previously appeared on covers of the French science fiction magazine *Fiction*, where perfectly endowed naked females either emerged from or morphed into a mixture of organic matter, extraordinary head-wear, jewellery or dreamlike imagery. Rarely in any way relevant to the content of the magazine, his covers were exceptional and Jim remembered that, although the schoolkids were fascinated by the Bertrand book and wanted it to be used in the magazine, the inspiration for its use on the cover was very much a last-minute thing.

The original plan was to use a David Nutter photograph but the idea didn't translate when the time came to set up the shoot.

'We couldn't get the cover to work,' he explained. 'It was our secretary dressed up as a schoolgirl, leaping about with a machine gun or something. Something really ridiculous, but it was really awful.'

It was the last night before going to print and at about three in the morning they hit on what at the time seemed like a brilliant idea. They would make a wrap-around cover using images from the Bertrand book, something they had originally planned to use as a centre spread inside the magazine, and where the image was a little too risqué, they would cover it up with a photograph of someone dressed in a schoolboy uniform. The wrap-around meant that another potential problem, the fact that in one image the woman was using a dildo, might not be noticed, as it would be on the back.

All the images were quite obviously the same woman but that didn't stop the prosecution at the *Oz* trial from later claiming the cover depicted a lesbian orgy. Raymond Bertrand's drawings were referred to by the judge, Michael Argyle, as 'extremely attractively drawn'; however, he was upset by what he constantly referred to as the 'dilldoll'.

Jim said afterwards, 'Felix and I had made this momentous decision. None of the schoolkids were around but they had seen the book and were quite happy for it to go in.'

At seven o'clock that morning the whole issue was taken to the printers and Jim remembered that, although the printers flagged their concern, they told them not to worry and that it would all be OK. The kids had loved it. As Jim put it, it was all 'naughty sexy stuff' and 'totally harmless and fun. But that's not the way it was seen.' As he ruefully remembered, 'And then, very quickly, the shit hit the fan.'

Like a 747 stuck in a holding pattern above Heathrow, the shit had simply been circling. A packed fuselage full of it was just waiting for the opportunity to be released, and in the guise of Detective Inspector Frederick Luff, it made a beeline for *Oz*. Later claiming he was driven by religious motivation, Luff had already been making a name for himself as a defender of British morality. Described by Richard Neville as 'fleshy faced', he favoured the burly detective look, with slicked-back hair and a beige trench coat.

On 16 January 1970, a couple of months before the schoolkids had made their way to Palace Gardens Terrace, he had led a raid on the London Arts Gallery in New Bond Street. As a big player in Scotland Yard's Obscene Publications Squad, Luff had been tipped off that the art gallery's exhibition, which had opened the day before, contained erotic drawings of a potentially obscene nature. Arriving with a warrant and back up, he raided what turned out to be John Lennon's *Bag One, the*

Erotic Lithographs exhibition. He took away eight of the works on the basis that the gallery had 'exhibited to public view eight indecent prints to the annoyance of passengers'. With the sort of heavy-handed tactics that the squad – already nicknamed 'The Dirty Squad' – were becoming known for, he insisted on detaining everyone in the gallery and taking their names and addresses. Later in court, when asked whether attendees actually showed 'annoyance', he was to say that yes, indeed, one of the 40-odd people at the exhibition had looked annoyed. Asked whether that person was so annoyed that they might stamp their foot in anger, he replied, 'Anger was registered on his face.'

Although John and Yoko were not in London for the opening of the exhibition, the raid ensured that Lennon, as a reader of *Oz* magazine, was given plenty of reason to offer support when the same squad piled into the *Oz* office later in the year. While preparing the evidence for the *Oz* case, Luff also tried to close down the show *Oh! Calcutta!* – but only after seeing it three times to convince himself it was obscene. His findings didn't convince the Attorney General, however, and the show moved to the West End, where it ran for three years. Actor Anthony Booth, whose daughter Cherie was to marry the future Prime Minister, Tony Blair, was one of the many actors who had stripped naked on stage for their art.

Although warnings were issued to news vendors, distributors and printers to convince them to wash their hands of *Oz*, Luff's tactics didn't work with Sid Spellman of Holders Press in Lamb's Conduit Street. According to a description in *Hippie Hippie Shake*, Spellman threw Luff and his men out of his office, likening them to Nazi police with leather coats and Alsatians. Interviewed in 1998, he didn't remember it in as much detail, but certainly recalled throwing them out as they didn't have a warrant. He got the impression that the police weren't really interested in him but were just finding ways to get at *Oz*.

'They only wanted to get the editors because it was so foreign to the sort of culture of the police and the establishment,' he said. 'Everyone was being heavily leant on because the establishment was petrified about what was going on around them.' He pointed out that he also printed *Janus*, the long-running spanking magazine of which he, somewhat ironically, said, 'Even Felix would have disapproved of.'

But the petrified establishment that Spellman alluded to was not a figment of his imagination. The glamorous Swinging Sixties were, in truth, confined to a small percentage of mostly middle-class youth, whose lifestyle was driven by a buoyant economy. Technology was making advances that those who watched the motor car overtake the horse and cart simply couldn't comprehend. A radio bought from Woolworth's had already brought a whole new world to children's bedrooms. A television, though limiting viewing to the hours between 5pm and 11.30pm, had introduced foreign cultures, and *Dr Who*'s Daleks were causing little children to cower behind chairs. Sean Connery introduced James Bond, while the original geek 'Q' thrilled audiences with technological possibilities. *Tomorrow's World* introduced the breathalyser to a generation who had watched motorways, flyovers and the Post Office Tower grow like alien planets before their eyes. England had even won the World Cup, and consumers contemplated the possibility of holidays in Spain, Italy or maybe even further afield. It was a heady time that politicians and community leaders found hard to keep up with. In fact, the apparent speed of change frightened many who worried that the effect would send society spiralling out of control. However, in reality, despite all the excitement and hope for a more liberal and open world, as called for by Mini cars, mini-skirts and *Oz* magazine, Britain was still essentially a somewhat prosaic and conservative society. A large part of the country was still in the grip of the fifties' straitjacket. Most of the population still adhered to a dull conservative style of dress, were stultified by a repressed attitude to sex and were fearful of change. The sixties' optimism wasn't shared by those who found security in a rigid social hierarchy, the rule of law and unquestioning respect for authority. It took until the mid-seventies for the truth to out. Luff's cronies turned out to be more crooked than anyone could have imagined.

It was that corruption that helped Felix Dennis evolve into a millionaire businessman. He later claimed that the class structure left him in no doubt about who did and didn't know what was really going on in the Dirty Squad.

Sitting in his Writer's Cottage in Mustique in 2014, he remembered the occasion with no dilution of passion. 'The working classes already knew,' he said. 'The working classes didn't need anybody to tell them that the police and the court system invent!'

He believed that the upper classes didn't need anybody to tell them either because they were part of the corruption, whether turning a blind eye or being on the receiving end themselves.

'The middle classes truly believed that there used to be people like *Dixon of Dock Green*. They truly believed that there were policemen like that. There were never policemen like that!'

Interviewed in 1998, Geoffrey Robertson, a young Australian lawyer and Rhodes Scholar at Oxford with Bill Clinton at the time of the trial, explained that as outsiders he and his Australian friends were a little naive when it came to their understanding of British policing.

'It was difficult for Jim and Richard and myself to believe the amount of corruption in Scotland Yard,' he said. 'We are talking about a period when the obscenities squad was dealing in obscenity, the drug squad was dealing drugs and the armed robbery squad was setting up armed robberies!'

Felix described the sort of scenario that might have occurred if he had had money at the time of the *Oz* police raids: 'You're after my little arts magazine,' he'd say. They would reply, 'It's not a little arts magazine. It's filth, isn't it? It's disgusting filth.' To which he would counter, 'Well, here's £5,000.' They would say, 'Well, that's very kind of you, sir, very kind. That's what I call open-handed, I call that, open-handed.'

With a mighty roar of laughter, Felix ruefully reiterated what has been said over many years about the effect the whole *Oz* trial had on him.

'That was never going to happen to me again,' he insisted. 'I was never going to go through all of that again because I didn't have any money – before I never even thought about money. I didn't care, I didn't need any money.' With the fire that was never far from his piercing eyes, he added, 'I worked at it night and day. I never stopped thinking about anything else, just about. I realised that, if I got that money, I was clear. Once you get the money, they'll eat out of your hand.'

In the period prior to the trial, Felix took full advantage of what were to be the twilight years of the hippie lifestyle in England. Courtesy of Capital Records, he attended the Essen Pop and Blues Festival, where the Groundhogs and Black Sabbath shared billing with The Keef Hartley Band and other heavyweights like Johnny Winter. With a growing confidence in his ability to see through the public relations conceit that was creeping into the music industry, he stormed out of a Deep Purple press launch, loudly proclaiming the event to be pretentious bullshit. He later returned to the bemusement and awe of the mute gathering of record industry executives and journalists.

In August 1970 he joined over 600,000 people at the Isle of Wight Festival, where Jimi Hendrix, the Who, The Doors and many others proved that the commercialism that was to follow hadn't yet completely taken over the music – despite Mick Farren's claim that the whole event was an example of 'capitalist interests seeking to exploit the energy of the people's music'. Although only about 50,000 people had been expected, like Woodstock before, it was overrun by crowds that no one could cope with. Fences were torn down as hordes of hippies gatecrashed the festival and a hill overlooking the site was as popular as, if not more than, the site itself. The festival created its own myths and planted itself into the hippie flower meadow of counter-culture history, but not without carnage and detritus. Farren remembered it as 'a Class One Rock Apocalypse'. For him it was *Mad Max* a decade before they made the movie; for many others it was the last great festival of the hippie movement. Although it may have been the last great festival, it certainly wasn't the end for the attempted change to libertarian values. However, it was to be one of the last times Jimi Hendrix played in public. Eighteen days later he was dead, attributed to asphyxiation from vomiting; his death was said to have been caused by an overdose of barbiturates.

*

It was Germaine Greer who was to pay tribute to Jimi Hendrix in the issue of *Oz* that came out after the Isle of Wight. In angst-ridden, soul-searching prose she looked into the heart of the future of the music industry and found it lacking. However, she also blamed the fans' thoughtless adulation for Jimi's early exit: 'We might piously cry that the gross commercialism of the op-pop-rock industry ground him to death, but really it wasn't that. It was the power of death in us, the people.' Although billed as the Travel issue, Jimi's pained face filled the centre of the 'O' in *Oz* on the cover, and there was little doubt that, on top of the debacle at the Isle of Wight, the loss of a legend was a sadness that would grow over the years. Later, one of the schoolboys, Charles Shaar Murray, was to write a much-admired biography of Hendrix. Charles had decided to forego his attempts at further academia and stay in London to become a writer.

On 7 November 1970, Felix made what was possibly his most famous TV appearance. A planned raid on *The David Frost Show* came about when Jerry Rubin, founder of the American Youth International (Yippie) party, arrived in London and stayed at Richard Neville's flat. Amusingly, Felix remembered him as someone who shouted even more than him. Rubin, along with two other Yippies, appeared as guests on the show to talk to Frost about the Yippie movement. When Rubin lit a joint and offered it to Frost, that was the cue for a group of hippies in the audience to descend onto the stage, bringing flowers and general mayhem. As the show collapsed into chaos, Frost asked Rubin whether he thought the childish disturbance would attract more people to his revolution, suggesting he was a reasonable man and could answer the question. Felix, off-camera at the time, was heard to say, 'He is not a reasonable man. He's the most unreasonable cunt I've ever met in my life!' That observation was to give him the reputation of being the first person to say the word 'cunt' on British television. Felix liberally squirted a water pistol at Frost and incurred the wrath of the TV host, who called him pathetic, childish and pointless as the show took a break.

Jon Goodchild, who was there alongside Mick Farren, Boss Goodman, Richard Neville and Jim Anderson amongst others, called it 'a serious piece of agit-prop' set up ahead of time to create maximum impact on camera. He remembered being surprised that the BBC had been so upset by the invasion.

'We all broke up and got out of BBC house by different routes,' he said. 'There were security guards everywhere chasing us. It was chaos. We didn't realise their response would be quite so nasty.'

Later, Felix told the *Guardian* that his mother didn't speak to him for three years.

Five weeks later, on 18 December, the *Oz* office was again raided by the Obscene Publications Squad and this time it was trashed, rendering it impossible to produce the next issue without a major clean-up and the return of many files. Illustrator Richard Adams remembered the raid. 'Luff really did go in there with all guns blazing,' he said. 'Swiping all the accounts, lots of artwork, correspondence files – lots and lots. It was really an exercise in just trying to knee-cap the entire collection.'

Realising the police were also planning to raid Richard Neville's flat, Felix raced around there and with typical bluster and aggression managed to get himself arrested. He was later released, but Neville was taken into custody on a possession of cannabis charge and only bailed the next day after solicitor David Offenbach managed to track down a judge on the golf course.

CHAPTER 6

TEDDY BEAR WITH A STIFFY

Eventually, on 18 August 1970, Scotland Yard issued their summons on *Oz* magazine and the three editors. Having previously been photographed dressed in school uniform, Richard Neville, Jim Anderson and Felix then posed for the press in convict suits. They were giving a massive two fingers to the establishment and, as Felix put it later, the police 'let themselves in' to his Wandsworth Bridge Road flat and threatened to jail him.

Richard, Jim and Felix were charged on five counts:

1) That they had conspired to produce a magazine that would corrupt the morals of young children and other young persons.

2) That between 1 May 1970 and 8 June 1970 they had published an obscene article, *Oz* No. 28, known as the SchoolKids Issue.

3) That between the same dates they had sent a postal packet containing a number of indecent or obscene articles in *Oz* No. 28.

4) That on 8 June 1970 they had possessed obscene articles, 252 copies of *Oz* No. 28, for publication for gain.

5) That on 11 June 1970 they had possessed 220 copies of *Oz* No. 28, also for publication for gain.

In theory, the charge of corrupting the morals of young children carried a maximum sentence of life imprisonment, an outcome that, although few believed might happen, still sent an occasional shiver of fear through the hearts of the three editors. However, as plans and meetings took place to organise the *Oz* Three's defence and Felix convinced Barclays Bank to open an *Oz* Obscenity Fund account, there were a few moments of light relief.

Didi Wadidi, the German editor of *Suck* magazine, the 'first European Sex Paper', which Germaine Greer had begun to write for, decided to come to London on a research trip. Didi thought it would be good to see which of the *Oz* editors would be best in bed. Richard Neville described her as slim and cream-skinned, with swirling dark hair. When she arrived at Palace Gardens Terrace and disrobed in front of him and Louise, she said, 'The three of us together, yes?' Sounding somewhat disappointed, Richard related that Louise declined, but did quip, 'Change the sheets when you've finished' as she left them to it. Purely to be supportive of the need for proper research, Felix also obliged, later claiming that Didi pronounced him to be the better lover.

Although the trial was covered comprehensively in award-winning writer and film director Tony Palmer's book, *The Trials of Oz*, which was rushed into print immediately afterwards and subsequently sold over 250,000 copies, initially and unsurprisingly the whole fiasco was reported in the press from more of an establishment viewpoint than objective observer. Malcolm Muggeridge, who had made an appearance in the second issue of *Oz*, wrote afterwards in a letter to *The Times* that the antics of *Oz* were 'squalid' and 'illiterate'. It was obvious from the start that efforts to thwart the *Oz* defence were already in place, when, with only days to go before the trial date, two possible defence QCs pulled out. Geoffrey Robertson had by then agreed to help with the *Oz* Three's defence and he and Richard Neville approached John Mortimer to see if he would head up the team. They tracked him down at a restaurant and he asked what the case was about. In answer they showed him the Rupert Bear cartoon, carefully shielding it from Mortimer's lunch companions, one of whom would later become his wife. He laughed and showed it to them, saying, 'Goody, when do we start?'

In Court Number 2 of the Central Criminal Court of the Old Bailey on Wednesday, 23 June, with Judge Michael Argyle presiding and Felix Dennis,

Jim Anderson and Richard Neville in the dock, John Mortimer rose to make his opening address. He described the trial as a case about dissent.

'It is,' he said, 'a case about those who are critical of the established values of our society, who ask us to reconsider what they believe to be complacent values, and are anxious, on that basis, to build what they think (and what we may not think) is a better world. Members of the jury, we are all of us totally entitled to disagree with their views, but this is a case about whether or not they are entitled to disagree with us.'

Tony Palmer and many of those present saw clearly that throughout the case the judge, through body language, tone and the use of his written record of witness testimony, was in no doubt that the *Oz* Three were not entitled to disagree with established views.

Justice Argyle spent much of the trial perusing an atlas with a magnifying glass and scowling at witnesses who stood for the defence. When a play re-enacting the *Oz* trial, written by Geoffrey Robertson, was first performed by the Royal Shakespeare Company in 1972, Robertson asked that the judge should be shown to have a magnifying glass with which to peer at Richard Neville. Apparently the director demurred, saying that even if it were true, which Robertson insisted it was, in a theatre the audience simply wouldn't have believed it had actually happened in the courtroom. In his book, *The Justice Game*, Geoffrey Robertson summed it up, saying, 'The most difficult thing about re-enacting the *Oz* trial is that it was the sort of life which art cannot imitate.'

Describing the defendants, Robertson said, 'Richard Neville had the boarding school mannerisms of Prince Charles, Jim Anderson was a gentle, gay ex-barrister and Felix Dennis, despite a south London abrasiveness, had all the makings of the multi-millionaire mogul he later became.' While Neville eloquently and intelligently defended himself against prosecution bullying, and Anderson remained committed to his own honest defence under questioning, Felix was determined not to be cowed by Treasury Counsel Brian Leary QC. As Robertson pointed out in an interview in 2000, Felix 'was the only person who had any kind of fight in him'. He remembered that there was a lot of time spent going through the cross-examination with him because they thought he might be the weakest link.

'But, in fact, a very interesting experience for me was to see that the very opposite was the case. Jim utterly crumbled and was the most hopeless witness you could ever find. Richard, like Oscar Wilde, spoke too much, made too many jokes and was tripped up as a result, but Felix was absolutely authentic. He was himself in the witness box and did by far the best under cross-examination.'

Felix wore a white suit, large silver-rimmed spectacles and had a well-cut beard on the opening day of the trial, but had changed into the dark-blue dungarees and the bright-yellow *Oz* T-shirt that they all wore when the *Oz* Three took the witness stand. By this time they had realised a farce was taking place and were determined to get as much publicity as possible. Felix affirmed as an atheist and described himself to the judge as a director of *Oz* publications and the one whose job it was to 'worry about money'. To describe his testimony as defiant might well be an understatement: he had no intention of letting the prosecution take him apart and his performance in the dock impressed everyone, even the judge.

Geoffrey Robertson explained later that at the end of the trial he had a conversation with D.I. Luff, which threw some light on the character of the establishment's bloodhound. According to Robertson, the Detective Inspector said, 'You know, I don't mind that Richard Neville, no one takes any notice of him, but it's that Felix Dennis. I saw the little bastard the other day with not one, but two young girls on his arm!'

Robertson said afterwards, 'What really got those working-class coppers, most of whom who were on the take, was not the chat show geniality of Richard Neville, it was that they were being taunted by someone, as it were, one of their own.'

The case was not conducted without humour. In the early stages of giving testimony, Felix explained the difficulties of producing a magazine when printers and distributors were being advised not to deal with them. He told the prosecution that he had begun to wear suits to meetings and to carry a briefcase to give credibility to the company and highlighted one occasion when a printer, without ever having seen an issue of *Oz*, told him it would be impossible for him to print the magazine. So he said, 'Well, you haven't even seen an issue yet, how do you know you've even got the technical capability to print it?' To which the printer replied that he couldn't print it because they were too close to Buckingham Palace. This seemed to coincide with some inner turmoil in the judge, who with a pained expression suddenly said, 'Now, wait a minute, wait a minute! Can we please keep the Royal Family out of this, do you think? We haven't succeeded in keeping many people out of it yet.'

When the representative for the Crown mentioned the existence of a 'dilldoll' on the cover photograph, the judge suggested they refer to it as an 'imitation male penis' to which Richard Neville quipped, 'The word "male" is actually unnecessary, Your Lordship.'

Later, Felix recounted a story about one of Luff's raids on the *Oz* office. Having been tipped off about the impending raid, he had arranged for a photographer and a news cameraman to be there.

'It is a fact,' he told the court, 'that newspapers and television and the mass media in this country have become extremely interested in the alleged harassment by police of certain underground publications. I do not think their interest is in any way illegal or irresponsible and I consider that to have a photographer and a responsible journalist present at a police raid on a magazine of any kind is not in any way being irresponsible, or in any way obstructing the police in the course of their duties.'

While history was being made in the courtroom there was no shortage of activity on the streets outside the Old Bailey. Already a one-man rapid response force, Felix was ably assisted by another Australian, Stan Demudjik, who had set up a Friends of *Oz* group to begin a campaign to bring the trial to the notice of as many hippies as possible, as well as to highlight anything that might be underhand or conveniently missed by the national press. Obscenity fund benefits were arranged at Middle Earth in Covent Garden and an *Oz* benefit film festival was held at the Electric Cinema Club on Portobello Road. Richard Neville remembered the *Oz* Police Ball benefit in March 1971 attracting around 1,500 people who 'boogied till dawn and screwed on water beds'. Hundreds of posters and leaflets were printed to galvanise people and raise awareness of the potential effect on the counter-culture's newfound freedom, as well as the attack on freedom of speech. One particular poster showed a Nazi Stormtrooper burning copies of *Schoolkids' Oz* above the words '*Oz* now. You next'. Honeybunch Kaminski, a cartoon character, was used as the *Oz* trial mascot and at one Hyde Park concert a 10-foot female dummy depicting Honeybunch, with enormous rouged boobs, was paraded through the crowd. The same mascot was to be included in the marches to the Old Bailey.

At the time a young artist called David Hockney was making a name for himself in the Pop Art world. Born in Bradford, West Yorkshire, he studied at the Royal Academy in London and later became one of the most influential British artists of the twentieth century. Amongst others, he was asked to produce a painting to be auctioned off to help raise funds for the *Oz* defence and agreed to do a drawing of the three defendants. Of all the works that were auctioned, Hockney's was to become the most memorable. He sketched the three of them nude, all sitting for him at different times, and produced a triptych of them together.

Richard Neville remembered feeling shy as Hockney, 'his eyes, huge through pop specs, coolly appraised my loins'. Small talk about the impending trial between artist and sitter was focused on the politics behind the trial. 'Do you think the Prime Minister's behind it?' asked Hockney. By this time Ted Heath's Conservatives had ousted Harold Wilson's Labour government and Felix would later claim that Heath was personally responsible for arranging the pursuit and eventual charging of the *Oz* Three. The Hockney triptych was to provide good fodder for friendly banter as the relative size of genitals was compared. Felix, it seemed, had won that one too. The Clytie Jessop Gallery in the King's Road hosted a fund-raising exhibition entitled *Ozject D'art*, which as well as David Hockney's prints included work by John Lennon, Yoko Ono, Germaine Greer, Gerald Scarfe, Philippe Mora and Martin Sharp in addition to Caroline Coon's first ever exhibited painting, 'Cuntopia'.

One of the biggest coups that the Friends of *Oz* pulled off, however, included one of the most famous voices to come out of the sixties. John Lennon had been a regular reader and supporter of the magazine from its early days and, when Stan Demudjik approached him about finding a way to help the three men who were about to go on trial, he suggested John write a song. He agreed to write, record and release a song supporting them but it would be a little more complex than that.

In an interview in *Sounds* magazine, Lennon recalled how it came about: 'Stan and some people from *Oz* rang up and said, "Will you make us a record?" and I thought, Well, I can't because I'm all tied up contractually and I didn't know how to do it. So then we got down to would I write a song for them? I think we wrote it the same night, didn't we? We wrote it together and the b-side. First of all we wrote it as "God Save *Oz*", you know, "God save *Oz* from it all", but then we decided they wouldn't really know what we were talking about in America so we changed it back to "us".'

The only way to overcome the contractual obligation was to use some-one else on lead vocal, so John enlisted the help of Billy Elliot, later to become known as half of the Newcastle duo Splinter, who signed to George Harrison's Dark Horse label.

The 'God Save *Oz*' song was to be recorded at Lennon's Ascot mansion, where he and Yoko later made *Imagine*. Felix remembered a motley crew gathered for the recording session, where he played congas, backing John and Yoko's vocal. Charles Shaar Murray recalled everyone piling into a van and arriving to a sumptuous buffet at John's house. His one regret was that, having strummed an acoustic guitar during the early takes, he suggested an electric guitar would sound better. Later, an electric guitar replaced the acoustic and his efforts weren't used on the final recording.

The Friends of *Oz* also planned a carnival parade, which would include the cartoon character Honeybunch Kaminski, and someone came up with the bright idea to also include an elephant. Unfortunately, Bow Street Police refused a permit for the creature but the parade, with John and Yoko at its head, did make an extraordinary spectacle for the people of London as it made its way to the Old Bailey, singing 'God Save *Oz*' and waving banners and placards in support of the *Oz* Three.

Behind all the public activity in aid of the *Oz* trial, Marsha Rowe and Louise Ferrier were working all hours alongside Geoffrey Robertson and David Widgery to develop the case for the defence. Days and nights were spent typing and preparing paperwork and over a hundred witnesses were sourced to offer specialist testimony showing the lunacy of the charges. Marty Feldman, Edward de Bono, Caroline Coon and John Peel all made colourful input, while other witnesses sombrely assured the jury that *Oz* was never likely to corrupt. The judge seemed to take quite a shine to Caroline Coon who, dressed in hot pants, proved to be a powerful and intelligent witness. He commented afterwards, 'Thank you, Miss Coon. You've lightened a dark and very dull afternoon.' Later, during his summing-up, he made a point of saying she seemed a 'very nice girl'.

Schoolboy Vivian Berger's cartoon of Rupert Bear with an enormous erection, racing towards a reclining grandmother and eventually deflowering her, was the subject of much comment and amusement. At one point, witness for the defence Dr Michael Schofield was asked what age did he think Rupert the Bear was.

'Oh, I'm very sorry – I'm not up to date with bears,' he replied. The question was pushed and Schofield explained that he might as well have been asked how old Jupiter was, eventually admitting to the prosecutor, 'I'm sorry, I'm obviously not as well informed as you are about little bears. I'm a psychologist.'

When jazz legend George Melly was asked about references to oral sex, he said he didn't think cunnilingus could be harmful, causing Judge Argyle to interrupt and say, 'For those of us who do not have a classical education, what do you mean by the word "Cunnilingtus"?' His mishearing of the word led to even more amusement when Melly explained what he meant.

'Going down or gobbling is another alternative,' he added. 'Another expression used in my naval days, your Lordship, was Yodelling in the Canyon.'

Geoffrey Robertson liked to think the term inspired the title of a later Eurovision song contest entry, 'Yodelling in the Canyon of Love', which didn't make it into the contest but was subsequently released as a single in 1997.

In the end it was Judge Argyle who proved to be the real bull in the china shop. After weeks of making it clear where his loyalties lay, he finally dug himself a deep hole by misdirecting the jury so many times in his summing-up that Counsel for the Defence knew the case had to be thrown out on appeal.

The jury, after deliberating for three hours and asking for a definition of obscene, which Argyle said the *Oxford English Dictionary* defined as 'indecent' amongst other things, found the defendants guilty on two of the three counts – the conspiracy charge was thrown out. Before sentencing, however, Argyle decided to send Neville, Anderson and Dennis away for psychological assessment, which led to another faux pas on the part of the authorities. While on remand in Wormwood Scrubs, warders decided to cut the defendants' hair, an action that began to tip the balance of public opinion against the authorities. What few observers really understood, but undoubtedly had crossed the minds of those who had really taken a dislike to the *Oz* Three, was that placing them in the company of hardened criminals might also put them in danger. Geoffrey Robertson said later that he and they had all feared that they might be mistaken for paedophiles and 'have their porridge pissed in or be beaten up', to put it mildly. Thankfully, Felix's aggression in court and Marty Feldman's comment that the judge was an 'old fart' had somehow endeared them to those inside the prison, and some even asked for autographs. Of course it still wasn't to be a pleasant stay, and, although Richard Neville later claimed that his boarding-school background made it easier for him, the time spent wondering what their sentence would be was to scar all three for life.

Felix later described what it was like to share a 9- by 5-foot cell. They got a cold bath once a week and spent 23 hours a day in the cell – 'Twenty-four, if it was raining,' he added. Describing the food as 'inedible', he said one of the prisoners had actually knocked a warder out with a loaf of bread on one occasion. Medical attention was available but lacked much sympathy: 'I once went to the doctor and told him I hadn't been able to take a crap for four days. "Dennis," he tells me, giving the beady eye, "constipation is not a treatable condition in the nick. It's a way of life. Get used to it!"'

The collection of weapons Felix observed was frightening: razors embedded in soap, ground glass for the child molesters and belts with the buckles honed to a sharp edge after hours of patient scraping on the wall. He recalled that he could practically smell the undercurrent of violent tension.

His cellmate had an artificial leg in which he kept a collapsible telescope, used to watch the goings-on in some flats across the road. He'd been doing it for so long he knew all the characters and their habits. On one memorable evening, perched on the top bunk, he gave a running commentary of a sexual encounter between a woman and her lover. Likening it to the final stages of the Grand National, Felix remembered his cellmate's excitement. Through a rising crescendo of whoops, he said, 'God, she's really getting it now! Give it to her, my son, and one for me, and one for the Governor. Come on, my beauty… My God, if her husband comes home she'll be for it … etc., etc.' As a thank you for his entertainment value Felix gave that particular cellmate all his cigarettes when he was released. On his eventual release after two weeks, still sporting a three-piece pinstripe suit, Felix told the waiting press that the people he had met inside 'were fantastic, but the conditions were abominable'. He added that he wished many of those who had been inside with him could have been released too.

While in jail, Felix was visited by supporters and friends, as well as his mother. In a handwritten letter using her own notepaper, addressed to her son at H.M. Prison, dated 3 August 1971, his mother Dorothy wrote:

Well, my dear, I am sorry to see you in this predicament. I feel so helpless because there isn't (or appears not to be), anything I can do to help at this stage. I do understand why you did it, what I can't understand is that I feel you knew what the end result would be – but you still produced Oz. However, as in most things we both can still manage to agree to disagree. My only sorrow is that you are where you are. Without your hair you must feel quite cold. Personally I think it will start a new trend amongst your followers, and also help trade, ie razors, scissors. I am thinking of you all the time and pray that there will be a happy solution for you. Personally I have felt, as you well know, that you are wasting your many talents, the compensating factor, however, being that you honestly believe that what you do is right. God bless you, Felix, my thoughts are always with you. Love Mother

For Felix, this was undoubtedly a heart-wrenching letter to receive but it showed a parent who had obviously gone through her own anguish, yet was capable of offering support and an open mind at the same time. Many years later, Felix was to learn that, 10,000 miles away, the press in Melbourne, Australia had managed to track down his father and hounded him for a comment about the fate of his son. Whether out of loyalty, shame or fear we shall never know, but Reg refused to speak to them. His brother Julian, who had been receiving copies of *Oz* by post from Felix, had kept in touch by phone and offered support when Felix suffered police harassment but he knew what was going on.

'I knew right from the start that when my brother started to tread this path with *Oz* that he was on a hiding to nothing,' he admitted, 'because there's no way they were going to put up with it, they just weren't going to stand for it. Anything they could do to divert attention away from themselves they'd do in a heartbeat. They were horrible bloody people that were running the country then and they could get away literally with murder and cover it up, so I couldn't understand why he kept pushing down the same road.'

When they eventually appeared for sentencing on 5 August 1971, the judge, awarding Richard Neville 15 months' imprisonment and Jim Anderson 12, famously singled out Felix Dennis as being of less intelligence than the other two, and therefore gave him a reduced sentence of nine months. Whether it was his 'boss-eyed' and slightly underdeveloped and rough look or his uncultured aggression that influenced him is anyone's guess, but Justice Michael Argyle saw Felix as somewhat impaired and decided to attempt some form of leniency.

The sentences were seen as an outrage. Newspapers began to report from a different angle, this time with more sympathy towards the defendants. The *Sunday Times* editorial on 8 August 1971 proclaimed '*Oz*: An Unjust Sentence'. It described the obscenities that had been on trial as just 'extended lavatory graffiti' and went on to say, 'the sentences have grossly inflated the offence and thereby created a specific and menacing injustice.' Describing the judge's actions as 'one man's blind lunge against obscenity in general', the piece finished with, 'Anyone has the right, and many think they have a duty, to make such a gesture: but not, without overwhelming justification, by imprisonment and deportation.'

At the other end of the scale the local *Surbiton Herald* surely must win the prize for the most cringe-worthy headline with 'Local Boy Makes Bad'. Even the *Daily Mirror* headline questioned the judge's action: '*Oz*: Obscene! But Why the Ferocious Sentences?'

The sentences and headlines combined to bring an enormous demonstration to the front door of the Old Bailey, where an effigy of the judge was burned as a steady rain failed to dampen the demonstrators' spirits. Eleven people were arrested and a fierce fire burned in the bellies of a horrified youth.

In Felix Dennis's archive there is a wonderful photograph of a young Rosie Boycott. Standing in a crowd outside the front of the Old Bailey, she stares at the camera with a stern, questioning look. She is wearing a denim jacket at least two sizes too large and her hair, like that of those around her, is bedraggled by the rain. A couple next to her hug, clutching each other for heat and comfort after an emotional protest, while others still mill about, some with and some without umbrellas. Behind her there is a small plume of smoke coming from the remains of an effigy of Judge Michael Argyle that she and others have just burned in protest at the judge's treatment of the *Oz* Three. As the effigy slowly turned from fire to soggy ash, protestors held hands and danced around the receding flames.

The Old Bailey sentencing of Richard Neville, Jim Anderson and Felix Dennis appalled everyone in the underground press. Not only because of its severity but also because, if it was upheld, it could have massive repercussions for all media.

'All the underground press in a way were involved,' Rosie Boycott said later. 'If you were going to call Honeybunch Kaminski pornographic, then there was a whole bunch of other things that you could describe as pornographic.'

At the time of the *Oz* trial, Boycott was working on another underground magazine called *Friends*. Initially started as *Friends of Rolling Stone* after the demise of the English *Rolling Stone* magazine, it had to change its name to *Friends*, and then, when no longer viable, it closed and re-emerged as *Friendz*. She and her underground press colleagues took the trial very seriously. Together with her then partner, Jonathon Green, she had helped to build the effigy of Judge Argyle and had carried it all the way to the Old Bailey from Piccadilly Circus. Later, she would become editor of the *Independent*, the *Independent on Sunday* and the *Daily Express*, carrying a deep-seated core of revolutionary zeal and quest for honesty into the mainstream media.

Turning up to court with wigs covering their shorn hair, the *Oz* Three had to wait for three days before their appeal was finally successful. At one point it seemed to John Mortimer that his magic had been lost on Lord Widgery, who was taking the appeal, and he feared they may go back to jail. Geoffrey Robertson would later suggest that, to see for themselves whether *Oz* was really pornographic, one of the appeal clerks had been sent to Soho with a £20 note to acquire a selection of available pornography, in order for Lord Widgery to decide whether *Oz* really was that bad. Inevitably the answer was, of course not, and according to Robertson 'in the course of his judgement he issued a resounding call for pornographers to be jailed. He was oblivious to the fact that the shops from which the samples had been acquired were being run in partnership with members of the Metropolitan Police.'

Later, Felix told Jonathon Green that one night while in jail the three of them had been taken from their cells and put into a police van. They were driven to a building that he recognised as law chambers and met with

Lord Widgery, who told them that he was under pressure to let them off on appeal. Ted Heath was being harangued by many MPs, he told them, who saw the case as looking bad for the establishment because it was so obviously weighted and without logic. He gave them each a sherry and told them that they mustn't work on *Oz* magazine after their release and must never tell anyone about the meeting. Neville and Anderson have no recollection of this, but Geoffrey Robertson later echoed the sentiment, explaining that Michael Foot, Tony Benn and many other MPs had been agitating and calling for Heath to do something. Thankfully, Judge Argyle had given him a get-out key.

As John Mortimer was to say on ITV's *South Bank Show* in 2003, 'The sentences were ridiculous. I mean, the judge by that time was past the bounds of sanity. We were very lucky to have that judge because a more intelligent judge might have directed the jury properly, and we wouldn't have won the appeal.'

There have been hundreds of pages of text written about the *Oz* trial and its effect on life beyond those heady days of protest. Within weeks, Tony Palmer's *Trials of Oz* made most of what happened in the courtroom available for public consumption and sold out immediately. Over the following years, a range of writers gave their opinions and the general consensus was that both *Oz* and the era that it had championed helped to create a more liberated and open society. Many of those who took part in that small, but vocal and highly visual world of the Swinging Sixties went on to carve niches for themselves in the creative and liberalised extended community that determined to live, if not the dream, then at least a variation of it.

Andrew Marr, in his *History of Modern Britain*, gives the *Oz* trial only a fleeting, though amusing footnote. Speaking of the Rupert Bear cartoon, he says, 'A teddy bear with a stiffy: it rather sums up Britain's answer to revolution.'

The sixties had started with one obscenity trial in 1960, that of *Lady Chatterley's Lover*, and finished with another, that of *Oz* magazine. The former could be said to have begun the process of heralding change – hanging was subsequently banned, divorce laws reformed, abortion laws changed and homosexuality between consenting adults over 21 was decriminalised. The other trial might be said to have carried on that process of change. By the beginning of the next decade, the *Oz* trial was almost certainly responsible for slowly exposing a deep-rooted corruption in the police force. The rot had spread and Operation Countryman subsequently found hundreds of crooked worms that were either relieved of their positions or sent to jail.

Detective Inspector Luff's religious convictions had shielded him from becoming corrupt and he was duly promoted to Superintendent Luff, going on to play an important role as a negotiator during the Iranian Embassy siege in South Kensington in 1980. He eventually retired, with some of the view that he was harrowed by the Iranian Embassy experience.

Judge Argyle moved back to the shadows after his 15 minutes of fame, though he still reigned supreme when it came to harsh sentences. He began to campaign for the renewal of the death penalty and eventually, still smarting from the *Oz* affair, he penned a patently foolish article in the *Spectator* in 1995, claiming the *Oz* editors were drug dealers. Although the *Spectator* was subsequently sued and had to print an apology as well as make a donation to charity, Felix and his co-defendants decided not to sue Argyle himself. It was to be a bizarre postscript to the trial.

Twenty years afterwards, the BBC ran a programme about the trial hosted by Jonathan Dimbleby. Titled 'The Trials of Oz', it showed an excerpt from a TV drama made about the trial and written by solicitor Geoffrey Robertson, which was billed as a true representation of what had been said in court. Afterwards, all three defendants – Felix, Jim Anderson and Richard Neville – were joined by Germaine Greer, Caroline Coon, journalist Janet Daley and Conservative MP Ivan Lawrence QC.

A lively discussion followed Dimbleby's question 'What was all the fuss about?' He asked whether it had been a landmark trial advancing the frontiers of freedom against the establishment, or simply a valid attempt by the forces of decency and moral sense to outlaw a 'perverse and squalid publication'. Despite the intervening years, the divide between those involved in the early days of sixties liberation was still apparent as they debated with the obviously right-wing views of those chosen to speak on behalf of the establishment.

Germaine Greer, still feisty, authoritative and eloquent, alluding to over-reaction by the authorities, pointed out that the magazine sold only about 30,000 copies and 'wasn't about to take over from Rupert Murdoch'. Caroline Coon explained that it was the beginning of challenging authority. An authority, she said, that had been cruel to women, to black people and to anybody who didn't fit in. With a full ashtray and an empty bottle of wine beside him, Felix admitted that, for him, *Oz* had been an introduction to an astonishing world.

'I'd never met people like that before,' he said. 'And I'm very proud to be associated with the magazine.'

The striking point that came from the opposition viewpoint was from Janet Daley, who explained that since the *Oz* trial it had become difficult to prosecute those who were doing 'much uglier things'. It was obvious that, 20 years after the event, there was still high emotion and questions remained. However, regardless of the legacy of *Oz* magazine and its sensational trial, in the early seventies the hippie dream appeared to be coming to an end, though Felix Dennis's adventure would continue – in ways that no one could possibly have imagined.

CHAPTER 7

A SONG FOR JOHN

Between the trial and the appeal Felix had gone back to his Wandsworth Bridge Road home but was besieged by press and well-wishers. The phone was ringing off the hook, and on his answering one call a voice said, 'I've got John Lennon on the line.'

Felix was about to start raining expletives down the line, thinking it was a wind-up and said, 'Listen, brother, I've just got out of the nick and I haven't got time for this crap!' when a distinct Liverpudlian voice said, 'Felix, have a look out of the window.'

He gazed out at the press and photographers gathered outside as John Lennon said, 'That's what I have to put up with all the time. Come on over and stay at my place for a while. I'll send a car over.' It was a show of the same sort of kindness and support that Felix himself would later become famous for, and provided not only a brief respite but also a few anecdotes for him to throw into what would become a vast repertoire.

While at the mansion in Ascot, Felix made himself useful doing menial jobs to help Phil Spector, who was producing *Imagine* and already exhibiting hints of the psychotic behaviour that would eventually put him behind bars. Running around to find him cans of Dr Pepper, Felix described him thus: 'Total hypochondriac,' he remembered. 'Mad already. If you got him a Coke, God help you because he was a health nut.'

Picking up bits of paper, Felix would ask Lennon what they were all about. 'Oh, just a new tune I'm working on,' John would say, as he scribbled lyrics such as 'Imagine no possessions' and 'You may say I'm a dreamer' – a few of those scraps of paper didn't make it to the waste-paper basket.

At one point, while sitting at the kitchen table, John asked Felix to sing for him. A natural extravert who had been singing in bands for years, he was, of course, happy to oblige and did a verse of Chuck Berry's 'Johnny B. Goode'.

'That's good,' said John. 'But it sounds just like Chuck Berry. Try something else.'

Felix tried another song, sounding not too bad, he thought.

'No, sounds too much like the original,' John insisted.

So Felix tried a third song, following which John fixed him with a friendly, though slightly world-weary look.

'You just don't have your own voice, do you?' he said. 'I hope you're not going to try and make a go of this. You haven't got a voice, you sing just like the last guy you've heard sing it.'

Hearing this verdict from someone he had admired for many years, Felix might perhaps have been utterly crestfallen, but being told that sort of home truth by someone with Lennon's experience somehow made it more palatable. 'What the fuck did he know anyway?' he would later joke.

As a condition of their bail, sureties of £100 each were paid by Tony Palmer and John Birt (later to become Director-General of the BBC). Both Richard Neville and Felix resigned as directors of *Oz* and Jonathon Green came in to edit the next few issues.

In the months leading up to the trial a new publication had been gestating. It had been dreamed up by Richard Neville, Andrew Fisher and Ed Victor (then a publisher at Jonathan Cape and now a leading literary agent). The publication was to be called *INK*, and it was envisaged as a weekly alternative newspaper. In his book, *Hippie Hippie Shake*, Richard Neville gave a tongue-in-cheek description of what he had hoped it might be like: 'a militant, muck-raking leper-rapes-CIA-agent tabloid of the Movement; where the *News of the World* and Rupert Murdoch meet the underground'.

Neville was very keen to involve Felix, especially as his prowess as the man who could bring in advertising revenue had grown.

'Richard was always singing his praises,' remembered Ed Victor. He recalled his first impression on meeting Felix at Palace Gardens Terrace. 'He reminded me of a short version of one of the three musketeers,' he said. 'He had that kind of hair, Louis XIV sort of hairstyle.'

Although distracted by the trial, Felix and Richard Neville both played a part in getting the first issue of *INK* onto the newsstands. Having raised the necessary funding to start the venture, Ed Victor and Richard were keen to recruit a heavyweight news reporter to ensure they would be reporting top news alongside the majors. In what appeared to be a huge coup they recruited what Richard claimed was 'a crack investigator from the *Sunday Times*, quick on his feet and sympathetic to the cause'. It turned out to be a monumental blunder. As Felix raced around London, trying to rustle up advertising for *INK* as well as for *Oz* from a market already saturated by underground press, Victor, Fisher and Neville spent a tense 24 hours up to press time waiting for a promised 'scoop' from their news editor. They got it, gleefully published it, and discovered to their excruciating embarrassment that their exciting tale of a 'Uranium Robbery' was in fact a year-old story.

Andrew Fisher remembered that Felix was never so enthusiastic as everyone else about *INK*, even though he was to be a director of the company. Although John Lennon and Mick Jagger were amongst those who had agreed to help finance the project and Felix had agreed to sell advertising and to do the marketing, Fisher later observed that Felix 'didn't give a fuck' about the paper. He was more interested in *Oz*, and, as Fisher also revealed later, it was 'Felix's pretty amazing instinct for what works and what doesn't work' that stopped him from getting too involved.

'I think he smelled bullshit about the whole thing,' admitted Fisher. 'And he was absolutely right and we were totally wrong.'

It wouldn't be the last time that Felix's natural commercial instinct was to put him a step ahead of everybody else but perhaps the most important thing to come out of his involvement with *INK* was the fact that *INK*'s production manager was a man called Dick Pountain. A solid Derbyshire man, whose interests outside of doing paste-up for *INK* included chemistry, mathematics and politics, he was to become one of Felix's closest friends and lieutenants.

By then Charles Shaar Murray had moved into the Wandsworth Bridge Road flat and remembered that Felix's only rules for living with him concerned milk, not alcohol.

'You don't have to pay any rent,' he told him. 'You don't have to buy any food. All I ask is that you make sure there is always a pint of milk in the fridge.'

Felix had an ulcer at the time and milk was the only antidote to his discomfort.

Murray also recalled that installing traffic lights on the stairs might have helped with the 'cavalcade of girlfriends' streaming in and out of the flat. At one point he remembered a black girl, who was one of the first to get silicone implants. Felix complained to him that her breasts felt like the 'Kaiser's helmet'.

As it was also one of the crash pads sometimes used by BIT, the organisation set up by author and community activist Nick Albery to help people find somewhere to stay when they came to London, Felix's flat also played host to a number of people seeking a roof for a while. The arrival of Latvian beauty Aina Vasilevskis and her friend Gerda McDonough brought many of the boys to their knees. Artist George Snow, designer David Wills and Felix were amongst those who could testify to her fiery charms as she swept in and out of Biba, the *Oz* office and Felix's flat. Felix wrote a heartfelt poem in memoriam after her untimely death in 2009.

Caroline McKechnie also stayed there. She worked as a typesetter on various underground magazines and remembered that for some of those who helped out payment was more likely to be from a slab of Afghan Gold cut up using the office guillotine than cash.

While on a trip through Europe from America, student Maureen Solomon decided to phone up and introduce herself to the editors of *Oz* magazine, a copy of which she had picked up on her travels. She remembered heady times at Wandsworth Bridge Road. Solomon became a lifelong friend of Felix's and with what most would have said was a massive understatement recorded in her diary: 'a lot of girls and guys were at his place at the time' and 'he seems pretty uninhibited'.

One evening she remembered when they were dancing together in a room full of people he had suggested they take off their clothes and have sex – 'shake off some of those inhibitions', as he described it. Solomon declined. Her understated take on London in those days was that, 'Americans were so uptight and Europeans were more relaxed about things.'

In an interview with Melvyn Bragg for the *South Bank Show* in 2003, Felix described the sixties: 'Having been brought up by a very loving but very strict mother and grandmother, it was just stupendous. Girls were prepared to have a lot of sex with you because they weren't going to get pregnant.'

That wasn't necessarily always the case, however.

On one occasion, hearing from a friend that she was in hospital after suffering an infection, Felix gathered up a bunch of flowers, a selection of books and some magazines and rushed round to see her. She explained that in fact the infection was in her fallopian tubes and had been brought about because she had just had an abortion. He had known about this because she had come to him to ask him to help her pay for it, although at the time she wouldn't tell him who the father was. When he got to the hospital he was a sympathetic and warm friend and offered to do anything he could to help her. It was only then that she admitted the child had been his. Recalling how the world of free love also meant freedom from care and responsibility, she later said, 'At the time it didn't even occur to me to tell him.' As far as subjects such as pregnancy went, you just 'didn't have discussions like that back then'.

Many years later she regretted Felix's lack of choice, saying, 'I was way too young to have a child and it didn't even occur to me that he might want a child.' At the time he certainly didn't, but, as someone who never did have a family of his own, whether the episode came back to haunt him or not is hard to guess.

At the time he and most of those around him were on a different planet. As he put it to presenter Melvyn Bragg: 'The music had improved a thousand per cent in less than two or three years and there was this whole feeling of freedom in the air. You could just taste it.' Having nearly lost that taste of freedom, Felix wasn't about to lose it again but it was yet another stroke of luck that would help him get a new home from where he could orchestrate both his social and business life.

His social life included looking after the elderly lady who owned the house he was living in. Having agreed to take over the lease on the flat when David Macintosh moved out to live with an American novelist friend in the West End, Felix spent a great deal of time ensuring his landlady, Mrs Brooks, was OK. A retired midwife, who was now quite hard of hearing, she would go out to the shops with him. He remembered how she would wander into the local butcher's shop, march past everyone in the queue and bang on the counter with her walking stick.

'I'll have a quarter pound of your best mince, and none of that fatty rubbish,' she would say, before turning round to exclaim, 'Oh, I didn't know you had anyone waiting!' The butcher would roll his eyes and Felix remembered her feisty but hysterical banter, which included telling the assembled shoppers how she had brought the butcher into the world and what an 'awful pain' he had been to his mother. 'Terrible delivery,' she'd announce at the top of her voice but they'd heard it all before.

Then it was off to the grocer's, where she'd order four Brussels sprouts. 'Four sprouts, not four pounds!' remembered Felix.

As she was hard of hearing she didn't mind the loud music that was played upstairs but she did question the fact that Felix had so many visits from the police, to which he explained, in a voice that was naturally loud enough for her to hear, 'I have a lot of friends in the police force, Mrs Brooks.'

She was a very organised woman who had a basement filled with tinned goods in case of emergency. School friend and fellow band member Bruce Sawford remembered that some of them dated as far back as the late thirties. She owned a bald budgie named Billy, for whom she had knitted a little waistcoat, but she didn't appear to have any other family and nobody ever came to see her. When she died in 1972, she left a request for Felix to look after Billy. As he was an animal lover he was glad to, but quickly saw that Billy was not only devastated and pining for Mrs Brooks, but also on his last legs, so he decided a better course of action would be to let Billy and

Mrs Brooks go into the ground together. When Billy breathed his last, with a little help from the gas ring in the kitchen, Felix popped his still-warm little body into the pocket of her midwife's uniform, which she had asked to be buried in. Once the undertakers came and closed the casket, Billy and Mrs Brooks left the house and went off together.

Soon afterwards, a relative, who had never been seen anywhere near Mrs Brooks while she was alive, appeared at the door and told Felix he planned to sell the house and that he would have to move out in three weeks. As Felix remembered the occasion, the man made the fatal mistake of looking down his nose at the scruffy hippie in front of him and was particularly rude. Felix, less than politely, put him in his place and pointed out that he had a lease. Had he been treated with a bit more respect, he may have negotiated and worked with the man but instead, finding he couldn't sell at the market rate because of the sitting tenant, Mrs Brooks' relative had to sell the house to a property developer, who was prepared to help Felix find alternative accommodation.

'I want at least three rooms and a kitchen in central London,' said Felix, pointing out that the rent needed to be no higher than he was paying at the time.

Even in 1972, London rents were high and so on the surface this was a ludicrous request and a bit of shouting ensued, but from the developer's point of view it was the best he was going to get. 'And about two months later the developer called me up at *Oz*,' remembered Felix. 'And he just said, "I want you to go to this place. Top flat, 10 Kingly Street, three rooms and a kitchen. It's a brothel, three girls going back to Edinburgh. It's in the *Standard* tomorrow but I got a tip."'

He told Felix to go immediately and make an offer for the fixtures and fittings, which would be his key money.

'Well, I went straight down there. Four working girls, beautiful sluts they were. All come together three years ago, saved up all their money, no ponces, no pimps.'

It was to be one of those occasions where his fame preceded him. One of the girls was an *Oz* fan and had seen him in the papers and even asked for his autograph.

Although Felix appeared to have landed on his feet, there were a few problems. He admitted later that he soon realised what he had let himself in for.

'First of all, one of the rooms had no joists. There were white lines that said, "Do not walk in the middle of this room". All of the windows were rotten. You couldn't lift a single sash window without it falling out in the fucking street.' And it turned out that the bathroom was two flights downstairs. 'Imagine running a brothel without a bathroom!'

However, the flat was above a pub called The Bag o'Nails, where he had been many times to see bands, and it had its own little roof garden. It was perfect for Felix and as a bonus, he later recalled, one of the prostitutes gave him a blow job before she moved out. 'Free of charge!' he declared. However, what really tickled him was the thought that the Crown Estate, owners of the property, had for once almost certainly been delighted to rent their property to a convicted hippie who worked on an anti-establishment underground magazine.

'Well, it was better than being a brothel!' he boomed.

While *Oz* rumbled on through 1972, with Felix gradually taking on the whole operation, he and Dick Pountain began to make plans for a world beyond the 'press' side of underground publishing. With his long dark hair, with a central parting and a beard, as a young man Dick Pountain had a touch of the Jesus look about him. He had enjoyed his student days politicking as a member of the Communist Party, and by the time things were taking off in London he had been influenced by the Situationists and was a founder member of King Mob, a non-violent but noisy group who liked to agitate about the futility of politics.

For a while he had worked as chief chemist for Steve Abrams, a primary member of SOMA, an organisation campaigning for the decriminalisation of cannabis, and along with other members of King Mob irreverently chanted, 'Hot Chocolate, Drinking Chocolate – Hot Chocolate, Drinking Chocolate' at the Vietnam protest in Grosvenor Square, when most of those around them were intent on making much more serious noises. Talking to Jonathon Green later, he remembered getting 'lots of aggravation from all the Trots around us'. After travelling around the States for a year, he returned to London to find there was a new crop of younger Situationist types with somewhat more radical views so he drifted off to find work. He and Felix would spend hours pasting up issues of *INK*, but it was failing fast and when the magazine eventually went under in February 1972 he became production manager at *Oz*.

Felix was at that time making a valiant effort to keep *Oz* going, even travelling to America to help promote a musical called *The Trials of Oz*, which ran at the Anderson Theatre in New York. Written by Geoffrey Robertson, although most of the music was written by Pittsburgh singer/ songwriter Buzzy Linhart, it also featured a song each from John Lennon and Mick Jagger. The script was based on the transcripts from the trial and it received mixed reviews, but being seen by some of the newspapers was what really mattered.

Mick Jagger's song, 'Schoolboy Blues', which was originally recorded for the *Sticky Fingers* sessions and is also known as 'Cocksucker Blues', was considered too strong for one reviewer, who called it 'the single most outrageous song you have ever heard in your life'. Explaining that she couldn't tell readers what the song was about in a family newspaper (the *Sunday News*), she wrote, 'You just won't believe your ears,' and went on to say, 'What all this is leading up to is that I loved the play and that you should run, not walk to the Anderson Theatre down on Second Ave, near Fourth St, to see not just what is a musically important event, but an extremely provocative show.'

Even though it was favourably received in the *New York Times* and the *Village Voice* as well, *The Trials of Oz* musical didn't run for long. Buzzy Linhart, interviewed on a local radio station later, put it down to the producers not having the courage to give it time. He said if they had waited another week the show was about to get a glowing three-page review in *Rolling Stone* magazine and then they would have had a hit on their hands.

When he first arrived in New York in December 1972, Felix stayed at the Chelsea Hotel, but soon moved in with Maureen Solomon, while making the rounds of the radio stations to promote the show. While there, he also followed up on a letter he had written to John and Yoko, asking for an investment of £7,000 to keep *Oz* alive. Solomon remembered how she and Felix waited for what seemed ages for John and Yoko to return his call. They eventually did so but only after Felix had gone out. Lennon agreed to help and was later allocated shares in the business. However, a combination of the fact that the counter-culture momentum that had driven circulation at the end of the sixties and during the trial had slowed, along with Richard Neville's waning enthusiasm and the growth of the music press was making it difficult to continue the magazine's success.

Back in London one day, Neville walked into Felix's office and said, 'I don't know about you, Felix, but I just can't whip up the enthusiasm to keep *Oz* going anymore.' Tanned, relaxed and fit after a vacation in Europe, he claimed that he hardly knew anyone working there any longer and suggested, 'Let's get out before the magazine degenerates into *Punch* or something.'

Felix was devastated. Exhausted from trying to keep it all together, he reacted angrily to Richard's suggestion, but as he wandered down the hall past a group of hippies slaving over typesetting, paste-up boards and camera equipment, he realised it was time to swallow the fabled bitter pill and admit it was over. The bills were mounting and there wasn't enough feed for the trough. In those days, if you couldn't pay your phone bill, the Post Office could legally close a business down and that situation was just around the corner.

'You're right, Richard,' he said. 'Let's knock it on the head. And let's do it today.'

The final issue of *Oz* was as much an editorial tour de force as a reflection of the changing times. Next to an illustration by Jim Leon, Felix penned an eloquent final editorial at 4pm, on 31 October 1973, an hour before the final copy deadline.

'For many of us "working" at *Oz* was the focal point of our existence,' he wrote, 'a hideous form of marriage between humans and an inanimate concept.' Likening the magazine to a wayward child, and illuminating the fact that it had controlled him as much as he had controlled it, he went on to say: 'We used and abused *Oz* for our own purposes, we hurled it bodily from one editorial extreme to the other, we left it and came back to it a dozen times, we cursed it, passed it around and then grew jealous of it. We treated it like a baby and it kicked us in the teeth. We shat on it, spat on it and wasted it. And now that it's an adolescent and leaving home, none of us can believe it.'

The issue contained powerful articles from contributors including David Widgery, Jim Anderson, Don Atyeo, Dick Pountain and Mick Farren and the review section seemed to have everyone kicking in. Caroline McKechnie reviewed *Strange Ecstasies*, a book of stories about drug experiences compiled by Michael Parry. Chris Rowley previewed his science fiction smarts with a review of *Billion Year Spree* by Brian Aldiss, and Charles Shaar Murray reviewed David Bowie's seventh album *Pin Ups*. Dick Pountain got his teeth into Philippe Mora's film *Swastika* and even Geoffrey Robertson had a few words to say about *What the Censor Saw* by John Trevelyan. The reviews section concluded with Mick Farren salivating as he skirted over the merits of the new self-titled Suzi Quatro album, somehow including the American rock band MC5 in the paragraph.

Richard Neville apparently dictated his final piece by telephone from Melbourne, in which he described Felix as 'psychotically persuasive' and before describing his new life Down Under flippantly said, 'So good evening, how are you, goodbye.'

The final cover was a photograph of a naked Felix, Don Atyeo and *Oz* ad salesman Jim Maguire, along with friends Maria Lexton, Marva Rees and Pat Woolley set against thumbnails of US President Richard Nixon in various undignified poses.

Many years later Felix was to admit that closing the magazine down was probably the right decision. 'A part of me has never forgiven Neville for not fighting on, of course,' he said. Together, they could have made it work, he thought, but he accepted that it wasn't to be. With a touch of irony he went on to describe Richard Neville as having an innate sense of timing: 'He showed it again by splitting for Australia almost immediately, leaving yours truly to sit across long tables facing creditors, receivers, number crunchers and a motley collection of slightly puzzled and occasionally enraged creditors.'

The likelihood is that a part of Felix was enjoying the role. However, he described those last few weeks sitting in the deserted *Oz* offices, packing up six years of his life as 'the worst I have ever endured'. Worse, he said, than Judge Argyle, facing the press or even prison life. With a sense of frustration and pain he summed up the crux of the emotion: 'It was the taste of defeat. A bloody nightmare!'

The year before the final issue of *Oz* magazine had begun with a coalminers' vote to strike and the deaths of 14 people after troops opened fire on a protest march in Belfast. Gradually there had been subtle changes to the way of life for those once part of the colourful hippie revolution. Few of them could have foreseen the rapid change to commerciality and the twin gods of profit and growth that were to rise from the ashes of the turbulent seventies, but there were a few who took their chances and searched for the golden lucre, Felix being one of them.

Already focusing solely on efforts to create a successful business, he was juggling his options and learning the benefits of searching out good contacts. In April 1972 when looking for a new printer, he and Dick Pountain took a train to Alloa in Scotland. A town long associated with the brewing industry, it was at one point home to nine different breweries. Alloa in those days was about a seven-hour train ride from London and Dick remembered it as a grimy industrial town, but found that the printer was very keen to print their magazine and decided to take them to lunch. The pub he chose was attached to the brewery and, as Dick recalled, was their official outlet.

After a long, boring train journey, trying out the local beer was a more than welcome relief and Dick described what happened: 'We go in there and he says, "You have got to try the local beer, it's unbelievable, it is just like cream."'

They started off with a half pint each and, sure enough, it was delicious.

Dick continued, 'He buys us about three or four of these while we are waiting for lunch. Suddenly we both realise we can barely move. This stuff is about 12 per cent proof. It is effectively barley wine.'

A combination of the long train journey and the strong ale turned their legs to jelly and the printer saw an opportunity to negotiate a good price from his new clients.

'Felix kind of gets up out of his seat and his knees are wobbling and says, "Where are the gents?"' said Dick. Later, he discovered that Felix had filled a sink with cold water and immersed his head in it. Shaking it dry like a dog after a swim in the sea, he returned damp but ready to haggle. 'He negotiated this guy under the table, chemical warfare!' concluded Dick.

Needing to branch out, Felix and Dick had decided to set up a new company to begin producing adult comics and so they launched Cozmic Comics, highlighting the letters *Oz* in the logo. Their new venture would also use Felix's old friend from the *Oz* trial, Honeybunch Kaminski, as part of the company name and logo. H. Bunch Associates Ltd was registered as a limited company in 1973 after Felix began travelling to California to try to rustle up partnerships and organise exchange deals to re-publish American comic strips in England.

On his 26th birthday, he wrote to Maureen Solomon, saying, 'Longevity is a dubious attribute seeing as only the good die young.' He had recently returned from his Californian trip and gloomily reported of England that the 'wretched' country was in the middle of yet another financial depression and the venture capital he had been trying to raise for *Oz* was hard to come by. Consequently, he explained to her, he had decided to liquidate the company and his next comments were heartfelt.

'As you can imagine,' he wrote, 'this was a bit of a blow for me and there's no point in me pretending otherwise. Bankrupting companies is an everyday procedure in publishing, of course, but I had grown a little fond of *Oz*.' He went on to point out how national newspapers had enjoyed a field day on learning of the demise of the magazine and had crowed with headlines such as 'Underground *Oz* is Going Under' and 'Hippie Magazine Bankrupt with £20,000 Debts'.

However, with a nod to Mick Jagger, he finished off by saying, 'Let them crow, let it bleed; we'll be back.' And he was right.

The company moved to Goodge Street and he described the experience as working in 'palatial splendour' in what he said resembled a 'psychedelic slum!' While one company party was notable for Dick Pountain's coup of booking a little-known band called Dire Straits for £30, one of the first Christmas celebrations at the Great American Disaster in Great Marlborough Street saw George Snow and Aina Vasilevskis making love on a restaurant table.

Snow remembered it as a riotous party and the evening that he first met Aina. He got very drunk.

'I was a green kid, who hardly knew anything,' he explained. 'I was very keen. I don't think I'd even taken drugs in those days.' A lamb to the slaughter with Aina, he ended up legless and outrageous, resulting in the restaurant owner asking Felix to get them to stop.

'We were knocking back Southern Comfort, which she could take far better than I could,' he, somewhat surprisingly, recalled later.

CHAPTER 8
MONEY FOR KICKS

In April 1974, a typically British event unfolded outside a cinema in Leicester Square, London – a queue formed. The new Bruce Lee film, *Enter the Dragon*, had been released in England and half an hour before the cinema was due to open, hundreds of Lee fans had gathered. They were a mixed bunch – mostly young, mostly male and many of them Asian and black – but they all displayed a characteristic combination of tension and excitement as they waited for the doors to open. Bruce Lee, a Hong Kong-born exile to Seattle, had died suddenly after filming *Enter the Dragon* in Hong Kong and, while most people over the age of 20 had been looking the other way, he had gripped the imaginations of hundreds of thousands of young men all over the world with films like *Fist of Fury* and *Way of the Dragon*. After moving to California and opening his first kung-fu school in Oakland, Lee had begun to establish himself as the West's foremost martial arts expert while at the same time developing a taste for acting. Small, wiry and looking like a series of copper pipes had been strategically placed beneath his taut olive skin, he exuded a simmering menace that attracted youngsters by the million.

As Dick Pountain later recalled, Lee attracted 'young teenage kids, mainly of ethnic, immigrant background', who felt intimidated by living in England. 'They just felt oppressed and anxious and suddenly this hero came along who said, "You're a weedy little Asian, but you can go around whacking the shit out of anyone you want!"'

He described the movies as all involving white gangsters with 'little five-foot-something Bruce Lee' kicking the hell out of them. Using a story formula that had been successful in just about every community for centuries, the films offered revenge porn for a new audience. As Pountain pointed out, for the target audience, it was 'unprecedented'.

Ironically, by the time he had been noticed in Hollywood, Lee had already pitched a TV series to Warner Brothers, which later became known as *Kung Fu*. However, instead of choosing Lee himself for the starring role, Warner Brothers had hedged their bets by picking Caucasian David Carradine to play the lead. Lee's sudden death shocked his growing fan club, and actors James Coburn and Steve McQueen were two of the pallbearers at his funeral.

As the queue at the cinema in Leicester Square grew, two men approached. Long-haired, with a general hippie demeanour, one of them wore a suit while the other wore jeans and a T-shirt. Later known as Don Won Ton and Felix Yen, editor and publisher of what would become *Kung Fu Monthly*, Don Atyeo and Felix Dennis were about to find out whether one of Felix's soon-to-be famous 'punts' would pay off.

Having seen Bruce Lee's face on the cover of a recent *Time Out* magazine, and also having watched about 10 minutes of the movie, Felix had decided there was a market for a magazine about kung fu and its greatest exponent, Bruce Lee. With little to go on except a need to keep the company afloat, they had cobbled together a poster magazine and decided to sell it to the kids in the cinema queues.

Atyeo remembered it well: 'It was a real underground kids' thing that no one had picked up on. We walked down with these big piles of *Kung Fu Monthly*, not knowing if they were going to sell or not. I remember this queue just broke and raced towards us.'

In the end, with the assistance of many street sellers, the print run sold out and they had to reprint it twice.

As Mark Williams, one of the original underground magazine writers remembered, there was very little material to work with. Few photos or biographical details were available and designer Richard Adams, who went by the name of Rik Kemo Sabi, had to use considerable ingenuity to produce even a simple poster magazine from what was supplied. However, it worked.

Don Atyeo recalled how he and Felix retired to a nearby pub after that first flurry of sales with pockets 'bulging with all this gelt!' They had a couple of drinks and just laughed. 'These kids had been hurling their money at us and we went back to the pub and gloated like a bunch of old scrooges.'

Atyeo is adamant that this was when Felix's attitude to money changed. 'That was the first time that Felix got a taste for money,' he said. 'Up to then he'd never seen anything like it and I think that was the turning point.'

After that first experience outside the cinema in Leicester Square, the 'monthly' aspect of *Kung Fu*, the magazine, became an instant reality. Although the decision to go monthly had been taken immediately, the logistics of producing a monthly magazine were not without difficulty, not least because they had very little content to use. However, as getting a jump on any possible competition was vital, and without more material the most they could have pulled together was a couple of issues, Felix packed Don off on an Aeroflot flight to Hong Kong to gather as much information on Bruce Lee as he could get his hands on.

'So off I trundled and we were ahead of the curve,' remembered Don.

Having completed the 'hippie trail' to get from Australia to London, Atyeo was no stranger to eking out an existence while travelling and so he stayed at the YMCA while he squirrelled around Hong Kong, looking for information on Lee and his films. After speaking to everyone he could find, including bit-part actors, producers, family and just about anyone that could give him a lead, he gleaned a suitcase full of it. He even turned up an interview that Lee had done for a local radio station and the station, not realising its potential value, gave him the reel-to-reel. On his return to England, Felix pounced on it and, before even listening to it, decided it would be sold as a cassette featuring 'the final Bruce Lee interview'. It became the first of a huge range of Bruce Lee merchandise to be advertised in the magazine.

In the meantime, Felix and Richard Adams, along with Dick Pountain, frantically worked on the next issue, hauling in Jonathon Green to help (he became Jo Nat Hong). Adams remembered that 'Felix got into a tizz about how it had to be done really, really fast.'

'Of course we were all well trained and honed after a few years working in the underground,' he continued. Production involved working something like two days and a night – 'It was really very, very fast.' Even Felix wrote copy, but, as Adams remembered, he was quick to hand that job over, especially as 'Atyeo was much more tongue-in-cheek as far as writing copy was concerned.' They managed to convince the president of the Bruce Lee fan club in England to supply them with whatever photographs she had but as Adams recalled, 'There weren't very many of them at all, but the fact that we did a poster magazine lent itself very healthily towards using few pictures, but big.' The production design allowed them to use one photograph on the cover and then duplicate it as the poster on the inside; the rest was fillers. But it wasn't enough to make a monthly magazine until Don Atyeo returned from Hong Kong with his goodies.

As the magazine progressed, sacks of post began to pile up in the doorway to the Goodge Street office as fans, eager to get their hands on anything to do with their hero, sent cheques, postal orders and cash. Bruce Sawford became the mail order king as that department grew. The mail order paraphernalia didn't go completely without a hitch, though.

At one point, according to Don Atyeo, the Bruce Lee Society Membership Kit was taken to task by presenter Esther Rantzen on her *That's Life* TV show and, after being hauled over the coals and accused of ripping off youngsters in front of an audience of millions, Felix thought the game was up. In fact, as Don remembered, it was exactly the opposite.

'Felix sort of said, "Oh fuck, we're buggered now," but the next day you couldn't get through the door for the mail sacks.'

The only thing that appeared to have been noticed from the bad publicity was that there was a Bruce Lee Society kit available. Enormous sums of money just kept rolling in.

Richard Adams remembered that merchandising became increasingly wacky. 'We all just sat around and smoked and drank, and thought up this God-awful crap,' he said. 'But the Bruce Lee pillow-slip was a winner. Sacks of mail started to arrive. Sometimes you could hardly get through the door because of the sacks of mail.'

There was even a Bruce Lee 24-hour candle, which according to Don only burned for about three hours. Ironically, despite the fact that at the time much of the motivation behind producing what they thought was pure tat was to make as much money as possible, there are still legions of Bruce Lee fans around the world who are proudly displaying their memorabilia. At the time of writing, some copies of *Kung Fu Monthly* were being advertised for sale at a multiple of five hundred times their original cover price.

As he would later explain in many interviews, Felix was developing a nose for how to exploit a brand and *Kung Fu Monthly* was the catalyst for many successes in the future. In addition to Bruce Lee merchandising, they hit upon the idea of doing Bruce Lee conventions, often with hysterical consequences. Bruce Sawford remembered the first one was in a cinema in Kilburn.

'By this time we were running the Bruce Lee Secret Society, which was another Felix idea,' he said. 'We decided to hire a local kung fu club to do a demo on stage and halfway through they summoned me onto the stage to hold this concrete slab that someone was going to kick in half. I was holding onto it and had no idea how to do it, 'cos there is a technique to it, and this guy went flying across the stage, jumped into it and went smack into my face.' With blood everywhere, poor Bruce was taken down to the local hospital to get cleaned up.

He remembered Felix attending another convention and being nearly crushed to death by the hordes of youngsters trying to buy memorabilia. With trestle tables heaving under everything from Bruce Lee candles to Bruce Lee protein drinks (banana milkshakes), Felix leapt onto one table, shouting 'Back, Back!' Even Bruce Lee packed lunches were on sale, which included boiled eggs that Bruce Sawford remembered as not being boiled. After Lee's younger brother Robert gave a rendition of a ballad about his famous sibling, they ran a section from one of the films followed by a Lee lookalike fighting with a Chuck Norris lookalike. According to Sawford, Felix had decided to bring bags of cash back to the office for safe keeping when the Chuck Norris lookalike, a well-known stuntman of fairly thuggish appearance, came to the side of the stage, aggressively looking for his money. After a word from Sawford, he was last seen racing after a cab, eventually finding Felix in the office in mid-count. Mikki Rain, an illustrator who worked for a time at Bunch, was able to give an impression of what the stuntman may have found. She remembered being alone in the office when she saw Felix scurrying up the stairs with plastic bags full of cash. After grabbing a camera, she snapped Felix as she recalled 'sitting there at his desk with bags of money around him, with a picture of Bruce Lee in the background and this sort of insane grin on his face'.

Another angle that Felix decided to exploit was books. At the time Wildwood House, a small publishing company set up by South African exile Oliver Caldecott and another colleague from Penguin, Dieter Pevsner, was trying to survive by producing highbrow books with an Asian philosophical bent. The *Tao of Physics* by Fritjof Capra and *Tao Te Ching*, translated by Gia-Fu feng and Jane English, were two of their more popular books. Somehow Felix managed to convince them that a biography of Bruce Lee would fit nicely into their current genre and they agreed. A happy marriage this was not to be but it did mean that Don Atyeo needed to make another trip to Hong Kong, where he unearthed Bruce Lee's mistress, Betty Ting Pei – at the time a real scoop. In the end, the effort paid off and the book, *Bruce Lee: King of Kung-fu*, written by Don and Felix, sold in great numbers, particularly in America, where it was published by Straight Arrow press.

As the operation became successful, Felix, always keen to keep a close eye on the numbers, hired an accountant named Sally-Anne Croft. At the time Sally-Anne worked on a freelance basis and helped out on a number of alternative-type projects. Interviewed in 1998, she described herself in those early days at Bunch as 'eccentric'.

She remembered how, in the early seventies, the company changed dramatically throughout the Kung Fu period. Prior to that, it just appeared to Sally-Anne that there were endless cartoonists wandering in and out. However, she remembered Felix as having a powerful energy.

'I remember him being approachable and cuddleable as well as being somebody to be wary of, because you never knew what kind of mood he was going to be in.' Although they became occasional lovers, she said he was a hard person to get close to, explaining that he was 'not really very good at letting people care about him'.

Sally-Anne's impression of Felix was to be echoed by many others but, when years later she was accused of plotting to assassinate a United States district attorney, Felix immediately dived in to help in any way he could.

Although many people, including high-ranking UK politicians, believed Sally-Anne and her colleague Susan Hagan were simply scapegoats for crimes committed by others, they were still extradited to the United States to stand trial and eventually convicted. Croft was sentenced to five years' imprisonment and released in 1998. Throughout the trial and her incarceration Felix wrote to her and offered financial support. She wrote back and Felix circulated her letters to people who had known her. It had a very positive effect. She said it was 'wonderful, because some of those people then wrote to me and I felt very connected to Felix's world again. Again he just does these things that are supportive or generous.' Sally-Anne believed that Felix's direct understanding of miscarriages of justice was part of the reason for his efforts.

'I think Felix has never got over his outrage about what happened to him,' she said, alluding to his incarceration during the *Oz* trial. 'And it was his way of expressing it. To support other people who are being done by the system.' Reflecting on how imprisonment can affect people, she added: 'When you are imprisoned the one primary experience is of powerlessness, of your life being controlled constantly by other people.'

While in prison she asked those who kept in touch to send photographs to her. 'The one that surprised me most,' she remembered, 'was a picture of Felix and his mum. I realised that I'd thought that Felix had kind of dropped from another planet and hadn't been born of woman.'

She wouldn't have been the only one to be surprised that Felix had a mother – it simply wasn't discussed at the time. A big part of the hippie philosophy was that background and family were irrelevant; it was uncool to talk about siblings or parents. Consequently, few people from those days would know anything about Felix's background until they read about it in newspaper or magazine articles.

It's fair to say that Felix's letters, especially to lovers and former lovers, most of whom would eventually become close friends, are very revealing. There were many people who met him and even worked with him who never really got to know him well, and many also that, despite knowing him for several years, never saw the gentle, caring, generous and often delicate aspect of his nature.

Writing letters, and later poetry, gave him an opportunity to show his warmth and tenderness. They could also be amusing, occasionally conjuring images of a wild-eyed, long-haired, slightly feral creature who barked at innocent passers-by – an image remembered by many who knew him with much affection. In a letter to Maureen Solomon in August 1973, he explained that he had been working 'like a maniac'. His words painted a picture that many would easily have understood.

'Crazy weather here is not improving my temper,' he wrote. 'Heatwaves, torrential rain, even a small whirlwind have all hit London in the space of the last few days. I blame the French Atomic tests (along with the most patriotic Britishers) and scream abuse to this effect at bewildered French tourists.'

In an early hint of his growing love of poetry and perhaps his perception of how he saw his role within his business and subsequently his social life, as well as an eerily prophetic image of where it might all end, he opened the letter with a few lines from one of his favourite poems, Tennyson's 'Morte D'Arthur':

> '...and all to left and right
> The bare black cliff clang'd round him, as he based
> His feet on juts of slippery crag that rang
> Sharp-smitten with the dint of armed heels...'

It is a poem to which he often made reference in a book he wrote many years later: *How to Get Rich*.

*

Felix's favourite description of his mother was: 'Like Mrs Thatcher – without the soft bits'. Their relationship was complex: he was in awe of her, he feared her, and in his own way he loved her. He was also hugely forgiving. Although Dorothy might have been accused of neglecting her children in order to train as an accountant when they were very young, he was often heard to defend her, saying she simply wanted the best life for her children. There was never any reason to think otherwise. Dorothy Coller grew up in an era when women were very much downtrodden. Her eventual success incited jealousy in the men around her and, when she wanted to buy furniture for their new flat in Thorkill Road, she wasn't allowed to sign the hire purchase agreement. As a woman she would not have been seen as a stable contributor to the household income, even though at that time there was no man in the house. Although she earned twice what her brother Cecil did, she had to get him to sign the agreement for her.

'And that's what everyone's forgotten!' boomed Felix. 'That was the world that my mother had to live in, where you shut your fucking mouth if you were a woman!'

He added that in those days women's jobs were to cook the dinner and organise funerals.

Sitting in a cottage in the grounds of his home on the private Caribbean Island of Mustique in early 2014, surrounded by the trappings of wealth, Felix said, 'I think I owe my mother everything.' As he gazed out over lush green trees at an idyllic, gently sighing bay, dotted with yachts costing many times what some would pay for a house, he pointed to the personality that helped make him what he became. 'The genes, the energy, the will to succeed' and 'the general restlessness', he claimed, all came from his mother.

Alluding to the relationship between the two families after his father Reg went to Australia and Dorothy began picking up her life again, he said, 'They loathed each other. You know, I know all about it. I understand why my mother won't allow us to delve into the past and she thinks I don't know.'

In the end, so many huge break-ups in families can often boil down to very little.

'Families have their secrets and they're just fucking sad,' he said. 'It's sad because there's nothing in them.'

There may have been rows over money but in the end, as Felix was to become acutely aware later in his life, relationships, especially with family and friends, have an infinitely superior value. When he co-wrote and published *The Beginner's Guide to Kung Fu* in 1974, he dedicated the book to his mother, using her maiden name of Dorothy Grace Louise Coller. In it he described her as 'not a kung fu fighter but a fighter just the same'.

As the business slowly moved onto a stronger financial footing, the social life that had revolved around Bunch expanded, especially as old stalwarts from the underground press days began to get work as a result of its success. Chris Rowley, who had made the transition from doing ad sales to writing, was also at the time keen on board games. He remembered how Felix had a wild idea to create a kung fu board game and so, along with some of the others, he developed a concept that included collecting cards and trading blows as players went round the board. Everybody was invited over to help develop it and also, as Richard Adams recalled, 'to get absolutely ripped' and play the game to test it out and see if it worked. He recalled people from *Oz*, *IT* and *Friends* magazines all coming together to play games and party. 'Lots of Jack Daniel's, lots of dope, lots of laughs' is how he described it. Although the initial reason for the gathering didn't produce a marketable kung fu game, the process included Felix going out to Hamley's toy store to buy various board games like Monopoly, Risk and Diplomacy, so a Friday night tradition was born. The games night became something for staff to look forward to after a hectic week of meeting deadlines, often by the skin of their teeth. It was remembered as huge fun, but also as being fiercely competitive.

Jim Maguire, another ad sales person, who had also appeared on the cover of the final issue of *Oz*, remembered how Felix hated to lose. 'He must have a photographic memory or something,' he said of his experience playing board games with his former boss. 'You can bet your life that he knows every question and every answer in those cards and you think, how's he done that?'

George Snow had similar memories of those games evenings. 'Felix always wants to win,' he remembered, 'no matter whether he's right or wrong. I have heard him defend indefensible positions and he knows he's wrong. He knows he hasn't got a leg to stand on and yet he'll sit there arguing with you.' Having often stormed out in disgust, Snow recalled one occasion when he decided to stand his ground. 'So I stood on the table and refused to come down off the table until he'd rescinded the point, which he didn't.' A more stubborn man might still be standing on the table, but like Arthur Dent before the Inter-Galactic steamroller, George relented and scurried off to the kitchen, where one of Felix's girlfriends taught him to play backgammon. With a weary sigh, he added, 'And you know you can't beat him because he's a bit of a bulldozer. He'll shout you down.'

Mick Farren sympathised with George Snow's anger during what he described as those 'monstrously cut-throat Trivial Pursuit games' that they played after he himself had moved to the States, although he claimed he was often the winner. The truly destructive game, however, was Diplomacy and as Mick recalled, 'You cut people's throats and you back-stabbed them and it was one of those evil fucking board games. You had to keep going into different rooms and conspiring with different people. You know, marriages would break up. It took forever. You would start Saturday lunch-time and go on until Sunday morning – needless to say, chemically enhanced.'

Mark Williams, who had worked at *IT* magazine and later at Bunch, felt the Friday night games nights ought to have come under a general heading of 'Sex, Drugs and Rock and Roll' instead of 'Games', but *Oz* ad salesman Chris Rowley also remembered them for their insights into the characters involved. Talking about when they played Diplomacy, he concluded that Felix was sneaky, which was of course one of the key skills needed to succeed in the game, but Dick Pountain was the 'real treacherous one', he added. 'Dick would be smiling in your face the whole while, and you have this ally against the villainous French and then all of a sudden...' Rowley eventually learned the strategy and discovered that 'if you weren't being mentioned, then you were in real trouble'.

As Jim Maguire would later say, 'Felix Dennis is a canny old fucker.' Whether he was alluding to his adeptness at games or his skill in the overall big picture is hard to know, but instigating and keeping the Friday night event was a canniness beyond what many realised at the time. Without ever having had a management lesson in his life Felix had grasped a firm understanding of the need to keep his staff happy.

Mark Williams summed it up. 'For most of us Friday nights at Felix's were something to look forward to at the end of yet another frantic week and precisely what was needed to maintain the social bond that had been so crucial to the company's early success.'

Don Atyeo, who lived at the Kingly Street flat for some time, remembered it for many other reasons, not least of all the state it was in when he first lived there. 'It was a tip,' he said, 'an absolute tip!' Already a man determined to keep hold of everything he had ever owned, Felix had moved all his possessions from Wandsworth Bridge Road, including what Atyeo remembered as a 'mouldy old stuffed Zebra head', which was moulting all over the place, as well as weird Chinese lanterns 'that he had collected from God knows where'. Sharing the flat for a time with Cozmic Comics cartoonist Ed Barker, his lasting memory is of Ed's pet parrot known as Quimby. 'She used to fly over and shit everywhere,' said Don.

A mattress lay on the floor in the front room and cracked windows were covered with clingfilm in a hopeless bid to keep out the cold. At three in the morning the bin men would thunder down the street, emptying bins, cracking jokes and loudly discussing the following Saturday's football fixtures, more often than not just after Don and whoever else was there had gone to sleep. But there was always an excuse to be awake long beyond the time that most people had gone to bed.

Putting it mildly, Atyeo described Felix's sex life as unconventional.

'He always used to come back with a couple of birds in tow and I would be asleep,' he recalled. 'He would stagger in at two in the morning with these women he had picked up somewhere and he would always drag me into it.'

They would end up having sex in the same room.

'Which was always bloody daunting because he always used to go at it like a bloody steam train,' said Don. 'I'd see him out of the corner of my eye, thinking I should be more energetic.'

Kingly Street had other benefits, though. In those days it was a hair's breadth from what might be called old-school Soho. Many years later, Felix would finance a book, *Characters of Fitzrovia*, written by former *Oz* magazine secretary and co-founder of *Spare Rib* magazine Marsha Rowe, along with Fitzrovia Association member Mike Pentelow. Through detailed vignettes of some of the inhabitants, it paints an absorbing picture of the colourful area, which was home to prostitutes, artists and writers and late-night drinking haunts frequented by an underworld fraternity whose lifestyle was both feared and revered. Felix was one of those featured.

CHAPTER 9
SHARES AND STIPENDS

While the early period at his Kingly Street flat provided fun and games, it also coincided with two very important changes: one to Felix's social life and the other to his business life. He began to supplement his sexual conquests and relationships by employing less complicated and more controlled adventures with prostitutes. It would later transpire that, apart from avoiding commitment on an emotional level, this also allowed him to begin to focus on what most people later realised was an extraordinary depth of commitment to his friendships. He began to develop a financial relationship or stipend with some of those that he wanted as part-time companions, as well as being there whenever any of them needed help.

It may have been the beginning of what Jonathon Green later called his 'philanthropic mode' when he became a kind of godfather of the counter-culture, paying for education, weddings, funerals and creating work for friends who might otherwise have not been there. It's fair to say that there had been signs of this philanthropic side to his character from very early on. Those who worked with him in the early days remember that he was never shy about buying the drinks and on many occasions when staff had overindulged in the pub or a nearby restaurant he would sneak in, survey the situation, pay the bill and disappear again. What confused some was the fact that, when it came to philanthropy, he didn't differentiate between prostitutes and lovers. He was loyal and generous regardless of anyone's position in society.

At the same time he also developed a more mercenary attitude to business ownership. Although it might be argued that the success of *Kung*

Fu Monthly precipitated the change in his attitude to money and also helped pave the way for a growing interest in sex without ties, Felix's past history and his complex character point to the likelihood that those changes had already taken root, even before the money started rolling in.

One close friend called Maria remembered an evening when she and her friend Marianne, along with Marianne's boyfriend at the time, were eating at a restaurant in Fulham.

'The waiter brought over a card which said, "My name is Felix Dennis. I am one of the ex-editors of *Oz*. I would like to meet you for lunch. Do phone this number."'

As she and Marianne were both attractive women she wasn't sure which of them the card was for, but eventually, to the boyfriend's immense irritation, they discovered that it was directed to Marianne. In time, both Maria and Marianne got involved in the Bunch organisation in one way or another, becoming known as the M&M Company. However, they were to have completely different relationships with Felix.

'Marianne eased out and I became more friendly with him,' remembered Maria. Partly, she thought, because Marianne objected to what she perceived as Felix's growing belief that he could buy anything he wanted, even women. It wasn't something Maria particularly had a problem with, but her abiding memories of him in those days were of his caring attitude.

One night in Dingwalls, which had become a sort of home from home for most of the Bunch crowd, somebody spiked her drink with LSD.

'Felix was great and he insisted on taking me to Casualty,' she remembered. The next day he complained, somewhat tongue-in-cheek, to the Dingwalls management. At the time Maria was embroiled in a relationship with a guitarist from a successful and fairly hardcore R&B band and she was surprised at Felix's attentiveness.

'I'd never known a man who would look out for you like that,' she said. 'I thought it was really decent of him.'

When she and a friend arranged to go on a long trip to America at the same time as him, Felix suggested that, if they would take turns to sleep with him, he would upgrade and pay for their hotel and travel costs.

Maria claimed that she purposely got sunburned in order to avoid keeping her part of the bargain and even disappeared for a while with what she described as an Al Pacino lookalike, who turned out to be a very successful pimp. When they returned to London, Felix offered to put Maria on a £25-a-week retainer to, as she recalled, 'meet for dinner and have a bit of a gossip' every now and then. Felix appeared to love gossip, but, as was later to become clear, it was as much to do with the value of information as the fact that he wanted to keep up with those he knew.

Outside of any ulterior motive, Maria was convinced that he was also trying to look out for her, especially as the man she was seeing at the time had turned out to be more psychopathic control freak than boyfriend. At one point when he turned up at Felix's flat looking for her, Felix stood naked in the doorway, refusing him entry. Whether it was his booming aggression or his full-frontal nudity that sent the guitarist scurrying away up the street is up for debate, but it's likely that the combination was pretty formidable. The voice was loud and the manhood proud!

The relationship had its moments of great hilarity too and Maria remembered Felix's penchant for winding people up, especially waiters and fellow diners in restaurants. He would offer her £100 to make sure one of her breasts was practically hanging out while the waiter was serving their food.

Describing it as 'such fun!' she said: 'The waiter would love it. Felix would enjoy watching the waiter and I would enjoy just chatting away as though I hadn't realised.'

There were, of course, times when even the stipend didn't give him the control he needed. Coming back from a two-week holiday in Greece, Maria remembered getting completely hammered on the plane after a disagreement with Felix. She got so drunk that she passed out and was asleep when they landed – 'But he had to wheel me out of Heathrow on one of those luggage things.'

Furious at her undignified behaviour, he took her home in a cab and told her that he never wanted to see her again. Maria woke the next day tanned, hungover and a little remorseful, but there have been few people that Felix completely cut out of his life and she was to feature in other adventures later on.

The other major change that occurred during the early seventies was Felix's attitude to business and shareholding. In his book *How to Get Rich*, he pointed out that ownership was 'everything'.

Felix and Dick Pountain's partnership, H. Bunch Associates, lived on a knife-edge during those early years, just producing comics, and there were many occasions when the business partners would have a serious heart-to-heart about whether they should, or even could, carry on. Dick remembered that they paid themselves a salary of £18 a week, which, although enough for a single man to get by on, was tough for someone like him, who had a child to bring up.

'I can remember on two or three occasions when we had to go home overnight and come back in the morning to decide whether or not we would wind it up,' he said. With *Kung Fu Monthly* their efforts were rewarded, and with typical understatement Dick described his feelings when it first looked like being a success.

'Extreme relief,' he said, 'that the cash flow was guaranteed for a couple of months.'

As he said later, 'The revenues from *Kung Fu Monthly* 1, 2 and 3 made everything possible because before that we had nothing.' It quickly became clear that they needed to set up a limited company and Dick recalled that Felix had decided he didn't want to have any other shareholders. 'At this point we hadn't actually set up the company properly at all,' he explained. 'There were no proper articles or anything, but it was a de-facto partnership.'

Felix argued that, because of horror stories about other businesses that had run into problems with shareholders falling out, he didn't want to issue any shares. In fact, he had decided his mother would be the only shareholder.

Dick takes up the story: 'As a result of that, Felix said, "No, I won't have any other shareholders. I'll make you a director and give you a profit-sharing deal but won't give you any equity." So I went away and sat down and thought about that, and thought, "What am I going to do, am I going to play hard ball and quit? This guy is definitely going places." I could see that even then. "This guy is a whizz at business and I hate business. I loathe business. It's not what I'm interested in at all. I've got to do something for a living. Do I walk away and try and do something else or do I stick with him?" And I decided I would stick with him.'

In effect, what he did all those years ago was to buy time. Thirty years later he was able to look back on that decision and point out that it had allowed him to do what he enjoyed without getting stuck in a role in which he had no interest whatsoever. He was probably the first to realise that hanging onto the coat tails of the Felix Dennis roller coaster would not only allow him to participate in the adventure, but also keep him in touch with one of the most extraordinary characters he was ever likely to meet. For Felix, apart from maintaining a bond that had grown strong over many lean years, he was able to control his own destiny and avoid the messy break-ups that can all too often devastate a friendship. He would also gain the counsel of an extremely clever colleague whose brain worked in a way that allowed him to maintain a professional relationship without being judgemental.

Another key ally in those early days was Tony Elliott, whose magazine *Time Out* was to live on for decades. Elliott remembered meeting Felix when he was working at ECAL. Interviewed in 1998, he described him in the old days as being 'as opinionated as he is now!' And he thought the general perception of the sixties was 'romantic crap'. According to him people thought it was just a whole bunch of people smoking dope, listening to music and having sex. This, of course, was true – and was often played out in that particular order – but Elliott saw all that as the superficial side of it.

'Underneath it all,' he said, 'there was a whole culture of people running and building organisations' – and any business that hoped to survive needed someone in there with a more conventional sense of how to succeed. During his time at Keele University, Elliott had started an arts magazine called *Unit* and eventually launched *Time Out*, which, by the time Felix was starting Bunch, had some money in the bank. They began a period of what Tony described as 'helping each other financially'. Over the years there was a series of transactions where he would guarantee Felix's overdraft and vice versa. On several occasions they would help each other pay the weekly wages of employees. At one point, when Tony and his wife, the journalist Janet Street-Porter were buying a house, Felix put up part of the money, and when Felix needed an office lease Tony was able to repay the favour. It was a relationship that was to span the decades – one of many where a mutual history with Felix proved he could be both a valuable friend and colleague.

Don Atyeo also has no regrets about Felix coming away 'with all the loot'. Although he, along with Dick Pountain and Richard Adams, was also hoping to get equity in Bunch, it wasn't to be and didn't particularly bother him. He later recalled with some humour having an argument with Felix at the time and stomping out, saying, 'I'll be a famous writer one day and you're going to suffer a cruel fate!' The writing on the wall was clear, laughed Don, when Felix bought a brand-new sofa for his own office.

'A really expensive sofa,' he remembered. 'And we thought, "Bugger, we're going to get ripped off here. Felix is just going to take everything!"' Which of course he did, but not without making sure that most of those involved were looked after.

All this was during a dire time in England. In a letter to Louise Ferrier of 1974, Felix described the effect of the miners' strike, saying that the restricted electricity meant dark streets and that Oxford Street looked 'like a Dickensian back-alley'. Party political broadcasts were clogging up the television and many shops were only open two or three days a week. One day he went out to buy a new bath and remembered the sales pitch as utterly surreal.

'Try to imagine a salesman,' he said, 'dressed in an impeccable suit and tie, with a distinctly upper-class accent, trying to sell me a bathroom suite with gold taps and fittings, while carrying a paraffin lamp and wearing a miner's helmet in a deserted and gloomy salesroom.' As he recalled, he 'freaked and got my ass out before he revealed his Oliver Reed dentistry'.

This was also a moment when the Conservative MP Enoch Powell was making a play for the big time. Felix watched as thousands of National Front members marched down Piccadilly. It was dark and they were all holding candles and walking in complete silence. Playfully describing the atmosphere as 'electric', he was touched and fearful at what he witnessed. He said they wore badges that read 'Heath Out – Enoch In' and waved banners declaring 'We Hate the Con Market' and 'Who Rules Britannia – Heath or Pompidou?' As he said later, it was a 'nasty sight, and the goose bumps on my neck weren't entirely due to the bitter wind'.

Following the success of their first book and a follow-up called the *Beginners' Guide to Kung Fu*, Don Atyeo and Felix convinced Wildwood House to commission another, this time about the legendary boxer Muhammad Ali. Felix wrote to Jim Anderson, saying, 'Don and I are locking ourselves away from drugs, women and all other pleasurable distractions to work on the Ali book.'

At the beginning of 1975 they rented a house in Norfolk to work on it but, as Atyeo recalled, it wasn't exactly a comfortable experience.

'It was the dead of Norfolk, it was awful,' he said. 'It had a wood stove and there was no heating. Every morning one of us had to get up and wipe the bloody snow away. The locals just hated us because we were hippies. We walked into the pub and nobody would talk to us for week after week.'

In a twist that hugely amused Felix, it was the local policeman who befriended them.

'We were sitting in the bar one day,' said Don. 'All the locals were sitting around the fire with their backs to us and not talking to us long-haired gits and the copper walked in and said, "I can see you're having a chilly time here with these locals", and their ears pricked up.' It turned out the copper had been drafted in from somewhere else and had also been ignored by the local community. The unlikely hippie/police alliance didn't go much further but he recalled the policeman suggesting the village was 'riddled with incest'.

Midway through writing the book in February 1975, David Sawyer, Felix's stepdad, died suddenly of a heart attack and Felix rushed back to comfort his mother and attend the funeral in Surrey. Many years later, in a letter to a friend who had just lost her own father, he would pass on a bit of advice he was given at this time. 'Let the dead bury the dead. Grieve for the living,' he told her. Soon after the funeral, he returned to Norfolk, where he and Don took to sparring round the sitting room to keep warm.

Back at Kingly Street, the following April, Felix woke very early one Sunday morning and took a stroll through freshly fallen snow. In the half-light, with not a soul around, he found himself in Golden Square, drinking in the silence that falls like an invisible cloak when the soft crunch of footsteps on snow suddenly ceases. He later wrote that while glancing idly around him the sight of four enormous, brooding sentinel trees caused him to catch his breath. Their magnificent snow-laden outlines would have a profound effect on the rest of his life. The four pyramid hornbeams, he said, were to change his attitude to trees from that of a child who loved them for climbing and a man who loved them for their beauty and usefulness in building and making furniture to a man obsessed with their haunting elegance, majesty and their place in the world.

A few years later girlfriend Olivia Toh dragged him off to Champneys, a health farm in Hampshire, where he claimed he lost half a stone. In a letter to Louise Ferrier in 1978, he described the place as 'magnificently equipped' but was irritated by the 'constant twittering of middle-aged women complaining about their wobbling fat'. However, the same trip afforded him an opportunity to observe and be horrified by the damage inflicted by Dutch Elm disease. On bicycle rides around the enormous grounds, which were surrounded by an ancient forest, he saw dead trees, fallen branches, rotting wood and enormous gaps in the hedgerows. He said it left him 'physically depressed'. Pointing out that like many city people he had a romantic vision of the countryside and especially its mature trees, he described the emotion that would one day help determine where his future fortune would be best spent: 'I found myself at one point wandering through an absolutely decimated copse, with not a single living tree in it, where there had once been twenty or thirty enormous elms.' He remembered hearing himself murmuring under his breath, 'the bastards… the absolute bastards.' Profoundly touched by the experience, he added: 'No doubt if we invested a hundredth of the funds spent every year on biological warfare in research on Dutch Elm disease we could have halted this swathe of destruction. Now it is too late, far too late.'

Although it was indeed too late for those trees, Felix would later be responsible for planting over a million British broadleaf trees in what would become known as the Heart of England Forest.

CHAPTER 10

CROSSING THE POND

While the death of Felix's stepfather may have marked for him the middle of a decade of change and growth on both a personal and business level, the second half of the seventies was to herald adventure, travel, new opportunities and maturity.

June 1975 in England was an extraordinary month. It began with snow, causing the cancellation of cricket matches around the country, and ended in what the media liked to call a heatwave; later, it went on record as being the warmest summer since 1947. Harold Wilson was back in power. Margaret Thatcher had defeated Ted Heath to become Leader of the Conservatives and, in a referendum, 67 per cent of voters had said yes to remaining in the EEC.

Against a background of political and economic turmoil, Felix decided to look further afield than Europe for expansion. With foreign rights for *Kung Fu Monthly* already netting decent money, he elected to make another foray into America to see if he could open up a market there for his new products. Arriving in New York at the end of June, he checked into the Americana Hotel on 7th Avenue, later citing their lax attitude to escorts at the time as one of the bonuses of staying there.

Suitably, it was a man named Lee who was to make way for the partnership that resulted from that trip – but it wasn't Bruce Lee. With his *Kung Fu Monthly* under his arm, Felix descended on the offices of Stan Lee of Marvel Comics. The comic book writer and producer who had launched

Spiderman, *The Hulk* and dozens of other characters had changed the face of Super Hero perception by giving his characters human frailties. He was to live to see them bring in millions of dollars in box-office receipts when they hit the big screen but, although he later claimed to be a big fan of Bruce Lee, at that time Lee wasn't about to add poster magazines to his business plan and unceremoniously showed Felix the door.

Next stop was a small business run by an Englishman named Peter Godfrey and his American partner Bob Bartner, whose names had been given to Felix by Tony Elliott. Godfrey remembered Felix giving him his first sight of the poster magazine.

'He explained what a poster magazine was and I thought, "God, that must be a money-making gem of an idea!"'

Felix and Peter immediately hit it off and they went back to Peter's house where, over a game of chess, they thrashed out the idea of forming a partnership in which Bunch would produce the copy and Peter and Bob's company would print and distribute the magazines in America. As the company was already involved in producing an adult magazine licensed by Paul Raymond, they decided to keep those brands separate and set up a new company, Paradise Publications, for the venture. It was the beginning of a partnership that would produce the bulk of Felix Dennis's wealth; also an opportunity for him to expand on his growing interest in America – politically, economically and socially. Like his old buddy John Lennon, he would later decide to live there for a time.

By 1976 Felix was beginning to feature in the newspapers again but this time as a success story. The Muhammad Ali book, entitled *Muhammad Ali: The Holy Warrior*, that he and Don Atyeo had written had been published in the UK and he wrote to Jim Anderson saying that London was bright and chilly. He also explained to Jim that, although he'd had an agreement to have the book published in the US, it had fallen through at the last minute. He considered taking legal action against the publisher but decided against it saying: 'It's not much use publishing a book with a publisher who is only doing it to fulfil contractual obligations.' He told Jim he planned to find another publisher.

As Concorde made its first commercial journey from London to Bahrain and ABBA's 'Mamma Mia' hit the number one slot in the UK charts, he was being interviewed by an *Evening Standard* journalist who described him as 'a trim, vital, wary, sharp figure with irons in every fire and views on everything'. She highlighted his belief in clichés 'because clichés are true' he told her, and quoted his fatal weakness as women. 'I love to talk to them. I love to go to bed with them. My best friends are women. The proper study of mankind is women,' he said. He also publicly reiterated his already well-known dislike of monogamy. 'Monogamous marriage absolutely revolts me, like seeing pigs eating from troughs,' he declared.

Anne Jousiffe, one of his many acquaintances at the time, already knew and understood his need for open relationships. Although their sporadic affair lasted over 10 years, it eventually suffered a fairly traumatic blow when a business arrangement went wrong. She described their relationship as 'very casual', saying that Felix was a good friend – 'Somebody who was very interesting, but it was never a love story.' At the time this suited her as much as him because she didn't want anything more. 'I never looked to Felix as a prospective full-time boyfriend or live-together situation or anything like that,' she insisted. 'To his credit he has always been completely open about his own feelings and the way he likes to conduct his relationships. I think the women in his life certainly seem to accept that, because otherwise they wouldn't see him.' She also appreciated his honesty, saying: 'He doesn't play games with any woman really, pretending that there is more there, or that it is going in that sort of normal progression of seeing each other and then more serious.'

If he had made clear his attitude to women and relationships in the *Evening Standard* article, he also made clear his business expectations, telling the journalist he planned to make his fortune before he was 30. At 27, he had three years left and was in what he described as 'a tough, nasty, unpleasant, disgusting business', which he said he loved to death, 'because I'm a tough, nasty, unpleasant, disgusting young man'. It was the type of comment he knew a journalist would pounce on and at the time, although part of the Felix Dennis bluster, it also sent a message out to those who might one day have to negotiate with him. In negotiations, there were few tougher.

New magazine ventures began piling up and press releases heralded titles such as *TV Sci-Fi* – 'a monthly magazine aimed exclusively at the youthful science fiction fan' – and *Which Bike?* – 'essential reading for anyone in Britain buying or selling a powered two-wheeler in 1976'. The company's first acquisition, *Hi-Fi Choice*, promised ambitious future plans with a broader editorial scope to reach the casual reader as well as the hi-fi enthusiast, while with breathless enthusiasm the company announced that 'the Skateboard revolution has hit the UK!' and launched *Skateboard* – 'the first magazine aimed directly at the fastest growing leisure sport in Britain'. Bunch and Felix's new American partnership powered along, launching new one-shot poster magazines covering *Star Trek*, *Grease* and *Charlie's Angels* amongst others.

Much as *Kung Fu Monthly* might have been seen as a sell-out by some of those who expected hardcore anti-establishment publishing from a member of the *Oz* Three, Felix was leading the way in terms of focusing on commerce, but it hadn't exactly been a well-planned manoeuvre. As Mark Williams, who had edited and published many of Felix's magazines, later admitted, 'We'd all moved from sort of idealism to straight publishing in a fairly haphazard way.' The joke that went around was that Felix had parlayed what was left of the counter-culture and successfully gambled it in mainstream publishing. He was more interested in a different kind of sell-out. After employing his old *Oz* friend Andrew Fisher to help license the poster magazine in different countries, travelling with him to Holland, Italy and Germany, Felix embarked on a series of ideas for other poster magazines that included such luminaries as *Starsky & Hutch*, *The Bay City Rollers*, *Earth Wind & Fire* and, most hysterically, *Crossroads Monthly*, which feted one of Britain's best-loved TV soaps at the time.

Although some schemes were hit and miss, especially one about tennis star Björn Borg, where the designer flipped a photograph, which made Borg appear to be left-handed, *Crossroads Monthly* provided those who worked on it with a few laughs. Felix's idea was that the cast of the soap, which was based on a fictional motel in the Midlands of England, should be interviewed in character instead of as actors. It made for a very surreal experience for fans who tried to plot the happenings on screen with those in the Bunch-produced magazine. The venture was short-lived, but, like the show itself, would always have a place in the hearts of those who followed its wobbly sets and stumbling dialogue.

Dashing back and forth across the Atlantic, Felix was kept busy launching one-shots and developing new magazine ideas. Although money was beginning to roll in and the staff count at the new office in Rathbone Place was growing, the business was not without its share of disasters. At the end of 1975 he learned an enormously important lesson when he discovered that they had used photographs of Bruce Lee without permission. The result was a painful payment of £25,000 to the owner. Copyright and ownership would never be an issue that Felix would lose control of again.

On another occasion Richard Adams remembered how Felix came up with a 'cracker of an idea' for a magazine to cover the upcoming 1976 summer Olympic Games. The plan was to produce an Olympic Games magazine template with general international information about the games that could be reproduced and tailored for any country. After a huge amount of work, the idea was stolen and sold to another publisher by someone who had been let into the loop.

'That just completely knocked the wind out of our sails,' Richard admitted.

At one point Moore Harness, the distribution company that Felix had used from the very beginning of his time at *Oz* magazine, having moved into shiny new premises in Islington, were caught out by the bank calling in their overdraft. They had to sell the business, leaving Bunch with an £85,000 shortfall. It was an enormous loss for a small company but they bounced back. As Mick Farren remembered, Felix had the resources to move quickly. 'We had a magazine on the street four days after Elvis Presley died,' he said.

In December 1977, on hearing that his former friend Maria was down on her luck and forgiving her for her drunken exploits on the flight back from Greece, Felix took her to lunch and suggested she should attend a party with him the following Tuesday. She agreed and he explained that the party was in New York and that they would travel there on Concorde. Living out of carrier bags at the time and staying at Joy Farren's house, Maria's main concern was making sure she signed on the dole that Tuesday and so, on the way to Kingly Street to meet Felix, she asked the taxi driver to stop at the dole office. By the time they reached Felix's flat there was a note on the door saying, 'Maria! Where are you? Get your arse to Heathrow as fast as you can'. The taxi raced to the airport and made it with plenty of time to catch the plane.

However, there was one problem. When Maria arrived she discovered that she had forgotten to pack her passport. They had breakfast and Felix tried to find a way of getting her passport there on time but it wasn't possible. He cashed in her ticket, gave her some money and she went back to London.

The party she missed had been organised by Peter Godfrey to celebrate a successful magazine about the *Star Wars* film. 'We'd made a ton of money out of this thing,' he recalled. 'So we rented a restaurant bar at a private airport in Danbury, near our office and we got the *Star Wars* folks to send us the Darth Vader costume.' By this time he and business partner Bob Bartner had been vying with each other to see who could throw the best parties, so Peter decided to push the boat out for this one. He arranged for someone to supply an Obi-Wan Kenobi costume and got a large friend to wear the Darth Vader outfit. 'We invited everyone and Felix came to the party,' he remembered. Nobody knew quite what was going on when, as they moved upstairs to the disco area, the theme music from *Star Wars* began playing, gradually getting louder and louder. Suddenly a deafening roar of engines filled the room.

'You have to remember we are at an airport now, on the second floor,' said Peter. 'Hovering at about the height of the second floor is a helicopter with a floodlight on the front. This is an ex-Vietnam helicopter. The sound of the rotor blades is building and the sound of the *Star Wars* music is building, and this thing hovers maybe 30 feet from the window.'

Inside the cab they had rigged up a spotlight to show the menacing figure of Darth Vader sitting next to the pilot. As the music battled with the sound of the rotor blades and the growl of the engine, the helicopter landed and Darth Vader emerged, complete with flashing sabre. Bathed in the spotlight from the helicopter he began to make his entrance, which Peter had previously arranged should be through the back door. However, nobody had expected the reaction of Felix Dennis.

'Meanwhile, I had gone behind the bar and dressed up in the Obi-Wan Kenobi crap,' said Peter. 'But what happened is that Felix is so overwhelmed by this that he roars downstairs and roars out to meet Darth Vader. It's kind of an out-of-body experience.'

The pair of them, Darth Vader and his wacky new sidekick, Felix Dennis, came bursting into the room like some kind of Batman and Robin team from a bad acid trip. At which point the dry ice that Peter had organised for the entrance exploded 'like Chernobyl' and the whole room, now filled with loud music, dry ice, shrieking guests and Obi-Wan Kenobi teetering on the bar counter, began to look like a scene from a *Mad Max* movie.

'Felix is just beside himself,' remembered Peter. 'He has lost his mind.'

Although at the time Peter recalled that Felix looked 'like a banshee' in the lights of the helicopter, he maintains that this was when they both began their love affair with helicopters. Peter and Darth Vader finished up having a mock sabre battle on the dance floor.

In the end Maria did get her dole cheque but she had missed one hell of a party.

Back in London, an executive at the Builder Group, a publishing house, was about to over-estimate his own importance, under-estimate a new client and take a holiday that would give Felix Dennis the opportunity to make his first million. And it all revolved around an ex-student journalist from the former Yugoslavia.

Angelo Zgorelec had arrived in London in 1965 on a student visa and claimed he had been dismissed from his job at home 'because I would not join the party'. His other reason for coming to London was because he wanted to join another party: the Swinging Sixties party. From where he stood, London offered a lot more fun than his home country. After waiting for five years, picking strawberries and working in hospitals, he got a full work permit, but not before he had come across *Oz* magazine. Zgorelec began street-selling *Oz* as well as distributing newspapers and other magazines, building up a little business, and in time he bought a small newsagent shop. He remembered Felix from those early *Oz* days and, when he found himself in the midst of a bidding war for a new magazine he had launched, his knowledge of Felix from those days was enough to give him an edge.

Still speaking with heavily accented English, Angelo explained how his good fortune in computer magazines came about.

'I started *Personal Computer World* in 1978 from my bedroom,' he said. He was producing it from a room above his newsagent shop in Bayswater. 'I was doing it all on my own for about a year and a half, 16 issues.' He claimed that because of the publicity about computers he could have sold it early on but, as he was selling 30,000 copies, he was covering his costs and having fun.

Stephen England (who would become the first managing director of Dennis Publishing) was reading his *New Scientist* magazine one day in 1978 when he spotted an ad for *Personal Computer World*.

'The logo was probably one of the most unpleasant typefaces you've ever seen,' he remembered. 'It was one of those cartoon bubble typefaces that somebody got on a cheap set of Letraset. It was really ugly. But I thought, "Wow, what a great idea!"'

As he was only spending about 60 per cent of his time selling space on another magazine at the time, he approached Angelo and offered to sell his advertising for a commission.

It was about a year later when Angelo Zgorelec decided that it was becoming increasingly difficult to compete with the larger publishers and it was time to sell.

'There were always a few bigger companies wanting to buy it,' he explained. His distributor at the time, Seymour Distribution, suggested he go with the Builder Group. 'I thought, "This is stupid,"' said Angelo. 'This is a publisher of building and construction magazines. Why would they?'

However, they made him a good offer and he agreed, although he harboured reservations because he felt they were an old-fashioned company. When it came time to sign the contract the executive in charge went on holiday.

Tipped off by a member of staff that Zgorelec wanted to sell, Felix called him on a Friday afternoon. It was too late, he was told. But then Angelo said, 'Are you the Felix Dennis of *Oz* magazine fame?'

'Yes, I am,' replied Felix. 'Then it's not too late,' said Angelo. They met that evening, and, as Angelo admitted later, Felix wasn't able to offer him the same amount of money as the Builder Group, but he said that he 'admired him enormously' and had closely followed the *Oz* trial. They eventually agreed a deal that allowed Zgorelec to keep 30 per cent of the business, something that he felt was very important.

As advertising sales manager, Stephen England was asked by Angelo to visit Felix prior to the agreement going ahead. His take on the situation was that Angelo had a choice – go with 'the old fart or the hippie'. He remembered his first visit to the Bunch office. 'I meet with this guy and he's a complete whack head,' he said. 'He talked 600 miles an hour. It was the first time I had ever met Felix. I didn't know what to make of him.' He went home and told his wife that he didn't know who he would be working for the following week. 'And then I started thinking, "No, don't let it be the hippie because he's just weird. He scares me." And of course it was.' In the end this was to prove a life-changing experience for England.

Felix taking on the role of international businessman only increased what most observers could see was a fast-moving success story but that didn't stop him from keeping in contact with those he had met along the way. He took the time to write letters to those who had stayed with him at Kingly Street, as well as those he had known in his teens and those who had worked with him at *Oz* and elsewhere. One letter he sent to his old girlfriend Sanchia Pearse was able to give her extensive details about many of those that they would have known during Felix's schooldays. His long, gossipy, typewritten notes brought people up to date with the lives of those around him as well as those from his past. In a letter to Louise Ferrier, in January 1978, he talked about a colleague who had recently asked him to invest in a house.

'I did not want to invest in property,' he told her. 'The thought of owning bricks and mortar fills me with a strange foreboding. I have always resisted the temptation without the remotest logical reason. It's the permanence of the idea that repels me. Even with a flat stuffed with belongings, I like the illusion of freedom.'

It was a mirror reflection of his attitude to monogamous relationships; however, in the case of bricks and mortar he ended up with the relative permanence of dozens of buildings. It's possible that at the time this attitude was tempered by the fact that he had just been burgled and consequently had had to have bars put on all the windows. With a hint of irony and memories from his days in prison he wrote: 'It's a little annoying, living inside rooms with bars.'

Louise had recently stayed at Kingly Street and he admitted that he missed her.

'You'll be surprised to learn that I felt a little lonely after your departure,' he told her, adding an asterisk to a handwritten note on the side saying that this was an understatement. He promised that within months he would go over to Australia to visit her, saying that the flat now seemed 'sort of empty'. In a later letter, detailing the comings and goings of those around him, mostly about couples pairing off and in one case getting married, he made a telling comment, joking that it might one day make an apt epitaph: 'I hope you are happy. I am not, but then I am too busy to notice.'

Felix's relationship with his family during these times was probably little different to what might have been expected of any entrepreneurial businessman coming into his thirties. At a Christmas gathering with his brother Julian he brought his new niece Alexandra a giant teddy bear 'standing at least three foot high!' However, his mother's dog took a fancy to it and in front of the assembled family began furiously humping it. 'My mother was hardly amused,' he said. Though he claimed tremendous affection for, and was fiercely loyal to his family, Felix wasn't rushing home at every opportunity. As he confided to one friend: 'Tribal gatherings can certainly be amusing if not taken too far… once a year suffices to overflow my own cup in that department.'

Like many siblings, Felix and Julian were completely different. Felix often found his brother's 'regular' life dull, although he did admit that at times he was envious of the fact that a person could be so contented. The irony of such a response wasn't lost on Julian, who said he had no use for money. 'A lot of people crave success,' he once said, 'but I crave happiness – for myself, for my children and my wife.'

As another decade came to a close in Britain, Margaret Thatcher got her feet under the desk at Number 10 Downing Street just in time to see in the eighties and watch a new recession hit the country. She and her chancellor, Geoffrey Howe, raised taxes, slashed spending and decided to cut back benefits for anyone going on strike. A class divide began to expand and unrest rumbled on. At one point in 1980 the staff from both the *New Musical Express* and *Melody Maker*, the two most powerful music weeklies in the country, were locked out after wage negotiations failed. Suddenly, as Mark Williams, who was writing features for music papers at the time noted, there was the potential that record company advertising and circulation income would be 'sloshing around with nowhere to go' and a plan was quickly put into place at H. Bunch Associates to hoover that up with a new weekly music paper. They had the talent and the staff but it would soon become clear they didn't have quite deep enough pockets.

While *Personal Computer World* was undergoing a transformation in terms of design and would eventually stumble through a roomful of geeks to reach a stadium full of eager readers, their new weekly music paper, *New Music News*, quickly began to suck cash and resources out of what was still, in many respects, a fledgling company. As the new punk on the block, the paper very nearly tipped the scales and Felix came close to breaking what he would claim in future was a cardinal rule – that ownership is everything.

He went to his American partners with an offer to sell 50 per cent of his company to them. Peter Godfrey remembered how close they came to being one half of Dennis Publishing.

'We got some way down the line of doing that,' he said. But at the last minute Bob Bartner and Peter's chief financial officer, having gone through the books with a fine toothcomb, advised against it.

'Felix was pouring money into this weekly beast,' said Peter, 'which ultimately failed.'

Whether that weekly beast was possibly a great success that stopped, Peter said he would never know, but in the meantime he knew it made the merger impossible to go through with.

'I'll never forget calling Felix up on the morning that we were going to close the transaction that would have changed all our lives,' he said.

Asking Felix to get together for a coffee before the meeting, he told him he wanted to pull out of the deal. It was a kick in the stomach.

'And I thought this was probably going to be the end of what had been a very lovely and successful relationship,' said Peter.

But Felix's response was: 'OK, mate, that's fine. We can still be friends. Business as usual.'

Together they walked into the meeting where bankers, accountants and advisers were seated and announced that it was time to have an early lunch – the deal was off.

Peter said later, 'I don't think we ever spoke another word about that and it is a great testament to our friendship over the years that it just happened, and there was never any ill feeling afterwards.'

In fact, they went on to make many hundreds of millions of dollars together. However, not before Felix had to clean up and put his house in order after the disappointment.

On 15 August 1980, he wrote a memo to 'All Personnel' explaining that a signing ceremony for a proposed merger between Peter Godfrey and Bob Bartner's company Fiona Press and Bunch had 'turned into a wake', and that weeks of negotiation and high hopes had been 'rendered useless'. He explained that, although the ultimate profitability of the business was fine, the Bunch Group was in 'serious difficulties' because of the drain on cash flow. He would do his utmost to try to sell *New Music News*, even for a nominal sum, so that people could keep their jobs, although he admitted to holding out little hope of that happening. He also announced the shelving of another project, *British & Commonwealth Stamps*, to help tighten the belt.

It was regretful to all and perhaps helped sow a seed of unrest that would later see key members of staff harbour ambitions of their own. Dick Pountain later maintained that, in the case of *New Music News*, Felix had let his heart rule his head 'because he absolutely loves music above everything else' and had always wanted to have a successful music magazine. In the end he did just that. Although perhaps not like the gritty *New Music News*, he did later launch a quite successful music magazine called *Star Hits*, in America.

The setback from the failed merger was further compounded by a lawsuit from Caroline Coon about a defamatory article in *New Music News* and also by Felix's failure to poach David Arculus from EMAP to run Bunch, something he would attempt to do twice. However, what most people would have seen as an even greater blow was just around the corner.

CHAPTER 11

EXILE ON KINGLY STREET

Sitting at home in his flat at Kingly Street on a cold November Monday in 1980, Felix was getting over a bout of flu. A get-well card from Bunch staff sat on a table and a pile of paperwork lay on his desk. Bruised and worn from the battles of the previous few months, and trying desperately to find a way to get beyond what seemed a perpetual state of survival, without any real forward motion, he was playing chess with a friend when the phone rang. The caller announced herself as Pam Dennis, his father's sister. As far as he could remember he hadn't ever spoken to his aunt before, and after wondering how she got his number, it took a minute to grasp what she was saying.

She gave him the news that his father had just died in Australia, also the name and address of his father's wife, Pamela Allery, and explained that she had found his number in the phone book. Felix had gone to great efforts to always keep the same telephone number so that anyone could contact him. He calmly put down the receiver and turned back to the chessboard, saying nothing about the content of the call.

It would be five years before he made contact with Pamela Allery and disclosed what he felt at the time of his aunt's call.

Explaining how he felt after Pam Dennis's call, he wrote, 'After she had rung off, I remember returning to a game of chess as calmly as if someone had merely called to make a lunch appointment. Perhaps I smoked a few more cigarettes than I normally would. Perhaps my end game was not as incisive as it could have been. And perhaps sleep came less easily than my usual head-on-the-pillow-instantly-gone habit. But I would be lying if I said that I shed tears or went into shock.'

The next day he called his brother Julian, who he said, 'seemed rather more upset than I'. He admitted that it took him some time to build up the courage to call his mother.

'Not because I do not communicate easily with her,' he said, 'on many levels we are more like old friends than mother and son. But instinctively I knew that this would be a difficult conversation.'

She was calm, though obviously deeply upset and they never mentioned the subject again. He was astonished years later to find she occasionally mentioned his father, even one day pointing to a pair of silver dogs she had just cleaned and telling him they had been given to her by his dad after he had returned from Burma.

'I looked at her with an arched eyebrow,' he said. '"He was in the forces," she replied. "He went to Burma in the war."' Felix said he knew his mother well and that the first sentence had come out accidentally. But the second, he said, 'came out like pulled wisdom teeth. But she got it out.' Something he claimed she had never been able to do before.

He remembered his father 'swinging me in his arms in a great circle and laughing'; he also remembered feeding the horse that came to deliver the milk to the shop. He remembered the sweets and jars on the shop shelf, but also remembered a time of 'adult anger' and his mother weeping and screaming down the telephone.

'I never heard her weep again in her life,' he said. 'Not once.'

He explained to Pam Allery that he harboured no resentment about his mother breaking off all links with the Dennis family.

'Knowing the hardships she endured to bring us up,' he said, 'the long hours she worked, her fierce determination to keep us together and to educate us… knowing all this, I cannot bring myself to blame her for that decision. Single-parent families are not so unusual now but in the 1950s and 60s it was a social condition virtually akin to living in sin.'

His loyalty to his mother has both baffled and impressed many of his friends over the years and much as she may not have appreciated aspects of his lifestyle, whether in business or socially, he maintained that his success allowed him to give her a good home and take her on exotic holidays, the like of which she might not have had otherwise. A year after his father died, he took her, along with an oriental girlfriend, on a cruise on the *QE2*. It was to be the first of many holidays, which she grew used to sharing with a wide range of Felix's female companions. But not before he was to conclude many successful deals.

Exactly three weeks after the death of his father, Felix's old friend John Lennon was shot dead outside his apartment in New York. Although he could have produced a particularly poignant tribute, Felix didn't rush to launch a one-off magazine to take advantage of the event. Although he hadn't seen John or Yoko in many years, he retained a respect for the man who had helped him out during his time at *Oz* magazine and made no effort to gain commercial benefit from his death. Instead, he persevered with the projects that were beginning to show dividends in the UK. After a bout of hepatitis, which had kept him housebound for many months, he wandered the streets of London, surveying the damage done by rioters.

Writing to Peter Godfrey, he said, 'In Central London I'm insulated from the main areas of trouble but it's pretty obvious that a couple of real riots last week from black and Asian communities in London and Liverpool have spawned a whole heap of "copycat" hooliganism and looting fever amongst out-of-work youngsters. Not quite the Armageddon the news would have us believe.'

This was the background to a period when Bunch was beginning to do well. *Personal Computer World* had developed clear market leadership and ABC figures put it around 11,000 copies in front of its nearest rival, *Practical Computing*. Having asked Don Atyeo to write the copy for a special on the wedding of Prince Charles and Diana Spencer, Felix admitted to having 'chickened out' of doing it after he discovered that there were 35 other 'specials' going to print around the same time.

Despite the previous year's pressures and difficulties, Felix's efforts were beginning to pay off. Having a market-leading magazine was starting to change the atmosphere at Bunch. Felix was feeling a surge of confidence and with what he remembered as 'Wolves in conglomerate clothing' beginning to call anonymously to make enquiries about the magazine, or 'the state of granny's health' as he called it, there was much to be positive about. Within a year he would walk away from an offer of £2 million for one magazine and a six-figure offer for another.

Although he had grasped the nettle of computer magazines with just a hunch that they might have a market, and in fact at one point he had told Peter Godfrey that they may just be a passing fad, there was another publisher who was sure that personal computers were the future.

Graeme Andrews, who worked for Dutch publisher VNU at the time, remembered that his chairman, Francis Koot, was convinced that 'personal computers were going to take over nearly all the functions in the world'. With this in mind they made a beeline for *Personal Computer World* and opened up what he recalled as 'very serious and lengthy talks' with Felix about acquiring the magazine. At the time he wasn't interested in selling, but VNU persevered and a year later returned with serious money. Negotiations got to the point of including lawyers, accountants, financial advisers and bankers, and VNU eventually made an offer of £2 million. It was an enormous amount of money that nobody in their right mind would have turned down but Felix, already several steps ahead of everybody in the room, left the money on the table. As Andrews said later, Felix was convinced that he could quickly make the company worth £3 million.

'I think that was quite brave of him,' he said. 'That was a big purchase in those days.'

The pair stayed in touch socially and less than a year later they opened up discussions again and this time settled on £3 million.

'Precisely as he had forecast it,' said Graeme.

With corporation tax hovering north of 50 per cent and higher-rate personal tax at 60 per cent, for tax planning purposes they agreed a convoluted signing ceremony that meant signing one part of the deal before midnight on 30 June and the other part on 1 July 1982. This entailed everybody involved, from the lawyers to the bankers, staying up until midnight. Graeme remembered a very good dinner, with a lot to drink and bleary-eyed executives announcing the deal the next day.

Felix returned to the UK and, along with his lawyer and tax accountant, celebrated the following evening in Miranda's nightclub in Kingly Street, where he got up on stage and sang a couple of Blues numbers with the band. The following day, having squeezed Felix for an extra few thousand pounds the day before the deal was struck, Angelo Zgorelec stopped the traffic outside Rathbone Place to show off his new Rolls-Royce.

When news of the sale broke, newspapers and magazines were keen to find out what price VNU had paid. In one paper Felix berated a journalist who had the cheek to ask such an impertinent question, while another, *Financial Weekly*, was so keen to know how much they had settled on they set up a competition offering a free computer to anyone who would give them the information. They were prepared to supply an Osborne 1, then one of the first portable computers on the market, to 'anyone who knows the real figure'. The offer, they cheekily said, was also open to 'Mr Dennis', should he wish to avail himself of a new computer.

Felix didn't take them up on the offer but what he did avail himself of was the opportunity to promote both his business and his thoughts on the industry. He announced the imminent launch of *MicroScope*, the first trade magazine for the computer industry, while at the same time taking a swipe at the fusty state of publishing in general. 'Publishing is still riddled with Hooray Henrys and chinless wonders,' he told Ian White in *Campaign* magazine. He said he was stupefied at how 'clueless' some of the chairmen of huge publishing companies were. With his by now signature brash, uncompromising approach, he railed at the state of distribution, calling for the need to put magazines into supermarkets. His industry was 'terrified of upsetting the newsagent trade', he said and pointed out that, although publishing was being run by those fearful of change, it was time to do just that.

Felix was being seen as a maverick making a name for himself as an outlaw, but he was also a sixties revolutionary who was being taken seriously. He told *Woman's World* that, although he didn't believe that he had changed or 'sold out', he had become one of the people that he and his fellow editors at *Oz* had been warning everybody about in the sixties. Most importantly, however, by getting his name in the press he was already discovering the marketing and human resources benefits of promoting himself as a ribald pirate.

Although he stayed on as a consultant to help VNU with their new baby and even helped them launch a new weekly computer magazine, *Personal Computer News*, as well, the tax threshold meant that by then Felix had decided to become a tax exile and move to New York. But not before launching *MicroScope* in the UK, taking a trip to San Francisco with his mother, offering to invest in the Chez les Ange restaurant in Frith Street, refurbishing the flat in Kingly Street and having one of his first Christmases in London for many years. It was to be a Christmas that he would remember for the crossing of swords of two of his friends.

Felix spent that particular Christmas Day in 1982 at Kingly Street with Yumi, a Korean companion. After he and his two other guests, Don Atyeo and Sue Ready, had had pre-lunch drinks, they enjoyed Yumi's starter of sashimi, followed by oyster soup. Felix replied to her efforts with a recipe of his own, which he later described as 'only slightly collapsed garlic and avocado soufflé'. This was a dish that he had first created when unexpected guests turned up for dinner and he only had five avocados, a few eggs and lots of garlic in the house. There was a certain amount of shuffling as his guests made a huge effort to look as though they enjoyed it. Before the main course he decided to relax the atmosphere by whipping out the Harrods Christmas crackers, in which he had secreted his own presents from the sex shop down the road. However, he mixed up the presentation and Yumi became the proud owner of Sunshine Erection Cream, while Don grappled with Electric Vibrating Loveballs.

Relaxing after a tasty goose served with all the trimmings, their moment of peace was interrupted by a ring on the doorbell. Pressing the entryphone and allowing whatever waifs and strays might be seeking the benefit of his largesse, Felix was surprised to be confronted by what he described as 'a walking flowerbed'. It turned out to be a chauffeur bearing a gift of flowers from another girlfriend, who had not only sent them via the chauffeur, but had, oddly enough, been passing by with her entire family at the same time. With little choice he invited them in to join the party. As they came in the door a voice from upstairs, with a decidedly oriental accent, whined softly, 'the little bitch!'

As Felix remembered it later, 'Dogs, mothers, fathers, cousins and half of the Hong Kong Jockey Club' began to climb the stairs and the moment arrived when he had to introduce the two women, who at different times had enjoyed both his affections and his increasingly diverse sexual fantasies. As they testily circled each other, verbally throwing punches like tightly coiled serpents, Don and Sue engaged the rest of the family in conversation. Felix recalled later that, while the mother was at her wit's end trying to stop the dog from attacking pieces of stray meat from the goose, the young brother, who was only 12 years old, was staring with 'rapt attention' at his oil paintings. The collection included black men and white women in furious sexual activity as well as a sex change portrait that he said must be seen to be believed. He described it as 'a kind of Jayne Mansfield with a dick the length of a small cobra'. With chaos reigning and the likelihood of a tornado strike imminent, Felix suggested they all retire to the lounge for drinks.

Although the friend's father, understanding the situation perfectly, found the whole afternoon hysterical, especially when the dog was nearly electrocuted after attacking the vibrating loveballs, there was a sigh of relief when the family eventually left. Visiting the bathroom later, Felix found a message scrawled on the mirror in glaring red lipstick: 'For a good time phone Yumi 555 4310. Major credit cards accepted'. He quickly wiped it clean but alas, too late! Yumi had already heard about it from Don and Sue. Coming out of the bathroom later, wiping her hands, she muttered with a traditionally Eastern grammatical touch: 'One never know where dog have been, eh?' Felix and the assembled company were left in no doubt about which particular dog she was referring to.

Although by now he had shown an appetite for oriental companions, Felix still showed an interest in all nationalities. Prior to leaving for New York he arrived to have dinner with Don and Sue at their flat in Clapham with his Italian friend Ornella. She looked stunning in high heels and fur coat and tottered in behind him. As she sat down, Sue suggested she hang up her coat.

'Oh no, darling, I can't take it off,' she said.

'Why not?' asked Sue, insisting it was warm enough and she had no intention of turning off the central heating.

'I'm not wearing anything much underneath, you see,' she replied.

A quick flash confirmed she was wearing lacy stockings and little else. To the displeasure of the assembled men, Sue then insisted on supplying a T-shirt and shorts to her dinner guest.

'Felix was furious,' she remembered.

Don later admitted to being a little disappointed himself.

PART TWO

THE
GLORY
YEARS

CHAPTER 12
HIPPIES AND SUITS

After the sale of *Personal Computer World* in 1982, Felix's life became, at least for the next two decades, a tale of two cities. But it also became the story of the development of one man's wisdom, ambition and personal growth – even if for a time it appeared to be disguised as an exercise in self-destruction.

Compared to the time it took him to make his first million, Felix's second major success happened relatively quickly. After boarding Concorde at Heathrow on the last day of the tax year in 1983, and flying across the Atlantic to New York alongside what he described as 'a plane full of tax exiles', his relationship with partners Peter Godfrey and Bob Bartner began to thrive.

Although his streetwise knowledge of London had served him well, New York in the early eighties was a world apart. It was gritty, to say the least. Graffiti, noise, traffic and crime were all part of the culture of daily life and the city had a reputation for being violent and unsafe. The iconic images of the era included junkies, homeless alcoholics and underground carriages daubed with gang names and provocative insignia. Daily life was reflected by kids cooling off beside gushing fire hydrants and middle-aged mobster-like Europeans lazing about in coffee houses and on doorsteps. Despite having visited and become familiar with the city from previous stays, Felix was mugged by an armed junkie on his second day.

'If there ain't 50 bucks in this wallet, my man, I'm gonna just have to get nasty,' he was told. To compound his early welcome to exile he also got stuck in a jammed elevator on the 25th floor of a tower block on the same day.

Susan Freeman, who worked for Bob Bartner and Peter Godfrey at the time, found him an apartment on East 64th Street, a busy but upmarket street a short walk from Central Park. From there, along with Susan's help, he set up Pilot Communications to develop new publishing ventures in America.

Asked what her first impression of him was in those days, Susan summed it up with one word: 'weird'. Talking many years later about what it was like to work for him, she made a comparison. She said she was a very organised person who liked to stick to routines and described herself as very precise. Felix, however, was 'the total opposite!' Although he was in fact a very organised person in many ways, to Susan his methods of doing business were different. She said then: 'He is not like anybody else. He lives life and deals with business in his framework and his way of doing it, which doesn't necessarily fit in with 98 per cent of the rest of the world.' But Susan's description wasn't pointing out any frustration, it was highlighting some of what she felt made Felix successful. She remembered him as 'brilliant'. Discussing a business matter, he would very quickly cut through the grey areas right to the nub of a problem, leaving her to wonder why she didn't see what seemed so obvious after he had pointed it out.

'He just had a knack,' she admitted. 'As the saying goes, when they made him they broke the mould.' Touching on a point with which any psychologist would have had a field day, she went on to say, 'I always figured Felix's mother must have had a very interesting time with him when he was growing up.'

Neither Peter Godfrey nor Bob Bartner felt the need, nor indeed had the time, to get involved with Felix's complex personality. For most of the time they worked together, they were in the eye of the storm and it wasn't until further down the line that they needed to tame the man who would terrorise and bemuse some business contacts, especially when they might include the U.S. Securities and Exchange Commission during the run-up to a successful venture that floated on the NASDAQ, the second-largest stock exchange in America.

Despite New York welcoming him with a bite on the ankles, Felix soon found his rhythm. On one occasion while out walking, he was propositioned by a prostitute who was jogging through Central Park. Although he thought he had seen everything, he was quite taken aback.

Eventually finding his voice, he said, 'Do you usually proposition gentlemen in your jogging outfit?'

Without missing a pace from her exercise she continued jogging on the spot and replied, 'Yes.' Felix looked bemused as she went on, 'The police can't accuse me of loitering, and in any case, it's good for me. I need to lose the weight.'

He chuckled and asked her if she didn't think men might prefer a more seductive outfit.

'That's easy,' she laughed and proceeded to open the tiny shoulder bag she was carrying. Inside was a pair of high-heeled shoes and what he described as a non-crushable evening gown. She then unzipped the front of her jogging suit to reveal enormous breasts snugly cushioned by a black lacy bra. 'I keep a G-string in my bag too,' she told him, 'along with my rubbers. Wanna see the rest?'

Of course he did.

Recounting the story, Felix boomed with laughter. 'I took her back to my apartment,' he said, 'and looking out from my balcony afterwards there she was, jogging back down the street. Only in America!'

Not all liaisons with prostitutes were as genial. Writing to his solicitor Michael Nixon not long after he got to New York, Felix highlighted what he called a 'knotty little problem'. He had been summoned to appear as the chief prosecution witness against a young lady who had stolen property from his flat in Goodge Street. Describing her as a 'nasty piece of work' who deserved whatever the judge should give her, he explained that he couldn't come back to London for the trial but would be happy to sign an affidavit if that would suffice. He explained that she was a prostitute but he hadn't known that at the time and only paid her what he said was a large amount of money after she had pointed out her occupation. He complained that, after buying her an 'excellent Dover sole at Wheelers', she then proceeded to steal his £4,500 wristwatch. Feeling more than a little foolish, he admitted, 'I am an absolute idiot.'

Thankfully, he spent his money on more than prostitutes. One of his first big purchases was to be the catalyst for the next major business success. In a roundabout way it was thanks to another internationally renowned businessman, Steve Jobs, who went on to achieve god-like status and eventually had his life analysed to a massive degree. Not only would Felix and Jobs share different levels of success in the same industry, they would also share certain character traits that helped to create that success.

After hooking up with a genius engineer and programmer called Steve Wozniak, Steve Jobs used his obsessive need for perfection to launch the first computer with a Graphical User Interface available to the mass market. The Apple Lisa was launched in 1983 and had a mouse, two floppy disc drives, a keyboard and a megabyte of RAM. It weighed 48lb and sold for $9,995 before sales tax. Felix pounced on it. Peter Godfrey thought he'd gone mad, and for a while Susan Freeman developed a computer phobia. For many months, Peter, Felix and Bob had been discussing the idea of launching a computer magazine in America but were unsure which way the market would go. When Felix bought the Lisa, Peter complained that he could have purchased a PC. Ironically, the Lisa was not a success for Apple and Steve Jobs was bounced off the project. His next effort, however, produced a product that would spawn Felix's next adventure – the launch of *MacUser* magazine, a year later in 1984.

But prior to the eventual launch it seemed to Susan Freeman that Felix rarely stayed in one place for very long. Although when not hunched over his Lisa, he was likely to be hunched over any one of a dozen lady friends, he was also racking up massive amounts of air miles. Before the end of the year he was to fly six trips across America as well as make a trip to Holland and he also went house hunting in Bermuda. The life of an idle tax exile was far from idle.

He also managed to develop an enduring love for New York. The place was brutal and dilapidated at the time. Washington Square was a cardboard city full of junkies and homeless people. Times Square was porn heaven and the murder rate regularly went over 1,000 people each year. Due to a glut of cocaine in the early eighties, dealers developed a solid form of the drug that could be smoked. Called crack cocaine, it quickly spread in popularity and its hugely addictive nature led to an increase in prostitution and crime. When one New Yorker decided to shoot four men who had attempted to mug him on the subway, many hailed him a hero. Writing to his friend, Managing Director of EMAP, David Arculus, later, Felix told him that he avoided the subway at all costs and kept a very heavy key chain in his pocket and 'a mean look in my eyes!' He later took a liking to the new form of what he described as 'Colombian marching powder' himself. Smoking crack cocaine was to feature in nearly a decade of his life on both sides of the Atlantic.

For Felix, New York in the eighties was electric. It crackled through the swarming crowds and gave him the sense that anything was possible. He described it as the only place to be. It was for him 'the centre of the universe, the middle of the vortex'. He explained that, although he had lived in cities all his life, nothing had prepared him for the sense of 'It Can Be Done and I Can Do It' that he felt during his 10-minute walk to work. He loved the fact that he didn't have to constantly apologise for having money in the bank and, in a letter to Louise Ferrier, he described feeling that the way forward was 'full speed ahead and damn the torpedoes'.

He told her what it took for him to become a New Yorker, saying it entailed 'enduring rudeness beyond belief from all and sundry'. He proudly confided that he had learned to steal other people's cabs as well as order 100 different types of pasta or 50 sushi dishes 'without glancing at the menu'. During a short visit to see him, his mother was shocked to see how brutally offhand he had been with a crazed bag lady. However, he explained, 'she hasn't seen what little old crazed bag ladies can do with a knitting needle and a length of razor wire.'

On a more positive note he grew to love the diverse and huge range of great restaurants, the bookshops that were open all hours and the live jazz and blues legends that played in small, smoky, downtown clubs. He even got to grips with baseball, describing it as 'sort of like rounders crossed with cricket'. He described health clubs as the 'national opium' and was amused during a drought when the mayor asked residents to urinate three times before flushing. But most of all he said the city was populated by a large number of beautiful Asian women, 'still a vital factor in my happiness quotient!'

After setting up an office on East 58th Street, he enjoyed walking around the buzzing streets and equally enjoyed starting a new company from scratch, albeit with a bit of finance behind him this time. Peter Godfrey remembered that, as they still hadn't decided where to go with launching a computer magazine, at first they went in a different direction.

'In the interim, with our efforts in Manhattan, we started *Star Hits* and another teen music publishing thread,' he said. *Star Hits* was a deal negotiated on a modest royalty basis with EMAP in order to emulate the UK magazine *Smash Hits* (to avoid any confusion EMAP wouldn't allow the use of the name *Smash Hits* in America).

Part of the negotiations with EMAP included bringing over a couple of staff to work in New York. As Felix was to describe it later in his book *How to Get Rich*, the magazine was destined for a short, though spectacular existence. British pop groups such as Duran Duran and Tears for Fears were popular in the US and the *Star Hits* association with its British counterpart should have given it an edge when it came to getting interviews, photographs and promotional material. One member of staff that made the leap across the Atlantic was *Smash Hits* editor Neil Tennant.

A North Shields boy, Tennant had cut his journalistic teeth writing copy for Marvel comics, but his real love was music. In New York, as Felix exuberantly described it, with *Star Hits* selling in the hundreds of thousands per month and sacks of mail from all over America piling high in their tiny office, Neil Tennant had become the editor of one of the country's hottest magazines.

'New York city lay at his feet,' wrote Felix. He could get backstage passes to any gig in the country, whether huge arenas or downtown clubs, and flew anywhere he wanted to interview whomsoever he chose. However, that wasn't what really took his fancy.

One day Neil wandered into Felix's office with a cassette tape on which he had recorded a couple of demo songs of his own. He told him that he wanted to leave and try his hand at becoming a successful musician. Never one to take the loss of an employee easily, Felix tried his damnedest to persuade him to stay, but he was adamant. One day, he told Felix, he would be on the cover of *Smash Hits*. As Felix later recalled, he was right. Within a year Neil and Chris Lowe, calling themselves the Pet Shop Boys, had released one of the songs, 'West End Girls', from that same cassette tape and they were on their way.

Pilot Communications churned out other projects as well as *Star Hits*, which included poster magazines with movie tie-ins as well as pop star magazines sold in special plastic display units. They even worked on a unique set of Trivial Pursuit cards, while at one point Mick Farren, who had by then moved to New York himself, helped produce a special one-off celebrating Elvis's 50th birthday.

While Felix, Peter and Bob were throwing around ideas about what kind of computer magazine to launch, fate stepped in – in the form of some disgruntled employees from another publication. Arthur Jacobs, who became Felix's lawyer in the United States for many years and helped set up the framework for various of their business interests, remembered the resulting scenario as a lesson on what extraordinary attitudes both Felix and Peter had towards their lives and their businesses.

One of the difficulties at the time was the fact that the computer industry, still relatively in its infancy, didn't have a glut of expert staff to put a magazine together. So when an approach came from five people who already worked in the industry, offering a business plan as well as their expertise in return for equity in the new venture, Felix and Peter thought their prayers had been answered. Jacobs remembered that they immediately prepared a plan for a new corporation, which would produce a magazine with a different editorial focus to that of their competitor. Over many weeks they negotiated, prepared documents, had extensive meetings, set up shareholder agreements as well as employment agreements, and put the legal framework in place to finalise a deal. Eventually, the day came to commit, and Peter, Felix and Arthur drove up to New Hampshire to sign the paperwork that would begin the process of launching a magazine focusing on the personal computer market.

As they arrived in the leafy, wide streets of Concord, New Hampshire in September 1983, the lawyer representing the five employees was standing outside his office waiting to greet them. However, he had bad news: his clients had got cold feet at the last minute, fearing they might be sued by their existing employer. As it happened, they didn't have contracts, a point that had been one of the deciding factors in Felix and Peter's decision to go ahead with the deal, but they weren't about to argue that particular issue at the time and, as Arthur Jacobs remembered later, in any other circumstances there would have been an explosion. He fully expected something more on the lines of 'Let's sue the bastards!' but instead was floored by Peter and Felix's reaction. They simply said, 'Well, that's awful. That's really bad. That's a big, big disappointment but such is life. What's the best restaurant in town? Let's go to dinner!'

They spent a happy evening with the New Hampshire lawyer regaling him with stories of business deals and life in England, as Arthur sat between them struggling to take in what he later recalled as a very surreal situation. What he saw that evening was two people 'who didn't miss a beat in terms of loving life and having a good evening'. After polishing off impressive amounts of wine and good food, they headed back to New York and, as Arthur said later, 'In typical Felix Dennis style he went on to another idea, which went on to be much, much better.'

Back in England, the culture change brought about by the sale of *Personal Computer World*, Felix's move to New York and Stephen England's new role as managing director was beginning to herald some changes. After a short spell working through a consulting role with *Personal Computer World* as part of the sale deal with VNU, England began the task of turning Bunch into the sort of company that could develop and thrive through the Thatcher years. Growth, consumerism and displays of affluence were beginning to permeate some parts of English society and the era of the laid-back hippie work ethic was slowly being consumed but not without a fight.

When Roger Munford was poached from a rival publisher to help launch a magazine called *Your Spectrum*, he found a line of cocaine on his desk when he got back from lunch on his second day. 'I didn't even know what it was,' he said. He remembered Bruce Sawford nervously suggesting it might be a welcome gift from some of the other employees. Asking what he should do with it, he was told just to leave it there – whoever had left it would be back looking for it.

'Sure enough,' he remembered, 'within an hour someone came in and said, "Er, do you want that?" "No, not really,"' said Roger and it disappeared before he could blink.

'Yeah, they were pretty much a bunch of degenerates and absolutely brilliant people,' he said later.

Roger's first job was to edit a satirical in-house Christmas magazine devised by some of those used to the long hours, the office banter and the sense of humour that traditionally supports skin-of-the-teeth publishing. Entitled *Your Scrotum*, it was described by Mark Williams as 'a piss-take on the sort of cheery, morale-boosting company newsletters that the much-bigger Dennis Publishing would eventually itself produce'. He remembered it as being 'full of scurrilous innuendo and outrageous pastiches of internal memos'. It included a hysterical 'Who'd Fuck Who?' chart designed in grid form, with men's names along the top and women's names along the side. Stars indicated who fancied whom, but, as Mark ruefully recalled later, the long hours precluded much chance of relationships 'carnal or otherwise'. Regardless, somehow they managed.

Your Scrotum was a roaring in-house success. The cover had thumbnails of Stephen England, with a headline that played on the Rolling Stones' 'Sympathy for the Devil', saying, 'Please allow me to reproduce myself'. Another headline offered: 'All new and used coke prices every month'. Roger recalled how it ripped Stephen England 'to shreds'. For his part, having originally agreed to it being produced, Stephen called it a 'clusterfuck travesty'. He described it as 'probably illegal in 90 per cent of the planet' and was on the point of firing Munford when he got a call from Felix, who demanded it be reprinted so he could send copies to his friends.

'It was probably 30 per cent abuse at Felix and 30 per cent abuse at me,' said Stephen, but to Felix, it was a valuable outlet for staff pressure and a healthy morale booster. Felix's response was a strong indicator of his inability to feel the pain of personal embarrassment. He would later explain that, although he certainly understood it, it never bothered him.

Stephen was aware that the company was beginning to suffer from the strains of the cultural change. He described *Your Scrotum* as 'the last Exocet missile from the hippies to the suits'. He had started at Bunch as the man in the suit and, as he described it, he was 'dealing with the first stages of de-hippifying Bunch'. In the end it wasn't the case that the suits outnumbered the hippies, it was more that 'the systems outnumbered the craziness, and that was more important. It wasn't really a matter of whether you took drugs or what you wore because those two cultures did a pretty good job of blending. We went casual; we got more secretive about where the drugs were being used. We kind of straightened up our act and the two came together, but we were running a real publishing company.'

On one occasion, Stephen had to sign off on the bill for a day at the Bike Show, where, out of £300, the only non-alcoholic item was a solitary plate of sausages. He remembered the chemistry between staff as 'incredible', though not always compatible.

'We would never hire normal people,' he explained. 'We would always have art directors who would literally rush around with a scalpel threatening to castrate anybody who didn't agree with their principles.' Magazines would have three people in charge and the publisher's job was to count the pennies and 'to stop the three killing each other'.

Although Felix had handed over the reins to Stephen and his move to New York gave the impression of taking a hands-off approach to the running of Bunch, it would be wrong to assume that he completely absolved himself of any responsibility for what was happening. He was still the proverbial driving force and his maverick style was to remain within the soul of the company always. Stephen grew used to a routine of late-night telephone conversations with the voice from across the pond.

'I actually think he was very, very good at negotiating late at night because he's a complete night owl,' said Stephen. 'And there's never been any logic to when he would call.'

Starting at 10–10.30pm, the calls would inevitably be a couple of hours long and, by the time he had got off the phone, Stephen remembered being what he called 'adrenaline saturated' and 'buzzed up to the eyeballs'. So, although the mornings became recovery time, they also began with a long list of things Felix wanted done. It was a routine that many people were to make part of their lives as his empire grew. 'So I'd always come in first thing in the morning with this cattle prod up my arse that Felix had put there the night before,' said Stephen. He would start 'lobbing hand grenades all over the building', barking orders at staff because he knew that Felix would be back on the line again by mid-afternoon.

Drinking his morning coffee in Manhattan, Felix would be bouncing thoughts, ideas, observations and orders all over again.

'He would never let go,' said Stephen.

Mark Williams, whose knowledge of the history of Dennis Publishing is extensive, related another legendary story about Felix's dictates from across the pond. When approached by another publishing house to help produce a computer partwork (a series of magazines that built up in volumes), there was a moment when it looked as though the first issue might be late. The nature of partwork publications means that the bulk of the advertising spend has to be made prior to the first issue coming out to ensure that as many people as possible are hooked into the product from the beginning. It's harder to convince buyers to start collecting a series of magazines if they have missed the first two or three, so in the case of this particular product there were millions of pounds at stake. TV advertising, newsagent promotions and binder deliveries were just some of the items that were key to a successful launch and if the first issue was not delivered on time then the consequences were serious.

As Mark recalled, when Stephen discovered that Part One might be late he had to ring Felix in New York to tell him and to seek his advice. Felix was, somewhat inevitably, utterly furious. He instructed Stephen to find out what it would take to speed up the production process and get the first issue out on time.

The answer that came back was: 'Five grand's worth of artificial stimulant.'

It produced a Nike moment when Felix blasted down the phone, 'Just do it!'

An assortment of freelancers worked day and night and the issue reached the newsagents on time and all was well. It was a somewhat unorthodox way of dealing with a production problem, and no doubt not in keeping with the new, more corporate Bunch envisaged by Stephen, but as Felix put it later, 'It was what it was.'

It was later remembered as a good call. The partwork went on to be a huge success, making money for both businesses.

CHAPTER 13

A FAIR FIGHT

Across the Atlantic, the US operation of Pilot Communications was growing and it was a bit of a journey for some of those who worked there. Susan Haung remembered when she first started working for Felix in the mid-eighties.

'I was deadly afraid,' she said. He was loud and he yelled, 'and he doesn't look at you when he talks to you.' She found Felix's yellow-tinted glasses disconcerting but soon realised that he was not so scary as her first impression. In time she became as much a personal assistant as secretary, organising everything from sending his Christmas cards to arranging work on his apartment. Because she spoke Chinese she also became a gatekeeper when Asian girlfriends would pester him. On one occasion, when a Korean friend was in jail, Felix instructed Susan to be sure to look after her.

'She would call me in the evening with whatever request,' she remembered. 'I had to buy her underwear, a Walkman.' Whether it was puzzles, books or newspapers, Susan would send them to the jail. 'That was just part of dealing with Felix.'

Despite his elevated position she remembered that he had no problem doing anything that needed to be done. If the sink was full of dirty cups he was likely to start swearing but was just as likely to get stuck in to cleaning them. His eating habits stood out.

Some days he would arrive at the office at 11am and his breakfast would be a Kit Kat. He would survive on that and tea, which consisted of two tea bags, an English breakfast and Earl Grey mix with milk and sugar. Later in the day he would need pastrami sandwiches and one day she remembered, as it grew late in the evening, his hunger got the better of him.

'I'm hungry, is there any food around?' he shouted to no one in particular.

'Oh, I've just thrown half a sandwich out,' answered one of the sales people, also working late.

'What kind?' asked Felix.

'Pastrami,' she said.

Felix came striding out of his office demanding to know where she had thrown it and retrieved it from the bin. He devoured it in seconds.

One day, when Susan's husband had been celebrating getting his captain's licence for the coastguard station, he and a friend spent the morning at a local bar and turned up at the office in celebratory mood. She put her husband in an empty office to sleep it off but his friend Sal wasn't so easily contained. He made a nuisance of himself wandering around the office and at one point followed Felix down a corridor, mimicking his 'penguin walk'. Felix just laughed and eventually suggested Susan take them home.

She stayed at Pilot for eight years and later said he was one of the best bosses she had, as well as 'one of the smartest men I have ever met'.

Speaking in 1998, Susan Freeman recalled how, because of his heavy smoking habit, Felix could never hide.

'You could always tell where Felix was,' she explained, 'because there would be this little trail of long ashes.' He would stand there with a cigarette in his hand or hanging out of his lips, 'and all of a sudden this giant ash would fall on the floor, or on your desk'.

Although she suggested that at times he 'got a little off-the-wall crazy' and was 'erratic in many ways', she also had high praise for him. 'I think he is a brilliant businessman,' she said. 'Felix is the type of person who you either love or hate him. I think there is very little middle ground because he is such a strong personality.'

Echoing a point made by so many of those who worked for him and describing the sort of delegation that had already become his management style, she went on to say, 'I loved working for him. He'll give you an idea. He'll sit and deal with the fermenting of the idea and then leave you to go deal with it. I think he trusts the people who work for him in terms of letting them get on with it.' Much as this was inspirational, it was also challenging.

She added, 'I think he is always demanding in that he demands the most and the best from people who work for him.'

Setting up the *MacUser* operation introduced a new group of people to Pilot. Telling Susan Freeman that the magazine currently serving the Mac market wasn't good enough, Felix said, 'I'm going to do a better one.' At the time there were six of them working on the teen magazines and as she recalled, 'All of a sudden we had, like, eight more people, eight weird computer nerds coming in to start *MacUser*. We had no place to put them, no equipment, no nothing.'

She remembered Felix's instructions about finding somewhere to put the new magazine. He told her, 'You have to find new offices and you have to find them fast. They have to be within 10 blocks in any direction of my apartment so I can walk to work. We have to be able to open the windows and we have to be able to control the air, and it has to be in move-in condition. Other than that, I have no specifications.'

In time everyone moved to the new office and it began to take on its own character.

'We had the music and computer stuff together,' remembered Susan. 'Slowly, more people started coming on board because *MacUser* was requiring a much larger staff than the music stuff. It was a very interesting combination of people.' She described the music people as 'very out there, kids really into music'. However, they worked alongside a very different animal, in many ways the antithesis of the American corporate style but very much fitting in with the pirate theme that Felix later liked to promote. 'Every time I fell into the editorial bullpen I thought I was in a throw-back era to the late sixties,' she said. 'The long hair, the jeans, the knapsacks, the whole nine yards.' Although he would claim that it wasn't done consciously, Felix's influence was creating a unique style for what would later become Dennis Publishing US.

The reason for the growth of staff was that Steve Jobs had launched the follow-up to Lisa. It was the computer that would begin a turbulent, but very profitable relationship with Apple. The launch of the first Macintosh or Mac on 24 January 1984 began with a TV advertisement based on George Orwell's book *Nineteen Eighty-Four*. Aired at the break in the Super Bowl two days earlier, it was directed by Ridley Scott and depicted a beautiful blonde athlete, dressed remarkably like a Hooters Girl, running from jack-booted police. With Big Brother lecturing from a massive grey screen to lines of empty-eyed, spellbound workers, she raced into the room and, Thor-like, hurled a hammer into the screen to release the world from the conformity of its grey zombified state. Although initially not popular with all of the Apple board, the advertisement was later hailed as a masterpiece.

IDG's *Macworld* magazine was very quickly launched, but as Felix later explained to Steve Bobker, an early editor of *MacUser*, it is often better to be second into a market than first because it gives you a sense of where the market is going and also gives you 'someone to beat'. Despite saying it wasn't good enough, Felix was sufficiently impressed with *Macworld* to arrange for a subscription to be airmailed to his brother Julian in England. Calling it a 'fabulous rag', he also planned to get all the back issues sent to him as well. So the launch of *MacUser* came along as the market for Macintosh was already being served.

As Peter Godfrey recalled, Felix came up with the idea of doing a Mac magazine a couple of months after the Macintosh launch. He suggested that part of the reason it was possible was that Bill Ziff, the major publisher of US computer magazines at the time, had decided against doing a Mac magazine and therefore left the door open. The arrangement between Felix, Peter and Bob Bartner was that Felix would handle the creative side of the publications while Peter and Bob would look after the printing and distribution. This meant that Bunch was able to launch *MacUser* in the UK before it was launched in the US.

Peter also remembered that initial dealings with Apple weren't warm. 'There were some difficult moments with Apple during this time,' he explained, 'because they wanted to control the market for publications.' From his perspective Apple were unhappy that they had no influence over them, while at the same time they needed access to Apple's user database to sell subscriptions to. As was later revealed in Steve Jobs' biography, *Steve Jobs* by Walter Isaacson, he was obsessed with control, from the inside of his computers to the colour of the glass steps in the Apple stores.

'So we went backwards and forwards with Apple,' remembered Peter. 'At one point, probably not foolishly, but ambitiously, threatening them with a lawsuit.'

A typical day in New York for Felix would have included back-to-back meetings and raising hell whenever necessary. He described what he remembered as a fairly standard day during the early *MacUser* days. Having slept late after a girlfriend had come back from a trip to Europe, he had rushed to a lunch meeting with a firm handling *MacUser*'s mid-West sales. It was followed by an editorial meeting to put fire into those who were slacking on deadlines. He then raced off a quick letter to Apple looking for mailing lists and followed this by checking over another Duran Duran *Star Hits* cover and working on *WOW!*, the new TV and movie star fanzine for Kable News. This was followed by a long evening in which he met with the owner of a small magazine that was a rival to *MacUser*. The owner wanted to sell and Felix made him a low offer. As he said later, his only interest was in the subscriber list. Next on the agenda, since anyone left to do business with had by then long gone home, was a short walk back to his apartment to await the arrival of girlfriend Yumi, whom he described as 'a crazy, mixed-up girl, but very likeable'. She eventually turned up two hours late. Having given up smoking and drinking for 12 days, Felix then stuffed himself with hot rolls full of Brie and salami before collapsing as the sun came up. If he ever saw a New York dawn it was usually because he had filled his nights with an excess of his favourite pastimes as opposed to rising early to join the early-morning commute.

Sitting in one of his exotic hideaways many years later, Felix explained that his stamina had often astonished even himself. Admitting there was no merit in it, that it was 'genes and nothing but', he recalled that he would work non-stop for 48 hours on magazines to make sure that they came out on time. However, he accepted that it wasn't entirely naturally sourced.

'I literally would take vast quantities of narcotics,' he said. 'Fuck the most beautiful girls in England. Go to sleep at four in the morning, get up at 8.30am, go in and do a full day's work.'

When he got home, he would do it all over again.

'How long could that go on?' he asked. 'Much longer than you could possibly imagine. So it is all about stamina. That's why I can do all this nonsense – and it *is* all nonsense.'

MacUser was ceremoniously launched at the *Macworld* Exposition in Boston in August 1985. As many potential advertisers as could be safely squeezed into a small riverboat were taken on a boozy trip along the Charles River and, while the main topic of conversation was Steve Jobs' boardroom clash with John Scully, the wine flowed, networking was done and serious contacts were made. As Steve Rosenfield, who had been brought in as ad director, remembered, it was a 'rollicking good party' that included a classically English touch of serving port and Stilton to the nearly 200 people on board. Felix had also flown Roger Munford over as the representative of Dennis Publishing UK. It was a memorable occasion for Roger, who had never actually met Felix and was concerned to make a good impression.

Booked into the same hotel, he and Felix were drinking at the bar after the celebratory dinner for those who had worked on the launch when a young girl approached them.

'Oh my God, are you British?' she cried. Fresh-faced and sporting hair over his shoulders, Roger was relatively casually dressed while Felix was impeccable in his tailored suit and silk tie. The girl asked whether Roger was a rock star and Felix was his manager. Although bristling at the ageist observation, Felix immediately went into charm overdrive. He kissed her hand and introduced himself as a magazine publisher from London. He then introduced Roger as 'the pride of my publishing company in England' and ordered more drinks while describing the business and how it was the largest independent magazine publisher in the UK. Following this he launched into a charm offensive with a detailed and amusing description of the various publications the company produced and an even more detailed description of what an important role Roger played.

'The girl sat down with this seductive speech,' remembered Roger. 'He was charming the pants off her.'

After a short time Felix disappeared and returned with a waiter bearing a tray of the hotel's best champagne. 'You two look perfect together,' he said. 'I want you to drink this champagne and have a great evening.'

With that he disappeared, leaving Roger to deal with what turned out to be a suicidal maniac from whom he didn't manage to extricate himself until two in the morning. It turned out to be a brilliant Felix ploy: spotting the potential for a nightmare scenario, he had magnanimously made his exit with grace and panache.

Sadly for Roger that wasn't the end of it. At lunch the next day, surrounded by more potential advertisers, publishers and assorted Mac aficionados, Felix held court and, having already launched *MacUser* in the UK, Roger tried to make a good impression.

At one point during the main course Felix shouted across the room, 'So, Roger, Roger...' The buzz of conversation slowed as people looked at the long-haired Englishman. 'Did you fuck her?' shouted Felix.

Struggling to swallow his food, turning puce and trying to remain cool, Roger muttered something about not kissing and telling and brushed it off as best he could.

The experience was a memorable introduction to his boss. As he put it, 'That was the first time I came across this "nothing matters" man.'

Felix may have understood Roger's embarrassment, but he certainly didn't feel it.

After the launch there was no shortage of angst with efforts to make *MacUser* a success. Up against what they perceived as the mighty *Macworld*, they put every effort into punching above their weight – something Felix had done time and time again.

Steve Rosenfield remembered that Felix's enthusiasm for all things Mac even included teaching him how to use a Mac, as well as how to use MacWrite. They worked in what Steve described as, by American standards, a pokey little office, where all the desks were squeezed tightly together. He remembered one occasion when to get cable from one office to another someone had to hang out of a fifth-floor window and throw cable across to Felix, who caught it on the end of a sweeping brush as he hung out of another window.

Felix also got involved in areas that he hadn't stuck his nose into for some time. Steve remembered one occasion when he was having difficulty closing a relatively small ad sales deal with a client who owned a small software company. He brought Felix to meet the client, who had a taste for fine wine. After numerous glasses of fine French wine and a promise from Felix to send him a case from his cellar the client signed the deal. Afterwards, Felix turned to Steve and said, 'OK, that's done, who's next?'

On another occasion when Steve needed to take a trip to LA to meet a client, he asked Felix's advice on where to stay.

'He flips open this huge Filofax,' said Steve, 'and said, "Pick one of these."' As it happened, he bumped into John Scully, who was president of Apple at the time and staying in the same hotel. 'He was surprised that someone from *MacUser* was staying at the same hotel as the former CEO of Pepsi,' remembered Steve. 'I think it left an impression that helped us crack Apple.'

One coup that made an enormous difference to their circulation list was the addition of *MacUser* onto the Apple warranty card. When new owners filled in their warranty card they were offered three free copies of *Macworld*. Arguing that the Apple community deserved a 'choice', they eventually got *MacUser* added to the card. As Steve remembered, the British-style design of *MacUser* made it the obvious choice for subscribers and their circulation grew.

'Once we got the card in the box we knew that we could overtake *Macworld* – because we had a better magazine,' said Steve. After a year of pestering and endless sales calls and presentations, Apple agreed to advertise in *MacUser* when all their previous advertising had been in *Macworld*. For Steve it was such a momentous occasion that he flew out to the ad agency just to thank them.

'They couldn't understand why I was there,' he said. 'I said, "You don't understand, I just want to thank you."'

As it became clear that those running *Macworld* weren't really taking their new competitor seriously, Felix and Peter Godfrey pushed harder and harder until a moment came when they knew they were close to getting beyond them in circulation. Despite Felix's lack of interest in God, Steve remembered them praying for divine intervention. Divine or not, the intervention came and they won the circulation battle.

In the end it became a tremendous success but not before Peter, Bob and Felix took some wild gambles.

'I'll never forget the summer of '86,' said Peter. 'Felix had made a very bold 100,000 circulation forecast for the first year. As we had started out with a quite modest 25 to 30,000 circulation for the first issue, we had a pretty big challenge to get the average to 100,000.'

It soon became clear that to do this would require a massive investment, several million dollars, which would have to come out of their own pockets.

Peter recalled, 'We would either go for it and spend all this money, and it might have been wasted, or we would back off.'

They went for it and succeeded, but later on found they had to do it again a second time to reach another magical circulation figure. Hands had dug deeply into pockets before Bill Ziff's people eventually decided to come calling and make them an offer for *MacUser*. The courage to stick his hand in his pocket in order to make a gamble pay off was to become a hallmark of Felix Dennis's business dealings for years to come.

After initial meetings with Ziff Davis had resulted in a split vote between them as to whether they should sell, it was agreed that Peter should take the job of going back for more discussions.

'We were anxious about competing with Ziff Davis,' he explained. 'It is not something you do lightly because Ziff had such a stranglehold on the computer publications business that they could launch any new magazine and sell advertising below cost until they got rid of the competition, and we didn't have limitless resources.'

When they were offered $5 million, Peter said he was flattered. 'Five million bucks for something that hasn't made a dime,' he said, seemed pretty exciting. However, Bob and Felix did a back-of-an-envelope calculation and concluded the figure should be closer to $21 million. Initially embarrassed and nervous about coming back and asking for more, Peter said he 'steeled' himself and made his presentation, stating the medium- and long-term value of their product. After a bit more batting back and forth, a deal was done. With an earn-out clause it would indeed be for $21 million. However, it nearly didn't happen.

As Peter recalled, Felix went to ground at the crucial last week of negotiations. He had taken his mother and a girlfriend to Jamaica for a Christmas holiday, and, although they spoke a couple of times on the phone, he hadn't had a chance to read the contract. On the day when it came time to sign, Felix at last appeared and decided he wasn't happy about certain aspects of the earn-out clause.

'We have got so far down the line at this point,' remembered Peter. 'He wants to participate in the negotiations – he is kicking and screaming. He is on the phone to Bill Ziff personally in Florida.'

Stomping, banging the desk and huffing like a bear with a thorn in its paw, Felix was roaring down the phone about the value of the assets in the New York office and whatever other incidentals that irritated him. At this point Peter held his head in his hands, incredulous.

'You are talking about the value of a few old Macintoshes and some furniture,' remembered Peter later. 'This is a $21 million deal, and he is screaming about junk.'

What made it all the more frustrating for Peter was the fact that Ronald Reagan's 1986 Tax Reform Act was about to come into force. If they didn't bank the cheque before the end of the day, they would have lost a sizeable sum due to changes in the capital gains tax law. But as the clock ticked on, Felix and Bill Ziff continued their long-distance arm wrestling. Felix alternated between waxing eloquent and sounding like a psychopath on crystal meth.

In the end Peter dragged him into another room and said, 'Felix, shut up. It's over! The fat lady's sung.' In a situation remarkably similar to the closing of the *Personal Computer World* deal with VNU, he calmly said, 'Oh, OK.' Like switching the light on in a room where someone was having a bad acid trip, Peter's intervention had the effect of pulling Felix out of what might also have been described as an obsessional rant.

On any other day that would be where the story ended, but by the time the arguing was over there was still every possibility that they may not arrive at the bank in time. Peter remembered racing across town in his Rolls-Royce. Realising they wouldn't be able to make it due to the traffic, they ditched the Roller and began to sprint to the bank. Like two crazed alcoholics chasing an escaping bottle of barley wine, they leapt over passers-by and drunks in the gutter, Peter gripping the cheque and Felix roaring with laughter. At one point a bearded European wearing a pirate's hat and selling a clutch of balloons leapt into a doorway to get out of their way. Felix was left with a lasting impression of an arm clutching a huge bunch of balloons sticking out of a doorway as bewildered children scattered across the pavement. When they eventually reached the bank's glass frontage it was already closed and people were milling about, getting ready for New Year's Eve.

Somehow they got in and, as Peter put it, 'I deposit the cheque, get the stamp on the back and get a copy of it and walk out and this deal is done, and we've made the first serious money we've earned.'

There had been tense moments followed by a rush of adrenaline and breathless relief, but there was also elation. Afterwards, there were even recriminations as Felix insisted that they may not get their earn-out and he hated his time spent babysitting *MacUser* for Ziff Davis, but as Bob Bartner said, it changed all of their lives 'very, very significantly'.

Despite their battles Felix grew to respect Bill Ziff. Speaking later, he related how he had been 'summoned' to have lunch with him one day after the deal was done. They met at a Japanese restaurant, were seated by white-gloved respectful staff and had food brought to the table. There was no time wasted looking at menus or deciding what to choose. After a civilised discussion about business matters and the state of the industry, Bill asked Felix if he would like a Cognac.

'I'd like an Armagnac,' answered Felix.

Bill requested their best 50-year-old Armagnac and, after the drinks were placed on the table, he sat across from Felix for a moment's quiet contemplation.

Eventually, he broke the silence with the words: 'You don't know how lucky you are, son.'

Felix replied that they were both lucky.

'No, I don't think you realise how lucky you are,' Bill repeated. He explained that Felix had lived with nothing. He had lived in a house with no electricity; he had bathed in a tin bath and had had to go outside to use a toilet.

'You'll always know what you did,' he told him. 'Everyone else knows what you did, but I will never know what I could have done.'

Because he had inherited everything he would never know the value of his contribution to his life, he explained. He would never know what it was like to start with nothing.

At this Felix pointed out that Bill had quadrupled his inheritance and created an enormously successful company. But Bill slowly shook his head, and then said a curious thing.

'In a fair fight, I could have beaten you,' he told him. From his point of view, a publishing battle with Felix could never be a fair fight because Felix had experienced having nothing and therefore had no fear about going back to having nothing.

'And he literally stood up, buttoned up his overcoat, got himself a candy stick and shook hands,' remembered Felix. 'We were both quite certain we'd see each other again, without any doubt. There was no great goodbye.'

He walked out and Felix watched as the chauffeur opened the limousine door. Bill waved and the car swept up the avenue.

'I never saw him again,' said Felix.

They spoke many times on the phone but never met again.

Although diagnosed with cancer in 1978 and told he might only survive a few years, Bill Ziff carried on working until his death in 2006. With none of his sons interested in the business, in 1994 he sold the company for

$1.6 billion. Felix wrote a poem about him called 'The Patrician', which included the words 'with an acre of linen across his lap', alluding to his wealth and style and the lunch they had shared. With a touch of pride that he was included in Bill's philosophy of life, Felix looked back on Bill Ziff with admiration.

'Whether he was envious of me or not, I don't know. But he was certainly envious of the fact that he never had the chance to find out,' said Felix. 'I certainly still think of Bill Ziff with huge fondness and the poem that I wrote for him, I hope, lives for many years.'

CHAPTER 14

THE EMBEZZLER'S BALL

What nobody on the Ziff Davis team could have been aware of was how much Felix needed the *MacUser* deal to go through. If Bill Ziff had alluded enviously to Felix's street smarts afterwards, he might have been doubly impressed with how he had handled another 'Bunch Crunch' that had taken place in the spring of 1986.

While meeting with the chairman of a distributor to finalise royalties due to Bunch from *Which Bike?*, Felix was informed of a rumour that his UK financial director, who Mark Williams recalled was nicknamed 'Jabba the Hut', had been negotiating with a printer to obtain capital to form his own publishing company. Felix immediately contacted Stephen England, who had also been approached the same day with information from an employee that confirmed the rumour. It was also rumoured that four other senior employees harboured similar ambitions and had planned staggered resignations to eventually set up a rival business. Although this might have been a serious blow, it was overshadowed by the shocking discovery that the financial director had also been embezzling funds from the company and throwing a smokescreen of confusion over the accounts department to camouflage his activities. His activities could not only have destabilised the company but would also have left it in a very precarious position in the face of a new competitor in the market. Especially a new competitor who knew everything there was to know about H. Bunch Associates.

Although Felix was known to be loud, abrasive and even brash, his temper tended to come across more like that of a breathless bear but this news could easily have produced a reaction similar to a wounded and angry rhinoceros. However, although his initial feelings of hurt and anger did threaten to explode into violence, his newfound maturity had been born from a natural canniness and survivor mentality. So, when it came time to face his deceiver, he flew back from the States, having engineered a board meeting on the pretext of discussing the sale of *MicroScope*. But not before first arranging an Anton Piller order (a court order that provides the right to search premises and seize evidence) to have the financial director's computers seized, along with files, computer disks and any other evidence that he might have wanted to hide. As Mark Williams remembered, Felix had to be really careful because some of those around him were incensed and would happily have beaten the man to a pulp.

Instead, the whole situation was dealt with calmly and professionally. 'Jabba' was accused of secretly signing cheques, falsifying invoices and hiding credit card records. In the end some of the money was recovered. The full amount of the deception was never disclosed but it was substantial enough to very nearly derail the company. It transpired that accounts for the previous year, 1985, showing a small profit were drastically wrong and in fact a substantial loss had occurred. Stephen England, although not in any way involved, fell on his sword and remortgaged his house to pay back a bonus that he felt he hadn't deserved since the whole debacle had occurred on his watch.

Collecting his own thoughts about the situation some time later, Felix regretted the fact that, as Bunch had made the transition from small to large business, it had lost many of those whom he could have trusted to spot what was going on and alert him in time to stop it. Having decided to write on a freelance basis, Dick Pountain was no longer there day-to-day, nor was Wendy Kasabian, who had been Felix's faithful PA and office manager since starting at Bunch in the summer of 1976. He was sure that, had she been there, Wendy would have 'blown the whistle' on the fraud. Knowing that both he and his managing director had so desperately wanted the new regime to succeed, they were prey to the 'good news, lads, we're making profits' routine that their new financial director had been peddling. In a long note that he made as an aide-memoire he recalled that his entire company was 'threatened with extinction' and 'all the jobs of the employees threatened with it'.

For a time he remained furious with some of his advisers, whom he thought should have noticed that something was wrong and even refused to pay part of one of their bills. When Felix argued with tax adviser Anton Felton over a £5,000 payment, Felton suggested a way to avoid bad feeling.

'It was one of those moments when we tossed the coin and I staked £5,000 to avoid the danger and nastiness that would have ensued if we had carried on painting ourselves into corners that we couldn't get out of,' he remembered. 'That I won the toss didn't matter, for now it was arm's length fate, and not Felix or I that had determined the result.'

Nonetheless, Felix was determined not to let the whole event damage the company and, with his already legendary knack of steadying a foundering ship, on 29 May 1986 he sent out a memo to all staff entitled 'The old order changeth...' Highlighting the great many comings and goings, including 'auditors in the basement, rumblings on the top floor, whispers in the hallways and a rash of resignations', he tried to still some of the 'more sensational rumours' by explaining what had happened. He told his staff that he would be increasing the profits of British Airways as he planned to devote more of his time and efforts to correct the current situation. Showing the leadership qualities that would later arouse such loyalty and conviction in both friends and employees, he said, 'We all know Bunch isn't a bad place to work but that isn't enough. I want to make it a *great* place to earn a decent crust and have a lot of fun doing it.' He announced that all staff and partners would be invited to the Bunch Embezzler's Ball at the Rasa Sayang in Frith Street, Soho the following week. Booze would be 'copious', the food would be 'prodigious' and the whole bash paid for by him and not the company.

As Mark Williams pointed out later, the night was a huge success.

'A wild time was had by all,' he noted.

Rotten fruit was handed out to anyone who cared to throw it at huge blown-up photographs of the embezzler and a classic wacky Bunch party was soon underway for staff, family, suppliers and many of those who had done business with the company. Stephen England remembered that it just happened to be around the same time as Felix's birthday and so Angelo Zgorelec, who had introduced the first computer magazine to Bunch, decided to arrange a surprise.

'This really big woman appeared in a fur coat,' remembered Stephen. Not wearing much underneath, but a completely different shape to Felix's beautiful Italian companion Ornella, she left quite an impression on Stephen, who recalled that whatever she had been wearing underneath the coat had been long lost from view, and that her stockings 'must have been made by some shipbuilder in Northern Ireland'. She came bouncing across the room, making a beeline for Felix and literally mounted him.

As he was being consumed beneath her more than ample breasts, he shouted 'Stop!' and was allowed up for air.

He quickly said, 'How much did they pay you to do this?'

She answered £100, and as Stephen recalled, he said, 'Here's £200, now fuck off!'

With £300 profit from two minutes' work she gleefully picked up her fur coat and wobbled off into the distance. Felix hunted down Angelo and, to everyone's amusement, verbally abused him for the next hour.

The whole evening was a canny way for Felix to show his suppliers, creditors and bankers that all was well within Bunch; he wanted it known that they had ridden the storm and that there was no need to feel threatened. He made a speech to that effect at the party but the real sign to anyone who might have worried was the party itself. It was two fingers to adversity to ensure that whatever was necessary to the survival of the business would be done. But behind the facade he was fuming; it was a lesson that he took to heart and refused to forget quickly.

It was also a lesson for Stephen England. Apart from giving back his bonus, he also had to sign every cheque drawn on the company bank account for the next 12 months.

'Hundreds of them every week,' he remembered.

By the end of the year his signature had become indecipherable.

If *Kung Fu Monthly* had given Felix a first taste of success and the sale of *Personal Computer World* had given him a taste of real money, then the sale of *MacUser* in 1986 put him in a different league altogether. But it also gave him a new problem: cash in the bank and advisers coming from every direction to tell him what to do with it. It was time to go shopping.

In the height of summer, when the lush, dense foliage of the plane trees in Berkeley Square offer shade from the sun, it is just possible to catch a fleeting moment of peace and tranquillity. However, it takes a strong mind, one with the ability to push the constant rumble of a city teeming with busy people into a place outside of their consciousness. Even on a cold January afternoon, with few leaves on the trees, a chill in the air and the insistent clatter of a jackhammer on a nearby building site, this was something that Felix could and would occasionally do. The proximity of stately trees whose bark proudly bore the scars of their hundreds of years in that small park would often put him into a Zen-like state. By now his love of trees and their gentle nobility inspired him. He could sometimes be found quietly sitting in nearby Golden Square gazing intently at a fallen leaf in his hand.

On one particular January day, however, a glint of sunlight on a window in the east of Berkeley Square caught his attention. Looking more New York than London, Berkeley Square House didn't exactly attract passers-by with its beautiful architecture, but the gleaming toys in the street-level windows spoke of wealth, power, status and extravagance. The gentle throb of a Rolls-Royce engine outside Jack Barclay's showroom brought Felix back into the world around him. He smiled at the Rolls-Royce badge that had inspired Richard Adams to produce the Bunch Books logo and strolled across the square into the showroom. As he gazed at the glistening, sleek-lined shapes before him, a smartly dressed young man strode across the floor.

Sensing the barely contained snobbery, Felix wasted little time with small talk and asked him how much a Rolls-Royce would cost. The salesman replied to the effect that, 'if Sir had to ask, then he probably couldn't afford it.'

It was obviously a red rag to a bull and Felix exploded, verbally ripping the poor man to shreds. He scuttled away to find his boss, who agreed to

Felix's demand to have the salesman fired. He then wrote out a cheque for £90,000 on the spot and told them to have the car delivered the next day. Still fuming, but also a little elated, he waited until he was around the corner before bursting into loud, hysterical laughter.

Having enjoyed the opulence of John Lennon's Rolls-Royce many years before, he himself was now the owner of a brand-new Fenland Sage-coloured Rolls-Royce Camargue. He would never drive it, of course – he had never wanted to drive and never would. But he was still chuckling as he climbed the stairs to his Kingly Street office.

Despite the success of the recent magazine sale, Felix threw himself into new projects while at the same time babysitting *MacUser*, but the purchase of the Rolls-Royce brought a new problem. He needed somewhere to take it – somewhere in the country. With Wendy Kasabian taking a sabbatical he despatched his new personal assistant Maggie Kayley on a scouting mission to look for properties within a reasonably short distance of London. He turned down many, including Cliff Richard's former home in Surrey and, ironically, considering he hadn't had any aspirations towards writing poetry at this time, it was a property near Stratford-upon-Avon, deep in the heart of Shakespeare country, that caught his eye.

The Old Manor in the tiny village of Dorsington was a chocolate-box picture of a Tudor cottage, owned at the time by a couple who had planned to use it as a weekend retreat. The owners, Mr and Mrs Billington, had their main home in Northamptonshire at the Manor House in Ashby St Ledgers. It was at one time home to the conspirators of the Gunpowder Plot. The Billingtons had spent a fortune doing up their weekend home, and Cathy Galt, who was looking after it before Felix's visit, had kept it aired, let in the cleaner and, as she remembered, 'fluffed up the cushions' once a week. Despite never having stayed in the house, the Billingtons had decided to sell up as they were moving overseas.

One spring evening in 1987, having returned to Heathrow via Concorde, Felix sat in the back of his new Rolls-Royce as his driver took the country route to Warwickshire. At the time there were no electric gates

Felix (right), with his mother Dorothy and brother, Julian, circa 1953.

Felix's father, Reg, with his younger brother Gordon, 1929.

Felix (left, with his leg in plaster) and Julian enjoying donkey rides, circa 1954.

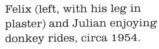

Felix (back row, far right), in a rare sporting moment,
posing with the St Nicholas Grammar School Under
Fifteen Cross-Country Team, 1961–62.

Working on editorial and design for *Oz* and *Ink*, 1972.

Felix (right), Richard Neville (left) and Jim
Anderson dress up to pose with copies of the
controversial *Schoolkids' Oz*, October 1970.

'Taking the piss'! 1970.

Felix (right) signs papers during the police raid of
the *Oz* offices by Scotland Yard's Obscene Publications
Squad in June 1970, with Detective Inspector Frederick
Luff looking on and Jim Anderson in the background.

From left, David Offenbach, Louise
Ferrier, Felix and Richard Neville
outside The Old Bailey, January 1971.

Felix, in his trademark suit, with his old mate
Don Atyeo larking around in London, 1974.

At home in Warwickshire with an array
of international editions of *Maxim*, 2000.

Felix and his US business partner, Peter Godfrey,
pose with *Maxim* girls at the '*Maxim* Farewell'
party, following the sale of *Maxim* in 2007.

Felix with Ronnie 'Wippo' Meckler,
Art Director at *MacUser* US, at the
MacWorld Expo, Boston Harbor, 1986.

Felix with J L Gassée of Apple
Computers, San Francisco, 1987.

On stage with Loudon Wainwright III, in 1998, at one of the annual village summer parties hosted by Felix at his home in Warwickshire.

Chilling out with Dana Gillespie and Mick Jagger in the Games Room at Mandalay, Felix's home on Mustique, during rehearsals for the Mustique Blues Festival, 2005. © Marion Hills

Felix, dressed as an elf, handing out Christmas
presents to the children of Mustique in 2011 – a
duty he took very seriously every year! © Marion Hills

Felix with his long-term partner and 'the companion
of my heart', Marie-France Demolis, at the Cotton
House, Mustique, 2000. © Marion Hills

Felix and Marie-France modelling the tour jackets for the 2013 *Did I Mention the Free Wine?* Tour.

Felix, dressed down in tour T-shirt, jogging bottoms and Uggs, boards a Gulfstream jet to fly from city-to-city on the 2004 USA *Did I Mention the Free Wine?* Tour.

Greeting fans and signing books in New York City on the 2004 *Did I Mention the Free Wine?* Tour.

Felix, surrounded by the tour crew, on the final poetry reading on the last night of the 2013 *Did I Mention the Free Wine?* Tour.

Felix performing on stage during the 2010 *Did I Mention the Free Wine?* Tour.

With Hugh Johnson planting the millionth
tree in the Heart of England Forest, 2013.

Felix sitting under his favourite cherry
tree in the garden at his home in
Warwickshire, 2006. © Dwayne Senior

An oak sapling destined for Felix's
Heart of England Forest, 2013.

The funeral party follow Felix's coffin
through the Heart of England Forest to
his final resting place marked by a bronze
statue and a sarsen stone, June 2014.

Felix prepares to go on stage for the last time at the Bloomsbury Ballroom in London on the final night of the 2013 *Did I Mention the Free Wine?* Tour. On his right lapel is the Légion d'honneur medal, a gift from a friend.

Felix and Marie-France at the launch of *Silva: The Tree in Britain* in London, 1999.

at the entrance to the Old Manor, so they drove in and Felix knocked on the door. He didn't get a reply, so decided to have a wander round. The back of the house looked out over a three-acre immaculately kept garden, with views over hundreds of acres of greening Warwickshire landscape. Standing by a cherry tree, he gently stroked its newly sprung buds and imagined the glorious display of life when it would blossom alongside the many other trees in this idyllic country retreat: he was smitten. The next day he made an appointment to view the property, and although, as Cathy recalled, he arrived two hours late, he proved to be the most charming and fascinating of the 30-odd people to whom she had shown the house. After caring for an empty house, wandering from room to room with her baby daughter in a Moses basket, Cathy was about to get on board the Felix Dennis roller coaster and would stay there to the end.

To save themselves the hassle of taking the contents to auction at Christie's, the owners had elected to sell the house with all the furnishings if they could find a willing buyer. With dark, chamfered, exposed beams and mullioned windows, it had been decorated and furnished in a style that appealed to Felix. Each item of furniture had been individually purchased to fit the house. From four-poster beds to hat stands in the hall, the antique oak pieces looked as though they had always been there.

As a man with little time on his hands, Felix was delighted to negotiate a deal that satisfied everyone. After handing over a cheque for £600,000, he moved in within a month. Although his first stay was short-lived for he had to get back to America, he now had a property that he could look forward to living in whenever he returned to England.

Back in America, Peter Godfrey later described the relationship between himself, Felix and Bob Bartner as being like the legs of a chair.

'A three-legged chair is a pretty stable beast,' he said. 'We all do completely different things. We are completely different people and we all stay thousands of miles apart.' Explaining that business and life are so much about conflict and resolution, he maintained that the fact that the three of them were never really in each other's pockets made it much easier to work together.

'Felix is the thinking Mr Energy guy, Bob the financial, and I'm the grunt that keeps on going, no matter what.'

One of the points that Felix had been arm-wrestling with Bill Ziff about at the end of the *MacUser* deal in December 1986 was ensuring that he could hold onto *MacUser* in the UK and other countries. It was a wrestle that he had won, much to the relief of Roger Munford, who was in the middle of working on the next UK edition when Felix rang from America with the news that he had sold the magazine. It was 9pm and Roger had a full team in the office, working frantically to get the next issue out. On hearing Felix's excited news, he blew his top before Felix explained that it didn't affect the UK. What he and the Ziff team had agreed to, however, was a non-compete clause with regard to publishing a Mac-related magazine in the US. But that wasn't a problem – they already had another idea.

One of the biggest sources of revenue for *MacUser* had been advertising from businesses that supplied components and accessories to computer owners. On one occasion, when a particular advertiser had had difficulty in paying their bill, Peter had paid them a visit and was amazed at how many calls they were receiving from their ads. Not only was the phone ringing off the hook but the office was badly run and in disarray. To make matters worse, many of their suppliers were withholding delivery of stock as they were in arrears with them also.

Peter elected to take the owners out to lunch and find out more about their business model. When he asked how much business they got from their ad in *MacUser*, they replied, 'Oh, about a million dollars' worth.'

Peter didn't need to give it a second thought. He immediately phoned Felix and, after another of their two-hour trans-Atlantic phone calls, they decided this would be where they would focus after the sale of *MacUser*.

CHAPTER 15

BOLINAS WEED

Although there were many who, in their own way, felt close to Felix, there were one or two individuals who refused to accept his no monogamous relationships rule and still hoped for a long-term commitment.

Suzen Murakoshi, a Japanese girl who had been brought up in Hawaii, had come to New York to build herself a career as an actress. Five foot two, with dark hair and brown eyes, Suzen brought an endearing smile and a childlike giggle to her many auditions, but when she answered a small ad in the *Village Voice* on 28 June 1983, she may not have realised the effect it would have on the rest of her life. The headline read, 'English Shogun seeks Oriental Geisha'. She later said she thought it was some kind of audition. It described a 35-year-old, intelligent English millionaire with 'reasonable looks', who was in 'full possession of his faculties'. The writer had just arrived in New York, had an aversion to singles' bars and was looking for a 'slim, beautiful Oriental woman' who might be lonely or bored by her present friends or lovers. He described himself as obsessed with his work and a 'mildly eccentric, adventurous and an unconventional person who does not suffer fools gladly'. He added that he valued kindness, good humour, wit, loyalty and the ability to appreciate silence. In essence the advertisement was a pretty concise description of Felix Dennis and the suggestion that he was 'absurdly generous' was sure to guarantee a huge response. Offering to provide those who responded with, at the very least, a wonderful meal and an 'interesting evening', he requested a recent photograph and telephone number.

Suzen was one of many to take the bait and sent in her standard headshot, accompanied by another photograph taken next to a Buckingham Palace guard from a recent trip to London. She had visited England to see the show *Cats* before auditioning for a part in the US production and was already intrigued by English culture. She was duly impressed with her first limo ride and dinner at Le Périgord on Beekman Place, and Felix was attentive and showed an interest in both her life and her cultural background. With millionaire style, he ordered a bottle of French wine that had been bottled on the day of her birth and regaled her with stories of his background in England and his business successes. He arranged for the sommelier to give the label to her as a memento. Sadly for Suzen, one of the memories of that evening was that she went home afterwards and became violently ill after consuming more rich food than she was used to.

Although she lived a gypsy-like existence, taking work wherever she could, while at the same time Felix criss-crossed the ocean building his business in the States as well as the UK, they still managed to develop a relationship. Suzen joined him at the Elbow Beach Hotel in Bermuda later that November, and, after proving herself to be what she later described as a 'klutz' driving a moped, elected to sit on the back of his while Felix chauffeured her around the island. The possibility of buying a property there was still in his mind and there was heightened excitement at the prospect of becoming a resident. Later, he bought Suzen a mink coat to keep out the New York winter and she was further impressed when he let her choose a $600 blouse at the Plaza Hotel boutique. Felix had long known the value of brash displays of wealth and the power that had to impress most of those he entertained.

It was very early on in their relationship that Suzen was to discover the depth of intellect that Felix could draw on when dealing with emotional issues. In January 1984, her father died and he sent a letter to her in Hawaii.

'Ritual condolences are little more than an expression of embarrassment,' he wrote. 'Frankly, death is a subject that most of us spend a great deal of time and trouble avoiding. When it comes, especially close to home, we are all the less prepared for its onslaught.' He suggested that perhaps some of the more primitive peoples of the world had it right, phrasing it as a question: 'The hair pulling, keening and semi-demented but at least fully expressed emotional and physical outpourings of grief must surely relieve the burden of helplessness in tribal African villages more thoroughly than the contrived funeral processions of the Western world?'

Although he might have been seen by some as a cold fish, he was never one to see any value in the very British practice of a stiff upper lip in the face of tragedy or adversity. To Felix that was simply dishonest. Having already gone through the loss of both his stepfather and his father, he had thought long and hard about the emotions associated with death. He told Suzen that 'falling apart' was a 'healing process of immense importance' and that it was 'the living who must face the abyss of loss and – by definition – their own eventual death'. His philosophy was that mourning was as much a preparation for death as it was a show of respect for the deceased.

On one occasion after going to the opening performance of *The King and I* to watch Suzen perform in the show, they went to a lavish after-show party. It was a glitzy black-tie affair with actors and actresses vying with each other to look good in front of photographers and press reviewers. An aged Yul Brynner, who was dying of cancer at the time, was the star of the show and his death scene had critics raving. As Felix arrived at the party, he helped Suzen out of the limo while dozens of photographers jostled for position. Taking two steps forward, he was blinded by the flashing paparazzi and tumbled to the ground, falling in an undignified heap. As he was helped into the club by a couple of flunkies, Brynner leaned over to him and said, 'Jesus, some people will do anything to upstage me!'

Although the champagne flowed, the general delivery of 'dahling!' from one actress to the next bored Felix to death. The one highlight he recalled was when a young oriental girl, the wife of one of the actors, got drunk and decided to treat the assembled audience to a striptease. Standing on the bar counter, she eventually tossed her diamond-encrusted dress into the audience, causing a riot. The dress was retrieved, but from where Felix stood, it looked as though it was short of a few gems.

Looking back on the early days of their relationship in the mid-eighties, Suzen remembered a classic courtship. They would have drinks at his apartment, go to dinner and take walks together. On one of their first Sunday afternoon dates they walked through Central Park.

'Just looking at the trees and being one of the people in the park, oh, it was really nice!' she said. 'That was really the best time.' Later, after learning that it was quite an unusual thing for Felix to sit through a show, she remembered that on one occasion they even watched one of her girlfriends in a play in Central Park. Suzen was also one of the few people that Felix took to a movie. They saw Eddie Murphy in *Trading Places* in Times Square, where she remembered that he did take a break to go outside for a cigarette. While producing one-shot magazines, he did also sit through a showing of *Star Wars*, but only after the insistence of the director, George Lucas.

In later years Felix was to maintain that not going to movies, plays or watching television had given him more time to be a successful businessman as well as time to hone the powerful intellect that so impressed friends and wrong-footed competitors.

There were times when their personalities appeared to be a mismatch. Suzen remembered how, on one particular Christmas holiday in Barbados, some of the other guests in the hotel completely misread their relationship. Although he enjoyed the warmth, Felix wasn't fond of sitting in the sunshine and would often spend many hours on their balcony reading while Suzen and his mother Dorothy would laze on the beach. One evening, while chatting to some other Brits staying at the hotel, Suzen remembered their surprise when she explained that they were a couple.

'Oh, we thought you were his nurse and he was terminally ill because he just never came out!' they exclaimed.

The truth was that Felix was never more content than when he had a book to lose himself in and nobody around to disturb him.

Regardless of the apparent differences between them, Suzen fell deeply in love with Felix and there were occasions when she discussed marriage and even the possibility of having children together. She felt she was the chosen one for socialising with business acquaintances and occasionally joined him for business trips abroad or around the States.

On one occasion she recalled Peter Godfrey and Bob Bartner discussing the possibility of him marrying her to become resident. His answer was instant: 'Under no circumstances am I going to marry anyone for tax reasons or for money.'

However, the serious marriage discussions that Suzen remembered were not to her liking.

'We talked about how, if we did get married, we might have two residences,' she said, 'and I would have to procure women for him. He is not, you know, monogamous. But that would be one of my functions and up to that point I hadn't really been doing that. I couldn't agree to that.'

Another side to the story regarding Felix's possible change of residency concerned a visit from the IRS, the American tax authorities. However, instead of grilling him about whether he had been paying enough tax in America, the representatives spent the meeting trying to coax him into becoming a US citizen to help him pay less tax in the UK. It might save him millions, they explained. Although he claimed he had been tempted, he proudly explained that he simply couldn't give up being English.

Apart from their social life in New York, holidays together and trips such as a helicopter ride around Mount St Helens, when Suzen was on tour with *The King and I* in Portland, Oregon, they would also spend time at a cottage he rented in Connecticut. It was one of the few places where Felix was able to unwind. It was a small, two-bedroom bungalow with a mezzanine floor that was used as an office and TV area, and it was set just a dozen steps above Candlewood Lake. Despite the fact that on sunny weekends it became a playground for those who enjoyed racing speedboats and jet skis along inland waterways, it was an especially peaceful place and Felix enjoyed a spectacular view from his window overlooking the lake. He never bought the place but leased it from the owner, who was delighted to have him as a full-time tenant, especially as he spent a vast amount of money decorating and improving it.

On quiet evenings away from the insistent hum of New York traffic, Felix would sit on the long balcony, either reading or taking in the beauty around him. On the jetty below, an oblong green canopy shaded his boat, the *Bearded Dwarf,* from the sun as it sat snugly in its stabiliser, protecting it from the waves. Facing due west, it was an idyllic place to sit and enjoy an early summer's evening. The cottage on Candlewood Lake was indeed an inspirational place and something about the way the last of the sun's rays dipped beneath the jetty under Felix's boat made it feel like the only beautiful place left on earth.

Here, Felix and Suzen would 'play house' as she put it. Despite holidaying with him in places like Jamaica, Curaçao, New Orleans and taking the Presidential Suite in the now closed Cerromar Beach Resort in Puerto Rico, Suzen also cited the cottage as the place that gave her some of her favourite memories, especially when it was covered in snow. When he was there alone Felix would potter quietly around the edges of the lake on his boat, trying not to disturb the wildlife. He was later to call it quaint, describing it as 'Swiss chalet comes to Danbury'.

Despite their special relationship, throughout his years in New York Felix's sexual appetite was relentless as always. He had made it clear to Suzen that under no circumstances could he be involved in a monogamous relationship and the only thing that the term 'in sickness and in health' could apply to was his need to participate in as many sexual encounters as possible – whether sick or healthy. Occasionally feeding this need helped to distract him from health issues.

On one occasion, suffering a serious back problem that kept him cooped up in his New York apartment, Felix was visited by a Korean heiress, who was in New York to look at property. Introduced by another girlfriend who soon left them alone, he described her as 'slightly plump, expensively dressed without much taste, halting in her use of English and monetarily perhaps the greediest person I have ever met'. Felix confided that as she appeared to be convinced that the English were a 'race of superior class and breeding' he lay staring at the ceiling, affecting a slight air of superior detachment. She described in detail how she had made a fortune by marrying a rich man 40 years her senior who was now dying, and up to then she had remained completely faithful to him and had nursed him through several life-threatening illnesses.

'I asked her to stop talking and get me a drink,' he remembered. She eventually managed to produce a whisky and ginger from the kitchen and thumped it triumphantly on the table.

'I found the glasses!' she exclaimed. Felix said nothing and she stared at him defiantly, eventually saying, 'I don't even know where the glasses are in my own home.'

Explaining that he was tired and in pain, he asked her to leave but the truth was that he was actually expecting another girlfriend to arrive. She phoned again that evening, wanting to see him immediately, so he transferred the call to his kitchen and arranged for her to arrive at 1am, giving him time to get rid of his current guest.

'She arrived in a ridiculous outfit,' he remembered, 'a kind of double-layered sheath dress and top. I should think it cost several thousand dollars, but her legs were too short and her heels too low to carry it off. She reminded me of Humpty Dumpty in a wedding cake.'

After some chatter about how lonely it was being a poor little rich girl, they ended up in his bedroom after she had arranged her clothes in an ultra-neat pile on the chair. Despite his back pain, he remembered that she was rampant. Quite obviously she hadn't had sex in some time and Felix was getting the benefit.

'She was voracious and masochistic at the same time,' he recalled. Slapping her behind as though she was a prancing mare, she screamed for more and Felix was able to completely forget his back pain. Eventually they fell into a sweaty heap, and, although she slept soundly, he did not and got her to leave early in the morning.

Later that afternoon 70 roses were delivered.

'I know there were 70,' he remembered, 'because I counted them when they arrived as if by magic in the elevator. It took all my strength to stagger into the kitchen with them.' Hidden in the tissue wrapping was a tiny, two-inch square envelope containing a pencil-scribbled note: 'Thank you for a very special time. S.'

'The discretion of her communication,' he recalled, was in stark contrast to the 'ostentatious outlay of $100 worth of flowers.'

The next day he was finally walking again, though finding it painful to sit. He had had nearly two weeks of confinement in his apartment and was going 'cabin crazy'.

To take his mind off the monotony he called up an oriental 'health club', who sent over a beautiful 20-year-old Korean girl, who went by the name of Suzie. 'Her face was a treasure, high cheeks, folded lids and flowing hair,' he remembered. However, due to some mix-up at the massage parlour, she had to go back and their sex was hurried and unfulfilling. He was, however, struck by her beauty. 'It's rare in a whore to find youth, beauty and shyness,' he said later. 'And her nature struck me as surprisingly kind – even trusting.'

Although he brushed off his reaction as feeble-minded, it was part of his nature to look beyond the veneer of those he came into contact with. One day he had been revolted by the greed of a multi-million-dollar heiress and the next touched by the inner beauty of a visiting prostitute. For Felix there was no shame in the world's oldest profession and later in his life he would show extraordinary levels of kindness and care to many of those whose lifestyles were frowned upon by the society they lived in. Hypocrisy and unkindness irritated him immensely.

Later that night a spectacular thunderstorm hit the city. Crackling lightning flooded his bedroom as staccato thunder pounded directly above the building. His tiny one-bed apartment shuddered under a frenzied torrent of rain. However, the overall benefit was that the storm washed away the stifling humidity and the next day was fresh and clear. It was cathartic weather. So much so that he called up another prostitute, who called herself Lisa. She was half-French and half-Vietnamese but rather a disappointment to Felix. His only memory of her was that she had a 'quite extraordinary ability' to slip a condom onto his penis before having sex. As he recalled, 'to be truthful, I didn't notice until sometime later.' To compound this disappointment after she had gone his back gave out again and went into severe muscle spasm. His immediate response was to have a temper tantrum, and as he recalled, being alone in the apartment he cursed 'with surprising vehemence'.

Throughout this time business meetings were conducted by phone or in Felix's apartment with him lying on the floor. On one occasion he even fired one of his editors while lying prone on the sitting-room floor. In notes to Peter Godfrey and Bob Bartner, he said he didn't expect to be in the office on a regular basis for some time and had been warned by the orthopaedic surgeon and the chiropractors not to expect to be able to resume normal life immediately and was told to rest for several months and to exercise frequently.

It was several weeks before he could walk again and in celebration of his slow road to recovery, he shuffled across 18 city blocks to the chiropractor, who put him on an automatic massage machine and performed 'excruciatingly painful' massage on pressure points in his back. As he was only 37 years old, the whole episode had scared him. He decided to try to get fit and, although he made no attempt to change his diet or alcohol and cigarette intake, he planned to put an exercise bike into his living room. He took up walking and, with a Sony Walkman hanging from his belt, joined the many thousands of New Yorkers who strode purposefully across the city, filling their lungs with petrol and other fumes. Walking by the river in an effort to get a taste of fresher air, as well as a hint of the smell of the sea, he would stride out to the sounds of Bruce Springsteen's 'Born in the USA'. However, he feared the coming New York winter and worried that one slip on an icy street could put him 'in hospital permanently'. Plans to visit the office in England necessitated booking three Club Class seats on a British Airways flight so he could lie down, and he redoubled his plan to find a house in Bermuda in which to regain his health.

If anything could equal Felix's voracious appetite for sex it had to be books. His thirst for knowledge and hunger for debate simply ballooned. Throughout his early years in New York he added to the growing library he had begun in London. He told his old friend Roger Hutchinson that some of his favourite books at the time included a biography of W. Somerset Maugham and *The War of the End of the World* by Mario Vargas Llosa, whom he described as a 'sort of South American, apocalyptic Tolstoy' that produced 'magically powerful writing'. He also recommended *The Name of the Rose* by Umberto Eco and *War Day* by Whitley Strieber and James Junetka – a fictional journalistic account of life in the US after a nuclear exchange. 'Scary but riveting,' he said. His holiday reading was often lighter but only marginally. Writing to his old friend from EMAP David Arculus, at one point he claimed to be looking forward to reading a clutch of John le Carré's novels during an upcoming break in Jamaica, though joked that he might also bring a copy of *War and Peace*.

Much as he was excited about his life in New York, at one point saying, 'Living here is like living in London on amphetamines,' he was also incredibly knowledgeable about life in the UK. Travelling back and forth by Concorde and doing business in both countries afforded him a prime position to observe the development of each economy.

'There is an air of electricity that runs through Manhattan streets,' he wrote to Roger Hutchinson. 'There is an optimism, a surging feeling of power and even wonder.'

England, on the other hand, was falling apart from his perspective. Consuming the *Guardian* and *The Times*, which he purchased from the news vendor around the corner at the United Nations building, he kept abreast of the arduous times back home.

'Arthur Scargill is a prat!' he exclaimed, alluding to the battle between government and miners in 1984. 'I cannot forgive his incompetence. He chose to fight on swampy ground and presented a "take it or leave it" negotiating position. This was interpreted by many people in the UK as sheer arrogance. Even a dimwit could see that a few of the totally unproductive mines must close.'

Showing his long-held sympathy for the Labour Party, he continued, incensed, 'He has severely damaged the Labour Party and given those wankers in the SDP yet more mileage. Margaret Thatcher's approval ratings actually increased in the first six months of the strike.

'I am not working class and have never worked in a mine. But I have voted Labour all my life, for what that's worth. I simply cannot forgive him. Best thing would be if he and MacGregor simultaneously resigned or committed hari-kari.'

Political leanings aside, Felix was losing all faith in the country of his birth.

'By living outside of the UK,' he said, 'I have finally come to see what my country really is. A poxy group of islands off the north coast of Europe that despite the most efficient farming in the world can hardly provide 40 per cent of its food; a nation that has rested on its industrial laurels for over half a century and is now worse equipped to face the coming decade than a country like Spain.' He went on to describe it as 'a small coalition of kingdoms that is still infested with delusions of grandeur and history (I can assure you that the only "special relationship" the USA thinks it has is with Japan!)' His rant went on, with him even admitting, 'It is an absolute embarrassment to be British in the big wide world.'

While Felix was more or less correct in his assessment of how the UK was perceived in those days, what was most striking was the fact that his communication skills, which might have been suspect to those who didn't understand him, were clear, concise and razor-like when using the written word. In person he was a powerful presence and, with tactics more bully-like than social, he could present a winning case, but on the other end of a pen he was almighty.

In between books, girlfriends, business dealings and debating the world's problems, there was the occasional party. Jim Anderson, who had been living in Bolinas, California for some time, came to visit New York for a Christmas break. On Christmas Day, in 1984, he arrived at Felix's apartment to start the festivities drinking sherry with Dorothy, Felix's mother. What began as a gentle enough opener soon descended into the sort of oblivion often more entertaining in the aftermath than it is at the time. Felix recalled that they all tripped off to the Plaza Hotel for an enormous turkey dinner with all the trimmings. As a rule traditional celebration of events such as Christmas,

Easter and Thanksgiving and such-like were not Felix's favourite pastimes; however, to keep his mother happy he always made a valiant attempt to, if not enjoy them, at least allow those around him to indulge their fantasy that they were having a jolly time. After a good meal, happily washed down with copious amounts of fine wine, Dorothy went back to her hotel for a nap, leaving Jim and Felix to venture further afield for more entertainment.

They piled into a cab and headed for Mick Farren's downtown apartment, where a party of ex-pats and assorted pirates was in full swing.

'By this time every single person at the Farren residence was absolutely shit-faced!' remembered Felix. 'It took 10 minutes for one of them to crawl downstairs to open the door.'

The flat resembled a disaster area, with half-eaten plates of food, empty bottles, cans, presents and general detritus everywhere. Half a dozen cats rampaged amongst the discarded food, while dodging drunks doing their best John Travolta impressions. Before it all got too fuzzy, Felix remembered that 'they had consumed three bottles of port, about 20 bottles of wine, several bottles of whiskey and untold beers'. After getting stuck in, Jim produced his by then famous 'Bolinas Weed' and, from that point on, Felix claimed to remember little more than loud music and sweaty bodies.

Eventually getting home at about six in the morning, he invited the mailman in for a couple of breakfast beers. As the doorman looked on in amusement, he handed over the post and wisely declined the offer.

With no one left to party with, Felix went to bed.

'I woke up around three in the afternoon with the world-beater of hangovers!' he declared.

CHAPTER 16
UNBURDENED BY NORMS

In 1987, while his new business in America, Mac Warehouse, headed up by Peter Godfrey, was getting underway with very little input from him, Felix was about to get yet another call from Lady Luck. For some time Bob Bartner had been urging him to launch a UK version of a successful US magazine called *Computer Shopper*. An unwieldy lump of a magazine with little editorial content to make it look attractive, few people at the UK company, which had been renamed Dennis Publishing, were keen to get involved with it. In fact, Colin Crawford, who had taken on the role of financial director, remembered that every time Felix came back from America 'every six weeks or so' he would bring back a copy of *Computer Shopper*, throw it on the boardroom table and say, 'Guys, you should be doing this.' They complained that it was a bit like *Exchange and Mart* and simply wouldn't work in the UK market.

'After a period of time, Felix got increasingly frustrated at this negative push-back,' said Crawford.

Until one day a curious thing happened.

The owner of the magazine had been approached by Ziff Davis, who wanted to purchase it from him. Knowing that Felix had experience, not only of selling magazines but also of dealing with Ziff Davis, the Florida-based owner, Glenn Patch, decided to ask him for advice. They met at his office and Felix remembered his surprise at seeing an alligator in a nearby culvert – a not uncommon sight in that part of America. After their discussions Patch wanted to know what he could do to pay Felix back for his kindness, and without missing a beat Felix came up with a suggestion that wouldn't cost him a dime: all he had to do was turn a blind eye if Felix launched *Computer Shopper* in the UK. They made a gentlemen's agreement that, without actually buying the rights to use the name in the UK, they would, by getting it onto the street before the ink was dry on Glenn's deal with Ziff Davis, already own the name by virtue of publishing it.

Stephen England remembered it as a stroke of genius on Felix's part that really wound up the Ziff Davis people.

'Right until the very end Ziff was not aware of the fact that he'd done this side deal,' said Stephen. 'They thought they were getting Europe – Ziff were in Europe by that time. They had a European operation and *Computer Shopper* was their mother ship. And they couldn't bring their mother ship to the biggest geography on the planet because fucking Felix Dennis had got the deal!'

Mark Williams related how Felix fired off a detailed memo to the board, telling them he wanted to launch *Computer Shopper* in the UK immediately. Soon afterwards he arrived at a board meeting and dumped a copy of the 800-page American version on the table and said, 'Do it!' The magazine became a major title for Dennis Publishing and Stephen remembered putting on his salesman's hat again to get it off the ground.

'I got in my car,' he said. 'I had to go to Watford, Cambridge and Birmingham.' He visited three companies in one day and ended up selling 84 pages of advertising, using a one-page fact sheet about the potential circulation, along with a copy of the US version of *Computer Shopper*.

Later, after Glenn Patch had closed his deal with Ziff Davis, he took Felix and Colin Crawford out to dinner to celebrate and even showed off a copy of his payment cheque. Colin remembered it as a great evening, where in the end it was Felix who picked up the tab.

'It didn't matter,' remembered Colin. 'It had been a great deal for Felix and Dennis Publishing.'

In the years that followed the launch of *Computer Shopper*, the UK company dabbled in the computer games magazine market, but without much commitment and therefore without the success that other publishers eventually achieved. However, although the launch and ownership of *Computer Shopper* was one in the eye for Ziff Davis, there was plenty to worry about when they decided to make a serious entry into the UK market. Dick Pountain recalled that not only did Ziff Davis invest huge amounts of money into their European operation but they also set about poaching as much editorial talent as possible by putting writers on retainer without ever launching magazines for them to write for. The writers were unable to write for any other publication, which meant existing publishers having to find new talent from blogs. As Dick recalled, that was how some of the talented columnists that write for the likes of *PC Pro* today initially got their chances.

Concerned that Ziff Davis would launch against *Computer Shopper*, in 1991 the company launched against themselves with a title called *Computer Buyer*, which not only survived for many years, helping to keep the competitor at bay, but was also successful in its own right.

One of the next key changes to Dennis Publishing UK was the move by Stephen England to America to work on Mac and Micro Warehouse and the subsequent shift of financial director Colin Crawford to managing director. Crawford recalled that, prior to his first interview with the company a couple of years before, he had decided to take a look at the offices in Rathbone Place from outside.

'I took one look at the place,' he said, 'and thought, "This looks like a hell hole. Why do I want to do this to myself?"' In the end he took the job after an interview with Stephen England. However, his first introduction to Felix was somewhat disconcerting to say the least.

'A few days after I joined, Felix comes into what was called my office, which was like a large broom cupboard. And he said he would like to take me out to lunch so we could get to know each other. And I think the first words out of his mouth were, "You know, Colin, I just want you to understand that I hate fucking accountants."'

It was an auspicious start but one that Crawford later said he had no problem dealing with.

He said, 'I'd worked for some very strong characters in the past, such as the chairman of a small entrepreneurial company who had been a colonel in the SAS. I'd also learned a technique whereby I didn't overreact to very emotional people and I would really let them have their say, let them take it in and then find a solution.'

This skill was one that he found he had to use quite often. He explained that Felix would 'come into my office and jump on the table and scream and tell me I was the worst accountant he had ever known in his life'.

Ten minutes later they would be going down the pub and having a drink together. It was the sort of interaction that many people experienced with Felix. His explosions were rarely personal and a long rant that one might be convinced was going to end in violence was more likely to culminate in a gentle question like, 'So, how are the kids?'

Crawford shared the view that Felix offered many people opportunities that they simply would not otherwise have had. Speaking in 1998, he said, 'I think one of Felix's greatest talents is that he can recognise when people have got an ability, and then he puts them into a position where he stretches people, and where he can get the best out of the individual. I think that's been part of Dennis's success – in all the ventures, not just Dennis Publishing, but the other things that he has done as well. He looks for talent and he doesn't care what age that person is or what their background is. That's totally irrelevant.'

Felix was always looking for something in those he met and usually it was characteristics that others might have missed, such as intelligence or passion.

'You know, talent moves on,' said Crawford. 'Felix isn't someone you want to work for for the rest of your life, but he's great at getting the best out of people.'

But Felix had his own take on this particular 'talent': as far as he was concerned it came easily. 'I love the idea of taking people on,' he said, 'finding out what they're made of and then thrusting them into positions of responsibility for which they are not ready, allowing them to make errors, backing them when they fuck up, allowing them to go back to the role as long as they don't make the same error again and again. And then people turn round and say you are a master of delegation. It's not very hard, actually.'

One of the more extraordinary moments that Crawford remembered was in 1988 when Felix and the rest of the board were wrangling with how to deal with the possibility of multiple attacks on their *MacUser* magazine in the UK.

'*MacUser* basically owned the market in the UK for Mac publishing and it was doing OK,' he explained. 'It was making a bit of money. Suddenly all our competitors both in the US and UK decided they all wanted to have a Mac publication. We heard of about six potential competitors all about to launch against us at the same time. And I remember the board meetings; Felix was there and the rest of the board and we were sort of looking at each other saying, "Oh God, what are we going to do here? This isn't much fun!" And in typical Felix fashion – he'd sold *MacUser* to Ziff Davis two years before and said, "Bill Ziff owes me one." And he got on the phone there and then to the owner of Ziff Davis publishing and put him on the speakerphone.'

Ziff's advice was simple: he told them to use his PC magazine model, which was to increase the frequency to fortnightly.

'And that we did!' remembered Crawford. 'And we moved very fast. We had to tell the team that they were going to have to work twice as hard for the same amount of money and we were going to have to go from an old technology to the new desktop publishing technology. And we had to do it all in a matter of two months.'

At the time of writing, *MacUser* is still a powerful brand read by creative professionals in many fields. Crawford's take on the situation was that it was 'a stroke of genius on Felix's behalf' to get advice from the right person, but more importantly, and a point that Felix would have admired, had it been done by someone else, was that, as Crawford put it, 'he didn't let anyone stand in the way of executing that strategy'. What completely bemused many was the fact that Felix was in no way intimidated or perhaps even aware of the fact that there was a grey area surrounding the idea of approaching a competitor for advice. He saw a problem, saw a possible answer and was not distracted by what was or wasn't the 'done thing'.

Although he spent just two years as a managing director, the shortest spell of all of Felix's MDs, in his capacity of financial director beforehand, Colin Crawford was able to learn an enormous amount from his time at the company. His insights and those of Felix's other UK managing directors, Stephen England, Alistair Ramsay and James Tye, paint a picture of a man who not only commanded phenomenal respect but whose level of achievement was obviously driven by more than just personality and intellect. However, like most of those who have worked for people with an intense inspirational and entrepreneurial spirit, there were times of exasperation.

'There were some days when I think I could have murdered him,' remembered Colin. 'Sometimes he just didn't know when to let up. Especially when you had worked so hard and it had been a really challenging year and you had given everything you could – and then he'd want more.'

He felt that there were times when Felix knew that he had gone too far but by that time it was too late. As he explained, 'You were about to jump off a cliff or jump to another company or whatever and he would then reach out and kind of pull you back.'

Stephen England also remembered having enormous respect for Felix, but not without also feeling some of the pain that came with the territory. Speaking from his home in Austin, Texas, he described Felix's management style in the early days as being like that of a barking dog: 'He's always been the guy that I look up to enormously. And he can tell me to do stuff in a way that can upset the crap out of me. I mean, he's made me cry dozens of times, but he is also so damned logical and such a good debater that in the end you usually can't argue with him. I'd try but I don't remember winning many.'

England was aware of what he called Felix's 'weird' moral compass. 'He can be a complete weasel sometimes but I've never seen him rip anybody off that doesn't deserve it.'

Stephen quit at least three times and can remember being fired at least twice, but on both occasions Felix's rant carried on for some time and by the end they parted, saying, 'See you in the morning.'

Conversations with Felix could go in any direction and it was important to get your point across quickly, remembered Stephen.

'You can't fricking just say no to Felix. It was always no "because…", or no "but…"' The 'but' or 'because' had to be very quickly followed by a good argument, Stephen said, because 'You've got to try to get all your bullets out at once before he starts firing back.' From his experience, Felix's 'firing back' didn't come from a normal mind.

'It could go either way,' he said. 'You're talking about schizophrenia, multiple personality disorder, ADD, Asperger's.'

Stephen believed that it may have been the complex mix of all of these neurological anomalies that made Felix so successful. The end result, he explained, was that Felix would take risks 'that normal people won't – because he doesn't care'.

Felix himself had shown an interest in autistic disorders even as far back as the mid-seventies when he visited a colleague, Anton Felton, whose wife ran a charitable unit for pre-school autistic children in their house in London. His interest in the children was described by Anton as 'incredible'. Discussing it later, he said, 'He was so sensitive in his observations and perceptions and in his intensity of attention and sensitivity to seeing autistic children.' Anton explained that Felix's connection to the children was intriguing. Watching a staff member interacting with one of the children, he said Felix was highly observant and 'very acutely aware of what was happening' between the two. He spent over two hours in the unit and on one occasion a packet of Smarties was emptied onto a desk and Felix commented on the speed with which one of the children was able to sort them out into different colour groups – 'Felix was quick to see the unique abilities of the children.' It was, as he and many others have said, one of Felix's key skills: the ability to see talent, and more often than not talent and ability previously hidden, even from those who possessed it, and eventually help it to blossom.

Anton felt that one of the secrets to Felix's success was his ability to ignore the grey areas.

'He either looks at the macrocosm or at the microcosm and doesn't obscure his vision by looking at the fuzz between the two,' he explained. 'One of the great things that he has is that he doesn't accept the axioms and premises on which most of us work. He examines many things from prime principal. And that includes the application of a moral dimension as well as logic.'

Describing a situation that many who had enjoyed full and frank discussions with Felix could understand, he went on to say, 'Felix would be devastatingly right, but I think that he could also be devastatingly wrong. Then he would catch up or circumvent it and learn from the experience. It is one of the interesting elements of original thinkers, they don't accept axioms that you and I may take for granted. Like all outsiders they are not burdened with all the norms and regulations of society, either because they don't accept them or because they don't know them.'

One of the anomalies about Felix's character that would become clearer as he got older was that, even if he didn't naturally feel something, he still managed to find a way to understand it.

Stephen England was also struck by Felix's interaction with autistic children. His sister-in-law, who had adopted three children, once came with Stephen to visit Felix at the Old Manor in Dorsington. Her daughter Lucy, who was 15 at the time, had been diagnosed as moderate- to low-functioning autistic, and when they arrived, Felix formed an immediate bond with her and showed her around.

'He is so good with her!' said Stephen. 'Literally nothing is too much trouble. Basically she could point to one of the cars and say, "I'd like that" and he'd bloody give it to her. But she'll point to, like, a book or just a little ornament, and he'd say, "Take it. Take it home."'

Stephen believed that Felix's ability to connect with autistic children was partly because he didn't have children of his own: 'He doesn't spend any time around children that are his. So, like most adults that aren't around kids, he doesn't treat them like kids. And the way you treat disabled people is very similar to the way you treat young people. If you coochy-coo them, you come across as a complete dick. So he talks to Lucy *pari passu*, on an equal level. And she responds to that.'

Felix's ability to treat an autistic person on an equal level meant he could have a better affinity with them than many others could. He was always pleased to see Lucy on their visits and always made time to entertain her.

In 2007, Felix held a ball in the grounds of the Old Manor in Dorsington to raise money for Springfield Mind, a local mental health charity that he had agreed to become a patron of. Although his support for good causes was numerous and mostly confidential, this was the only charity that he had ever agreed to lend his name to and the ball raised over £100,000.

CHAPTER 17

MASTER AT PLAY

Throughout the mid-eighties, while becoming one of Concorde's most familiar passengers as he dashed back and forth across the Atlantic, Felix carried on with his buying spree, purchasing property, art and antiquities. To help decorate his New York apartment he shipped in thousands of dollars' worth of Guy Colwell paintings that he had bought years before and then spent $7,000 on a nineteenth-century carved rosewood chest and a silk carp painting. Placing an antique Edgar Brandt cast bronze cobra lamp, which he had purchased for over $4,000, in the corner of his sitting room overlooking 2nd Avenue contributed an imposing presence. A barber's chair, a Tiffany lamp and an oak swivel chair set him back another $7,000.

Seemingly having forgotten his comment to Louise Ferrier about never wanting to own bricks and mortar, Felix added 39 Goodge Street in London to his portfolio before a splurge over the next 20 years saw him eventually own more than 6,000 acres in Warwickshire. At one point, while being interviewed on a breakfast television show in the UK, he pointed out that he had 28 kitchens and joked that he had cooked in all of them. This brought a wry smile to the faces of many of the 70-odd personal staff who looked after him and ran the kitchens that he owned.

What became apparent and surprised many was that his investment in land was not just for property development. He was also looking at a long-term legacy plan that would leave a lasting mark of his personality and spirit on England's green and pleasant land. However, an event in

September 1988 very nearly thwarted that dream: he had the first of many brushes with the Grim Reaper.

Felix was never the world's fittest man. In later years one of his employees was to describe him as a huge character that had been squeezed into a small body. Although he was alluding to the enormous achievement and intellect as opposed to excessive weight, it was a body beset by health problems throughout his life. He rarely took exercise and, even though he proudly pointed out that he had been on the cross-country running team at St Nicholas Grammar School in Northwood Hills, there was little else that impressed him when it came to participating in sporting activities. When he first bought the Old Manor in Dorsington there was a tennis court in the middle of the garden and, although Richard Adams has a recollection of Felix playing once, it wasn't with any great gusto. He huffed and puffed his way around the court, still wearing a suit, while Richard and the other guests were dressed in tennis whites.

Felix didn't like taking part in team sports and any attempts to get fit, whether by running or using a personal trainer, usually ended quickly and badly. His favourite mode of transport, on his estates in both Mustique and Warwickshire, was by Segway, the two-wheeled electric vehicle that he took great delight in showing off to visitors. If it hadn't been for his love of walking amongst his woods in Warwickshire, his sedentary lifestyle, love of smoking and drinking, and his drug addiction might have earned him an even earlier exit than he had.

After flying on Concorde to New York and then on to Boston for a visit to the *Macworld* Expo, Felix travelled to Los Angeles. While there he complained of headaches and a feeling of tiredness, but assumed that he was either suffering from exhaustion or had picked up a flu bug along the way. By the time he had decided to return to the East Coast he was running a temperature and was alternating between chills and fever, his whole body ached and he struggled to make it to the waiting car at the airport in New York. His chauffeur suggested that he visit the A&E department of the nearest hospital but, as Felix later admitted, he had arranged for a Korean girlfriend called Tammy to meet him at his cottage in Connecticut and insisted they drive straight there – even in the beginning stages of a serious illness his sexual urge was stronger than the bug that was attacking his body. Thankfully, Tammy had her wits about her.

By the time they reached his cottage on Candlewood Lake it had become obvious that something was desperately wrong. Sweat was pouring from his body and he began rambling and complaining of shortness of breath. Tammy rushed next door to neighbour Clark Varnun, who unceremoniously threw Felix into the back of his pick-up truck and rushed to nearby Danbury Hospital. There, after what Felix later described as terrifying but effective measures to get his temperature stabilised – which in his delirious state he recalled included having iced water poured onto his genitals – he was diagnosed as having contracted Legionnaires' disease.

He wallowed in a state of fever and fear, while in more lucid moments promising himself that if he got through this he would change his lifestyle and do whatever it took to get healthy.

Eventually discharged from hospital, Felix was described on his discharge papers as a 41-year-old English man who had been suffering from fever for four days. The doctors confirmed that his temperature had at times reached 104 degrees. For him it was a frightening experience. Not for the first time, nor indeed the last, he would hallucinate and mix reality with fiction and for years to come the whole episode would be reported as a life-changing moment. He later joked that, at one point, he was asked if he would like to see a minister or a priest and replied, 'No minister or priest, thank you, doc. But do you have a venture capitalist handy?'

He also pointed out that his particularly unfit state hadn't helped him, explaining that Legionnaires' disease was 'especially lethal to coked-up, overweight, cigarette-smoking, malt-whiskey-swilling idiots with too much money, who believe they are built of titanium'. Although this should have been enough of a shock to his system to make him moderate his excesses, it didn't. Weak as a kitten, he spent time recuperating by the lake but on returning to England became ill again and was firmly instructed to stop work and recover properly at the Old Manor.

As the whole episode had coincided with an outbreak of Legionnaires' disease in Los Angeles, where four people subsequently died, Felix later boasted that he was one of the few who survived the outbreak. In the history of outbreaks of Legionnaires' disease in the United States, the event is ominously highlighted in the marketing materials of many air conditioning duct-cleaning companies, usually upping the death toll to seven.

A couple of years later Felix would cheat death again when on a Concorde flight one of the engines failed, sending stewardesses and luggage tumbling down the aisle. He later wrote a hysterical piece for the *Oldie* magazine with descriptions of fellow passengers, including an opera singer and a supermodel. He claimed he had lifted his legs from the floor to turn himself into a pivoting fulcrum in order 'to avoid spilling what was probably going to be my last drink – a large gin and tonic'.

While his period of recovery from Legionnaires' disease at the Old Manor included time spent avoiding alcohol, that didn't last forever. He began to build up a wine cellar that would later become the envy of wine connoisseurs around the country. In typical Felix style he read everything there was to read about the subject and slowly populated his cellar with Premier Crus from the top French vineyards and decided he would not drink any wine unless it was French, and damn good too! He also began to fill his garages with wines that he could share with friends when they came to stay, whether he was there or not. His relationship with French wine also coincided with a new relationship, one that was to sustain him through some of the darkest days of his life.

Initially invited to join a party at the Old Manor by a friend from London, Marie-France Demolis began to cook for Felix and those he entertained on weekends when he would escape from London and his growing business empire. Born in the lower Alps, one of nine children from a Catholic farming family, Marie-France moved to England as an au pair after a spell at boarding school and eventually got a job at a London hairdresser's. Tall and slim, with long dark hair and brown eyes, she and Felix immediately fell into the only sort of relationship that they could both cope with – she didn't want any commitment and neither did he. In fact, as she recalled later, one of the attractions for Felix was the fact that she wasn't particularly impressed by him at all at the beginning. There were similarities in character traits between the two and their mutual lack of need for emotional entanglement quickly gelled.

After a spell cooking, entertaining and, as she remembered, leaving small chocolates on his pillow after turning down Felix's bedding, she gradually became a constant feature in his life. The fact that she was one of many girlfriends didn't bother her. However, despite taking her on holidays with his mother, it took a long time before she was accepted.

'She was always telling him he should have a better girlfriend,' she recalled. In fact, it took 10 years before Mrs Sawyer told Marie-France that she should call her Dorothy.

'By that time it was too late,' she laughed.

With the sort of resilience that one would have expected from Felix, she shared in some of his more difficult years.

Felix's description of himself as 'coked-up, overweight and whiskey swilling' was, at the time, perhaps a little light on the truth. In fact, although a brush with death from a potentially lethal disease might have been enough to frighten most men and give them a wake-up call about their mortality, he was already delving into an area of experimentation that was dark. Darker even than many of those close to him would ever know.

Fuelled by cocaine and his passion for sex, his obsession with women at times took a sadistic twist. He listed some of the women from his New York life with notes about their origin as well as their sexual interests. One was Taiwanese, married and had a young son and he remembered her as 'sadomasochist'. Another was Korean and 'new to the game', while another was Japanese and he noted 'masochist'. Another Japanese girl was 'practised', while a girl from the Philippines showed expertise as a 'mistress'. At one point he was seeing 14 oriental girls, not all of whom were prostitutes.

His relationship with most of them explored various forms of sado-masochism while one or two also had an agreement that they would participate in sexual adventures while he was away or when they themselves were travelling. Writing to Felix, one of them referred to him as 'Dearest Master', while he called her 'Filth'. He complained that she whined down the phone to him whereas her 'clear duty' should have been to 'be inventive in sending material to amuse me and remind me of your pitiful existence'. He instructed her to 'ensure that at some point in the next ten days you send me photographs of some worthless individual humiliating you. Man, woman or both is immaterial.' She complied, sending long descriptive letters detailing sexual exploits with other men and women, which included one long, handwritten note where she described a threesome that featured harnesses and ankle restraints. Another old friend came over to 'abuse me a bit before I saw you on Monday,' she told Felix. 'He slapped my butt with his hand, as well as a few for good measure across my face.'

A photograph placed in the classified pages of the New York magazine *Corporal* by one of Felix's girlfriends at the time showed a scantily clad woman in black stockings and bustier. She described herself as beautiful and athletic and asked for a 'slave playmate'. The ad went on: 'Must be under 30, thin, attractive and submissive. Limits are respected. Cleanliness and utmost discretion exercised'. The plea for a playmate pointed out that if she failed to find one she would be beaten but, 'if I succeed, he may let me use the London Rolls-Royce'. Amongst his many talents, an understanding of the attraction of money and power was something that Felix had begun to use liberally.

Much as he managed to keep his business lives between the US and the UK apart, his obsession with such multiple sexual adventures, along with a growing addiction to crack cocaine crossed the Atlantic with him. What's more, his need to tell the world just how little he thought of its moralistic stance flowed. He talked to newspapers with little or no guardedness. To the dismay of many of those who worked for him, he became perfect fodder for journalists looking for a 'millionaire crack addict orgy story'. As they gleefully reeled off descriptions of his travelling harem, he regaled them with tales of his escapades and snippets of his philosophy on marriage and monogamy.

One of his favourite stories was to explain how his mother dealt with questions about the dozen or so girls that would come on holiday with him.

'I believe he's become a Muslim and they're all his wives,' she would say.

However, she was not amused and if Sigmund Freud was alive he might have had questions about Felix's attitude to his mother. Dorothy was a strong woman and Felix treated her with a mixture of fear and reverence. A favoured theory is that those attracted to masochistic partners often have deeply rooted mother complexes. Felix was far too complex a character to neatly fit any theory but another suggestion is that he got a taste for S&M during the sixties and early seventies, when what had been the domain of the rich became a plaything for some of the more daring and adventurous in the counter-culture. Bondage and S&M was nothing new and had been a subject for filmmakers from as far back as the thirties. Sexploitation, sadism and rough subjugation was the content of cult films such as *Olga's House of Shame* in 1964 and *The Defilers* (1965). The opening scenes of Stephen Woolley's 2005 biopic *Stoned*, about the death of Rolling Stone founder Brian Jones, depicted bondage and whipping as part of the hedonistic sixties lifestyle.

One of those working girls who experienced Felix's particular fetishes remembered the trepidation that preceded a meeting with him.

'When you go in there, you just don't know what to expect,' she said, 'because there would be like six, seven of us at a time. And it was like, Oh no, what time are we going to come out? What's he going to be like? Is he in a good mood? And things would have to get done perfectly, but after, like, 14 hours, you used to get paid really well for it. So that was good. I used to go for the money, really.'

She also exploded the myth about Felix's orgies, explaining that if there were six or seven girls around at a time they were just waiting until they were called. He saw them all separately and, with a stamina that would have confounded a racehorse trainer, called them in one after the other.

'Very rarely did he see two girls in one, because he's quite intimidated with two girls,' she explained. However, that made the whole experience more difficult. She continued, 'It was a nightmare as well sometimes. He was bloody hard work. It was all this, sit like this, you had to sit like that, and you got cramps for hours later, backache, brainache, mouthache – and just putting up with his shit. But at the end of the day we did get paid.'

In his darkest moods, in the grip of waves of crack-fuelled paranoia, he would degrade the girls as much as he possibly could.

'We were made to stand in the garden naked,' she recalled, 'just stand there. Just stand there "because you're useless". That's what he liked. Be submissive – "You're just nothing but waste." The more you degraded yourself, the more he liked it.' The order of master and slave ensured that he maintained control.

'He never likes you looking at him either,' she remembered. 'You always had to look on the floor and call him Sir.'

Some of those who knew Felix found it remarkable that so many women were prepared to put up with his demands. However, there were many that experienced their own pleasure, either in the game or in the resulting emotional catharsis. Writing to him in the mid-eighties, one girlfriend, who had become frustrated about the lack of direction in their relationship, explained why she enjoyed their trysts.

'Your toys,' she said. 'I think of them. I love leather – the smell of it, the look of it, the primitive attraction to skins of dead animals. Restraints are new to me, and like all toys, newness is enough to make them interesting for at least a little while.'

In a long psycho-analytical description of what she got out of their relationship she went on to reveal what their sex life really meant to her.

'I'm very fond of your body, Felix,' she said. 'But the truth is, I'm more fond of my own. You are only as valuable to me as you lend yourself to my pleasure. If my catering to you makes you happy, fine. But I'm not doing it for you, I'm doing it for me.' She confided that she had never liked psychology; from her point of view introspection was like masturbation, 'boring to all except the participant'. Nonetheless, baring her soul was its own reward. She apologised for her embarrassing grammar and excessive verbiage. 'But having gotten this down on paper at last,' she added, 'it's time to move on.'

By this time Felix's paranoia had already dictated one rule that he happily announced to journalists that interviewed him: he had given up penetrative sex. An old girlfriend whose occasional relationship with Felix came before his dark period remembered a story about a hospital nurse who rattled off results from a blood test that he had had on one of his hospital visits. Going down the list, answering 'negative' to most of the options, when it came to HIV the nurse said, 'Positive' and Felix's face went deathly white in disbelief. He remembered that he could have heard a pin drop. As he was about to stammer a question, the nurse then said, 'Just kidding.' The transformation from white face to red and then a blazing purple was instant and Felix exploded. A fear of HIV was one of the reasons he had decided not to have penetrative sex again.

Felix would later explain that his attitude to sex meant he couldn't bear being with women who were inexperienced. Sitting in the Summerhouse at the Old Manor in Dorsington many years after his sexual appetite had waned, he said, 'I've had families of women. Especially women who are slightly masochistic and of a certain shape and type – and very clever – they had to be bright. But they do have to be slightly masochistic in their sexual tastes.'

With signature contradiction he went on. 'They've got to be sassy and answer back; they've got to dress beautifully. I'm not interested otherwise. And they've got to be absolutely filthy. I am not remotely interested in girls that want to be corrupted. I've never corrupted a girl in my life. I'm not remotely interested. Please do not send me any virgins – I wouldn't know what to do with them! I'd send them back to you. I want girls that really, really want to enjoy sex and a lot of it, and pretty wild sex, and I truly believe I've probably had more sex than four or five, six or ten guys that I know put together. And I feel sorry for them. I just go for it, and I always did, and I knew women liked that.'

Although there were times during that sinister period, while in the grip of his vicious crack cocaine habit, when Felix's actions and game-playing left some women crying and emotionally bruised, his conviction that people deserved the same respect, whether a nurse or a prostitute, meant that many of his women became extended family members.

'They've been a family,' he said. 'It sounds crazy, doesn't it? And they've stayed a family.'

He was aware that his friendship and generosity not only helped offer many of those in that extended family a little comfort, but he also knew that on some occasions it offered more.

'A few were so completely useless that they had to be put on some sort of pension, otherwise they'd just starve in the street,' he explained. 'We've done away with most of those now and got them places, but there are still one or two.'

Felix's life was littered with expressions of gratitude for acts of kindness as diverse as paying for drug rehabilitation to offering either business or personal advice when it was most needed.

Speaking about his drug addiction to Melvyn Bragg on the *South Bank Show* in 2003, he explained – in the hope that he might pass on good advice to anyone who was dealing with the same problem – that the drugs had been fun, but he was lucky to have survived his time with them. After what he often called his 'lost decade' he had learned that his addiction was yet another life that had been lived, without much understanding of what was going on. If he had managed to do anything more than visit his inner turmoil throughout that decade, then he had more time to begin to make sense of it when it would resurface later after he began writing poetry.

Talking to the audience at a poetry reading in Stratford-upon-Avon in 2002, he selected the oft-quoted line that 'Cocaine is God's way of telling you that you have too much money'. Not wishing to alienate any members of the audience who might have thought he was being somewhat holier than thou, he said he wasn't in any way acting the hypocrite.

'You must do whatever you are going to do,' he said. 'Just know that – especially if you get used to crack cocaine – it will bankrupt you, it will turn you into a criminal, you will lose your friends and the only people you will have left are the other people that take cocaine. But in the end, even if you have a will of iron – and believe me, underneath this sweet exterior, I do – it will break that as well.'

With his audience spellbound, he smiled and added, 'However, it is the best drug that I have ever had in my life! Its only downside is that it kills you.'

CHAPTER 18
LOOPY LOU

Barry Miles, known to his friends as 'Miles', first met Felix Dennis in his *Oz* days but they really didn't get to know one another that well until they were both part of a New York ex-pat group in the eighties. A motley crew that included Felix, Miles, Mick Farren and Motorhead's Lemmy, they celebrated Christmas and any other excuse for a party as often as possible. While liberal amounts of cocaine, amphetamines and whatever other drugs were available at the time may have kept the party going, Miles recalled that Felix's drug use wasn't necessarily as heavy as that of many of those around him. In fact, as he put it, Felix 'was a tremendous advocator for the more hedonistic side of the sixties culture, particularly the sex side, but was never very into drugs as I recall'.

Marsha Rowe, who had worked at *Oz* magazine and was part of the defence team that burned the midnight oil to help fight their case, agreed. She didn't see Felix as someone interested in the drug culture in those early days. Speaking about the enthusiasm for experimenting with drugs, she said, 'That idea of the transcendence of consciousness of the drug experience, that didn't interest Felix whatsoever!'

As Felix himself explained later, there were some drugs that suited him and others that didn't. 'Acid, I took a few times,' he said, 'quite a few times. It was quite fun, but I've got a vivid imagination and it was probably a bit intense.' More importantly, acid didn't enhance his core interest. 'It also got in the way of me having sex, and you cannot have proper sex on acid. And anything that interfered with me having sex was absolutely not acceptable. It was completely unacceptable. In the end I just packed that malarkey up. So that was no good. But of course once a decent Colombian marching powder became available, that was a completely different matter!'

The fact that Felix used cocaine wasn't much of a surprise to those who were close to him throughout the seventies and eighties, but his descent into smoking crack was news to many. Friends and work colleagues were bemused by the stories he later told in newspaper articles, often attributing his tendency to bullshit when talking to journalists to the drugs. Only Marie-France and a select few of the girls servicing his sexual needs were aware of how far he had fallen. Others heard the occasional rumour but were not close enough on a day-to-day basis to know how bad things had become.

Don Atyeo and his wife Sue recalled an occasion when they were travelling from Hong Kong to France and had planned a few hours' layover in England. Before leaving, they had spoken to Felix, who said, 'Come to the Manor' and they were collected by his chauffeur-driven Rolls-Royce at the airport. As it was a beautiful day, they sat in the garden amiably chatting to Marie-France, while waiting for Felix to appear: he never did. Marie-France would make occasional trips into the house to try to get him to come down, but after a particularly rough night smoking crack, Felix refused – he didn't want his best friend to see what state he was in. He told her to make excuses, but, more importantly, to also make sure a pipe was ready beside the bed.

As Sue recalled, 'Marie-France came down and finally made some excuse about how he had eaten a bad prawn or something the night before.'

Discovering later that Felix had been smoking crack, she was astonished.

'I couldn't believe it,' she said. 'He was the least druggie of anyone, really the least druggie.'

Don was surprised too. Although he remembered Felix taking cocaine, he pointed out, 'He wasn't a hound for it. I mean, he was running the business.'

His other long-time girlfriend, Suzen Murakoshi, was also aghast at the thought of Felix smoking crack cocaine. First discovering it on a holiday in St Vincent, when three or four other girls were invited on the trip, she made it very clear that she wanted nothing to do with it.

'That was sort of the beginning of the end for us,' she said. Felix explained that his nose just couldn't take cocaine any more so this was another way for him to enjoy it. But Suzen was unimpressed, and, although she tried to make him see that it wasn't going to end well, she was fighting a losing battle.

'In the end, my relationship with Felix lasted longer than anyone else's,' she said. 'He was committed to me for the long term, in his own way. Ultimately, he knew I could take care of myself.'

Many years later she mused about whether Felix would have been able to achieve as much as he did without his experience of crack.

'His vision was so maniacally expansive after his addiction,' she said, 'that it must have changed his brain.'

His PA at the time, Maggie Kayley, recalled how he would hide rocks of crack around the Old Manor, often in places as daft as a toaster, and to her it became obvious. 'He was getting mega paranoid,' she recalled. 'It was just complete overload.'

It was affecting his work and she was very aware of it.

'He just wasn't being productive at all,' she said. 'Rather than being the way he used to be, really getting people on their toes. He was respected for that. But then he completely lost it and began pissing people off instead of motivating them – which he was so good at doing before. It was so hard.'

She agreed that he disguised his habit well but that was partly due to the fact that he was already known as a difficult character.

'It was hidden a bit because it was in his nature to be like that anyway.'

Tantrums, especially over little things, were not unusual. In fact, it was usually the little things that set him off. His reaction to an untidy room was likely to be much more explosive than the loss of a million dollars, so, when he became paranoid and jittery, many of those around him didn't think to question whether something was wrong. However, Maggie could see that he was becoming delusional and, since Felix had been such a huge part of her life, even giving her away at her wedding in Barbados and laying on a special party for her and her friends, she found it hard to deal with.

'It's not easy seeing someone destroying themselves and not being able to do anything,' she explained.

Joking with Maggie that she was the night shift while Maggie was the day shift, Marie-France was driven crazy by Felix's antics. 'He wasn't very good at it,' she revealed. 'Some people can't take drugs. He's an addictive personality. He'd take one puff and then go crazy.'

She recalled how he would stomp around the house in a state of heightened paranoia, telling her to check that the doors were locked and to make sure the curtains were closed. He began to believe there were people snooping around the gardens and heard voices upstairs.

'He'd send me Loopy Lou,' she admitted.

At first he had tried to control his drug use. Marie-France remembered how before he really used crack they would have a proper dinner in the dining room at the Old Manor with whatever girls were down for the weekend, and Felix would have little folders of cocaine deposited in different places around the house. He would insist on taking a rest after dinner and would then go off to read for a couple of hours. The girls would sit around bored to tears, as Marie-France recalled, 'waiting, waiting' for him to decide it was time to party. But once he had declared it was time to begin, the rest of the night would be both riotous and on occasions harrowing.

Felix's brother Julian, despite not living in his pocket, was aware of the impact his brother was having during his crack years.

'He was out of his mind, he couldn't speak,' he recalled. 'The people I feel sorry for are the people that have had to put up with him, especially whilst he was doing crack cocaine and God knows what else. He was really rude and horrible to everybody.'

Julian remembered urging Felix to apologise to those people before he died, 'because you've got no idea what you were like,' he told him. Alluding to the fact that both during the crack years and afterwards people would take advantage of Felix's generous nature, Julian tried to point out to his brother that, during this time especially, he was being used.

'He was throwing lavish parties,' he recalled. At a big fireworks' party Julian spotted one family arriving with fistfuls of plastic bags and they then began putting all the free drinks into the bags. He approached them, informed them that he was Felix's brother and told them to put all the drink back, saying that, if they didn't, he was 'going to level every one' of them.

'But he can't see that happening,' he said at the time, 'because he's out of his mind on something or other – if it's not two bottles of wine a day, or three bottles, or a bottle of brandy. That's what annoys me,' he continued. 'He knows that eventually it's going to catch up with him but he still does it.'

As crack began to get more of a hold on Felix, his paranoia reached new heights. One evening, alone in his flat at Kingly Street, he convinced himself that he was being stalked by the CIA. He ran into his tiny kitchen and grabbed a claw hammer from a drawer. Opening the door from his little kitchen to his even tinier roof garden, he roared into the night and quickly closed and locked the door, putting the chain on for extra security. He then raced around each room, checking windows and looking behind sofas. Unconvinced of his safety, he retreated to his bedroom. It was a dark room with a strategically placed mirror over the bed and he was surrounded by African masks that seemed to mock him. Standing on the bed, he faced the mirrors on his wardrobe and began to shout at his own reflection.

'You have no fucking clue who you are fucking with!' he screamed, shaking the hammer at the wild-eyed creature in the mirror. 'Just fucking try and get me!' As the dawn crept over the plants and flowers on his roof garden, he eventually collapsed only to wake hours later, slumped beside the bath in his bathroom. It was an episode that he remembered for the rest of his life and one that he held onto when later battling with withdrawal.

On one particular Monday morning his chauffeur, Lloyd Warren, had been summoned to come and collect him at the Old Manor. Arriving a little early to make sure he had time to pack Felix's things and ensure everything was perfect, Lloyd turned up to find the kitchen door open. He peered inside and called out but there was no reply. Assuming Felix was upstairs, he went to the bottom of the stairs and called out again but there was only silence. Lloyd didn't like to wander around the Old Manor, so he slowly climbed the stairs, calling as he went. In the study he found Felix slumped in his chair with his bathrobe open and a book fallen on the floor.

Lloyd stepped back and loudly called, 'Mr Dennis!' His first thought was that Felix was asleep, so he should shout as loudly as possible. Since this didn't have any effect, he remembered looking at Felix's chest to see if there was any movement.

'I couldn't see anything,' he remembered. 'I touched his face and there was nothing, so I thought he was dead!'

Battling with the concept of giving Felix mouth-to-mouth resuscitation, Lloyd froze and suddenly Felix groaned and struggled to open his eyes. It was obvious to Lloyd that his boss had overdone it and on the spur of the moment he made a decision that was likely to lose him his job. He went downstairs and got a black plastic bin bag and collected all Felix's crack pipes and other paraphernalia and put them all in the bag. Felix, still struggling and too out of it to do much, began to complain.

'He was spluttering and swearing,' recalled Lloyd, 'really going off and red as a beetroot.'

Lloyd proceeded to stamp on the plastic bag, smashing everything inside. Felix was furious – he had paid a fortune for his hand-made crack pipes. He shouted at Lloyd that he was fired and that he should take his money and go, never to come back to the manor. Lloyd left, assuming this was the end of more than 10 years in the job – a job that had led him on many adventures, many amusing and some terrifying.

Later that day, sitting in a cafe, he got a call from Felix, asking him to return.

'It was as if nothing had happened,' said Lloyd. 'He just said, "Lloyd, I have a big collection of VHS tapes and I want you to collect them up and sell them."'

He told Lloyd that, whatever he got for them, he would split the proceeds between them. By the time he had collected them, he had nearly a dozen bin bags full of VHS tapes. It turned out to be enough pornography to get a small shop started. Lloyd took them to Soho and remembered getting nearly £600 for them, which pleased Felix immensely. They split the proceeds and the episode of smashing the crack pipes was never mentioned again, but it was to be part of a change that may have kept Felix alive for a few more years to come.

It was at Marie-France's insistence that he eventually stopped at the end of 1997.

'I got so tired of it,' she recalled. She told him, 'You have to stop that crack. You don't behave. You have one pipe and you're a total monster.'

One of the few people with the courage to tell Felix the truth, she pointed out that he was ruining his health and that people were asking questions.

'The business is suffering and you're missing appointments,' she told him.

Remarkably, he simply said OK and told her to go away and not see him for three weeks. He then locked himself away and wouldn't see anybody until he had beaten it, a process that he was determined to go through alone.

'Then we met in Mustique and he never asked for it and never did it again,' she concluded.

With his custom-made crack pipes and anything else that might have tempted him now destroyed, Felix always claimed that he quit crack cocaine with willpower alone. That may have been the case but his was no ordinary willpower. There were aspects of his character that made it impossible for him to go back to an addiction and even more impossible to lose a battle with it. He had to beat it – in the same way that he had had to beat every other adversity that came his way.

Sitting in a small cottage that he called the Summerhouse in the garden of the Old Manor many years later, he declared that there was no merit to how he quit crack.

'I was never, ever going to allow addiction to rule my life,' he declared. 'I don't mind getting addicted, I'm quite happy to get addicted but if it starts to interfere with my life and is starting to annoy me, or annoy people and all that, then I would just stop it. I don't think it's very meritorious, because I could just do it.'

CHAPTER 19

TROJAN HORSE

For years after Felix became known for his business success, he claimed that a lot of it was due to luck. To a certain extent this was true. In the mid- to late eighties, after he and his partners had successfully sold *MacUser* to Ziff Davis, the cost of computers, accessories and software began to fall. Although his Apple Lisa had cost him over $10,000, the new Apple Macintosh, introduced in 1984, cost a comparatively paltry $2,495. Even the first portable Macintosh, effectively the first Apple laptop, which was launched in 1989, still retailed for a lot less than the Lisa at $6,500. With new software and other accessories making the products more accessible to businesses and soon individuals, a market quickly developed and Mac Warehouse soon began to make profits for its three owners: Felix Dennis, Peter Godfrey and Bob Bartner.

With extraordinary foresight and canniness they had included 24 free pages of advertising in *MacUser* as part of the sale deal and since they had agreed a non-compete clause, stopping them from launching a new Mac magazine, they also took the subscriber list with them to their new enterprise. Not only were they launching a new business to a market that was looking for somewhere to find the products it wanted, but they had also tied up access to that market.

From their initial idea they soon created a catalogue system that was to make them the biggest supplier of hardware and accessories around the world. Also realising that PCs were in the ascendancy, they then launched Micro Warehouse and applied the same template to any other computer accessory area that they felt there was a market for. Peter Godfrey described the launch and rapid progress to profit as being like a 'nuclear explosion'. The partners' initial investment was $250,000 each. Although later they would have to give a personal guarantee when extracting a $6 million credit line from one supplier, their start-up investment would look paltry compared to the eventual return.

Peter likened the development of their market to a Trojan horse in the sense that they initially sold to corporations via the Mac enthusiasts such as graphic designers. So when these businesses decided to expand computer operations, especially in the field of PCs, Peter, Bob and Felix's company was already a point of contact. However, as Peter remembered, the development of Micro Warehouse wasn't all plain sailing.

'The PC business was a lot tougher,' he said, 'lower profit margins and much more competitive, plus a very established corporate sales environment. The Trojan horse was the Macintosh business into corporations and then offering the PC products later.'

Looking back on it afterwards, he described their entry into corporate America as coming in 'stormish fashion'.

Although a little luck in their timing was useful, they needed something special to get buyers to trust their system. Peter called it their 'magic ingredient'. They were setting up a mail-order system in an area of industry that wasn't accustomed to it, nor had any reason to trust it. Consumer America had some experience of buying mail order since the advent of the Sears' catalogue had offered products for the home. However, corporate America needed more security. It needed to know for sure that, when it laid out thousands of dollars for computer equipment and accessories, those products were going to arrive on time, if at all. The whole concept of mail order to business was in its infancy.

'What transformed that hesitancy,' said Peter, 'was the introduction of overnight delivery. So we offered overnight delivery for $3, which was a mammoth undertaking and immediately the uncertainty went out.'

They quickly transformed the computer business.

'Our deal was order until midnight and you will have it on your desk at 9am, $3 shipping charge.'

In many ways they were paving the way for the likes of the behemoth Amazon today.

'It really set the stage for the internet in as far as people widely became accustomed to ordering via telephone and getting stuff quickly,' Peter added. The relatively high price of computer equipment had made the low delivery charge possible. 'You had a gross margin that allowed you overnight shipping that was affordable to the customer.'

The company's growth was phenomenal. 'Fairly early on we had a $500 million business,' remembered Peter. The whole process wasn't without growing pains. Things were happening so fast that logistical decisions had to be made without time to think them through. 'We were knocking walls down,' he recalled. 'We'd say just knock that wall down, put the computers out there, the phones in there and we will figure out what to do with them later. It was just crazy – just crazy.'

On one occasion, Peter remembered a meeting where they were struggling with the need to tighten up their delivery system.

'Our problem at that point,' he explained, 'was that we would deliver by truck from Lakewood, New Jersey, which was a two-hour drive to Newark Airport and the plane would then fly into the hub just outside Cincinnati, Ohio.'

Once at the hub, the packages would then be put onto other planes at about 4am to be delivered to wherever they were going. The company's problem was that they needed to be able to get more packages to the hub at Cincinnati. While senior logistical staff and company heavyweights grappled with the problem around a boardroom table, the solution came from what Peter described as 'a kid from the IT department'. When they were discussing larger planes, different airports and bigger trucks to deal with what Peter explained was a '$300 million to $400 million increase in business annualised', the kid from IT said, 'You know, it's the same shit that we send every day, only the label changes. So why don't we just store the stuff where the planes are and just send the labels?'

It was another magic ingredient.

As Peter remembered, 'Within weeks we opened a warehouse and then we built a 400,000 square foot warehouse. And now, when you go to the hub of Federal Express and Airborne Express, as far as the eye can see are warehouses, and we were the first.'

Ideas for the growth of the business came from many places, but as Bob Bartner was later to say, Felix was very much 'a visionary' with 'basically brilliant ideas' and he could make things happen. This proved to be the case at Micro Warehouse too. Although, as Bob agreed, Felix wouldn't have been the best person to put in charge of the day-to-day running of any business, his input into the look and feel of the catalogue was vital.

'We needed to figure out how to get money from the manufacturers and the software developers,' remembered Peter. 'So Felix came up with the idea of the blind listings – the snake, as we called it, the A–Z of all products.' The free listings were to include all products but to support the listings manufacturers and suppliers needed to take advertising space in the catalogue. 'So they got the line listing free and they paid for the advertising,' Peter explained.

The process of laying the groundwork for developing a sales strategy was also credited to Felix. While talking to Stephen England on one of his trips to the UK, Felix pointed out that he looked like he needed a holiday and why didn't he and his wife go and stay in the cottage in Connecticut? They duly took his advice and enjoyed a well-earned break with a weekend in Boston, a weekend at the Manhattan apartment and the best part of two weeks on Candlewood Lake. While in Connecticut, they also went to dinner with Bob Bartner and saw a side of the American lifestyle led by successful businessmen.

'It was all great fun,' remembered Stephen. 'And we kept saying, "Oh, I could live here, I could do this!"' It had been a great escape and a tempting taste of the lifestyle that America could provide. So, when three weeks after their return Felix phoned Stephen and asked him to come to dinner with him, he wondered what it was all about.

'I've got a personal matter I'd like to discuss with you,' said Felix, leaving Stephen with no clue as to whether he was to get a dressing down or a pat on the head. After general chit-chat Stephen remembered asking Felix outright, what was the reason for the dinner?

'How would you like to move to the States and go and work at Warehouse?' asked Felix. It was exactly what Stephen wanted. Although in some ways this might have been perceived as a sideways move, he saw it as an opportunity not to be missed and later questioned Felix as to whether the whole offer of a holiday in Connecticut had been a set-up, but Felix always denied it.

'I believe him,' said Stephen, some time later. 'I don't think it's some kind of plot. If it was, who gives a shit? Got me to the States. Bummer!'

Stephen remained in America and has felt indebted to Felix for the move ever since.

After developing a smokescreen story to cover the fact that he was leaving Dennis Publishing UK, while Felix was deciding who should take over, Stephen began making plans to move his family to America and once there quickly got stuck into developing a sales system that was to become the envy of sales operations around the country. However, there were two more key events that helped the eventual success of the business. One of these was finding Roger Munford, who had left Dennis Publishing to spend time in America, but eventually came back to the fold by accepting a job offer from Felix to run the publishing operation in New York in the early nineties. One of Dennis Publishing's great editors and publishers, Roger was asked to help overhaul the Mac and Micro Warehouse catalogue system in order for the company to cut costs and take advantage of all potential revenue sources.

One of the major costs for the company was the expenditure taken by producing and printing the catalogue and it had proved difficult to get people to include it in their advertising budgets. Talking to Mark Williams many years later, Roger recalled one of the turning points.

'I remember sitting in one meeting with all these pages on the floor that were going to be in the catalogue,' he said, 'and these guys were talking about whether they should go from eight issues to nine issues, or why don't we do 10? After a while Peter looked at me and said, "Is there something wrong?" And I said, "Yeah, you're all talking about doing eight, nine or 10 issues a year, but you're getting money from the same people that buy ads in magazines. Magazines come out 12 times a year, and they've already got their budgets for that – so why would you do anything other than 12?" And that was the first time that Peter Godfrey kissed me on the cheek. I ended up moving there and staying six-and-a-half years in Connecticut.'

The other major change that helped bring in more business was an idea brought about by Felix's eye for a pretty girl. Seeing what he allegedly called 'cheesy motivational posters' around the offices of Mac Warehouse, he complained that they looked tacky, but Peter argued that they were a key part of keeping up employee morale. As they were having this discussion, Felix gazed around the room and, as he later told Mark Williams, he noticed an attractive woman on one of the workstations.

'The girl on 137 is fantastic,' Felix said to Peter. 'I'm going to ask her out.'

Horrified, Peter made it clear that this wasn't a good plan. However, it did give Felix the idea to get her photographed with her telephone set on her head and put her on the front cover of all of the catalogues. Her name was Kerry and, with her blonde hair, brown eyes and all-American cheerleader looks, she became something of a company mascot. Putting her on the cover to entice people to pick up the phone was the perfect call to action. Thus was born a hook that was a huge marketing success and was to be copied by many catalogue companies afterwards. Next to her photograph was the line: 'I'm Kerry, call me'. Suddenly every girl that answered the phone became Kerry and another customer service coup was born.

Mac and Micro Warehouse became runaway successes and Peter, Bob and Felix decided to take the company public, though not without a little bit of resistance from Felix. Peter's argument was that a public company would give them legitimacy with what were called the 'big box manufacturers'. Companies such as IBM and HP weren't coming on board and the stamp of a publicly quoted company with all the financial muscle that brought could get them to agree to sell their products through the business. He was looking for a tipping point where the sales volume would get so big that it would be 'irresponsible of them not to let us sell their brands'. However, Felix's natural need for control made him very hesitant: he didn't like the whole process, nor did he like the scrutiny that came with due diligence and an IPO (Initial Public Offering). But he was outvoted, and as Peter later recalled, keeping Felix at a distance from much of the activity associated with a public flotation gave him something of a mysterious reputation.

'Felix was somewhat the man behind the curtain,' remembered Peter. 'Investment bankers noted his reluctance and distance.'

However, he did his bit. Peter recalled one meeting where Felix kept his rebellious personality so in check that 'we could have brought in an actor to play the part'. Writing about the process in his book *How to Get Rich*, he later admitted that it wasn't his scene but he had been forced to 'listen to enough lectures and to sit around enough tables and listen to sufficient legal eagles to gather that my partners and I were entering a different world. We were about to be entrusted with massive quantities of the public's cash. And if we screwed up in any one of a hundred ways, then it was chokey for us, go straight to prison, do not pass go, game over.'

The thought of going to jail had a special effect on Felix and, even if his private life was going off the rails, he was astute enough to know when to step back. He described 'endless meetings with investment bankers and their ferret-faced lieutenants' and lawyers droning 'incomprehensibly to each other about gobbledegook, with faces that look like they are sucking a lemon'. Felix was later to express his irritation that, after the business had floated in December 1992, everybody wanted to meet the guy who had done no work but made masses of money.

'Absolute bollocks!' was his response. Later, it was reported that by the time of the stock offering Micro Warehouse was receiving up to 10,000 calls a day.

'That's a lot of Kerrys!' laughed Felix.

The IPO was a success and all three partners made a substantial return on their investment. Felix gave most of the credit to Peter, who he explained had led the project through the stage of going public. He described it as Peter's tour de force, adding that through that process he had done his best, offering 'unhelpful entrepreneurial suggestions' but in effect he was 'way out of my depth'. The business was eventually reversed back into the private sector via a sale to a huge investment consortium. Ironically, it was sold in

January 2000 just after the millennium bug (or Y2K) scare, at a time when a shiver went through the computer and accessory sales market.

Even more ironic was an anecdote at the end of the story. Bob Bartner, originally the chairman of the company, had decided to jump ship early on as he wanted to semi-retire as well as pursue what became a successful theatre producing career. However, he also admitted that part of his reason for leaving was that he had seen something that the others hadn't. Discussing the company in 1998, after he had left but before it was eventually sold, he explained that his reasons for leaving were philosophical.

'The philosophical difference was twofold. I didn't think the international markets were the most logical way for the company to expand.'

From his point of view they had turned out to be more difficult than anticipated and, even though the company had affiliated businesses in five European countries, he didn't believe they were the most effective route to growth.

'Second of all, they viewed themselves as a computer company that sells direct to the consumer, whereas at the time we started, and still to a large extent today, they are one of the best direct marketing companies in America. They have a relationship with their customers and my view is that they could sell them a lot of other gear other than computer software.'

What Bob saw then is what Amazon later became. From a struggling start, selling books from a relatively clunky website, they became a juggernaut; fixing a stranglehold onto the consumer market where they were to sell just about anything through their website and affiliated companies.

PART THREE

TAKEN
AT THE
FLOOD

CHAPTER 20

HEROES AND VILLAINS

Despite his later claim that he had lost a decade and $100 million living it up with prostitutes, drugs and alcohol, the nineties was far from an unproductive time for Felix Dennis. In fact, it represented a period of enormous achievement for him. During that decade he began to develop some of the initiatives that would help to define him and his legacy, and pave the way for an intellectual and cultural explosion. He may have ended the nineties by reining in what looked like a trail of self-destruction, but he still managed to play a vital role in the development of Dennis Publishing, and many of the choices that he made during that era were to have a profound effect on both his bank balance and his status as a publisher. However, in order to facilitate that personal and business growth he needed to invite new people into the mix.

Despite the launch and success of *Computer Shopper* in the UK and the growth of Mac Warehouse in the US, Felix's companies were cash poor. His determination to fly by the seat of his pants, take chances and gamble on new ideas and new people had left him with a few disasters, especially in the accounting department. It was time to find someone who could put his business on a sound financial footing. After refurbishing his Kingly Street flat, throwing an office party to boost employee morale and then throwing a poignant and at times emotional party for the twentieth anniversary of the *Oz* trial, he began the search for a new finance director for Dennis Publishing. What followed was the most unusual interview that one young Kiwi had ever experienced.

Ian Leggett, who had arrived from New Zealand in 1979 on a two-year work secondment, had stayed in the UK and risen through the ranks of some of the larger accounting firms, but found himself out of a job when he had been forced to put his previous employer into receivership. He applied for three jobs, one of which was a company he knew little about, but he diligently did his homework and was initially successful in an interview with the board of Dennis Publishing UK. His next task, however, was to meet the owner, which began with a 10am economy flight to New York.

'Felix was this mysterious guy in New York,' he recalled, 'and I arrived in New York at about 5pm and checked into this really cruddy, rat-infested hotel.'

He called Felix and was told to come round to his apartment. Expecting to be asked about his background and his vision for the future of Dennis Publishing, he had armed himself with information about how much revenue different magazines might be making, but this preparation appeared to be in vain.

'I sat in a meeting with Felix for two hours and didn't get a word in,' he explained.

Felix did what had now become his trademark interview, which was to talk endlessly about himself and his businesses while weighing up the candidate and subtly determining their suitability by seeing how they reacted to his monologue and his booming laugh. It was as much an apparent lack of people skills as a canny way of giving the potential employee a chance to see what they were getting into, and it also allowed him to see how they might react to his nonconformist nature. He was setting the stage for the alpha male role that he liked to present to new colleagues.

Once or twice Felix did ask Ian to tell him a little about himself 'but I'd get two words in and he'd butt in!' he remembered. After a couple of hours Felix said, 'You seem a decent enough guy, how about we go across the road to the wine bar?' The monologue continued for some hours in the wine bar until Felix suggested they go to a nearby Italian restaurant for some food. At this point, Ian, fresh off a seven-hour flight from London and beginning to feel the five-hour time difference, was trying to keep up drink for drink with Felix.

'I really wanted the job,' he explained later.

The evening wore on and, at about 11pm, Felix suggested they go back to his apartment for a nightcap. With his girlfriend Suzen in the other room, Felix then said, 'Now the interview begins.'

It had been about eight hours since they first met.

Felix continued, 'There's one thing that I need to have, Ian, and that's an honest financial director. Tell me, do you have any convictions?'

Ian happily replied that he didn't and decided he should show his own need for honesty.

'And I wouldn't like to be on a board with anyone that has either,' he said. 'So I should ask you the same.'

The question was asked in all innocence. Although Ian had done his homework on the financial side of Felix Dennis's magazines, he knew nothing of Felix's background.

'I was a Kiwi, I didn't know,' he explained later. 'There was no internet then.'

In classic style, Felix never broke stride and simply fixed Ian with a poker-faced look and answered, 'Nothing that stuck.'

Six weeks later, Ian was offered the job.

Ian later pointed out that when he joined the company it was in dire straits. 'Serious, serious trouble,' he said. His first tasks were to cut overheads, renegotiate leases and slash spending – a course of action that, although painful, did eventually pay dividends.

When the time came to hire a new managing director for the UK, Felix turned to his friend from EMAP, Robin Miller, for advice. He suggested that, if Felix was going to hire someone from outside, that person had to be at least 25 per cent if not 30 per cent better than the person from within. It was a 'devil you know' situation. Hiring someone from within, you already knew their faults. Likening it to the process of talking to someone on a first date, he explained, 'You're meeting the outsider in their best make-up.'

Felix considered Alistair Ramsay for the position. Having trained at VNU and been able to bring useful sales training and systems experience to the company, Alistair had grown through the ranks after starting out as a sales manager on the weekly trade magazine *MicroScope* many years before. By the time his name had gone into the hat for the new MD's job, the company was, as Ian had suggested, in serious trouble. Alistair agreed – struggling with the term 'annus horribilis', he settled on calling 1992 a 'shit year'. The company had a weekly football magazine called *90 Minutes*, which he said was 'haemorrhaging money' and Felix had dramatically announced that, for the first time in the history of the company, they would have to make cutbacks. Amusingly, during the board meeting in which Felix made this announcement, he was interrupted by his PA Maggie Kayley, who urgently needed him to sign off on the purchase of some very expensive llamas for his Warwickshire estate. Alistair was sitting next to Felix at the meeting and remembered being amused that there was a freeze on paper clips but money for exotic animals.

His own recollection of the interview for the top job was that he didn't actually apply for it. Instead, Felix took him out to lunch to tell him that he wouldn't be considering him for the position.

'What we require is a real bastard,' he told Alistair. 'I want a ruthless bastard to run a tight ship to get us back on an even keel, and you're not a ruthless bastard.' He explained that Alistair wasn't old enough nor experienced enough, but that he would like him to work towards being a future MD. Knowing he wasn't going to get it, Alistair wrote a long memo to Felix, explaining what he suggested needed to be done with the company, and was surprised to get a reply offering him the job.

'I wasn't particularly ambitious for it,' remembered Alistair. 'Nor had the confidence to think I could do it.'

Around the same time Felix promoted Irishman Stephen Colvin, who had risen through the ranks after a start in advertising sales, to the board and announced that he would see how the 'young Turks' would do. With Ian on board, Alistair in the hot seat and Felix as the 'guy with the entrepreneurial ideas' and the creative talent, as well as being the 'ideas man and strategist', things began to improve for a while. This was helped in no small part by the flotation of Micro Warehouse in America and the injection of much-needed capital.

Alistair remembered that period as a time when Felix could 'do whatever he wanted to financially and he was going to enjoy it. He stepped aside and started becoming a gentleman farmer in Warwickshire.' In reality he was doing more at the Old Manor than becoming a gentleman farmer, but it was certainly one of the personas that he began to project.

Buying up land and property around him in Dorsington, Felix gradually started to establish a vision of the sort of estate in which he wanted to live. While the Old Manor was a great location in which to entertain, it was also a place where he could escape to enjoy his ever-growing obsession with books. He expanded on his earlier collection, acquiring first editions and bound anthologies as well as finding somewhere to store his assortment of *Oz* and sixties art. Later, he would become an avid collector of the work of designer Eric Gill.

However, the collection of sculpture that began in a small field that he had purchased next to a run-down barn on the lane beside his home was to become another of the attractions that helped to define Felix Dennis: he called it the 'Garden of Heroes & Villains'. The purchase of the location itself was thanks to a chance meeting with a neighbour, whom Felix described as a 'formidable woman'. She told him that the barn was to be auctioned off that day and that she didn't want strangers to buy it.

'So, get yourself into that fancy car of yours and go straight to the auction and buy it,' she told him. He followed her bidding and bought the property but, other than taking some friends down to view it and drink champagne from plastic glasses afterwards, he did nothing more with it for a few years. However, he grew to love the view and, despite the wind that howled through the open ruin, he felt a tranquillity that was absent from the bustling Old Manor, with its growing band of maintenance staff, cleaners and gardeners. As his enjoyment of the location grew, so too did a plan to create a totally unique garden.

An idea had slowly been germinating that would help show the depth of interest he had in literature, as well as display his appreciation of the achievement of others. Like many before him, Felix wanted to build his own folly and at its core there would be a maze and a tribute to the time when he and his friends, Richard Neville and Jim Anderson, made their own bit of history.

In early 1995, while Felix was buying yet another property next door to the Old Manor, work began to clear the site around the barn after decades of neglect. Brambles and tangled vegetation were uprooted and trees were pruned, and, if really necessary, some were removed. The first thing to be created was the *Oz* maze, which required the planting of 580 yew trees. The circular maze was mirrored on the other side of the barn by a circular topiary garden that sat at the head of a lane of trees, around which Felix planned to place a series of sculptures.

After holidaying in Bermuda many times, beginning in 1979, he had begun collecting smaller works by a Bermuda-based sculptor called Desmond Fountain. Coincidentally, while on a trip to see a foundry in England, Fountain decided to deliver one of those small pieces himself.

'I'd never met Felix at this point,' he recalled. 'I was a total innocent about how important Felix was in what he did.'

He was impressed by what he described as the 'picturesque environment' that Felix lived in and they soon fell into a discussion about Felix's idea for life-sized sculptures to use in his new project.

'He started talking to me about the *Oz* trial,' recalled Desmond, who at the time was only vaguely aware of *Oz*. They arranged to meet again and that was when he discovered the true depth of not only Felix's generosity, but also his commitment to getting memories of *Oz* correct.

Arriving at the second meeting, Desmond was shaking with rage and emotion because of tribulations in his personal life. Felix noticed his hands were shaking so much that he could barely hold his wine glass. They concluded their meeting but Felix told him that he shouldn't drive and insisted one of his drivers take him on to his next destination, despite the fact that it was in Berkshire. He arranged to have Desmond's car delivered back to him the next day and they went their separate ways, each in a different Rolls-Royce.

Having commissioned the sculpture of the *Oz* defendants, Felix was determined to ensure that everyone was going to be happy with it, so he sent Desmond and his partner to Australia to meet Richard Neville and Jim Anderson.

'I wanted to take measurements,' remembered Desmond, 'to make sure the sculpture was going to be right and get to know them a little bit.'

The plan, which was the theme for the whole sculpture garden, was that each sculpture was to depict a moment frozen in time. In the case of the *Oz* defendants, it was a moment when all three were wearing girls' school uniforms and Desmond had an idea to add an extra dimension to the finished work: the three men were to be cast in bronze but beneath the uniforms they would not be wearing any underwear.

Alluding to the 1971 David Hockney triptych of drawings of the three *Oz* editors naked, he explained, 'I measured them stark naked under these skirts they had as schoolgirl uniforms. So anybody who goes along and peers up underneath can see what David Hockney saw.'

Although many other sculptures were installed beforehand, the *Oz* sculpture was eventually placed in the middle of the maze in November 2000 and Desmond paid tribute to Felix's vision. Speaking of the concept, he said, 'I would give my eye teeth to be able to draw from my imagination and do the kind of things, in the same way that Felix can. It's magical. One can be very envious of him for being capable of following his imagination – his whims and what have you.'

Throughout the rest of his life, Felix indulged his whim of commissioning sculptures for his Garden of Heroes & Villains. When he began to open the garden for charity, people flocked in their thousands to see the sculptures and roam the pathways. Children laughed as their parents became lost in the maze and as the project developed there was always something new to see each year.

Sculptor Ian Rank-Broadley, who produced sculptures of Josephine Baker, Billie Holiday and Lord Rochester for Felix, specialised in figures and portraits, which are mostly in private collections; however, almost everyone in Britain will have touched his handiwork at some time in their lives: his image of HM The Queen has appeared on every new UK and Commonwealth coin since 1998. He could see that Felix's inspiration for freezing a moment in time didn't come directly from visual observation.

'He is very cerebral,' he noted. 'He is a voracious reader and very often he tries to conjure up figments of his intellectual experience, and that is how he arrives at what he wants in terms of sculpture – instead of being led by his eyes and tactile qualities.'

Knowing Felix's deep appreciation for singer, actress and dancer Josephine Baker, Ian made him a small medal of her belly button as a birthday present, hoping that 'in a loose moment, when he is stuck on the aeroplane, he can pull it out and stroke it'.

Having begun the Garden of Heroes & Villains, Felix became something of a patron in the world of sculpting. Altogether he commissioned 25 sculptors to work on more than 60 pieces. Michael Rizzello, the son of an Italian tailor whose work included plaques of the Queen Mother to go alongside those of George VI at St George's Chapel in Windsor and the Royal Chapel in Sandringham, described Felix as a 'sensible and humane individual'. Speaking in 2004, he said that Felix was 'the nearest thing to a proper patron'. He likened him to the patrons that existed in the eighteenth and nineteenth centuries, explaining, 'You had rulers and families commissioning works of art, sometimes on a whim. And some of the greatest works have been produced like that.' Echoing the thoughts of many of those commissioned, he added, 'Long may he carry on.'

Sadly, Michael never lived to finish his piece, *Battle of Thermopylae*. Depicting a moment during the famous battle between Spartans and Persians, he had found it 'gripping and absorbing'. The piece was eventually finished by John Ravera, who had created sculptures of Geronimo and Einstein for Felix.

Anthony Stones, who produced a sculpture of Shakespeare as a young man and another of the Chinese inventor of paper, Ts'ai Lun, as well as one of Potemkin for the Garden of Heroes & Villains, went on to open his own sculpture park in China. He was inspired by Felix and said, 'I always respond to passion and enthusiasm and Felix has got that. And what I like about him is that he doesn't give a stuff for the art establishment and their critical blah blah blah, and neither do I, because I think they are going up a blind alley and will run into a wall.' He believed that as a patron of the arts Felix brought a level of earthiness to his projects.

'It is great to meet somebody who is not infected by that tripe at all,' he declared. 'As president of the Society for Portrait Sculpture, I can only applaud somebody who is spending this kind of energy and money and time in promoting figurative sculpture.'

He also applauded Felix's diverse range of subjects, explaining they were not monopolised by any particular political focus.

'If you are going to have heroes you have got to have a proper spectrum of them and he certainly has. They are not all Labour trade unionists, or whatever. He has cast his net quite widely for his heroes and heroines!'

Dutch sculptor Marjan Wouda, who made many pieces for the garden, also had a special interest in sculpting animals. She supplied a pair of ravens that were particularly in tune with Felix's enjoyment of intrigue, mystery and the wish to keep business opponents on the back foot. The ravens were called Huginn and Muninn and had been given the ability to speak by the Norse God Odin. He would send them out across the lands to find out what his enemies were doing. They would return and sit on either shoulder, whispering into his ears. When she first made them, Marjan set them on a kind of plinth so that one could stand between them to listen to their news. Felix placed them outside his conservatory, facing the door of the Old Manor and often referred to them as 'the first drones'.

A walk around the sculpture garden also gave an insight into a hobbit-like world that said as much about Felix's need to live within dens created to cocoon his own solitude as it did about his fascination for the world outside of those sanctuaries.

A telling remark by one of the sculptors that contributed to the garden, John Poole, summed up the views of many who later grew to love Felix's poetry.

'I find him a tragic chap,' he said. 'I don't envy his life.'

CHAPTER 21

TREASURE TROVE

Much as Felix had endlessly travelled back and forth from England to America and brought his influence to bear on the UK operation as well as the American company, it was the US dollar that contributed to the bulk of his fortune. From the sale of *MacUser* US in December 1986 through the flotation of Micro Warehouse and the eventual sale of *Maxim* US in 2007, he earned hundreds of millions of dollars. Having started his life in what polite company might call humble circumstances, or which he once referred to as a 'fucking hovel', he had gradually built up a small empire.

Before heading off to the auction for the land that would house the Garden of Heroes & Villains, he had begun to buy other nearby property and one of his first purchases of 1988 was a small bungalow about 50 yards from his back door. It was called Highfield, and, although it certainly didn't warrant the price, Felix was happy to part with £200,000 to the young couple who lived there. It was to be many years after the actual purchase that work would begin, but he started to develop a plan to create a building unlike anything ever seen in England before.

The building was to reflect his passion for trees and wood as well as his love of barns, but most of all it would be built to indulge the child hidden deep beneath Felix's blustering exterior. He wanted a timber building because he had fallen in love with timber structures while living in America.

'I am familiar with wooden structures and I know that they work,' he told Dennis Publishing director Teresa Maughan when she wrote a foreword to a privately published short book about the project. 'The only reason Britain doesn't have wooden homes is because it doesn't have any trees. Ninety per cent of all homes in America are wooden.'

The house was built in the style of a seventeenth-century barn and it was the biggest green oak-framed building built in Britain for 300 years. The frame was constructed off-site and then assembled using only pegs and dowels, no nails or screws. When in place the final structure actually comprised one huge, aisled barn with two smaller timber structures attached: one housing the kitchen, the other containing the changing rooms. Although the term 'leisure centre' is simply misleading, that is how it has at times been described. It housed a swimming pool, a Jacuzzi, steam room, sauna, cinema, bar and gym, as well as a kitchen, dining room, bedroom, changing room, library and, most importantly, a private office simply known as The Quiet Room. Later, it was estimated that if you laid all the electric cable in a straight line it would have gone from Stratford-upon-Avon to London. Nine years after the purchase of the old bungalow, Highfield was looking like one of the most magnificent new buildings in the country. However, on the eve of Good Friday in March 1997, just three weeks from completion, disaster struck.

Sitting at home in the Old Manor, Felix was in night-owl mode. Marie-France had been delayed on a trip to London and he had instructed her to stay there and not come back until the next day. Without any other distractions he focused on work, and at 2.30am, he was looking over some of the final preparations for the launch of *Maxim* in America when he thought he heard the sound of breaking glass outside. His first thought was that it was vandals but he dismissed that later, saying, 'We don't have vandals around here.' However, he did decide to investigate and saw a large column of flame bursting out of the study window of Highfield. Less than 50 yards from his back door, he could see that it was serious so he ran back inside to phone the fire brigade. After making the call he thought about grabbing a fire extinguisher but within seconds the flame was higher than the nearby trees, so fearing that it might spread to the house he grabbed a coat, hat and a camera and began to try to get around the site while taking photographs from a safe distance.

By the time the first fire engine had arrived, the night sky was lit up and the village had begun to look as though it was hosting a late-night sporting fixture. The fire had reached the roof and burning embers were beginning to fall to the ground. They seemed to be sending further embers flying towards nearby properties, some of which sported brand-new thatch.

'There was an enormous risk to the surrounding buildings,' Felix recalled.

Later, they discovered that the baize of a snooker table in the conservatory of the flat next to the Old Manor had burn marks, where embers had fallen through the skylight. As the firemen began to spray Highfield and hose down nearby buildings, the water pressure dropped and, as Felix later recalled, there were times when the water jets were simply dribbling. More fire engines were called for and in a surreal moment a group of firemen arrived on foot when their engine had gone off the road and ended up in a ditch. Villagers began to arrive in their night clothes and, as a request from the chief fire officer to Severn Trent Water to turn up the pressure couldn't be accommodated, they managed to get water from a village pond that Felix had only dug out a year previously.

'The roar of the fire was deafening,' Felix recalled. 'Beams weighing three quarters of a ton came crashing into the pool and roof tiles smashed down to the ground.'

Thankfully, the fire was controlled enough to stop it spreading to other buildings but the destruction of Highfield was complete. The next day, as builders, surveyors, architects and project manager Bill Taylor surveyed the scene, there was devastation and tears. Architect George Godsman remembered crying at the site and Bill Taylor said, 'I had grown men here, very, very tearful on that day. Hard builders were shedding tears.'

Felix tried to bring a sense of perspective to the assembled group, putting an arm around Bill Taylor's shoulders and saying, 'Don't worry, there's no one dead.' After two years of building and nearly £3.8 million spent on the project and a mood of utter desolation, perspective was a concept that was hard to swallow.

Despite his efforts to console those around him, Felix was angry and searched for someone to blame. Coincidentally, David Arculus, whom

Felix had failed to poach from his job at EMAP, had by this time moved on to become chairman of Severn Trent Water, the company in charge of supplying water to Dorsington. In need of someone to lash out at, Felix rang up his old friend and berated him about the problems of getting enough water to fight the fire.

'Felix was rather cross with me and thought that Severn Trent should have supplied a very large water main just in case his barn burned down,' laughed David, remembering the irate phone calls.

It took quite some time for Felix to make a decision about what to do after the fire. Much as he tried to project a positive attitude, he was bruised and torn. Years of effort, energy and excitement had been demolished in a few short hours. What had grown from nothing into one of the most extraordinary pieces of contemporary wood structure in England was now a smouldering pile of ashes. After visiting his old friend, cartoonist Ed Barker, who was dying in hospital, he decided the only way to go was forward and gave the order to rebuild.

One consideration that came into the decision to rebuild was the effect it might have on the village. For the best part of two years locals had put up with a constant stream of builders, carpenters, electricians, plumbers and specialists in a complex and diverse range of services. In general they had dealt with the noise and disruption well but could they go through the whole process a second time? After Felix found a generally positive and at times generously supportive response, he then had to deal with sourcing the wood. The project would need to find trees and after that it would take a huge leap of faith and positive energy to get everyone enthused again. An investigation concluded that the fire had started in the cinema area, probably by the malfunction of a lighting or electrical circuit.

The second incarnation of Highfield became a magnificent building. The rebuild brought an opportunity to make some changes, one of which included enlisting the advice of an interior designer who had done some work for Felix on the small flat next to the Old Manor. A nephew of the great cookery writer Elizabeth David, Johnny Grey had set up a small design studio after studying at the London Architectural Association School of Architecture. Inspired by spending so much time in kitchens with his aunt, he began to develop an aversion towards the trend for fitted kitchens. Instead, he created a new trend encompassing a looser, more user-friendly, yet more comfortable kitchen. Before long his keen eye and sympathetic sensibilities led to a unique style that he would later share by publishing many books and articles on design, especially in kitchens.

One of the first and most immediate changes that Johnny implemented was his recommendation to create a huge fish tank inside the door. Initially the design called for the visitor to face a wooden wall on entering. As the theme for the building was to be based on Felix's love of Robert Louis Stevenson's *Treasure Island*, Johnny suggested that looking through water as you entered would set the scene perfectly. The final result was a breathtaking tank filled with a vast array of beautiful fish that was one of the largest fish tanks in private hands in England. The 17-ton structure had to be winched onto the site and then placed on boards and rollers to allow it to be squeezed in through the front door.

Turning left past the huge bank of water, the visitor then enters an open kitchen area, which Johnny had designed to give the feel of a seventeenth-century ketch, a small sail boat that carried tea and later opium from India to China. Beautifully crafted with curved lines, a central island echoed the construction of a ship's hull. Beside it a tapering cupboard cleverly conceals a spiral staircase to the basement bar, games room and cinema. Finishing the cupboard, however, was not without its trials and tribulations. It had been given 25 different coats of paint before the final finish was arrived at – by accident. While the artist was sanding off yet another coat, Felix walked in and said, 'Stop! That's it!' By sheer luck she had given the cupboard a dappled look that gave the impression of water. She then had to spend several weeks trying to recreate the random rippled effect over the whole cupboard.

The kitchen set the scene for an entrance into a small but opulent banqueting room. Inevitably, the area featured an eclectic mix of Felix's collection of small sculptures as well as paintings and later a wall of framed pages of some of his poetry that had been printed in *Tree News*, but to create a division between the dining area and the pool, Johnny had designed a rood screen carved in English oak. Panels highlighted some of the objects that were landmarks of Felix's life. These included an open book, a quill, the scales of justice and a computer.

Touches of Johnny's design transformed the original vision but not without the occasional explosion. The en-suite bathroom for the only bedroom in the building included a grotto complete with over 500 fibre optic lights that twinkled amongst a wall of sea shells behind the toilet seat. The bath itself sat inside marble housing, which was made from hand-finished Italian Carrara marble.

Showing him the design for the en-suite bathroom, Johnny explained to Felix that the grotto around the toilet alone would cost £10,000. It didn't go down well.

'Ten grand for a toilet!' exclaimed Felix. 'OK, Johnny, but you can pay for it.'

In the end Johnny had to get creative with the costs but he did get to design an extraordinary bathroom.

The new design also included an inside walkway around the building and a balcony at the back on which to watch the sunset. Site manager Bill Taylor fashioned a shovel out of wood and personally dug the residue from the fire out of the swimming pool to ensure that the delicately designed mosaic floor was undamaged. The shipwreck design was created with 450,000 glass mosaic tiles on the bottom of the pool. If you stacked the tiles on top of each other, they would have formed a column over a mile high.

A central feature made up of huge Californian preserved palm trees rose 33 feet up into the rafters to provide a tropical feel while also cleverly concealing the air conditioning, and no less than 50 square metres of Lincoln sandstone was quarried for use around the pool. The Main Deck kitchen, though rarely used for cooking, was fitted with everything a Michelin-starred chef could dream of.

Overall, the nautical theme embellished by Johnny Grey's witty and flamboyant treatment gave the building a sophisticated adventure playground feel, and with dressing rooms adorned with porthole windows and the use of 750kg of shells to decorate some of the walls, the overall effect was breathtaking.

The downstairs cinema and bar were given an Art Deco design and 1,500 sheets of 33-carat gold leaf were used for decorative gilding and moulding. To complete the wacky picture a huge turntable was built into the garage below so that Felix's Rolls didn't need to do a three-point turn to come out. A thoughtful touch considering he would never get behind the wheel himself.

Although there were changes along the way, including the cancellation of a Jacuzzi hidden inside a volcano in the middle of the pool, it was local planning that put paid to one of Felix's more avant garde ideas. He had hoped to install a basket at the end of a motorised pulley system that would allow him to rise up above the bed into a glass dome-like structure, where he could then sit and enjoy 360-degree views of his estate. Although it was pretty harmless-sounding, the idea didn't get past the planners.

The final result, after two building attempts, was a masterful feat of design, engineering and craftsmanship that Felix shared with friends and colleagues. Guests staying in cottages around his estate splashed happily in the pool, enjoyed saunas and Jacuzzis and drank liberally from Felix's wine cellar and bar. It became another playroom for Felix to entertain in, as well as a space where he could indulge his growing interest in collecting art to his own taste.

It was a style that Johnny Grey eventually grew to appreciate, despite his team's initial reluctance to be associated with the *Treasure Island* theme. Speaking many years later, Johnny said he felt closer to Felix's vision of good taste, suggesting that it had a 'huge element of open-mindedness' and 'spirit of play'. Explaining that although he had had the occasional difficult client, he had also worked for some wonderful people, Johnny added, 'Felix gets pretty near the top as the one whom I think has the most independent spirit.' He believed that as Highfield grew so too did Felix's confidence in his own sense of style and, although there were those who felt his taste was brash, Johnny described it as 'steam punk' and suggested that, although Felix wanted exuberance, 'he doesn't want to completely abandon an element of aesthetic sophistication.'

Few of his friends or colleagues would have described his taste as artistic or sophisticated in a traditional sense, but his early interest in graphic design and the influence of sixties art from the psychedelic work of Martin Sharp to the wild drawings by some of those whose work he published in comics helped Felix develop his own unique style. His sense of humour even extended to commissioning a fake van Gogh of Robert Louis Stevenson, which he placed above the mantelpiece in the Quiet Room in Highfield. To compound the joke he even had it alarmed. On one occasion when Toby Fisher, one of Felix's personal assistants in Dorsington, was dusting the painting, he found himself red-faced when a piercing alarm went off after his feather duster had connected with more than cobwebs. It was a story that Toby enjoyed telling visitors while giving them a tour of Highfield, when Felix would open his garden to raise money for charity.

Much as Felix avoided art galleries, theatres, cinema and most other traditional seats of cultural activity, that didn't mean he had no love for art. Indeed, he made a point of supporting the work of those he appreciated and his encouragement of Suzen Murakoshi's theatrical career showed no lack of financial commitment. But his collection of work tended to be defined by the era he lived in, as well as his love of nature. In other words he was rarely influenced by fashion or historical significance, unless it could be related to the written word. However, on one occasion he was happy to support an exhibition at the Central St Martin's School of Art & Design.

After an approach in 1998 from the course director, Don Grey, he hosted a group of students at the Old Manor as they grilled him for information that might help them follow a new project brief. In response to a quote from a newspaper article, where Felix had suggested he might like to build a pyramid on his estate as his burial chamber, the director had suggested that his students devise an exhibition of work based on unusual memorials or burial chambers that might be used after Felix's death. Although he later said that his remark about the pyramid was flippant, Felix did admit that it 'had a kernel of truth in it'. He recalled that the students had asked him to choose favourite objects, had taken many photographs and 'measured my bones and took plaster casts of certain portions of my anatomy'. The end result was an exhibition called *Dennis Desiderata*, which was staged at the Lethaby Gallery at Central St Martin's College of Art & Design in Southampton Row in London on 12 November 1998. He sent out invitations to close friends, confiding that he had not been permitted to view any of the exhibits and expected to be as surprised as they. The exhibition was described as 'A celebration of the death and life of Felix Dennis in the presence of the deceased'.

Although perhaps not an international success, the show was both amusing and poignant and there were many fascinating ideas contributed by over 30 students. One artist suggested an inverted subterranean pyramid, pinning the earthly remains of Felix to the English landscape. Another came up with the idea of a latter-day Babylon reached by an underground labyrinth, while another envisaged glass kites interlacing in the sky above an avenue of perpetual trees. There were many references to ideas that Felix had already implemented, such as the Garden of Heroes & Villains, but after spending a day with him there were also those that fully absorbed the humour of the event. Elie Zaccour suggested a large piece of jewellery that Felix's friends could wear, which would be used in sex games, while another student devised a bubble-gum vending machine that would dispense items from Felix's will as a series of lucky dip prizes. Kelly Ho produced a revelatory cube, which unfolded to reveal Felix's infatuations of books, trees and women, while Louis Segal decided that Felix should survive after his death and appear as a four-armed puppet. Three arms would count money, drink fine wine and make telephone calls, while the fourth would offer two fingers up to the rest of the world.

An article in the *Express* gleefully reported on the exhibition with the headline 'I'm the mad geezer who loves a good party, in life and in death'. Felix was photographed beside the exhibits and even hopped into a coffin to give the photographer something to amuse readers. As well as the humour there were some ideas that may have tickled his ego but thankfully weren't used when the time eventually came. For example, one artist suggested the production of a funeral party invitation distributed in CD form that would be based on Felix's idea of heaven – 'to spend all his time with women, books and trees'. Another suggested a CD that could be distributed to guests as a souvenir, while the one that might have left Dennis Publishing executives reeling was a multimedia piece about moments of death and renewal, which the artist suggested could be distributed with one of the company's PC magazines on his death.

Lucy Charlton, a ceramicist from Tunbridge Wells, produced a piece that Felix kept in a drawer in the Old Manor. It was an impression of the inside of his right hand, cast in solid silver. She had included ambergris in the original design. A secretion of the sperm whale intestine, ambergris is used in the production of perfume and Lucy wanted to show his status because silver and ambergris signify wealth. Felix was quite taken with the design and bought it from her at the end of the show.

He had also put up a prize for the winning entry and chose the bubble-gum vending machine. The winner got to be taken by Rolls-Royce to the restaurant of their choice, where they were at liberty to hammer their own impression on his credit card account.

CHAPTER 22

EVERYTHING
THAT MATTERS

If the *Oz* reunion party at the beginning of the nineties had rekindled old friendships and brought back both painful and amusing memories, an article in the *Spectator* in May 1995, written in response to a review of Richard Neville's new book, *Hippie Hippie Shake*, gave the *Oz* trial a new boost of publicity.

Michael Argyle, the Old Bailey judge, who had sent Felix down for nine months, was incensed at John Mortimer QC's review and penned what became, for him, a disastrous response. It not only accused Mortimer of being on the side of 'peddlers of porn, soft drugs, terrorists and the rest', but also accused Felix and his fellow *Oz* defendants of selling drugs to schoolchildren. He said they had been selling drugs and *Oz* magazines at the entrances to schools and youth clubs and that 'the stuff was pouring in by ship, in huge lorries from Scandinavia and the Low Countries'. He even suggested that, during the time that Felix, Richard Neville and Jim Anderson were behind bars, the drug traffic into the UK had slowed down and had increased as soon as they were discharged. He had also intimated that the defendants were responsible for threats on his life.

'During the sitting of the trial, a police dog handler with an Alsatian sat outside in the judges' corridor,' he wrote. 'Three more armed police lived in the house night and day for weeks.'

He went on to describe how, although the officers drank all his whiskey, they did look after his pet yellow canary, Gustavus Adolphus. Much of the article was seen as farcical and the product of an unbalanced mind. It finished with a description of Argyle's dreams of fighting the SS alongside the Jewish brigade in deep Italian snows 'advancing across a valley carpeted with the dead'.

Some of those reporting on the article and its subsequent court action assumed that the *Spectator* had published it thinking an Old Bailey judge's word would not be questioned.

However, it was questioned – and with no lack of energy – by Felix Dennis.

Although pushed by many to sue Argyle, Felix decided the man was possibly deranged, and as he was at the time 80 years old, he later said he didn't want to make him a martyr for the right-wing establishment. Instead, he sued the *Spectator* and got them to pay £10,000 to a children's charity and the National Library for the Blind. In their letter of apology the magazine agreed that an accusation that Felix and his co-defendants had been importing and peddling drugs was 'groundless'. They also pointed out that Judge Argyle's protection by Special Branch and police dog handlers had been because of death threats the judge had received from 'someone entirely unconnected with the defendants and *Oz* magazine'.

It appeared that the *Oz* trial, an episode in Felix's history that had served to give him a taste of life behind bars, as well as offer him a major boost to his street credibility, had come to elevate his profile again. *Oz* had originally given him a platform on which to stamp his feet and damn the establishment, and in that pattern of good fortune that he so often referred to, it had handed him the lucky dice once again.

Remarkably, as if Lady Luck was not content with pouncing just once in the same month, she paid Felix another surprise visit. Somebody dropped off a new magazine to his Kingly Street office, which was to help bring yet another fortune. He quickly scanned through it and put it in his briefcase. Later that day, as his chauffer Lloyd drove him back to the Old Manor, he read through the magazine again, this time page by page and article by article. Carefully placing it back in the briefcase, he turned to the window to catch a glimpse of majestic oaks and ancient chestnut trees silhouetted against the late spring sky. He remembered closing his eyes and composing a note to send to the magazine's owner. Later, he claimed that from that first read he was smitten, 'addicted' and 'hooked'. While awaiting the result of his writ against the *Spectator* he wrote the note to journalist and ex-deputy editor of the *Telegraph*, Jolyon Connell, whose magazine, *The Week*, had made such an impression on him. It was a note that was to launch Felix and Dennis Publishing into another and wholly different publishing adventure.

Jolyon Connell's career in journalism began in Aberdeen but after he moved to London he worked his way through the ranks to become the *Sunday Times* defence correspondent, then Washington correspondent, and before launching his own business he helped start the *Sunday Correspondent*, was deputy editor of the *European* and later deputy editor of the *Sunday Telegraph*. Tall, thin and with hair later described as 'wilder than Felix's', it was during his tenure at the *Sunday Telegraph* that he hit on the idea for *The Week*.

'I'd had this vague idea about doing specialist newsletters for different professions,' he recalled. 'They would tell them what was in the newspapers that might be relevant to their professions.' He pointed out that, although he was in the newspaper business and read as much as he could, often there were times when someone would mention a story that he had simply missed and he realised that this must happen to many people. People were getting busier and newspapers were getting bigger, and as he explained, 'Our time to read them is getting shorter and shorter.'

Staying with his mother in Scotland after the death of his father, he took a walk around a nearby lake and began to formulate the idea of a digest of the week's news and comment, highlighting what he later described as 'the most arresting and original ideas, the funniest stories, the most interesting articles from abroad', as well as the best houses on the market. He wanted to produce 'everything I would like to know all together in one succinct, easy-to-read package'.

It was January 1994 and most of what readers currently enjoy in *The Week* was thought out on that walk. Jolyon tested his ability to summarise articles using a piece in the *Mail on Sunday* about fox hunting, which had been written by John Mortimer. Little did he know when he chose it that he would eventually go into business with one of Mortimer's most famous clients from the early seventies.

Having resigned from his job, sold his house and produced the first few issues, he then lived through the pain that new business owners suffer in those early, heady days of launching a new venture. It looked as though making the magazine work might be a lot tougher than he had at first thought.

'I had no business sense whatsoever,' he admitted. He later suggested that, although he had hired the very talented Jeremy O'Grady to help him sort through the daily newspapers to compile the different sides of news stories, he had spent far too much time trying to do everything himself.

'I made the classic journalist mistake,' he said. 'I wanted to be involved in everything.'

One day, sitting at his desk in the converted garage that served as their office, he opened a letter congratulating him on his new magazine and inviting him for beer. He waved it in the air, saying, 'Has anyone heard of Felix Dennis?' Not noticing any response he stuffed the letter into a drawer and a couple of days later mentioned the name to publisher John Brown, who immediately advised him to go and visit Felix.

Jolyon's description of his first visit to Kingly Street said as much about the difference between him and his new business partner as it did about his courage to take the venture forward.

'I'd never come across anybody quite like him in my life,' he recalled. 'It was hard to take him seriously, really.'

Felix had gone into monologue mode and was sizing up Jolyon by telling him about himself, his wild excesses and his success in magazine publishing. Jolyon began to question what he was hearing: has he really made all this money? Is he bullshitting me? Is this some kind of rubbish and why is he telling me all about his private life? Felix had launched into his favourite subject, explaining to Jolyon that he hadn't had penetrative sex in 10 years. Despite the point of the meeting being to look at the possibility of investing in *The Week*, Felix couldn't help but, spin a few stories in the company of a journalist. Jolyon remembered him as 'like a character from a cartoon. He talked all the time but, to give him his due, he sold himself.' However, despite his concerns that Felix was somewhat of a fantasist, two thoughts stayed with him: 'He's jolly, and he's got the money.'

When it came to success and money, however, Felix wasn't really faking and Jolyon was to discover that one of the great advantages of achievement, along with access to money, is the ability to take a good idea and turn it from a fledgling start-up into a raging success.

Having brought those skills to a number of previous ventures, Felix had already decided that he wanted to bring them to *The Week* and he and Jolyon agreed to meet again, this time at the Old Manor. Sitting beneath Felix's favourite cherry tree on a beautiful July afternoon in 1995, he explained to Jolyon that he would be happy to take a stake in his venture but that there was one caveat. He would eventually try to take complete control of the magazine; ideally he wanted to own 100 per cent of the business. They did what later became known as a 'back of an envelope' deal and Felix agreed to take possession of 33 per cent for a sum that Jolyon thought would be plenty to see the business grow and eventually prosper. What Felix knew, but Jolyon didn't, was that they would soon need more. Less than a year later, Jolyon came back for more and Felix brought his interest up to 51 per cent, and with that control of the company. Not much more than a year after first setting eyes on the magazine, Felix had made it his own.

'I know now I should have done a loan stock deal or something similar,' said Jolyon later. 'The thing about a weekly is that you are a clattering train. You can't stop. And if you start becoming successful it doesn't cost less, it costs more.' Felix, of course, had been through the anxiety of running a weekly magazine, initially with the very painful *New Music News* in 1980, and the lessons he had leared from that were to prove invaluable in the growth of *The Week*.

However, he not only brought his own experience to bear on the development of the magazine, in time he also brought the talent and experience of different departments of Dennis Publishing in to help, but prior to that he introduced someone who had inside experience. Richard Howell, by now working as a freelance publisher, had worked on *New Music*

News back in the Bunch days and had been responsible for bringing *Hi-Fi Choice* to Felix in the early years. He came on board as publisher in 1997.

'It was an excellent editorial product,' remembered Richard, 'but it had no systems, just no management or control to it. There was nothing fundamentally wrong with it, it was just getting the marketing right and getting the costs under control.' Apart from being an excellent product there was something else that caught Richard's eye. It had a subscriber list that he said read like a *Who's Who*. He described it as a 'very sexy subscriber list'.

Jolyon and another early employee of *The Week*, Kerin O'Connor, who would later become one of the dynamic directors of Dennis Publishing UK, began mining the weekly list of new subscribers for suitable names to request testimonials from.

On one occasion, seeing the name John Cleese from Lansdowne Crescent on the list, they wrote to him, asking if he would like to offer a comment about the magazine for publication. Mr Cleese wrote back, thanking them and saying that indeed he was John Cleese and that yes, he would be delighted to offer them a testimonial, but perhaps they were mistaking him for another John Cleese?

Slowly and surely circulation began to grow, and more and more people began to ring the office to express their gratitude and praise for what they thought was a much-needed and excellent magazine.

After living in Moscow publishing books prior to joining *The Week*, Kerin O'Connor was a relative newcomer to the UK publishing industry but according to Richard Howell he was 'very bright' and 'very sharp'. He was also a fast learner and was fortunate to have Felix Dennis as his mentor.

'Felix realised early on that the reader was king,' remembered Kerin. 'He also understood that *The Week* needed to be put on a solid foundation as a subscription business and the investment needed to be appropriate to allow that to happen. The more money you put in, the more money you got out.'

To that end Felix didn't interfere. His changes to the magazine were very minor. With Richard Howell gently nursing the team towards the idea of including advertising, Felix changed the paper from newsprint to semi-gloss so that both readers and advertisers had a better-looking product. He added a couple of extra editorial ideas but in general left them to it. By the time he came to launch the magazine in America, he was describing it as being like heroin on paper. Felix's belief in *The Week* was as passionate as, if not more so than, his belief in any other publication he had ever owned or been involved with.

Talking in 2010 about how he invested heavily in the American version of *The Week* with a launch in 2001, Felix claimed he spent $48 million over seven years to make it a success. He pointed out that the money wasn't the only investment in the venture.

'It's the opportunity cost,' he said. 'Just for once the bean counters have got it right and us mugs who just make things and do things and run things, we're wrong!'

He pointed out that not only could that money have gone into launching other magazines or websites but the bank interest on it alone, over those seven years, would have made a tidy sum.

'And they said look, not only have you lost the money, OK, you've lost what the money could have done!'

When he first began rolling out *The Week* in America, the *Wall Street Journal* ran a headline asking, 'Is Felix Dennis Mad?' His new magazine was up against powerful brands like *Newsweek* and *Time* in a weekly news category that was not only hard to break into, but was itself struggling for direction with growing interest in the internet. That of course was just the kind of incentive he needed to keep pouring in the money, and in the end his terrier-like perseverance eventually paid off. However, one of his business partners didn't at first share his enthusiasm. Peter Godfrey even wrote out a personal cheque to Felix for $1 million, begging him to take it and shelve his ambition for the magazine.

The US launch editor was Bill Falk, who had been poached from New York's *Journal News*. Bill had what had become the standard interview with Felix.

'I was expecting to be grilled by him on all sorts of things,' he remembered. Felix spoke for about 55 minutes of the one-hour interview. 'And when it was all over, I sort of staggered out, a little stunned.'

He was thrown in at the deep end and given four months to launch the first issue from a standing start. In April 2001, *The Week* launched in America to a lukewarm response. As in the UK it was a slow burn and, as Mark Williams put it later, 'The US and UK experiences growing *The Week* resembled parallel evolution.' He saluted what he called the 'backroom heroes', whose mastery of subscription acquisition and renewal techniques and strategies had gradually built up readership, thereby creating a base to attract blue chip advertisers. Felix's belief, coupled with deep pockets, the tenacity to persevere, along with teams of committed people, eventually brought it to profit on both sides of the Atlantic.

Of those now based in America, perhaps the one that knew the most about Felix and his history was Sir Harold Evans, who had been hired as editor-at-large for *The Week* after its US launch. Speaking in 2014 about his memories of Felix, he recalled how in 1967, not long after he had been made editor of the *Sunday Times* in London, he heard about Felix before the *Oz* trial had made headlines. He explained how he remembered 'this scruffy kid flogging magazines along the King's Road in Chelsea'.

As editor of what he called 'the greatest newspaper that ever was', Harold didn't take much notice until one of his childhood heroes, Rupert the Bear, whom he recalled 'used to be on the bottom of my porridge plate' was suddenly at the centre of an obscenity trial. With a twinkle in his eye and the skilled delivery of a man adept at amusing an audience with an interesting anecdote, Sir Harold explained that the *Sunday Times* had decided to take a sympathetic attitude to Felix 'not because of Rupert the Bear, but because Scotland Yard had laid its heavy hand on these Australians and this crazy Felix Dennis'. At the time, he recalled, Scotland Yard were questioning him about railway lines while Felix was being questioned about much more interesting stuff. 'I thought, "Christ Almighty, he's much more glamorous than me. He's got all this sex stuff!" I was kinda jealous.' Sir Harold then lost sight of Felix and his life until: 'Next thing I know, he's a bloody millionaire and I'm still flogging myself for 30 quid an hour!'

Sir Harold became a great promoter of *The Week* in America and he and Felix spent many hours debating the rights and wrongs of the world, both in publishing and society in general. Friendships such as this, along with the distinction of being the owner of a magazine like *The Week*, brought Felix a level of respect that was lacking in all his previous publishing successes. In later years he sometimes regretted not going into the newspaper business himself, but on one occasion, talking to Charlie Rose in an interview for PBS television in America, he suggested that it would be a very dangerous thing for him to do. He pointed out that whenever people start owning newspapers their prejudices start showing.

'I'm not sure that I want the temptation of all that power in my hands,' he told Rose. 'I sound off enough – I don't think I need to bore the rest of the universe with my opinion!'

CHAPTER 23

DANCE THE BLUES

It was on a Christmas holiday in 1994 with Felix's mother, Dick Pountain and his partner Marion Hills, and of course a selection of girls including Marie-France, that the possibility of owning a property in the Caribbean came a step closer. Felix had booked up half of Young Island, an idyllic Caribbean resort just 200 yards from the southern shores of St Vincent, and, although he had previously contemplated buying houses as far apart as Spain and Bermuda, his interest in having a home in the sun had waned slightly. He was already turning over ideas for the Highfield development at the Old Manor and was busily buying up more land and houses on the Warwickshire estate. So when Marion Hills pointed out an interesting property being sold by David Bowie on the nearby island of Mustique, Felix's initial response was disinterest. He told Marie-France that he already had homes in New York, Connecticut, London and Warwickshire. Why would he want another? Knowing when not to push her luck, Marie-France said OK, but asked if they could go and have a look at the famous Basil's Bar on Mustique.

Three miles long and one-and-a-half miles wide, the island of Mustique boasts some of the most beautiful beaches in the world. The sand is fine and white, the waters turquoise and inviting, and when a cooling tropical breeze drifts through the trees and gently ruffles the spectacular wild flowers there is little to match its beauty. It is one of the few populated Caribbean islands without acres of electricity and telephone poles lining the horizon. Watching an evening sunset over Britannia Bay, with the accompanying sounds of tree frogs and crickets, is a spectacular experience and, although he knew little about it, as far as Felix was concerned, an expedition with a full entourage was always good for a laugh.

Thirty years after that first trip, sitting on a deck overlooking Britannia Bay with David Bowie's former home a few yards behind him, Felix remembered that visit very clearly.

'I knew the girls would be very keen to meet David Bowie, or look at his house anyway,' he recalled. 'So I said, "I'll go and look at it but I'm not buying it!"' After arranging a helicopter to take everyone over, which took a couple of trips with the girls 'dressed up to the nines', Felix arrived at what is today known as Mandalay. He recalled that everyone was really impressed.

'David Bowie wasn't there. Very sensibly he'd gone off to Barbados,' he said. The girls lounged around. 'And I thought it was really great. I liked the dark entrance when you walked in. And then you got this lovely sea view.'

He also liked Bowie's Balinese decor: 'He'd had a Balinese fairyland built. Very minimalist: nothing inside, bare light bulbs, no lighting in the garden. You were given a torch. It was a very different house from today.'

Although Felix remained insistent that he wouldn't buy the house, he came back again a few days later with Marie-France and decided he wanted it. It seemed his luck had followed him to Mustique as well for he bought it for what he later described as a very fair price.

'I didn't realise that Mustique was in one of its periodic slumps and that nobody had sold a house for a year and a half or something,' he said. 'And they were all getting really nervous.'

Managing director of the Mustique Company Brian Alexander later told him that what he had paid was a good price. According to Alexander, the value of property on the island would eventually rocket. He was right, and Felix was later to buy two more houses there.

At that time Felix knew very little about the island. 'I'd never looked it up, there was no internet,' he explained. He knew nothing about its aristocratic history or the fact that it was frequented by royals and the very rich. Mustique had never been on his radar and he suddenly found himself in a relatively alien world, which, although it had neighbours that included Mick Jagger and Bryan Adams, was a bit of a social bubble. As it happened, that bubble later suited Felix, who, prior to his time there, had spent many years escaping into quiet corners to be alone with either his books or his thoughts.

If it had been luck that brought Felix to Mustique, coincidentally it was another fluke that brought David Bowie to the island all those years before. Stranded when his boat broke down after visiting Mick Jagger and his wife Jerry Hall, he had gone for a walk and come across the plot of land on which he eventually built the property. With the help of architect Arne Hasselqvist and designer Robert J. Litwiller, he had built the house that Felix, as before with the Old Manor, had insisted on buying, complete with all fixtures and fittings.

Felix remembered that it was very different when he first saw it. There was no sundeck and the bar was 'the size of a broom cupboard'. With a hint of disgust he remembered it had 'inadequate staff quarters, to put it mildly. And that's being polite.' Felix would later cause quite a stir on the island when he decided to tackle the issue of staff accommodation. In the meantime, however, as chance would have it, despite warnings from what he called 'old codgers' down in Basil's Bar telling him he was crazy to waste his money, there was the equivalent of a property boom on the island and soon afterwards the value of his investment rose. It rose even more after he made enhancements that turned the house into a haven and a playground for his friends and colleagues.

David Bowie had taken a few things but agreed to leave most of the furniture in place.

'He took his piano,' recalled Felix. 'He asked me if I would not sell his towels and things like that as souvenirs. And I didn't, I never did.'

Joking that after his death his estate manager would probably sell them, he said he had kept them in a cupboard to honour Bowie's wishes but imagined that 30 years later they were unlikely to be in a good state.

It took him about 10 years to complete the refurbishment but Felix reeled off a list of the improvements like it was yesterday. 'Garages, staff quarters, kitchen, laundry, chef's kitchen, guest kitchen, office, study, media room, huge sun deck, games room, bamboo lounge, studio, put an extra bedroom down in the studio, writer's cottage, woodwork shop…' He stopped for breath and then added that he had even built a nursery to grow his own plants and vegetables for the house. 'The Mustique Company was trying to charge me like $10 a plant. Fuck that!' he declared.

Today the house has its original horseshoe shape, with the entrance through the closed end. Two fire-breathing dragons light the way on top of the gate leading to a pavilion entrance guarded by two mythical stone Indonesian warriors. Entry through the intricately carved pavilion is a breathtaking experience. The sight of the sea view below is over a series of pools, the first, landscaped and filled with koi carp, flows into another beautifully designed pool below. It seems as though the pools must end in a waterfall down to the sea. As Felix described it they appeared to drop 'Niagara-like into the waiting ocean below'. Around the edges he had placed more Indonesian stone carvings and an eclectic mix of sculpture and exotic plants. Below that a kidney-shaped infinity swimming pool, built to look like a natural pond, with pebbled floor, faces west out over Britannia Bay. It proved an idyllic place to watch stunning Caribbean sunsets and Felix would happily wade around the pool, picking leaves out of the water.

To the right of the entrance an open dining area appears to float over the pond. On balmy Caribbean evenings he would entertain friends around a marble table that seated up to 12 people. It had been shipped in from Bali. Strategically placed spotlights and hand-painted glass lamps that Felix had commissioned from an artist in New York bathed the area in a warm light.

Despite the length of time he spent on the house, it didn't take him long to integrate himself into the politics and management structure of the island. The first couple of years were a time of uncertainty, at least from the point of view of some of the other homeowners. Felix was still in the midst of an adventure with crack cocaine and, although he kept himself to himself for a while, he still brought an entourage of girls to the island, which caused a bit of a stir amongst some of the residents. Occasionally over-enthusiastically enjoying Felix's hospitality, some of the girls would loudly parade themselves around Basil's Bar or the Cotton Club beach, upsetting some of the more sedate homeowners.

Dick Pountain remembered one occasion when Felix took him and Marion Hills on a boat trip to a nearby island with some of the girls in tow.

'He was hanging out with a pretty rough bunch of hookers, most of whom haven't stayed on,' remembered Dick. They arrived at a jetty and trooped off for a pizza to the restaurant of a nearby hotel, where a snooty waiter made it very clear that they were unwelcome. 'All of these girls had been snorting coke and drinking rum the whole journey across,' said Dick. And one of them 'just went ballistic and started jumping up and down and chattering like a monkey. She was wearing a mini-skirt that barely covered her ass, and swearing torrents in sort of Korean and New York slang. The waiter just kind of fled for his life. We did actually get the pizzas brought down to the boat on plates covered in cooking foil.'

Speaking in 1998, before Felix had really made an impact on the island, the local doctor, Michael Bunbury, explained that he had met Felix early on and had taken to him straightaway. Often he would visit him for an evening of good conversation over a few whiskeys, and he found Felix's intellect remarkable. He said he was often confounded by his knowledge of medicine. Some people 'had preconceived ideas about Felix. They weren't happy that I was up there all the time,' he recalled. Explaining that Felix's behaviour rubbed a lot of people up the wrong way, he said that, even though they hadn't met him, 'there were an awful lot of people thinking that he was just a nasty piece of work.'

Perhaps not able to understand what people found unacceptable, Felix was bemused by their reaction to his travelling harem and often claimed they were not being that outrageous. He put their angry response down to snobbery. As Michael explained, it wasn't Felix who was behaving badly but it was he who was held responsible.

'It was the girls making all the noise, he was actually in the background somewhere.'

In time things changed and, as was his habit, Felix soon became an expert on the island's history. He also quickly developed his own philosophy and opinions on what was right and wrong about those who had helped create it and those who had come to live there. He divided Mustique's history into three categories: the early or pioneering years, the intermediate years and the later years, and placed himself in the intermediate category. The early years, he said, were when Colin Tennant, or Lord Glenconner, was said to have bought the island for £45,000 and began building houses on it.

'Prior to that there wasn't even a jetty,' Felix explained. 'You had to get into the water up to your dick. Mosquitoes so bad that you had to get into the water for three hours every evening or you die! No fresh water, no proper food. People were living on fucking spam!'

By the time Felix arrived on the island, Colin Tennant had helped to develop its reputation for exclusivity by giving Princess Margaret a wedding present of a plot of land on which to build a holiday retreat. Architect Arne Hasselqvist had also begun to build the kind of houses that attracted those with deep pockets and a wish for privacy. Although Colin Tennant eventually relocated to St Lucia, Felix did have some dealings with him when purchasing another plot of land after he had renamed David Bowie's house 'Mandalay'.

'By the time I arrived there were about 40 or 50 houses here already,' he recalled. He claimed that he was the last man to negotiate with Tennant, whom he said referred to him as a 'pleb', although Felix claimed he had called him a 'well-mannered' pleb – with a sense of humour. Felix had little time for Tennant and he thought the feeling was probably mutual.

Although Colin Tennant still owned some plots of land, the island had been sold to the homeowners when he left, and one of Felix's first encounters with the Mustique Company, the organisation responsible for the running of the island, was when he met Brian Alexander. Explaining how the company worked, Brian described it as 'part local town council, part nanny and headmaster, and part company'. They had annual general meetings, a memorandum and articles of association and directors elected for up to two years.

In time Felix was to take his place on the board, but as a new homeowner he had decided that it would be nice to have somewhere to land a helicopter so that he and his guests wouldn't have to take the five-minute drive to the airport.

Felix remembered the encounter well – 'He said of course I could have a helipad.' Brian had brought with him a three-dimensional map of the island and of the area around Felix's property. He pointed out two or three places where Felix could build a small helipad.

'You can build as many helipads as you like,' he told him. After a practised pause he added, 'But you can't land a helicopter on them.'

After his initial excitement, Felix was ready to explode but soon fully understood Brian's reasoning. He explained that if they allowed helicopters on the island the place would be crawling with them and the noise alone would create havoc, let alone cause resentment at the loss of privacy to homeowners. It was permitted for helicopters to land at the small airstrip but nowhere else. This was an explanation that Felix completely took on board and a few years later, when a suggestion was made to extend the small airstrip to allow private jets to land on the island, he was one of the most vocal opponents. Using his promotional expertise he led a campaign against the initiative, making up posters, flyers and even T-shirts proclaiming, 'No JFK on Mustique'. He remembered that some homeowners were appalled but he knew that the noise of private jets would damage the attraction of the island.

Brian, who would later speak at Felix's funeral, saw many good qualities in him and was impressed by his straight talk. 'He's straight in your face and then it's over,' he remembered. 'I think that's a very admirable quality. He doesn't mind confrontation at all, it's one of his strengths.'

As the island was inhabited by some very powerful people, Felix's brashness, lack of fear and keenness to make things better meant that he was able to bring his will to bear when it was necessary.

'You're getting a huge amount of management expertise for free,' said Brian. There were times when he relied on Felix to bring some balance to situations. Alluding to the fact that many successful people got what they wanted through rough treatment and bullying of those around them, Brian pointed out that there were times when the board or a committee would get some strong characters.

'And I'd always try to get someone like Felix on as a counter wave,' he recalled. 'You get the sort of alpha males and you need the Felix alpha male to balance that.'

Felix's influence came in many ways. On one occasion, after arriving at the airport, he noticed a little pile of books in the corner of one of the small wooden buildings. When he asked what they were for, he was told that this was the island's library. He was naturally incredulous.

'There were more books in my toilet!' he said later.

It didn't take him long to decide what to do and by 1997 the building of the Mustique Community Library, donated, instigated and overseen by Felix Dennis, was underway. To ensure it was properly maintained and manned, he arranged for a librarian's cottage to be built next door and insisted that anyone who came to visit him brought a book for the library. It was a classic Felix Dennis gesture that inevitably drew criticism. There were those who felt that he had spent an exorbitant amount of money on a library. Why couldn't he have spent that same money on something more useful for the island's residents? Couldn't he, for example, have bought everyone a refrigerator? Wouldn't a modern appliance have been more practical and useful? Perhaps it would have, but Bud Fisher, who had lived on the island before Felix's arrival and became his first manager at Mandalay, summed up both his and Felix's thoughts on the subject.

'I think it's a far more positive gesture in the long run,' he said. 'If you have a refrigerator, it changes your lunch.' But a library, he explained, could change lives.

In his first years there, Felix also arranged for a huge firework display to entertain everyone on the island and ensured that the event happened as early as possible so the children could enjoy it too. He then organised another memorable experience for the island's children: he planned and paid for a student exchange with some primary schoolchildren from the Isle of Eigg, a small island off the east coast of Scotland. Eigg had a tiny population, and an exchange with children from an island in the Caribbean was a unique idea, to say the least. Felix had pointed out to Bud Fisher that, on finishing primary school, the children on Mustique had to leave the island for further education and that it was the same for those from the Isle of Eigg. He wanted to give them a chance to experience something completely different.

Bud, whose wife Patsy helped organise the trip, remembered how he and Felix went down to the school one day as all the children were preparing for their trip. Patsy had brought a map and was giving them a briefing. Inevitably, Felix took over and chatted to all the children about what they would see. He had arranged for them to go to London and visit Madame Tussauds, go to the Zoo and other attractions. Wide-eyed and excited, they were all clutching luggage bags that had been specially inscribed and supplied by Felix.

'And the children sat there,' remembered Bud. 'And one little boy put up his hand and said, "Do we get to keep the suitcases?"' The plan had been to keep the suitcases and pass them on to the next group if the exchange carried on each year, but as Bud recalled, 'Felix just folded right there and looked into this little boy's eyes and said, "Yes, you can keep the cases."'

Arriving at Eigg, the children participated in classes with the locals and described their different cultural backgrounds, especially in music and dance. They attended the local regatta and watched a yacht race known as the Eigg and Spoon race. They marvelled at the tug of war and also attended a local ceilidh. However, one of the most memorable things for the children on both sides was the difference in the weather. One little boy from Mustique was wide-eyed on discovering that the rain on Eigg was cold, and as Bud recalled, so too was his teacher.

So even before Felix had first taken a seat on the board of the Mustique Company, he had made quite an impact. Having rebuilt his own staff quarters, he grumbled about the state of the accommodation that local construction workers were living in. Brian Alexander explained later that as properties were often scheduled to be completed before the Christmas holiday there were times when between 350 and 500 workers were based on the island.

'The problem was that the numbers were changing all the time,' remembered Brian. 'The construction companies were responsible for their housing and sometimes accommodation was provided on each building site. As you can imagine this accommodation was sub-standard.'

Although Felix was not on the board at the time, Brian recalled that he was very much a driving force to help change the workers' conditions. Brian explained how they dealt with the problem.

'We capped the numbers at 350,' he said, 'and decided the company would build a better standard of house in one location and rent these houses to the construction companies for their employees.' In order to ensure that the area was properly managed and the properties kept in good condition for the workers, the Mustique Company nominated Felix 'as the sort of camp commander or Quartermaster', as Brian called it.

'Felix was, as you can imagine, a powerful driving force in making it happen quickly and correctly.' It was his job to set a standard of care in employment, which Brian explained was, at the time, 'the best in St Vincent and the Grenadines'.

Not everything was quite so serious on the island or indeed at Mandalay. After quitting his crack cocaine habit, Felix entertained, opening his house up to guests, as well as inviting other homeowners and their guests to enjoy his hospitality. As always, he was more at ease when the party was at his house and, as the refurbishment gradually finished, his gatherings would take place in different parts of the house. The bar that was once the size of a broom cupboard became the Bamboo Lounge and grew big enough to comfortably accommodate a coach-load of people. There were occasional parties that made Felix chuckle, such as the time when a large group of beautiful young women arrived. Tickled that he had attracted such a glamorous audience, he began to regale them with tales of his youth, only to find them all turning away when Robbie Williams appeared. Although Felix realised that he wasn't the main attraction, he took solace in the fact that Robbie took more notice of him than the girls.

'He was a nice lad,' Felix said later.

On another occasion, when a large group gathered in his downstairs games room, complete with bar, pinball machines and a fully equipped sound stage, he was bemused when an actor best known for a role as James Bond asked him whether the door would lock.

'Of course it does,' replied Felix. The actor insisted he lock the door and then cadged a cigarette from him. Felix soon realised that his guest was having a sly fag.

'Let me get this right,' said Felix. 'I've got 007 in my games room and he's frightened that his wife is going to find out he's smoking?'

This was indeed the case, nodded Bond. Felix howled with laughter as he related the story, especially when he explained that his guest then asked him if he had any mints.

'You get that kind of amusing idiocy in Mustique,' sighed Felix.

With unusually self-deprecating tones he related a story about another occasion in his games room that embarrassed him slightly. A fairly large group had gathered and were in party mood and his staff were under pressure to serve drinks to everyone, so he was helping out.

'We'd got about 30 people down there,' he said.

He noticed one girl sitting alone, feeding a little baby. Felix decided to introduce himself and described the exchange.

'I sat down with her and said, "So do you like Mustique?" "Yeah." "Having a good time?" "Yeah, fine…" "What are you doing, my dear?" She went, "I'm Kate Moss."'

A little embarrassed that he hadn't recognised her, he looked to the man standing next to him, who turned out to be Jefferson Hack, Kate's then boyfriend and father of the child.

'You aren't very good, are you, Felix?' he said to him. Laughing, he went on, 'You're not much fucking good in company, you didn't ought to be let out! Who did you think it was?'

Burying himself even deeper into whatever hole he had just dug, Felix replied that he thought she was somebody's wet nurse. Howling with laughter as he remembered the story, he said, 'I must have been having a brainstorm – there haven't been any wet nurses in the Western world for the last 25 years!'

Another humbling event Felix liked to relate was how he bumped into Lou Reed walking down a track to a nearby beach. Reed recognised him from one of the books left lying around in the house he was staying in. Felix recalled Reed's first comment. 'You're that guy who writes poetry,' he said to Felix. 'Why don't you put some of it to music? Who wants to fucking read poetry?'

One of the many things that Felix loved about Mustique was the annual Blues Festival, which was held at Basil's Bar at the end of January. An institution on the island and the first port of call for anyone wanting to enjoy a rum cocktail on the waterfront, the bar became a playground for party-loving Princess Margaret and her friends in the sixties. Basil Charles was later nicknamed the King of Mustique as he hosted countless celebrities and became associated with the high life after setting up home with the late Viscountess Royston. He received an OBE in 2005 for his work on underprivileged children's education with the Basil Charles Educational Foundation. The Blues Festival became a vehicle to promote the charity and helped attract sponsors and contributors.

The festival not only gave Felix an opportunity to try to upstage his neighbour Mick Jagger, but it also provided him with an excuse to talk about his favourite musical subject with some of the best blues musicians around, and all in the comfort of his own backyard. The festival itself began thanks to an old friend of Felix's, Dana Gillespie, who first met him back in the early seventies at his Wandsworth Bridge Road flat in London.

Dana was a London girl who started her singing career on the folk circuit in 1964. And although her career spanned various musical genres and included film success and appearances on stage in shows as diverse as *Tommy* and *Jesus Christ Superstar*, she said that blues was her first musical love. Sitting in Felix's study at Mandalay after another successful opening night at Basil's Bar in January 2014, she explained that she had first come to Mustique 35 years before with her stepfather. She had fallen in love with the island and recalled that, when she had first started visiting, there were only a handful of houses. She became friendly with Basil and remembered how one evening in 1994, when most of the customers had gone home, she had picked up the microphone and started singing.

'I started singing some blues,' she recalled. 'And Basil, who always wears a kaftan, was up on the table, dancing. In the end I'd literally sung for about an hour and a half.'

Sitting down afterwards, she turned to Basil and said they should start a blues festival. She said, 'If you get a piano, I'll get some musicians and the only way it's going to work is if it's free.'

The following year, Basil found a piano and Dana brought her musicians and a new festival was born.

Dana recalled that it was because of a dinner table discussion that Felix first got involved.

'We did about two years and Felix didn't even put in an appearance,' she said. 'My mother used to come to Mustique with me and one time my mother was having dinner with Felix's mother, and somehow the blues got mentioned.' Dana asked, and Felix obliged. 'He'll be the first to say he's not the greatest singer in the world,' she laughed, 'but he's such a front presence. He's just like a dynamo on stage.' Explaining that there were times when Felix might do two or three songs, Dana remembered that on one occasion he followed Mick Jagger.

'He was the only one that didn't mind that Jagger was his opening act,' she said. Arriving on stage after Mick's powerful performance, Felix thanked him for performing in aid of the children of St Vincent and the Grenadines. He went on to explain that just before Mick went on stage he had asked him to do him a real favour.

'Would you warm the bastards up for me?' said Felix.

Wearing beige chinos and a blue Hawaiian-style shirt, he then launched into a raucous version of Willie Dixon's 'Wang Dang Doodle', followed by his old favourite, 'Johnny B. Goode'. Felix played air guitar, air piano and generally played the buffoon on stage to the delight and bemusement of the audience, most of whom had no idea who he was.

Dana remembered that there were occasional rehearsals on the stage in Felix's music and games room, which was equipped with guitars, amps, drums and a range of instruments that included an electric piano, which she would often borrow for gigs. She recalled that Felix loved the rehearsals.

'He's colourful, he's joyous and in a weird way he's full of love.' Not the first to use a cliché when describing Felix, she added, 'He's an enigma and, when they made him, they broke the mould, simple as that.'

The festival produced a CD each year and the proceeds were donated to the charity. Although Felix featured on most of them, he also produced his own CD, *Blues in Paradise*, in 2014, which featured 14 live tracks from 1999 to 2013. As well as featuring a couple of Felix's poems, the songs recorded were backed by a range of superb blues musicians, along with additional vocals from Dana. In an introduction to the CD, Felix wrote that, when he bought his first property there, Mustique was then 'a byword for celebrities, artists, entrepreneurs and royalty behaving badly in one of the most beautiful environments in the world. Sounded like my kind of town!' In time, it did become his kind of town but not necessarily just for bad behaviour. It became a haven in which he was to write poetry, write books and orchestrate philanthropic activities. He would even dress up as an elf to join Basil Charles on Christmas Day, giving out gifts to the local children.

There were times when even the beauty of Mustique couldn't suppress the natural frustration that would build up inside Felix, though. Eric Shaw, a lawyer who had worked for the Mustique Company since the eighties and also spent time as chairman of the company, often stayed with him. In fact, when Eric married his wife Caroline, Felix flew over to New York to be the best man at their wedding, and even arranged for the London taxi cab that he used as a company vehicle in New York to take them to City Hall. As a wedding gift he gave them an all-expenses-paid holiday for 14 people in Shogun, another Mustique property that he bought in 2006. Eric saw how sometimes Felix would find life on the island too much.

'He'd spend nearly four or five months on the island and become rather impossible,' he recalled. 'He would start to complain about construction noises or if someone was speeding he would phone security to try to get them arrested. By about four or five months he would be ready to either leave, or blow up the island.'

Brian Alexander remembered one occasion when Felix spent three months on the island and began to go what he described as 'a bit nuts'. He would ring up complaining about the least little thing and Brian eventually suggested he go back to England 'for a rest'. He later described Felix as suffering from 'island fever'.

It seemed ironic to some that anyone would need to go from a Caribbean island paradise to England for a rest, but many residents understood the feeling of claustrophobia and few of the homeowners spent the entire year there. They preferred to rent out their properties through the Mustique Company. However, in time, Mustique became Felix's true second home. The London address in Kingly Street became his private office and his base for business, with his private flat on the top floor. The Old Manor in Dorsington had become his country retreat. There, he could entertain friends and colleagues in Highfield, take walks amongst his Garden of Heroes & Villains and enjoy the acres of land on which he would plant trees and build a forest. But island life made a place in his heart, and in time Mustique represented a sizeable percentage of the world he built around him after the early days of his latch-key youth in London's Surbiton.

CHAPTER 24

FIERY DELICACY

By the time Felix had begun to make an impact on the island of Mustique, he was already well beyond the description of over-achiever. Interviewed for the *Marshwood Vale* magazine in 2013, he admitted that perhaps his excesses with cocaine had given him an edge because he stayed awake longer than most of those around him, but he was careful not to recommend that to anyone else. He did take every opportunity to tell any journalist the story of his lost decade and the $100 million that he said he had wasted during that period, but, although he could at times give the impression of being a little melodramatic, he always tried to use it as a cautionary tale.

Outside of the time he spent smoking crack cocaine, buying property, building houses, developing an utterly unique garden and running his business, he also found time to take his mother to the Buckingham Palace Garden Party and open his own garden to the public, eventually raising tens of thousands of pounds for charity. In 1998 he threw a party after the open gardens event at which American singer Loudon Wainwright III was the main guest. An enormous fan of Wainwright, Felix was bemused by how few people in the audience were aware of him but took great delight in sharing a raucous version of the classic American road song 'Route 66' with him.

Having initially offered to buy Miranda's, the gentlemen's club below his office in Kingly Street, in 1988 and been unsuccessful, Felix managed to take a controlling interest in it in 1996. He was thrilled to bring friends and colleagues to the club to show off his investment.

On one occasion he took his old friend Alan Marcuson there after they had enjoyed an enormous Japanese meal. Editor of *Friends* magazine, Alan had been part of the underground press during the late sixties and early seventies and eventually became a successful and well-respected antique carpet and textile dealer.

Speaking of his visit to Miranda's, he said, 'I'd never been into a joint like that in my entire life. They had big mirrors on the wall and naked girls on tables. They were cleaning the mirrors with their bodies.'

Felix joked with him that he would make £12 out of every punter in the club and that this would be his pension scheme. Much as he enjoyed his interest in the club, he sold the majority of his stake in it in 2006, preferring to fund his pension from other sources.

Throughout the nineties he also embarked on an association with the Labour Party, meeting with Tony Blair, whom he said he admired, and Peter Mandelson, whom he described as a 'loathsome creep'. However, that didn't deter him from supporting the party and he donated more than £1 million. He was offered a knighthood but turned it down, requesting that it be given to someone else, and he later confided that he had also turned down a place in the House of Lords.

Whatever government was in power at the time he made a point of paying his taxes and proudly showed off copies of the cheques that he had sent to the Inland Revenue. Ian Leggett did a little analytical number crunching in 2014 and concluded that, in the last 20 years of his life, Felix had employed, in trading companies and privately, some 780 members of staff with a total salary bill in excess of £300 million. He estimated that, in that last 20 years alone, the level of employment and income taxes had been in excess of £258 million. It was quite a positive impact on the British economy, especially for someone once described as not very intelligent by an Old Bailey judge.

There was one occasion regarding the Inland Revenue that caused as much mirth as it did anger at the time. After receiving a tax demand in December 1996 for nearly £8 million, Felix delivered the cheque to the local tax office in Stratford-upon-Avon. As the due date was a Sunday, when the office was closed, he delivered it on the Monday morning. The staff were delighted and, according to one local paper, they crowded around and applauded. A photograph was taken of the cheque and blown up to commemorate the occasion.

However, a few days later, the pleasantries and general bonhomie was forgotten when head office decided to issue a fine for late payment. Felix was duly presented with a bill for £1,342.81 on top of his nearly £8 million. He was furious. Stomping around his kitchen in the Old Manor, he yelled expletives at the Inland Revenue as he instructed his advisers, both accountants and solicitors, to fight the demand. Local and national newspapers picked up the story and had a field day. He was said to have been prepared to go to prison rather than pay and claimed the Revenue were trying to screw the last drop of blood from a stone. Jessica Gorst-Williams in the *Daily Telegraph* likened the whole episode to a pantomime farce, while the *Black Country Evening Mail* called it a fiasco, describing Felix as a 'Midland millionaire'. In the end he had to pay the bill but the publicity was the source of some amusement and Christmas spent in Mustique was enough to help him overcome any pain.

There were many highlights for him to look back on in the nineties but there were also moments of high emotion and of great sadness too.

He and Marie-France travelled by helicopter to visit his old friend, the cartoonist Ed Barker, before he died in Gillingham in 1997. A year later, his lawyer, Michael Nixon, who had become his right-hand man in dealings going back to his early days in Kingly Street and whom Felix had held in such high regard, died in London. Felix and Marie-France had urged his chauffeur Lloyd to forget all speed limits to get them to Michael's bedside in time to say goodbye. On arrival at the hospital, Felix tried to help Michael to the bathroom but they both fell to the floor. He would later relate the story of how they appeared to be wrestling amongst saline drips and bedclothes.

The following year, his old friend and mentor at *Oz* magazine, Jon Goodchild, died of cancer in California while finishing the design for a book that Felix had commissioned. The book, *Silva: The Tree in Britain* by Archie Miles, was described as the ultimate book on British trees, their history and uses. It was dedicated to the memory of Jon Goodchild and it was in the preface to this book that Felix described his encounter with the pyramid hornbeams of London's Golden Square. He wrote: 'Nothing in the world gives me greater pleasure than to lay hands on the bole of a young sapling planted a few years back, imagining in my mind's eye the day it will reach its maturity, its roots nourishing the earth, its leaves shading the ground, its fruits feeding wild life of all kinds and its beauty freezing the heart of humans yet to be born.'

Losing people that he cared so much about, all of whom had played an important role in his life, was a blow that may well have helped Felix in his efforts to clear the demons from his life. But another incident that contributed to him staying straight also happened at the end of the nineties. Ex-employee and old friend Mark Williams had been found guilty of money laundering and sent to jail in America. He had been caught transporting a large sum of money for his then girlfriend and, despite efforts from Felix and others, it looked as though he was likely to be imprisoned in both the UK and the US. Felix's support was never in question and he immediately paid whatever expenses he could, as well as all legal fees. When Mark was released and then sent to jail in the UK for the same offence, Felix visited him and again stood by him to help in any way he could. Some of those close to Mark believed it had been a cautionary tale for Felix, a case of 'it could have been me'.

'It was incredible, his loyalty,' recalled Williams afterwards. 'I've never come across that loyalty in anyone before.'

He later came back to work on a couple of projects for Dennis Publishing and also produced for Felix a definitive history of the company's activities from 1971 to 2012.

While loyalty to friends and colleagues was a huge part of Felix's character, he had long been making an impression on those within the business community. And even though his biggest success in America was later to realise $240 million, his counsel and advice were freely offered, whether required or not. Chris Anderson, the man who founded Future

Publishing around the time Felix was moving from *MacUser* to Mac Warehouse, remembered meeting Felix at a time when Ziff Davis was threatening the European market.

Speaking in 1998, he remembered Felix's extraordinary energy, saying, 'Felix and I had dinner. In his usual extraordinary table-thumping manner he proclaimed to me how ruthless and evil, yet skilful the Ziff Davis empire was, and how the whole of Britain should take up arms to fight the enemy and what he was doing.'

Chris recalled having a couple of 'great, great dinners with him' when he would sit 'agog' at the level of energy coming from the other side of the table.

'Felix has just a unique way of anyone I have met of really, really, really getting energised about stuff, and driving home his point with the most colourful language and ideas and force that you can imagine. Fortunately he is, contrary to what the judge in the *Oz* trial said, actually very smart.' He went on to describe Felix's canniness as a 'combination of reading the situation right, reading people right and then hammering through like a bull in a china shop.'

Later becoming the owner of the very popular website TED Talks, Chris said that he and Felix couldn't have been more different in character and lifestyle. However, they faced some of the same challenges and hit it off on a few occasions really well.

'I'm in awe of his combination of lifestyle approach and perhaps management style and yet his evident generosity,' he said. 'He is just an extraordinary, extraordinary man.'

His feelings towards Felix were thus despite the fact that Felix at one point took him to court in a battle over the name of a magazine.

'It was clear that *Computer Shopper* was doing really well,' Chris remembered, 'and we wanted to have a buyers' guide for the Omega.' They planned to launch a magazine called *Omega Shopper* and, when Felix found out, he begged Chris not to launch using that name.

'I'll pay £100,000 into your favourite charity to not go ahead with this name,' he told Chris, who replied that there was no way Felix could control the use of the name 'Shopper' as much as he could control the word 'practical' or 'user' – 'or any other funny little words that go into magazine titles,' he said. They did eventually go to court and Felix lost but there were no hard feelings.

'It was entertaining to see him in action and he got very, very worked up about it. But once it was done, it was a done deal. Clearly the launch of our little title made not one jot of difference to the success of *Computer Shopper* in the long term. Rather a storm in a tea cup.'

Chris maintained that there was 'no one remotely like him in the UK'.

Chris Anderson was also partly responsible for an anecdote that was enjoyed by many who knew Felix well. One of his very successful publishers, Kevin Cox, who had launched *Computer Shopper*, had decided to move on from Dennis Publishing and take a job with Chris's firm, Future Publishing in Bath, Somerset. Future were getting serious about publishing games magazines and it was an area where Kevin's expertise would have been very useful to them. However, Felix was not noted for coping well with employees leaving to join the competition, especially good ones. He would always say that if anyone was to leave, even to set up their own business, he would wish them well and support them. He based this on the reasoning that, if they didn't succeed, they might come back to the fold and work even harder.

Ensconced in America when he heard that Kevin was leaving, he quickly put a plan in place to try to tempt him back. Alistair Ramsay, who was soon to become Dennis Publishing's third managing director, remembered that Felix did his bear with a sore paw routine, shouting to whoever would listen in London that Kevin must be put on a plane to America immediately.

'Put him on a plane to New York,' barked Felix. 'We'll get a limo to pick him up. No, better still, we'll get a helicopter to collect him. We'll make sure that he's really wowed by the steps we are prepared to take to keep him.'

Before he could decide which cardigan to jam into a suitcase, Kevin was whisked off to New York, where Felix decided to take him out to a Korean restaurant. In expansive mood and sporting his most expensive watch, Felix sat across the table and began extolling the virtues of his publishing life – how wonderful New York was, and what a great future the company had.

When the waiter brought a small plate of appetisers, Felix, with a worldly air, said to Kevin, 'Try these, they are wonderful – but hot. Be careful with them.' As they both gingerly nibbled on what Felix had insisted was an oriental delicacy, it became increasingly clear that they were indeed very hot, and although neither man admitted it to the other they were also disgusting. Felix called for cold beer and he and Kevin gratefully gulped down pints of soothing lager onto scorched throats until the waiter returned with a further tray of delights. However, before putting them on the table he took out a match and set light to what was left of the 'delicacy' that Felix and Kevin had been nibbling.

It turned out to be tiny pieces of Twiglet-shaped charcoal. Not another word was said on the subject, but the story got out and, as such stories do, it took on a life of its own. A few years later when Roger Munford coincidentally dined with Felix in the same restaurant, the waiter brought out a small dish of charcoal after they had sat down. Roger kept his mouth shut, but the look on his face must have alerted Felix as he simply said, 'Yes, Roger, it's true, now let's move on.'

In the end the whole episode didn't change Kevin's mind and he went off to spend many happy years working for Future Publishing, but the story was a good indicator of two of the things that many people could attest to about Felix Dennis. One was his determination to keep good employees and the other was his total lack of interest in food. Much as he had claimed he could understand sushi menus and order any of a dozen types of pasta in New York, his enjoyment of food and restaurants was limited to the kudos gained from being somewhere exclusive or exotic, rather than from any enjoyment or interest in the food itself or even the dining experience.

As Dick Pountain later pointed out, Felix didn't like to go to a restaurant where the chef was more famous than he was.

CHAPTER 25

BEER TRUCK IN THE DESERT

Felix's determination to hold onto what he later referred to as 'talent' would become one of the attributes of which he was proud. It also proved on many occasions to be one of the reasons for his many successes. When another top-level executive from Dennis Publishing UK, Stephen Colvin, was courted by a major publisher in the US, Felix swept into action to try to keep him on board. A small, wiry Belfast man, Colvin thinks fast, talks fast and pulls few punches.

The story that Felix liked to relate was how he had brought Stephen out to his cottage in Connecticut and taken him out on the lake in his boat. He didn't have a plan as to what to offer him until that moment when he had switched off the engine on the boat and they were quietly drifting along the water. Stephen explained that he really wanted to live and work abroad for a while and he had been offered a job on the West Coast as vice president of a division within a competitor's publishing empire. Felix simply said, 'Wouldn't you rather be the president?' To which Stephen replied that there was nothing in the US company to be president of. The business at the time, as far as he could see, didn't have much going on and there was no prospect of anything else happening. Felix then suggested Stephen get involved in *Blender*, an interactive CD-ROM, which at the time was looking like it had huge potential, although it was later overtaken by the internet. Mac and Micro Warehouse had taken Felix's eye away from magazines in the US and the only real publishing was being done in the UK office, which was not somewhere that Stephen felt he could progress.

At this point Felix had to think even faster and said, 'So, why don't you find new products and launch them?'

Stephen remembered that, to close the deal, Felix threw in another offer. 'And then he said, "As part of the deal you can use this cottage at weekends when I'm not there."'

It was a huge temptation.

'He had me,' said Stephen. 'He threw that big carrot in and it was obvious that was what was going to close me.'

What Stephen remembered best was the fact that the whole meeting took place, not at a Four Seasons Hotel or a fancy restaurant, but on a boat in the middle of a lake in Connecticut.

'I was amazed,' he said. 'That was a very special moment, really. And I went, "And what was the job again?" That was special.'

It was from this conversation, with Felix winging it as best he could, that the framework from which to launch *Maxim* US was created and it was to become one of the great successes, making Felix and his partners hundreds of millions of dollars.

Alistair Ramsay was well placed to remember how *Maxim* came about. Launched in May 1995, the original idea to do a 'lads' mag' had been presented by two music journalists, Matt Snow and Lloyd Bradley. At the time, according to Alistair, the only other magazines serving the men's market were very much targeted at urbanites. He described them as aimed at a fashion-conscious, London-centric audience. Snow and Bradley believed there was a market for what Alistair later described as 'a normal type of magazine for men that was not so pretentious or so fashion-oriented'. The idea gelled with Felix's thoughts also, but as Alistair explained they didn't just leap in and launch a new magazine straightaway.

'We'd be silly to just go and launch,' he told Felix. 'Why don't we do something we haven't done before? Let's pretend we are a real company and let's actually do some research.'

Felix agreed and they set Snow and Bradley the task of producing a dummy issue. This took some time and investment.

'In the meantime,' remembered Alistair, 'we also immersed ourselves in looking at the men's market in general.'

However, when the dummy pages were produced and sent off to research and focus groups, the response was that it wasn't going to work. The articles were too long and, as Alistair recalled, popular wisdom at the time suggested that the people they wanted to reach had shorter attention spans and didn't want to read in-depth, six-page articles. The research they were doing was coincidentally saying exactly what Jolyon Connell was at the same time thinking about *The Week*. To further confirm their findings, another men's magazine, *Loaded*, had been launched by IPC and, as Alistair explained, 'Men were fed up with being politically correct, and it had humour, it had crumpet and it had lager.' With both the research and the experience of an already launched competitor proving that the original idea wasn't going to work, Felix and Alistair decided to produce a very different magazine. Describing their thoughts afterwards, Alistair explained that the magazines on the market at the time were on the one hand like the *Sun* and the *Mirror* and, on the other, like *The Times* and the *Telegraph*, and what Dennis Publishing tried to do was be like a newspaper in between the two. 'We tried to be the *Daily Mail*, the mid-market mag,' he said.

One evening after work in the London office, Felix took various members of staff down to the nearby Ship Inn for a brainstorming session to come up with a name for a new lads'-style magazine, and, after worthy suggestions such as *Gotcha*, *Men's Life* and even *Felix* were discounted, a decision was taken to use the name *Maxim*. It had all the ingredients a 'lads' mag' should have: it would translate easily into different languages when the time came to license it, and it even had an X in the middle that could hint at content that might attract red-blooded males.

Although one would expect that, with a formula based on 'beer, babes, gadgets and fashion', *Maxim* would be best launched by a man with an interest in just those subjects, this wasn't the case. What was to surprise a few people and prove to be a stroke of genius was that the first editor-in-chief chosen to launch the title was female.

From a background as editor of *Cook's Weekly* and *New Woman*, Gill Hudson certainly had editorial experience, but would she really be the right person to launch something so potentially macho? Talking in 1999 about her experience with Felix Dennis throughout the launch and beyond, she admitted that at first she had baulked at the thought of editing a 'lads' mag'. When the idea was initially pitched to her, she said that if she were to launch such a magazine it would be very different to what was already on the market. She explained what she had in mind and was surprised to discover 'that was exactly what they wanted'.

She remembered that it was a new direction for Dennis Publishing and she thought 'most of the Dennis board didn't want to do it, they thought it was too risky. But Felix did.' She had already accepted the job before meeting Felix and, apart from the engine-like shaking of his leg, the one thing she took away from the meeting was that she didn't really get a word into the conversation. In fact, it wasn't what one could call a conversation. It was a fairly typical Felix interview, where he made his judgement based on how the other party dealt with his monologue.

Gill was given 14 weeks to get the magazine launched and Felix didn't interfere. In fact, the next thing she heard from him was after the first issue had arrived on his desk. She got a message saying, 'Felix called, call him immediately.' It sounded ominous so she steeled herself and dialled his number.

'So I rang him back and thought, "Just be bold."' She asked him what he thought. 'And he just said, "I'm coming over," and slammed the phone down!'

Subtlety in interpersonal communication was not Felix's strong point and, hearing his gruff tone, Gill spent the next few hours assuming the worst. She even contemplated her future and thought about clearing her desk. It was eight hours before Felix made an appearance, and it was only thanks to a conversation with his secretary that she discovered that in fact he had loved it.

'He's sending copies out to all his friends,' she was told.

For Gill it was a lesson in the incomprehensible way that Felix Dennis handled employee relations. He had resolved to make her sweat, she decided, 'because Felix's worst nightmare is that people get complacent'.

She explained that he could be capable of 'incredible kindness and thoughtfulness', sending crates of champagne and saying, 'brilliant issue', but 'he cannot stand complacency or the fact that people are just sitting around, coasting'.

As an introduction to the wily ways of Felix Dennis, it was a hard lesson.

'It was such a mismatch of expectations and attitude that it nearly finished me off,' she admitted. 'It took about a year off my life!' Thankfully, *Maxim* UK was a huge success. 'The whole thing just exploded in a way no one expected,' she recalled. 'No one would ever have known that we would have sold 350,000 copies.'

In fact, she remembered doing a dance around the office when they passed the 100,000 mark.

Although the credit for the success of any one magazine could rarely be given to Felix alone, Gill was one of those who saw first-hand some of the aspects of Felix's personality that made him remarkable.

'He is very brave,' she said. 'I'm not sure the company is as brave as he is.' She pointed out that Felix had some great ideas, 'But you have got to have balls to carry them through.'

After *Maxim*, her career included many years as editor of one of the largest-selling magazines in the UK, *Radio Times*, after which she headed up *Reader's Digest*. Her experience at Dennis Publishing was hugely valuable and later Felix was to applaud her achievements at *Maxim*. Even though he would become known for putting the credit squarely at the feet of the 'talent' that he hired, she summed up what many realised over the years, saying, 'Felix is a great tribute to what you can do on your own.' What had already become legend was the fact that whatever it was that he was doing, whether alone or around a boardroom table, his inspiration built platforms for an enormous number of successful careers.

The next stage in the *Maxim* story was to include Stephen Colvin, who had accepted Felix's offer to run the US operation. However, launching *Maxim* in America was a huge gamble, especially as it went against all the received wisdom of consultants, industry experts and focus groups. Felix was already seeing his investment and effort in Mac Warehouse turn over millions of dollars and he was relying on Stephen to open up the market for *Maxim* in America. However, as Stephen later recalled, they were advised that it simply couldn't work in America.

'There was a lot of wariness,' he admitted. 'It was a big investment, big risk. If it didn't work, then obviously there was a lot of money at risk.'

In the end, after another session with consultants advising them not to go ahead, Felix and Stephen went for a drink and decided to go with their gut. In fact, as it transpired later, both Bob Bartner and Peter Godfrey put up the cash while Felix invested his American company's resources, which, according to new financial director Ian Leggett, at the time consisted mostly of just staff and debts. But some of those members of staff were worth their weight in gold.

Stephen explained that when British people come to the States they are surprised at how thin magazines are. The reason is that it's a huge country and therefore circulation has to be very high to make an impact and consequently print and distribution costs are also high. The market is also capable of dramatic changes in loyalty from one day to the next. Sitting amongst the noisy mid-morning coffee drinkers in Pershing Square on New York's 42nd Street, Stephen buzzed through memories of strategy and industry expertise.

'The trouble with launching anything in America,' he said, 'is that, even though you think you've got the best product or whatever, the whole thing is saturated. You can get noticed for a minute but then you're forgotten.'

Whether it was getting subscriptions or newsstand sales, he said, to be successful you had to be smarter and get what he described as 'share of mind' in some sort of lateral creative way. 'And that's the challenge – you've got to hit people over the head.'

One of the lateral ways they came up with to get people's attention was using the Howard Stern radio show. Stern was one of America's most popular radio DJs and he hosted a show that was syndicated across the country. Tall, irreverent and known for an 'in-your-face' presentation, his popularity with the sort of market that *Maxim* wanted to reach was key. Stephen explained that he had on numerous occasions tried to bring the magazine to the attention of Stern's manager and the producer of the show but with little success until he hit on a way to get Stern to talk about the magazine on air. Discovering that in many cases American radio DJs actually read the adverts themselves, they produced an ad that they hoped would make Stern look at the magazine.

They had published a list of the top '100 Reasons Why it's Great to be a Guy', which included such politically incorrect items as 'Everything on your face gets to stay the same colour', 'You can go to the bathroom without a support group' and 'Wedding plans take care of themselves'.

The irreverent and occasionally self-deprecating tone of the list was right up Howard Stern's street and, having read the 30-second advert on air, he took to reading out some of the 100 reasons each morning. A huge success with listeners, it drew them to the magazine in droves.

Another idea was to get scantily clad celebrities to grace the covers of the magazine. In theory, that should have been relatively easy in a world where stars hunt for publicity. However, the magazine just wasn't well enough known and, having scoured LA only to be rebuffed by PR companies, Stephen and editor Mark Golan decided to throw the 'best party LA had ever seen' – 'and that's what we did,' remembered Stephen. Held at Circus Maximus in Hollywood, it was enormous fun and not only pulled in some big advertisers but got them into the event business too.

Maxim parties became the hottest ticket in town but not all of them paid off. Kim Willis, former director of marketing at *Maxim*, remembered how one particular party put her at the end of a bit of stern advice from Felix.

It was August 2000 and LA was sweltering. After three months of planning and over $1 million spent on production, Kim's team had converted a run-down motel into the *Maxim* Motel for what she described was to be a night of wild debauchery. The motel featured 21 themed rooms covering a variety of the wackiest ideas people could come up with. One was even completely covered in edible cheese. Every detail had been carefully planned, right down to the ashtrays, which had 'Stolen from the *Maxim* Motel' stamped on them. As Kim recalled, Marilyn Manson, Carmen Electra and 'pretty much every Hollywood b-list celebrity of the era attended'. They had even partnered with *Yahoo* to live-stream the event online. The coverage was so intense and the interest so huge that thousands of people turned up, trying to get a look inside, causing the LA fire department to close the event down.

'I pulled down a security fence to distribute sponsor gift bags to the swarming crowd,' remembered Kim, 'and was soon ticketed for inciting a riot.'

The party had lasted a total of 45 minutes and, with $1 million looking like it had gone down the river, Kim was convinced she would surely be fired. Felix was indeed furious and berated her the next day by telephone but, before he hung up, he screamed one last bit of advice down the phone.

'Kim,' he said. 'If you're going to fuck up, fuck up BIG!'

Maxim went on to become huge in America, reaching millions of readers. At one point its circulation grew so large that advertising rates were competing with those of television. They had to rein in the promotion or agencies would use their budgets to place TV adverts instead of print. Covers featured musicians, actresses and celebrities such as Catherine Zeta-Jones, Pamela Anderson, Bridget Fonda, Beyonce, Shania Twain, Mariah Carey and Helena Bonham Carter. Felix loved working on cover copy and never tired of running his eagle eye over them. Often he threw in his own ideas for straplines. However, it was one of his earlier efforts that proved most enduring when he came up with: 'XENA LIKE YOU'VE NEVER SEEN 'ER!' for a 1999 cover with Lucy Lawless as the Warrior Princess Xena.

Andy Clerkson, who had walked into the H. Bunch Associates offices in the early days and asked if they had any jobs, worked through many publications but believed that *Maxim* had a dramatic effect on American publishing.

'I think *Maxim* scared the life out of a lot of American publishers,' he said. Indeed, it hit the demographic that everybody wanted, which at the time was 'young guys of 18 to 34'.

Interviewed when *Maxim* was on its way up, Clerkson noted, 'These guys are going to spend money on ridiculous crap.' He also believed that *Maxim*'s target market were 'brand loyal' because they were in a sense like dogs who blindly followed their master. At the time they were the Holy Grail to advertisers.

John Mack Carter, who was editor of *Good Housekeeping*, also praised *Maxim*'s success. He believed that no one, not even Felix, really had any sense of just how successful the magazine was going to be. John agreed that it reached 'that young male audience, which was very much in demand for the advertising market in the US'. He explained that 'all the British companies and the European publishing companies wanted to get over here and get a hold on this market, this wealthy market'.

John also emphasised Felix's own role in *Maxim* and in his many other magazines.

'Felix found people who would edit publications to his specifications,' he said, 'and to his voice.'

He was not suggesting that Felix controlled his editors. On the contrary, although he was very hands-on and got involved in making sure covers hit the mark and design had readers at the core, he employed people to do their jobs because he believed they were better at them than he was. However, the perception from John's perspective was that, when people in America talked about *Maxim*, Felix was the *Maxim* guy.

'The voice is Felix's and the interests are his,' he said.

With an uncanny sense of tying readers and advertisers together, by launching *Maxim*, Felix had not only filled a niche, but created an enormous beast too.

When it came to the launch and growth of *Maxim* his vision showed a strategic thinker who could read a market by understanding how large chunks of people think. Bringing *Maxim* to America, he explained, 'exported an attitude'. It was the attitude of challenging political correctness – or, as Felix put it, fighting it 'tooth and claw'.

The point that Felix grasped early on was the fact that no one was publishing magazines for men in a way that they published magazines for women. He realised that the men who went to bars after a hard day's work in America and watched sport, talked about girls and ate chicken wings were the same men who went back to work the next day and built rockets, performed brain surgery or managed hundreds of employees in vital businesses around the country. The mistake that people made, he said, was to assume that the way people acted when they were 'off-duty' defined their entire personality, interests and intelligence. These men, he believed, needed to be catered for with the same editorial diversity and respect that women were given in their magazines.

Talking to Charlie Rose in an interview for PBS in July 2001, Felix explained that men around the world were pretty much the same. 'And women are too,' he observed. 'Women around the world have always had a wonderful general interest magazine press.' It stretched from *Good Housekeeping* to *Cosmopolitan* and beyond. 'Men never had that,' he added. There was never a general interest men's lifestyle magazine because 'conventional wisdom in our industry has always been the same on both sides of the Atlantic, and in France and in Germany and in Italy – you can't do it, it can't be done.' The general consensus, he said, was that all magazines aimed at men had to be specialist – 'And I always thought that was baloney, complete baloney.' He never understood why men should buy so fewer magazines than women, so he consciously went out to challenge that understanding. In doing so, he turned American magazine publishing on its head.

His intuition wasn't the only thing that brought success with *Maxim*. His forensic understanding of his market and the publishing industry and how it worked led to a formula that he would later emulate with magazines *The Week* and *Mental Floss*. Although he would later sell the UK title, he launched *Stuff* magazine in the US a little after *Maxim* in July 1998. It was a rearguard action that not only ensured that those who didn't feel *Maxim* spoke to them were still buying a Dennis Publishing magazine, but also made sure any competitor coming into the market didn't have much space to squeeze into. Felix saw *Stuff* as being edgier than *Maxim* and therefore reaching a slightly different audience. Where *Maxim* reached the equivalent of a 'college senior', *Stuff* was reaching out to the 'freshman'. In American terms, Felix called it 'covering all the bases'. As Stephen Colvin recalled, '*Stuff* was a good opportunity and a good brand – it just about ruined the market for our rivals.'

John Lagana, chairman of Dennis Publishing US, remembered the tremor that Felix caused with *Maxim*. After working with Malcolm Forbes,

Lagana had moved to become chief financial officer with Jann Wenner at Wenner Media, owner of *Rolling Stone* magazine. 'We were sitting there, thinking, "How do we compete with these fucking Brits?"' he recalled. 'We started putting a sexy woman on the front. *Esquire* had never done that, *GQ* had never done that. All of a sudden they are all doing it because *Maxim* newsstand sales were 1.2 million per issue! *Rolling Stone* on average would be 100,000 a month over two issues. *Esquire* would be under 50,000, same with *GQ*. Advertisers were being charged four times the amount that *Maxim* was charging for a lot less reach.'

Although he loved his time at Wenner Media, after 14 years Lagana was intrigued by an approach from Dennis Publishing and just after the Twin Towers horror of 9/11, he and his wife Maggie flew to London to meet Felix. They were amongst only seven people on the 469-seater plane.

The interview was conducted in classic Felix style. It consisted of three days of relaxed time spent in Dorsington, enjoying Felix's hospitality and the delights of the Warwickshire countryside. As they prepared to catch their flight back to New York, John and his wife wondered why there had been no interview until Felix called him into the Quiet Room in Highfield and asked him to sit down.

'Well, I'm not supposed to say this, but when can you start?' said Felix. John replied that surely there were things that needed to be discussed. 'Aw, fuck all that!' said Felix. 'How much do you want? When can you start? And let's get going!' In yet another stroke of business genius, and in his own inimitable way, he had snagged one of the best financial controllers he could ever have found.

John, on the other hand, arrived at a company that had superb assets in *Stuff* and *Maxim* but was struggling with the pressures brought about by its own success. He was, however, impressed by Felix himself and his 'leadership qualities'.

'One of Felix's qualities was that he treated the people lower down with respect,' said John. 'It was genuine. When people presented to him he was genuinely interested in what they had to say. He was always a friend to everybody in the organisation, so, from a business perspective, as the leader of the company, he had complete loyalty and support from people at every level.'

John explained that when you have hundreds of people working on both sides of the Atlantic those are the qualities that people are romanced by. 'He had the ability to make you feel that you were the most important person to him at the time. That separated him quite a bit from the other smart business people. Felix was all that, but he had that quality that many politicians have. One thing about politicians is that if you are in a room with them, regardless of what your politics are, you usually like them.'

Indeed, Felix knew the business back to front so he could talk to anyone. As John explained, 'It was almost like watching a master artist painting a portrait. Investment bankers would walk away from a meeting, saying, "This guy is a fucking genius!" He was always connected with the different steps along the way.'

Felix would often say that the reason for *Maxim*'s success was because 'it was the first beer truck to reach the desert', but anyone involved in delivering that beer knew it couldn't have reached the desert without Felix behind the wheel.

CHAPTER 26

BETTER THAN SEX

One of the most common characteristics of Felix's growing success observed by his friends and colleagues over the years was the fact that he never seemed to change. His booming voice and confidence had long become hallmarks of his personality, but, despite his growing millions and his life of apparent luxury, his friendship and generosity never wavered. Perhaps on the surface his suits developed more class but there was little in his demeanour or attitude to those around him that would have heralded any real transformation. However, there were subtle, imperceptible changes rumbling inside him. At the same time his battle with ill health was never far from his mind.

In September 1999, while returning from a court hearing where his impassioned character reference hadn't managed to keep Mark Williams out of jail, he was taken ill on the way to a pub. His chauffeur Lloyd recalled leaving Felix sitting on a wall outside while he went in to get him a pint of Bass. Returning, he found him crumpled on the ground. Barely able to speak, he hissed to Lloyd to get him to a hospital, while his PA, Wendy Kasabian, found him a doctor. Within an hour he was at a Harley Street clinic, where he began what seemed like an endless series of tests.

Later diagnosed with thyroid deficiency, he described the process.

'I became dangerously ill. Little by little, I was losing the use of my arms and legs. My face was bloated and I suffered from constant fatigue.'

As well as these symptoms the most alarming thing for Felix was, 'when I spoke, my words were slow to come and slurred'. He described how, day to day, he wandered from consultant to consultant and clinic to clinic, enduring 'CAT scans, angiograms, bone scans, ultrasound and a score of other indignities too tedious and gruesome to recall'.

To bring him up to speed with the latest gossip he wrote a letter to Mark Williams, in which he also talked about the endless tedium of doctors and tests. However, one particular day of testing in Harley Street was to change his life yet again. Sitting on the edge of his bed, certain he was dying and simply wanting to get it over with, a poem came into his head. It was Dorothy Parker's 'Resume', which ends with the line 'You might as well live'.

Felix asked for a piece of paper and, as the nurse's station only had Post-it notes available, he scribbled his own response.

Called 'Travel Advisory', it was an eight-line poem following the form of Parker's poem.

Felix didn't write another poem for nearly a year, and, as he recalled, that was only because the first two lines had raced around inside his head, 'like a dog shaking its lead at a reluctant owner'. However, by October 2000, he said, 'The dam burst and I became engulfed in a tidal wave of poetry.' To the growing astonishment of many around him, he became obsessed and spent virtually every waking hour not dedicated to business writing.

It was no surprise to Marie-France, though. During those early years he would show her every new poem, often giving her the original copy. She recognised his new preoccupation as part of his character.

'He was very obsessive,' she noted. She believed that the compulsion to write poetry was a replacement for his crack addiction.

At the time Felix said he didn't know why he was writing. 'Nor do I want to know, all I know is that I cannot stop,' he added. 'Walking in the woods or in the back of a limousine, in board meetings or in the middle of making love in a Gulf Stream jet 40,000 feet above the Atlantic, or just lying in bed.'

He was consumed and fascinated with poetry, and as was always his wont he quickly became an expert, devouring everything he could read on the subject. By the time he had written over 350 poems and was ready to publish his first book, he was a match for any professor of poetry in knowledge and could happily joust with anyone on the subject.

Driven by a need for technical knowledge of sonnets, stanzas and poesy, as much as to pour forth, he admitted that he had found himself 'adrift in a sea of verse'. He claimed that he even tried to stop but it was useless, he said – 'The words and metre, the rhymes and ideas rise unstoppable and un-encouraged until I sit down and give them tangible form.'

Later, he recalled that at the time he joked about it, he worried about it and he even resented it. He said he felt marooned in a sea of verse and believed it unlikely that he would ever again see dry land.

Perhaps inevitably his ego and self-belief overcame any concerns he had about telling friends, colleagues and even competitors about his new-found love. In his book *How to Get Rich*, published in August 2006, he mentioned how his old friend Robin Miller had pleaded with him not to publish under his own name, but to use a pseudonym. However, Felix had already recognised the bigger picture and seen the possibility of poetry tours, applause and adventure. If he didn't use his own name, then he wouldn't get to enjoy the ride. His first book was published by Hutchinson in 2002, with a quote from the *Independent*'s John Walsh on the cover: 'If Waugh were still alive, he would fall on Dennis's verse with a glad cry of recognition and approval.'

Although initially slated to be called *Better than Sex*, proving Marie-France's suggestion that this new obsession was a replacement for his previous excesses, the book was eventually published as *A Glass Half Full*. Felix dedicated it to Marie-France and to his mother, and suggested in the preface that he might now be 'growing up'. Containing 200 poems, it was the beginning of a new journey that would show him opening up his soul and sharing many of his thoughts, though only a millimetre at a time. Over the years, as he gradually grew in confidence and slowly began to look into his own life with less guarded eyes, he began to open up.

A Glass Half Full was the first step in a 14-year odyssey, where Felix unravelled his life year by year, day by day and minute by minute. In his exploration of the world around him, he began the slow process of learning about himself. Starting as he meant to go on, he also added a spoken-word CD so buyers of the book could enjoy listening to him recite each poem in the voice that was such a powerful part of his character.

After a trial event in Mustique in August 2001, he gave his first poetry reading at the Groucho Club's banquet suite in London the following November, but the real test for him was launching into an 11-date tour on publication of the book, the following year. Naming it the *Did I Mention the Free Wine?* tour, based on a conversation with Mustique neighbour Mick Jagger, he arranged to open up his wine cellars and offer free wine to anyone who came to listen. It was a blatant marketing ploy by someone who had the money to promote himself and he happily admitted this to Melvyn Bragg on the *South Bank Show*, later saying, 'I did it because I was frightened that nobody would come.' Inevitably, the ploy incurred the ire of many poets who didn't have the same resources. However, there was no mistaking the potential of what Felix had to say. Over the years he had proved that his intellect was powerful and, if poetry was the distillation of profound thoughts and truths, then Felix was going to use it to its full advantage.

Artist and filmmaker Fiona Prendergast, who had worked at Bunch after a short career in the music business, filmed and produced a documentary of the first tour called *Did I Mention the Free Wine?* It included footage from a reading he did at the RSC's Swan Theatre in Stratford-upon-Avon in 2003 and showed Felix dressed in a yellow shirt and mustard waistcoat, an outfit that was to become his poetry uniform. With eyes popping out of his tortoiseshell bifocals, he engaged his audience with confidence and humour.

A new poem, 'The Summer of Love', which was to appear in his second book, *Lone Wolf* (2004), laid out his qualifications as a baby boomer who had enjoyed all the excesses of the sixties and further proved his fitness by pointing out that he couldn't quite remember it. His opening voiceover in the film told viewers that he knew two things when he was growing up: one that he was born lucky, and the other that he was not going to be poor.

'Under no circumstances would I stay poor,' he said. 'Seems silly now, but I was in deadly earnest back then.' To further prove that he had moved away from his humble beginnings, which had included an outside toilet and no electricity, he was seen arriving at readings by helicopter.

As well as poetry fans, those tempted by the wine and others simply curious to see who was the guy with the helicopter, the audience included many old friends and colleagues. Faces in the crowd included his mother, his brother Julian, Dick Pountain, Don Atyeo, Ian Leggett, Alistair Ramsay, the poet Michael Horovitz and a host of others.

Dr Sam Hutt, also known as musician Hank Wangford, explained that we all need a kind of artistic expression. He said of Felix: 'Out of the blue, after an illness, he's found this amazing expression.'

Richard Adams, graphic designer and friend from the early days, admitted he had been very surprised, describing Felix as 'somebody who is a philistine where poetry is concerned, a self-confessed philistine. Somebody who never goes to the cinema, never goes to theatre, never goes to the opera and has never been to a poetry reading.' However, he found this new expression a 'revelation'.

Broadcaster Melvyn Bragg, also enjoying a visit to a reading, said he liked the short form and liked the attack and the dramatisations, and found that some of Felix's poetry reminded him of other poets like Kipling and Blake. He explained that 'all poets remind you of other poets. That's what poets are like; they pinch from other poets all the way along the line. That's what they do.'

When writing in 2011 about his favourite 10 Felix Dennis poems, the Scottish poet and writer Christopher Rush agreed. He described them as coming from 'the undefiled poetic well of the past'. Of reading Felix's poems, he said, 'One of the incidental joys is to be taken back time and again to poems you may not have read for decades.' In Felix's poetry he saw Kipling, Housman, Masefield and Betjeman, as well as what he described as 'the boys of the old brigade'.

In later years, Ian Leggett would pinch some of Felix's poetry and change the words for use at employee leaving speeches, often to hilarious effect. As he later pointed out, agreeing with Melvyn Bragg, borrowing the metre and changing the words was what Felix did in many of his works anyway.

MORE LIVES THAN ONE

One of Felix's early poems, 'I Have a Secret Servant…' published in *A Glass Half Full*, is a classic example of how he liked to draw a veil of mystery over himself. Proving that his poetry was as much a vehicle for advancing his own mythical persona as it was a vessel for drinking from the mysteries of life, he suggested that he had his own secret daemon on his shoulder that advised, cajoled and occasionally forced him to do its bidding. When performing the poem on stage, he used his voice to great dramatic effect and gradually built up the story to alert potential competitors to the fact that there was another dimension to his actions; that there was another level to his negotiating power that no one could ever challenge. He alluded to the fact that he had no fear and that his daemon would make him bet all his money 'lose or win!' It made great copy, great television and great theatre, and was yet another weapon in the arsenal of Felix Dennis idiosyncrasies.

The first poetry tour was not short of amusement or drama. Due to read at a hotel in Grasmere in Cumbria in November 2002 for a special evening with the Wordsworth Trust, there was a panic when low cloud made it difficult to get a helicopter close to the site. Staff waited anxiously while PA Wendy Kasabian juggled options of nearby airports and chauffeur dashes. In the end there was a break in the cloud and a remarkably calm Felix took to the stage. Being the Wordsworth Trust, he was reading to an audience that one suspected might have damned him. However, they didn't.

Interviewed afterwards, Dr Robert Woof, director of the Wordsworth Trust, said, 'As usual, Felix is challenging. He is actually reassessing his whole life for the benefit of other people. You just feel that he lived it so richly and so dangerously so that he could be so wise for our delight.'

At a venue in Brighton some of the staff at Dennis Publishing enjoyed the show and the cameras were still rolling at two in the morning to capture some of their reactions. One senior manager said, 'Felix's ability to be a raconteur and poetry reader and to hold an audience is second to none, and that's his absolute forte and I'm inspired and I admire him for it.' As he turned to walk away, one of his colleagues wanted to hear more and said, 'Don't walk away,' to which he replied, 'I'm not walking away, you're staggering backwards!' If anyone could be aware of the benefits of free wine, it was Felix and, when it came to entertaining those who worked for him, he was a master.

At a Glasgow venue, Bruce Sawford, who played the role of tour manager, had the unenviable task of explaining to the audience that, although it was a non-smoking venue, Felix had been given special dispensation that allowed him to smoke on stage. It appeared that Felix had paid dearly for his 'vital stage props'. He later encouraged audience members to throw their empty glasses at the hapless sound crew, who were easy targets at the back of the hall.

On another stop, at one in the morning he was found loudly debating with students at the Oxford Student Union. He became passionate, shouting at the top of his voice during a heated political discourse about Europe. Afterwards, as he wandered out the door surrounded by the students, as if chatting to the owner of a local cafe he casually observed, 'You've got a nice gaff here.'

After one reading, Chris Hughes, publisher of *Good Housekeeping*, described the evening as 'like pop songs without the music' and was asked what he thought about Felix as a magazine publisher becoming a poet. He replied somewhat insightfully that he thought Felix was a magazine publisher by accident, that he was really a pirate and an enthusiast.

'He's a joy to have as a British person,' he declared, 'and he does whatever the hell he likes and he's very successful at it.'

Musing on the purpose of his own life wasn't something that Felix liked to participate in publicly, but he often made comments that proved penetrating and aware. On the tour he recorded how he felt about poetry becoming part of his life's journey: 'I sometimes feel as if my whole life was a preparation for this. The early poverty, the blues bands, the sixties underground scene, getting sent to prison, books, travelling, crack cocaine, going cold turkey, a passion for trees and the countryside. All of it is just a preparation for writing poetry.' This was a comment born from a deep need to be accepted by the poetry fraternity, something that Felix always knew would be an uphill struggle. Because he was seen as wealthy, there were many who couldn't see beyond the publicity and marketing. They couldn't see where he had actually come from. Some, of course, didn't know his modest background, but of those who were aware that Felix Dennis had grown up in humble circumstances and fought his way to the upper echelons of the *Sunday Times* Rich List, there were a few who chose to ignore it. Thankfully, what many might refer to as his thick-skinned determination to succeed allowed him to take the criticism and carry on.

All in all, the first poetry tour was a success. Those with grave reservations and gentle scepticism breathed a sigh of relief, while others who accepted Felix's 'full speed ahead and damn the torpedoes' attitude looked forward to the next instalment. It proved to be one that might have sent the sceptics running for cover when he casually said, 'Maybe I'll be the first poet in history to tour the USA in a Gulfstream jet.' As usual, Felix was looking at a much bigger picture than anybody could have imagined.

After the UK tour, he spent Christmas of 2002 in Mustique, where he finalised plans for the building of a private retreat beside Mandalay. It was to be called Writer's Cottage and it became a haven where he would spend his days reading, writing and refining his craft. Already he had arranged to purchase another property on the island for Marie-France and with the assistance of Brian Alexander, managing director of the Mustique Company, he also unveiled, to a mixture of delight and bemusement amongst residents, a new sculpture by Marjan Wouda of two enormous copulating tortoises near the entrance to his home. Announcing it as the first public sculpture in Mustique, at the unveiling Brian Alexander said of Felix, 'He's not an average man and this is not an average sculpture.' The 'humping tortoises' later became a must-have photo opportunity for visitors.

What proved difficult for many people to understand was that, despite his obvious obsession with, and concentration on poetry, he still had time to maintain his business interests, run his properties and private office, develop his estate and progress his ambition to grow trees.

Steven Kotok, who eventually became president of Dennis Publishing US, believed that Felix was misunderstood by those who saw him as a businessman who got involved in other activities.

'He's really just a wild man for whom business is one of his outlets,' he explained. Describing him as a very intense, adventurous person with many interests, he added, 'It just so happens that business is one of those pursuits. He could have been a rock promoter, he could have been a great writer.'

Felix had launched *The Week* in the US in 2001 and a month later followed it with the launch of *Blender*, a product that started life as a magazine on a CD-ROM. *Blender* had been Felix's vision for the future but had been hard to sell and eventually led to the start of Dennis Interactive. *Blender*'s launch in the US in 2001 was a revival of the brand name as an ink-on-paper music magazine. Steven remembered it as a difficult time for Dennis US.

'We launched *Blender* print magazine a month after *The Week* so we went from a two-magazine company to a four-magazine company. It was just a strain on everything. Neither title was performing as expected, so it was a strain on cash flow.'

Back in the UK, Felix had continued expanding his Warwickshire estate with the purchase of more nearby properties. He loved his new country lifestyle and some of those close to him hinted that part of the reason he bought houses close to him was because he hated the sound of people mowing their lawns and decided that if he owned the neighbouring cottages then he could have the lawns mown when he was in London. That didn't help him when small planes from the local airfield did aerobatics in the sky above the Old Manor. On one occasion, sitting naked in the kitchen while Marie-France cut his hair, he became so incensed with the noise of a nearby plane that he jumped from the chair, ran naked from the house and leapt about the garden, shouting at the sky. His dog, Bitter, who had been sitting quietly at his feet, joined in the melee, barking wildly. Bitter never learned to accept the noise of the planes and from then on would always bark at them. In later years, when Felix was recording poetry at a makeshift studio and the sound of a nearby plane distracted him, he would send his farm secretary, Kathy Collins, out on a mission to ask the airport owners to call down the offending pilots. On most occasions they were happy to oblige.

His new estate manager, David Bliss, who had jumped off a combine harvester when first summoned to Dorsington to see what he could do about helping turn Felix's farming and tree planting activities to profit, remembered their first meeting as brusque.

'He just said, "So what the fuck can you do to make this estate better?" I just said, "A lot more than you are doing now."'

It was a classic Felix teaser and, although ready at that minute to walk away, David stayed. He moved his family into a nearby farm and gradually took over the running of the estate.

In London, Dennis Publishing UK had moved from its offices in Bolsover Street to seven floors on Cleveland Street and purchased *Evo* magazine to add to its portfolio. Subscriptions to the UK edition of *The Week* had overtaken the *Economist* and, a few years later, the company would buy IFG, adding *Viz*, *Fortean Times*, *Bizarre* and *Jack* to its stable of magazines. A business that had started publishing comics in a garret in Goodge Street had long since grown up, and, with much inspiration but little interference from Felix, it was becoming a well-oiled machine, ideally placed to weather whatever storms would hit the world of ink on paper in the years to come.

In the meantime, having completed his 500th poem, 'Landfill', while in Mustique, Felix decided to work on his earlier idea for the next poetry tour. He had written enough new poems for a second book and his first, *A Glass Half Full*, was to be published by Miramax in the US. It was time to organise his threatened US poetry outing and this would be the first leg of an expedition that was to span two continents. He decided that in 2004 he would travel the US reading his poems and immediately follow that with a UK tour. And, again, stretching the 'talent' as much as he could he determined that it would be with the help of a somewhat surprised Steven Kotok, who had no previous experience of arranging such a thing.

'But then, I wasn't qualified for any other job he had given me before,' remembered Steven. He tried to suggest other people that he thought more qualified for the job but Felix was insistent. Making contact with a promoter whose speciality was bringing British comedians to America, Steven embarked on what would become an extraordinary journey, both physically and emotionally.

Together they planned an 18-date tour that would begin in Minneapolis and end in Miami. Felix followed through with his earlier threat to travel by Gulfstream jet, though added what he later called a 'Johnny Cash' bus for the sound, video, lighting equipment and crew. Although it hadn't actually carried Johnny Cash around the US, the vehicle had hosted bands like Limp Bizkit and Eminem. Never enjoying travelling by plane with Felix, Marie-France chose to join two of his personal assistants and follow the tour on the bus.

One of Steven's first headaches was to figure out how he could get the venues filled for a man that few people knew, but who was determined to get people to come and watch him read poetry. The answer was to work the *Maxim* list.

'Amazingly, we did get hundreds of people to come to each one,' he said. 'On the *Maxim* list we didn't push the poetry. It was more like "an evening of free booze with the *Maxim* guy". *Maxim* here was a much bigger phenomenon culturally than in the UK so during that poetry tour he wasn't just a rich guy, he was "the *Maxim* guy" – essentially Hugh Hefner.'

In the end the venues hosted a mixed but very interesting crowd that Steven described as one-third *Maxim* readers and one-third people interested in poetry. They had also advertised in local papers so the other third were those who just liked to do fascinating things.

The next headache was arranging Felix's accommodation. On his previous UK tour he had insisted that he fly home after each gig, something he also did for all subsequent tours. But America was a big place. Booking hotels was Steven's only option, and, as Felix wasn't necessarily easily pleased, he remembered it as a bit of a nightmare.

'Every hotel was the worst hotel he had ever been in,' he recalled. 'Every traffic jam was the most maddening experience of his life. He never wanted to explore a city. He'd find the hotel and immediately demand to be in a nicer one.'

Steven would bicker with him, explaining the tour was costing a fortune, but if Felix was in a $1,000-a-night hotel, he would complain that he should be in a $10,000-a-night one.

'He wanted everything vaster and bigger,' said Steven. 'You just had to ignore him.'

Delays at the airport were another source of tension. Steven developed a system for trying to calm Felix in these situations.

'When he was agitated, I would always ask him about cricket,' he explained. 'He would spend 40 minutes explaining how cricket worked. That was my ace in the hole if I needed to keep him focused.' Despite Felix's professed lack of interest in sport, his brain didn't allow him to ignore it completely. He still had to at least be an expert in how it worked.

On stage, Felix was as passionate as he had been on his first UK tour. His eyes pierced those close enough to see them, sweat crept around the edges of his beard as his powerful voice rose and fell and his arms waved. At times it looked as though he was trying to pummel the air around him into submission. He stalked around the lectern, his voice and body alternating between an angry caged beast and a wise old sage.

Some of the poems that recounted tales from his life in England simply wouldn't resonate with an American audience but he had many gems that hit the mark. 'To a Beautiful Lady of a Certain Age', a gracefully delivered poem decrying the need for plastic surgery, was a hit in every city and he started each night with 'Never Go Back', the poem inspired by his mother. On the first night in Minneapolis, although the arena was not full, there were many laughs and whoops of approval. One lady insisted on shouting repeatedly that she loved him. Afterwards she purposefully strode up to him, grabbed his hands and pushed them into her underwear. For once, he made his excuses and left.

Another of Steven Kotok's jobs was to ensure that there was as much press coverage as possible before each reading. This meant Felix doing something he hated – talking on a mobile phone. He conducted interviews using Steven's mobile and, as local papers, regional magazines and even the *New York Times* were lined up for Felix to charm, he became less than enamoured with their attitude.

'Another interview, another stitch-up,' he was often heard to exclaim.

Steven recalled, 'He would talk about wanting to bring poetry back to the people and away from the ivory tower, but it didn't matter. Because he was rich, they didn't want to know. If it was some formerly homeless person, which you could argue Felix was, from a longer perspective, it would be a heroic story.'

Much as this was true and would have made a more palatable story, unfortunately the fact that he travelled to his gigs by private jet made it a challenging tale to sell. The irony that wasn't lost on Felix was the fact that, had it been a 'born with a silver spoon' rock band travelling to gigs by private jet, no one would have batted an eyelid.

Another bone of contention was the post-9/11 security that made it difficult to get in and out of buildings, including radio stations. Arriving at one station for an interview, Felix was asked by security to show his ID.

'I don't carry any bloody ID!' he declared. Steven explained that, as Felix was from the UK, he wasn't used to having to carry identification with him at all times. The security man was polite and conversationally asked why offices in the UK would not require ID. 'Because we don't live in a police state!' barked Felix. He was not a patient man and fortunately Steven was able to get a member of staff to come down and escort them in. He asked Felix to remember to bring his passport the next time.

A couple of days later, they turned up to another radio station. Felix, of course, hadn't brought his passport along and stubbornly shouted that, if they didn't want him to do a bloody interview, they didn't have to let him in. The security guard in this instance wasn't as understanding and took great offence to Felix's growing belligerence. As Steven tried, unsuccessfully, to get hold of someone from the station, Felix and the security guard prepared to lock horns.

Felix huffed, puffed, grunted and snarled until, in a moment of inspiration, Steven whipped out a copy of one of his poetry books and showed the guard the photograph of Felix on the cover.

'The security guard wavered, happy to have me hanging on his decision,' recalled Steven.

He agreed to let Felix in, but told him he would have to improve his attitude.

Relieved, Steven turned to Felix, expecting a grateful smile but instead felt the full force of a passionate verbal explosion.

'Improve my attitude!' Felix roared. 'Are you here to protect us from terrorists or to enforce respect for yourself, you officious little fucker?'

His rant went on and there were few people within a block of the building that wouldn't have heard every word. Oddly enough, the Felix tornado got away with it and the security guard let them through. Once on air, Felix wasn't finished and immediately launched into a description of the altercation for the listeners. As Steven remembered it, 'The radio host turned out to be a far-left political commentator and he and Felix got on famously, agreeing about the absurdity of the creeping police state.'

The following week in Los Angeles, Felix was scheduled to do an interview with Steve Jones, former guitarist with the Sex Pistols on his show, *Jonesy's Jukebox*. His guests were to be Felix and actress and musician Courtney Love. Fearing the same security problem, Steven had phoned ahead to explain that Felix wouldn't have his ID and he was assured it would be OK. On arrival, they were given neatly handwritten name tags to allow them access around the building. Ignoring Steven's silent pleas for sanity, Felix slowly peeled the back off the sticker, dramatically slapped it onto his forehead and slumped into a sofa in reception. Splayed out across the seat, he tipped his head and gazed up at the ceiling. When eventually called into the studio to join the show, the premise of which was that Steve Jones could do whatever he liked without direction from station management as long as it was within FCC rules, Felix allowed the sticker to fall from his forehead and genially chatted to Courtney Love about Mustique (she had visited the island as a guest of Kate Moss). Courtney read his poem, 'All the Young Dudes', and then announced that she no longer abused drugs and alcohol. It was a surreal radio experience.

The final reading of the US leg of Felix's two-continent tour was at the stately Biltmore Hotel in Coral Gables, Miami. A majestic building, featuring one of the largest swimming pools in the continental United

States and liberally decorated with grand architectural ornaments, it was an opulent setting for the last night. With a mixture of relief and emotion everyone, especially Felix, enjoyed the show. Nearly every member of the audience bought a book and, although too exhausted to participate in a raucous wrap party, the crew descended on a small restaurant for a late dinner together. Glasses were raised and Felix even hugged Steven Kotok, telling him he was great and calling him 'a fucking scholar'.

The next day, Felix flew from Miami to Coventry to prepare for another 13 dates in England.

Caroline Rush, who had joined Felix's private staff in 1998 and arranged his powerhouse poetry reading at the RSC Swan Theatre in Stratford-upon-Avon in 2003, had gradually become a lynchpin in the team that published his books and organised his poetry tours. She remembered her first interview as 'bizarre'. Having waited for over two hours for him and listened to Wendy Kasabian's many apologies for his tardiness, something she was to become quite adept at herself, she eventually saw him as she was leaving. Felix boomed his apologies and rambled on about what a nice group of people she would be working with. He had been sitting in the garden at the Old Manor and, as she stole a glance at the people he had been talking to, she was taken aback to find that one of them was a bronze sculpture of Mark Twain sitting on a bench. It was her first sight of one of the many sculptures that was to help fill the Garden of Heroes & Villains, an initiative she oversaw for many years. The next day she had a call, asking when she could start. Wendy's advice was to be broadminded, resilient and to have a good sense of humour too.

'He can be quite tricky sometimes,' she explained.

By the time they returned from the US leg of the 2004 poetry road trip, Caroline was on a high, but, like everybody else on the team, she was utterly exhausted. The next leg of the tour was to promote Felix's second book, *Lone Wolf,* which had just been published by Hutchinson in October 2004. Starting in London, Felix travelled by helicopter to readings across the country, from London to Liverpool and Brighton to Glasgow, while the rest of the team travelled by minibus around the country.

Although the attempt to break into the American market and the launch of the *Lone Wolf* collection and tour had helped Felix to reach more people than most poets could hope to reach in a lifetime, it was still early days in his career, and there was one thing that would never stop bothering him. For once it wasn't a little thing. In the preface to *Lone Wolf*, he opened up about the pain and anger he felt at how some in the poetry community mocked him. Written a year before the book was published, he admitted that it was penned with passion and that he should have toned it down somewhat, but following the advice that he often gave to others he went ahead and printed his response to what he called 'Mr Well-Known-British-Poet', who in a magazine article had called Felix a 'philistine', who would never be a 'true poet.' However, if the slight had had any effect, it was positive.

As his old friend Richard Adams later explained, Felix was deeply hurt, perhaps as much as he had been stung by Judge Argyle's comments many years before.

'He knew there were people out there that were prepared to really rag him,' said Richard, 'but he was determined as ever he had been at the start.'

Felix gave a powerful account of himself in his response and in the same way that he had been spurred to great success in commerce he became an over-achiever in his newfound passion for poetry, gaining friends and admirers from every class and quarter. Back in July 2001, he had told Charlie Rose in an American PBS documentary, 'I'm going to become a famous poet, Charlie,' and he meant it.

And he did just that. In time, fellow writers, poets, critics and musicians all paid tribute to the genius within Felix's poetry. Mick Jagger, Paul McCartney, Stephen Fry and Dawn French were amongst those who lauded his words. Benjamin Zephaniah, the Birmingham poet who was listed in *The Times*' list of the 50 greatest post-war poets, described his poetry as having moments of real genius. 'The audience that listen to poetry want to hear what you've got to say,' he said. 'They don't care if you are rich, poor, what your trappings are or what the venue is. They don't care if you're gay, straight, white or black. They want to hear what you've got to say and I think, at the heart of Dennis's work, there is something very interesting.'

Zephaniah took some of his family to hear Felix read his poems. It included a devout Muslim, a devout Christian, a 15-year-old girl and a five-year-old boy. 'And all of us have found something,' he declared afterwards. He believed that in some poetry circles there was 'criticism' of Felix's showmanship on stage but insisted, 'That adds another dimension.'

Author and critic Tom Wolfe, who claimed Felix was the 'best poet writing in the English language', was hugely impressed by his poetry performances and explained that it was his firm belief that literature's first duty was to entertain. Alluding to Felix's ability to hold an audience, he said, 'If it can go on from there and do incredible loops in the sky – great. But first of all it has to entertain.'

Writing in *Agenda* magazine, the poet Alison Brackenbury, who had sat on many judging panels, including the Poetry Society's National Poetry Competition, explained that, once a type of poetry is defined and accepted, it is relatively easy to agree on the worst and best examples. 'The really ferocious fights,' she said, 'are about what types should be valued.' Suggesting that defining Felix's work as popular poetry was to use a clumsy label, she added, 'I strongly approve of popular poetry, although I consider a couple of its most successful practitioners to be lightweight and unconvincing. These do not include Felix Dennis.' She went on to describe Felix's work as having 'strong bones', particularly liking his ability to turn a story on its head – 'The shocking twist – the flick of the wrist – is a particular gift of Dennis.'

Felix had become known for championing the merits of old-fashioned rhyme and metre. He disliked free verse and after judging a poetry competition for the *Marshwood Vale* magazine in 2007 explained: 'Personally, I happen to prefer traditional rhyme, metre and poetic forms – a dangerous heresy in what the American author Tom Wolfe calls "the poor old mallarme'd and ezrapounded world of contemporary poetry". But personal preference is not the cardinal issue. What counts is surely whether a poem touches us, amuses us, entertains us or moves us.' Felix's poetry had the gift to touch, amuse, entertain and move his readers and live audiences.

His old friend Dana Gillespie recognised where much of that gift came from. 'I think he channels all the energy that he used to put into sex, drugs and rock and roll into his poetry,' she said, 'and if that's the result of his illness, then yippee! He's a bright boy so he turned a disadvantage into an advantage.'

CHAPTER 27

A SLIVER OF RAZORED ICE

Before poetry had gripped Felix's imagination, his maverick style and pirate swagger had helped create a mystical persona, one that he loved to promote. The legend that Americans called the '*Maxim* guy' also fascinated many in high places. Lance Ford, another Englishman who had moved to the States and worked at Condé Nast before jumping ship to join Dennis Publishing, remembered an occasion when *Maxim* was enjoying huge success in America in the nineties. Graydon Carter, editor of *Vanity Fair*, asked if Lance could arrange for him to meet Felix. So Lance organised what he described at the time as the 'ultimate meeting of the publishing minds'.

Felix and Lance went to the Times Square headquarters of Condé Nast, where *Vanity Fair* publisher Pete Hunsinger and Graydon Carter had booked a private dining room so that Felix could smoke. They sat down and began chatting about magazines and were soon asked if Si Newhouse, chairman of Condé Nast, could join them. Si came in and the two immediately launched into a discussion about the world of publishing.

'Christ, maybe he's going to make an offer for *Maxim*,' Lance remembered thinking at the time.

As word got out that Felix Dennis was in the building, the little gathering grew. Steve Florio, then president of the company, insisted on joining them, as did editor-in-chief of American *Vogue* Anna Wintour, who remembered Felix from when she worked at *Oz* magazine in the late sixties. Felix later recalled that he recognised the sound of Anna's footsteps coming down the corridor long before she entered the room.

'Felix was holding court with some of the top people in his industry,' said Lance. 'It was as if he had a right.'

And perhaps by then he did. At the end of the nineties, he was the cocky new kid on the block and, as Lance remembered it, the publishing community loathed his success. Lance described the magazine world at the time as a very 'buttoned-down, blue blood publishing industry', likening it to a 'very neat neighbourhood'. When Dennis Publishing came along it was as if they had 'bought one of the houses in this nice little neat neighbourhood and took the wheels off the car, stuck it up on building blocks, and started having late night parties'. He believed that the industry needed Felix Dennis at the time because it was 'not evolving, not relating' and demanding vast sums for advertising. That needed to change, he said.

'There's a new kid on the block,' he declared. 'Success breeds respect.'

Felix's success had bred respect on both sides of the Atlantic. Sir Robin Miller, knighted for his services to the publishing industry in 2003, was CEO of EMAP and later chairman of HMV and a non-executive director of British TV station Channel 4. He became a close friend after he and Felix spent many years as rivals. Although they did collaborate on an agreement for Felix to publish *Star Hits* in America, Sir Robin remembered it as a relationship that in the early days was about 'deals that didn't happen'. He thought they had a deal to buy *Personal Computer World* for nearly £2 million from Felix and that it had more or less been cemented after a drunken night in Miranda's nightclub in Kingly Street, but the deal was scuppered by VNU's higher offer.

'I just can't walk away from it,' Felix had told Sir Robin, who remembered him being 'hugely apologetic'.

Ten years later, they got some way down the line on a deal to work together in the American market, which didn't pan out either. But the lack of success at consummating deals didn't stop Sir Robin from having huge respect for Felix.

Describing his meteoric rise, he said, 'To start with nothing, and have the energy and balls to build up what he did, was indeed some amazing achievement.' He believed that part of Felix's success was driven by his experience at the *Oz* trial: 'He was determined to show those bastards – whom he despised – what he was made of and how he could succeed and have influence.'

He also pointed out there were traits that Felix displayed that, although difficult for those around him, were key to his success: 'He was an impatient man and people who succeed in this industry are not necessarily patient people. And then he could be an unreasonable man, but then again sometimes people who succeed are not reasonable people. And he could be very unreasonable.'

Describing Felix's audacity, he also alluded to the loyalty that he showed to those who had worked for him. He remembered a time when they had both come to visit Mark Williams in jail and Felix turned up in a Rolls-Royce, more rock-star royalty than astute businessman. His distinctive style stood out amongst the rest of those who had come to see friends and relatives; Sir Robin described it as a most bizarre visitation.

'He loved that sort of stuff. He had an ego as big as the moon but he was lovely with it.'

Mike Soutar, once editor-in-chief of *Maxim* US and now owner of Shortlist Media, a successful London publisher of 'freemium' magazines, remembered that Felix was at times 'not an easy man to work for'. Sitting in his office at Emerald Square in Bloomsbury in 2015, Mike described Felix as 'idiosyncratic and particularly demanding on small detail'. However, he believed those were some of the qualities that made him so exciting to work for.

Mike's interview, conducted in Dorsington in 1999, was in standard Felix style. Mike recalled that it was less an interview and more a case of Felix 'laying out his hopes, dreams and strategies for the next couple of years'. What made the whole experience of working with him such an education was the fact that those dreams and strategies were so much more achievable when orchestrated by Felix. 'He would open a very expensive bottle of wine and issue various thoughts and commands and ideas from behind a cloud of smoke and I'd do my very best to keep up with his grand ambitions' said Mike. But what made it really exciting was that Felix could work so fast. Talking about their competitors, Mike explained, 'He was brilliant. By being so fast he made everybody else look like they were wading through treacle. He would constantly provoke them and tweak their noses and they would respond slowly and cumbersomely and clumsily.' As Mike described it, Felix could make 'the heads of Conde Nast and Hearst look like lumbering, uncertain, indecisive lumps'.

Felix 'styled himself a buccaneer in every single respect', said Mike. He understood the attractiveness of a Wild-West spirit and most importantly the value of being an underdog. As Mike described it, Felix gave a master class in exploiting being the underdog. 'Even though we were really big by that point we were still the plucky insurgent operating on a cost base of a fraction of everybody else.'

Another friend from those early magazine publishing days, whom Felix had on more than one occasion tried to poach from EMAP, also received a knighthood. Sir David Arculus, along with Sir Robin Miller, was credited with taking EMAP from a small regional publisher to a comparative giant in the industry.

Sitting in Felix's Kingly Street office in late 2014, Sir David remembered Felix coming up to see him in Peterborough, all those years ago. They went out to what Sir David remembered as a smart hotel for lunch and Felix outlined his proposal for Sir David to become a director of the company. He admitted that in some ways he regretted not taking the offer.

'I was really tempted,' he conceded. 'Felix and I were kind of opposites but we complemented each other. He knew how to create things and I knew how to run things. I think we were quite a good team from that point of view.'

The reason he didn't accept Felix's offer was that he had young children at the time and didn't want to jeopardise the security that his existing position afforded him. It was a situation that, although Felix understood on one level, wasn't something he could truly empathise with.

'He had incredible energy,' Sir David added. 'He never let himself be tied down by domesticity. He had great confidence, I think it derived from his energy. He had 10 per cent more to chuck at everything.'

As Sir David stood at around six foot five inches and Felix a good foot shorter, he and Felix might have looked a slightly incongruous team but they respected each other's abilities immensely. Sir David went on from EMAP to become an adviser to the governments of both Tony Blair and David Cameron, but he also shared an interest in trees with Felix. As chairman of Severn Trent Water, he was involved in supporting the National Forest and on one occasion invited Felix to a special presentation in the hope that he might support the planting of some trees. Felix decided to travel by helicopter but low cloud made landing difficult. Sir David and his colleagues waited in a field with the sound of the helicopter above them as it looked for a break in the cloud. Eventually, Felix landed, pulled out his chequebook and presented them a cheque for £100,000 to plant a wood. What surprised everyone was that he didn't want the wood planted in his own name: he had decided to name it after someone else.

Sometime later, Felix's managing director Alistair Ramsay recalled how he first heard about the wood.

'It was 25 May 2004,' he recalled. 'I was summoned to the Manor with little notice and no agenda. This was unusual. I wondered if I was to be sacked.'

Felix's luxury Mercedes Maybach arrived to collect him, and Ian Leggett joined him for the journey. After a nice lunch, washed down with wine from Felix's cellar, Alistair was still none the wiser about their reason for being there.

When a helicopter landed in the field nearby, Alistair thought, 'That's the point! He has bought a helicopter and we are having a spurious meeting just so he can impress us by then flying us back to London.'

However, that wasn't the case.

They got into the waiting helicopter and flew north. Alistair later claimed that he was secretly hoping that Felix had bought his favourite football team, Nottingham Forest, but when they landed in a field where a small group of officials and a photographer greeted them, he was still utterly bemused. More wine was poured and they were shown some small baby saplings that had been planted.

'There was then a little ceremony and the unveiling of a plaque,' said Alistair.

The wood had been named 'Alistair's Wood'.

On the flight back, they stopped a few miles from Felix's house to visit Spernal Estate, which Felix would later make a central part of his ambitions to plant a broadleaf forest in the heart of England. More wine was consumed and, by the time Alistair arrived home in Surrey, it was very late. Much the worse for wear after all the wine he was not feeling great either.

As he recalled, he was in the doghouse, big time.

'Hence the reason I remember the date,' he said later. 'It was my wife's birthday – ex-wife now.'

Sir David recognised the dichotomy around Felix's generosity and care for those around him. Pointing out that his kindness was directly opposite to his inability to let anybody get close to him, he said that Felix's life was all one continuum.

'A lot of us have a private life and a public life,' he said, 'but actually it was all the same to him.'

He explained that, when meeting with Felix or going out for dinner, the conversation would be about everything that Felix was doing, nothing was from a different part of his life.

'A lot of people put their lives into compartments but he didn't have that other compartment,' he added.

Someone else with whom Felix shared an interest in trees was another competitor: chairman of Haymarket Media Group Michael Heseltine, now Lord Heseltine.

After founding Haymarket in 1957, he was a Member of Parliament from 1966 to 2001 and a cabinet minister. He was deputy prime minister from 1995 to 1997, before becoming a life peer in 2001.

Felix would meet him for lunch at Wiltons in Jermyn Street to discuss the industry and anything else that might be to their mutual interest. In his book *How to Get Rich*, Felix mentioned a story about how Lord Heseltine bought one of Dennis Publishing's titles, *Stuff* magazine, from him in 1997 for what Heseltine later called 'peanuts'. Felix cited it as one of his business errors and recalled that this wasn't his finest hour.

Speaking from his office in London in 2014, Lord Heseltine described Felix as a 'one-off'. He explained how he had enjoyed their lunches together and said that, as he saw it, *Stuff* magazine was a flanking protector of *Maxim*.

'He wanted to try to make it difficult for someone to come in and compete with *Maxim*, so the best way to do it was to put a protective Maginot Line around *Maxim* and he did that with *Stuff*. My people saw that this was a better property, concentrating on the technology and the electronic kit and all that, not the girls. The girls ceased to be part of our activity. I have to admit that I was against the purchase, even at the very low levels we paid. But that simply reveals the age gap. I simply was not familiar with the use of the word "Stuff" in that context.'

'He was highly voluble, very self-centred, opinionated and original in his approach to life,' Lord Heseltine added. 'He was better at talking than listening, I think.'

Although their respective companies didn't have an enormous amount of comparable magazine titles and Felix would have been seen as much more of a maverick, Lord Heseltine agreed that there were similarities between them.

'I think probably we had a buccaneering spirit,' he said. 'I think that our publishing interests revealed a sort of entrepreneurial flair, and wherever we landed, we would have exploited the qualities that made us publishers and businessmen.'

Pointing out that he had a copy of Felix's CD, *Mustique Blues*, on the desk in front of him, he went on to admire his ability to self-promote.

'You were never short of information about Felix. He was a self-publicist in a very professional way. And why not?'

If anybody can understand the value of self-publicity, it is a politician. Spending their lives under the scrutiny of journalists ever eager to expose anything that might deviate from their chosen mission statements yet needing exposure to promote their careers, they know only too well how important it is to spread their own gospel. In most cases, however, they don't get the opportunity to offer a controlled insight into their lives until their careers are over and they take the time to pen their memoirs. Felix, on the other hand, had the opportunity to promote his own beliefs and philosophy at a time when he was on the upward slope of yet another adventure.

Although he employed a researcher, Susan Bandy, in 1998 to talk to many of those with whom he had worked over the years, it wasn't until 2005 that Felix began work on a book that was to offer snippets of wisdom as well as fleeting glimpses into some of the moments from his already well-publicised career. Having promoted his lifestyle by flying in private jets and helicopters, being driven in a fleet of Rolls-Royces and Maybachs and owning properties in England, America and Mustique, one of the most obvious subjects for him to write about was wealth and, as he called it later, 'the getting of money'. Although the subject was also influenced by hundreds of requests from people wanting to know how to make money, it was likewise something that had consumed the greater part of his life.

The book was entitled *How to Get Rich* (2006) and, early on, Felix explained that, although making money had been, and, still was, fun, it had wreaked havoc on his private life. He told how it had consumed his waking hours and led him to a life of narcotics, high-class whores, drink and consolatory debauchery. Most importantly, and perhaps poignantly, he admitted that these 'afflictions', as he called them, had undermined his health.

The book is one of the most fascinating treatments of the subject of devoting one's life to the purpose of getting rich. Full of wisdom about the psychology required for the pursuit of capital and possessions, it is also one of the few works that highlights the pitfalls in a way that allows the reader to avoid going down that road with no loss of pride. After its publication and success, Felix pointed out that the title was an attempt at irony and that he hadn't expected people to use it as an instruction book, but more as a memoir of the pros and cons of wealth creation.

He did examine some of the benefits of affluence, explaining that the most precious thing that riches can offer is time. In his case it gave him the time to read, to walk in the woods, to see friends, commission art and to contemplate his philosophy of life.

As Felix put it, 'To do just about anything really, as long as it does not involve day after grinding day, making money in an office or a factory for somebody else.'

He also discussed the importance of growing a thick skin, however. Those interested in the pursuit of wealth would have to be unmoved by the mockery that sometimes comes with failure. Failing publicly was part of the journey and, if there was any inkling that embarrassment might be an issue, it was time to go back to the job market. Caring about causing worry to family, spouse or a lover also wasn't an option.

'This is not a calling for the faint-hearted,' he declared.

He also quoted a line that he attributed to Winston Churchill: 'Success is never permanent; failure is never fatal. The only thing that really counts is to never, never give up. That's that old windbag Winston Churchill again,' wrote Felix. 'But he was bang on the money there.'

As he had outlined to many of his colleagues over the years, there was nothing wrong with taking a good idea and making it work for your own ends.

'If you never have a single great idea in your life,' he wrote, 'but become skilled in executing the great ideas of others, you can succeed beyond your wildest dreams.'

How to Get Rich, much of it written from the comfort of his hideaway Writer's Cottage in the grounds of his home on Mustique, became a great success but left many readers somewhat confused. Felix had made it very clear that riches hadn't made him happy, nor did he believe they had made anyone happy.

'Never have I met a self-made rich man or woman whose family or personal relationships were not plagued by the burden of creating a fortune, even a small fortune,' he wrote.

He pointed to rocky marriages, lack of time spent with children and the substitution of expensive gifts to repress guilt as just some of the more obvious pitfalls of a life devoted to making money. Also, that in order to succeed in gaining great wealth one needed a slightly sinister nature.

'Somewhere in the invisible heart of all self-made wealthy men and women is a sliver of razored ice,' he wrote. 'The love of another, or of family (or of their God, if they have one) can help contain it. Seeking great wealth will release that sliver to grow. It is in the nature of the beast. If you do not wish it to grow then quit any dreams of becoming wealthy now.'

In his lifetime, he never appeared to permit love of any kind to dull the sliver of razored ice that grew inside his heart. Somewhat prophetically, he also explained that having too much money isn't really important.

'Breaking your neck is important. Getting cancer is important. Having nothing to eat is important. Losing someone you love is important. But too much money is absolutely not important.'

Alluding to the alienation created by wealth, he wrote that the constant demands from others for a share of one's money become so tiresome that many rich people insulate themselves. However, that insulation breeds paranoia, arrogance and loneliness – 'And rage that you only have so many years left to enjoy rolling in the sand you have piled up.'

Felix had a postcard designed to be sent as a response to most of the thousands of begging letters he received to his office, which gently pointed out to the writer that he simply couldn't help everyone who asked. There were many of them too.

Steven Kotok was shocked at the amount of people who stood in line to have a poetry book signed as a ruse to hand over a business plan or request help in some way or another.

'Every single person that approached him wanted something from him,' he recalled. 'It was like a gauntlet of humans with their hand out, one way or another.'

Despite bemoaning the irritation of such attention, Felix knew it was part of the territory. In fact, his philanthropic activities became one of his hallmarks. His contributions to charitable causes were numerous and were one of the few activities that he was determined to keep completely confidential. As one colleague pointed out, Felix was a sucker for the last story on the evening news, which was usually designed to tug at the heartstrings of the viewer. One newspaper clipping that he kept in his archive, which told the story of how an anonymous businessman had paid for successful IVF treatment to enable a couple to have a baby, has a handwritten Post-it note attached to it, saying, 'The best £10,000 I have ever spent'.

Published at the end of August 2006, *How to Get Rich* was at the top of Amazon's business category by November and number four in Foyles' all-category list. Its mix of anecdote and advice struck a chord with a wide range of readers, from those with business interests to others who simply enjoyed Felix's 'tell it like it is' philosophy. By the end of 2009, he was working on the follow-up, *88 The Narrow Road*, which he claimed was written for those determined to attempt the getting of money but who were 'willing to shoulder the consequences'. It contained distilled and rewritten thoughts inspired by the previous book and comprised 88 sections of advice covering everything from raising capital, through negotiating, delegating, trusting one's instincts and friends, to dealing with rivals and courting Lady Luck. Dealing as it did with the attributes and focus needed to follow the narrow road towards riches, he couldn't resist a section on happiness, again stressing that, although wealth was preferable to poverty, it was not conducive to contentment.

Years before, in a *South Bank Show* special, Felix had explained to presenter Melvyn Bragg that 'Making a lot of money is just a trick, it's a facility. It literally does not make you an iota brighter. I don't know why people place quite so much importance on it. As far as making money is concerned, I'm a one-trick pony. It's a hell of a pony but it's just a trick. Magazines happened to work out. If they hadn't worked out, I'd have switched immediately to something else where I could have made a lot of money. It's a good job that I didn't spend that time in prison; I'd have been a brilliant criminal.'

Felix had come a long way. A front-page article in the *Observer* of September 1988 had included his name on a list of 'subversives'. It had allegedly been published by a right-wing organisation called the Economic League. According to the journalists who had unearthed the list, Paul Lashmar and David Leigh, it contained the names of individuals who might be blacklisted from working with businesses in the UK and had been financed by a group of UK companies. Less than 10 years after the article was published, Felix Dennis was not only admired and respected by many people in the business and corporate world, but he was also one of the select few able to take his mother to meet the Prime Minister, Tony Blair, at Number 10 Downing Street, as well as attend HM The Queen's Annual Royal Garden Party.

CHAPTER 28

HARD WIRED

Despite Felix's obvious love of poetry and writing, it was business as usual at Dennis Publishing. Just before the publication of *How to Get Rich* in 2006, the company readied itself to bid farewell to its longest-serving CEO, Alistair Ramsay, and Felix set about the task of finding a replacement.

A nominating panel of Stephen Colvin, Ian Leggett and Dick Pountain had seen seven candidates that included prospective employees from companies such as IPC, Future and Hachette, as well as Dennis Publishing. Four of them were recommended for a second round and Felix's later impressions were telling. In his opinion the standout candidate had impressive man-management skills, 'had definitely thought through the future of the magazine business' and had strong and robust views on the digital and online future that mirrored Felix's own thoughts. However, he had stated that his family must come first, so, although he was prepared for early starts, he would not work late at night. Another candidate, Felix recalled, would 'work like a demon to prove himself', while yet another had 'covered himself in glory' at his current employer.

All in all, Felix and his senior management had a seriously strong list of potential candidates to take over the company and guide it forward at a time when the changes being introduced by the internet were about to become dramatic. In the end, Felix followed the advice that Sir Robin Miller had given him many years before and chose an internal candidate based on the theory that none of the external candidates was more than 30 per cent better than the one who already 'knew the company backwards'. At the beginning of 2006, James Tye took over as CEO of Dennis Publishing.

James had been at Dennis more or less all of his working life, although he didn't actually meet Felix until he had been there for four years. He remembered his first encounter was at a time when he was working in editorial. Felix brought all the editors into the boardroom and told them that all their covers were 'crap'.

'I was really impressed by him,' said James. 'My first impression of Felix was him shouting at me.'

It wasn't until 2000 that he made his first presentation to the board with Felix present. Already ambitious and determined to learn everything about publishing, he had moved from editorial to production and presented the idea of a complete overhaul of the production process.

'I told him that I could save him a million quid,' recalled James. 'He was engaged by that.'

Felix later thanked him for turning what had looked like a very dull subject into something interesting.

The management change was at a time when worldwide sales of *Maxim* were booming, especially in India and Russia, but a plan was underway to sell the brand. Codenamed 'Project Dorothy', it was eventually finalised in 2007, netting $240 million for the sale of *Maxim*, *Blender* and *Stuff* to Quadrangle Capital Partners. The sale provided useful cash for Felix, who had not only continued his build-up of property in the UK, but had also decided to purchase another house in Mustique. It was a luxury villa called Shogun that sat on five acres of land next to Mandalay and it became a stunning addition to his growing portfolio of properties.

By this time Felix had also published a new poetry book entitled *When Jack Sued Jill: Nursery Rhymes for Modern Times*. It contained his take on the follies and absurdities of daily life and included many rewritten nursery rhymes that he had previously introduced on his poetry tours. A single insert in *The Week* sold 1,098 copies. He also compiled a selection of his poems for a book called *Island of Dreams*, which he planned to publish privately to raise money for the Mustique Community Library.

If the nineties had seemed like a productive period of Felix's life, the noughties would prove to be just as busy. His poetry and prose was flowing, he had built up great teams running his companies on both sides of the Atlantic, his estate in Warwickshire was expanding and his role on Mustique was gaining him respect from both homeowners and employees so it was somehow inevitable that something would go wrong. And in true Felix Dennis style it went wrong in a very public way, all thanks to his need for the approval he sought from self-promotion.

Throughout the latter half of 2007, Felix had begun to feel worn down. In June he completed his one thousandth poem, 'I Just Stepped Out'. It was a beautifully crafted reply to those who loved him and might one day miss him, and it tipped more than a nod to WH Auden's acclaimed 'Stop All the Clocks'. Published in *Island of Dreams*, it would become a favourite with many of those who admired Felix's poetry. However, within a month of writing it, he began to feel that, yet again, something was very wrong. He complained of feeling utterly exhausted. Discounting as unlikely the possibility that he might have contracted Legionnaires' disease again, he wondered if he had pneumonia and began a series of tests with doctors both in Harley Street and later at the Old Manor. With no immediate diagnosis, he underwent bone marrow tests in London and was also seen at the Alexandra Hospital in Redditch.

After conferences with many different doctors, including his doctor in Mustique, he was diagnosed as having haemolytic anaemia, a condition that, if severe, requires prompt treatment. He began a series of treatment, including a course of steroids and in time started to feel better. However, he ignored advice not to mix alcohol with his medication and after a particularly long interview with a journalist, where he liberally dispensed wine from his cellar, he became a little over-zealous in his wish to appear interesting. The result was a front-page article in a national newspaper claiming he had admitted to killing a man. It was a great story but those who knew him well simply rolled their eyes. Reading between the lines, they saw a classic case of Felix Dennis fabrication and embellishment. Some said they wouldn't have been at all surprised if Felix had dreamt of doing such a thing, but the possibility that he had was laughable.

Afterwards he withdrew the story unconditionally, explaining that he was drunk and that the combination of the wine and the medication had led him to talk nonsense. Licking his wounds, he went to his cottage in Candlewood to prepare for the launch of *How to Get Rich* in the US. But as James Tye said later, he was bruised. Not long afterwards, James visited him at the Old Manor and asked him how he was. With an uncharacteristic lack of bluster, Felix hesitated and admitted that he felt a bit silly. James knew him well enough to know that, since much of his day-to-day discourse was theatre, this was a rare moment of complete openness.

'It's very rare that you get to the real Felix,' he remembered later.

Although those who knew him well saw through the shield of drama that Felix used to avoid exposing any weakness, his craving for success meant that this same penchant for melodrama had become one of the weapons that he used to great effect in business.

In November 2013, he explained that his attitude to business deals often began with his favourite opening position: 'You appear to be under the impression that you're dealing with somebody who gives a shit. Allow me to correct you. I absolutely don't give a shit. We're either going to come to an agreement, or if we're going to remain as rivals, I'm going to destroy you. And I absolutely will destroy you. And if you think I can't, you're wrong, I will. I don't want to. I'd much, much rather that we came to an agreement here, because it wastes so much time. But do you honestly think you can stand against me? And the answer is no. So stop fucking about and pretending, and let's just get down to the business of who's paying who what, for what services.'

This is a maxim that he said had served him all his life. It had been proven time and again that, if there was higher ground to be had, it is likely that Felix had not only scoped it out but had built his own fortress on it before anyone else had even arrived.

Stephen England remembered one particular lesson that he learned during his early days with the company. It was regarding dealing with the issue of buying print. The standard practice was to have a nice lunch and then arm wrestle, figuratively speaking, about business issues after the meal was over. The printer would want an increase and the buyer would want a discount based on increased business. If all went well, the outcome would be no change to the print cost and everyone would go home relatively happy.

On one occasion as he and Felix were arriving at L'Etoile, a genteel restaurant in London's Charlotte Street, Felix turned to Stephen and gave him a look that said, 'Watch this'. As everyone sat down, Felix made a point of refusing to take his seat, telling the waiter to 'piss off' when he offered to pull out his chair.

'Suddenly he grabs the back of his chair as if he's about to say grace,' remembered Stephen. 'And we all think, "Shit, he's going to say grace, we'd better stand up!" But instead he looks over at the printers and with a voice that silences all the other diners in the restaurant says, "Basically." Just then, another waiter arrives to ask if anyone would like to order a drink and Felix tells him to "Shut up and piss off!" So, with half of the restaurant staring at their food and pretending not to listen, he says, "Tell you what, guys. This is really boring. If we are even going to be talking about an increase, I'm going to leave." As his adversaries begin to balk, Felix says, "Look, guys, let's just make a decision." With every face in the restaurant by this time looking over at their table, the printers just stuttered and said, "OK, just the same price."'

As Stephen remembered, with huge relief they all ordered gin and tonics and proceeded to have a great lunch. He would later refer to it as the 'Gin and Tonic Exocet' – 'because nobody expected it'.

But Stephen didn't believe that Felix pre-planned his attack. 'I think the wiring from Felix's brain to his mouth is very short and is really thick wiring,' he observed. 'I think it was just a wacky idea that he had. He probably thought it up on the way up there.'

Stephen was also interested in management theory, something Felix detested. Occasionally, he would carelessly leave a copy of a book about management techniques on his desk, which on more than one occasion resulted in Felix either burning it or throwing it in the bin. The only one that Stephen remembered being allowed to keep was a small book called *Leadership Secrets of Attila the Hun*, which he described as being 'about using kinds of military iconography and metaphors to manage people in a very Felix way – which is to lead from the front, balls to the wall'.

Jim Maguire, who first worked for Felix at *Oz* magazine, put it another way, describing Felix as a man with a 'rapier-sharp mind in the hands of a ruthless opportunist'. He added that, being a Gemini, there were two sides to him.

'He can be a very charming man,' he said, 'but in business he uses these attributes to mesmerise his prey before striking for the kill. It is nothing personal; it is just the way it is. Felix doesn't take prisoners.'

While most journalists that interviewed Felix came away thinking they had just spoken to a dozen people, his brother Julian, in an interview with the *Sunday Times* magazine in November 1997, summed up that experience.

'People have said to me, "Felix has three or four different faces." And I say, "He's got more than that. And I know every one of them." These faces range from total outright anger to the most charitable person you've ever met.'

In his book *The Trials of Oz*, Tony Palmer related Felix's description of himself as being 'Geminean with schizophrenic tendencies'. At the time he was alluding to the fact that Felix worked in many roles – as business manager, designer and editor – but, as mentioned before, both his brother and many of those who knew him often found it difficult to understand which personality they were dealing with. Felix later admitted that he had his own fair share of Obsessive Compulsive Disorder (OCD) and, in an interview with journalist and friend Jon Snow for a Sky Arts documentary in 2013, he hinted at his individual traits when responding to Jon's question about his 'linear' style. Perhaps giving a clue to his own observations of some of his idiosyncrasies, he said that there were many people like him.

Some people believed that one or two of the idiosyncrasies that Felix displayed might have been attributed to those identified by Austrian paediatrician Hans Asperger, especially when he appeared to display a lack of understanding about how hurt some of his less thick-skinned employees could feel when he berated them. He didn't believe in social niceties, and the concept of telling lies or avoiding the truth in order not to hurt feelings struck him as plain stupid. However, it was those particular traits that not only made him fascinating company, but also gave him some of the edge that made him so successful.

Others who knew him hinted that Felix may have hovered on the edge of the autistic spectrum. On a business level, the fact that he wasn't distracted by the potential to feel hurt meant he could cut through the small talk and get to the point quicker than most. It also allowed him to ignore the grey areas that other people can become mired in. On a personal level, he quickly discovered the best way for him to deal with the emotions that he couldn't quite feel in the same way as everyone else was to keep his relationships on a structured level: he offered friendship and generosity while never really feeling the depth of emotion that many of those he encountered felt. However, that is not to say he didn't have feelings. He did, but they were simply less complex and more childlike.

Despite many people's attempts to label Felix's individuality, perhaps Jon Snow's observation may be closest to the truth. Sitting in the ITN newsroom, surrounded by the bubbling ferment of world news, he explained that he believed there wasn't a classification that Felix could fit into: 'I've met a few autistic and aspergic people in my life,' he said. 'I don't think Felix fitted into that. I don't think Felix fitted into anything, not even a normal human being. He was not normal, he didn't live a normal life. He was a complete one-off individual.' As far as labels went, Jon believed there wasn't one for Felix. 'I'd never got round to giving it a name,' he said. 'It was uniquely Felix.'

What became very apparent when Felix began to write poetry in the latter part of his life was the depth of intellect he was able to draw on when needing to understand situations that did not engender natural emotion in him. His poetry was to become not only a vehicle through which he could analyse the world around him, but also something he regularly used to analyse himself. And although he often hinted at this use of poetry and the distillation of his hard-won philosophy, he would never like to admit it outright.

Pam Harbord, who worked at Bunch in the days before Felix moved to New York, found it strange that he had been attracted to her. Although their relationship was brief, she thought her socialist tendencies were part of the reason they enjoyed each other's company.

'He used to like arguing with me,' she recalled, describing him as an 'aggressive dynamo'. Although she said that he would 'absolutely loathe anybody trying to psychoanalyse him', she could see similarities in their characters that would have created an attraction. Part of that, she said, came from the fact that she had been orphaned at quite a young age. She thought that Felix had a similar background and said, 'All of us with that background like to control our surroundings and I just feel that perhaps Felix likes to control his surroundings more than the rest of us.' However, she agreed that analysis could go on forever, pointing out that 'all of us know aspects of Felix' but nobody, she believed, could actually 'really' know him.

But there were a select few who did get very close to him.

One of his two closest friends, Dick Pountain, also felt that, although it didn't define Felix, the disappearance of his father at such a young age clearly affected him. However, Dick saw the effect as being more indirect.

'A lot of the keys to Felix's attitudes and behaviours are his father's desertion and the effect of that on his mother,' he explained. 'But his mother is probably like that in any case. And that may have been the cause of the desertion, I don't know.'

As Felix admitted, his mother didn't show a great deal of warmth and it would be easy to assume that he didn't benefit from the same sort of love that most mothers give to their children. Dick felt that this definitely influenced Felix's view of how others behaved.

'It affects his attitudes to other people who do the same thing,' he said. 'I mean, he's ferocious about people impregnating girls and not doing the right thing.'

Despite Felix living in a very free and liberal age, he occasionally showed strong traditional values at odds with the supposed ethos of the permissive era. His upbringing, the traits that informed his character and the years through which he came of age made for a complex nature and a definite fear of allowing anyone to get too close too.

Dick pointed to the macho stance that Felix took when it came to relationships.

'His attitude to women, his expressed attitude to women, was that all men pay for it, one way or another. If you don't pay for it with a prostitute, you're paying for it by being married, which is an utterly cynical sort of libertine attitude. How much he actually really believed that, deep down, I don't know. But he definitely had what they nowadays would, in therapy speak, call fear of intimacy.'

What made all this the more confusing was Felix's loyalty to those he befriended.

'He's exceptionally loyal to women that he thinks are in need of his protection,' said Dick. 'And he bestows that protection without any reserve at all. And without any time limit either.'

He felt that Felix may have what he called 'an instrumental view of getting hold of women in the first place' but, once they came into his radar, he would not throw them on a scrap heap.

'Never discarding them – not at all,' he said.

Don Atyeo, Felix's other close friend and cohort from the seventies, was once described by *Time Out*'s Dominic Wells as a 'blunt Australian of scabrous good humour'.

Don also saw the influence of Felix's mother as a factor in how he developed.

'You have two sides of it,' he explained. 'I think he was badly neglected by his mother, who was out being ruthless and single-minded and turning herself into an accountant and bringing home the bacon.'

And while Felix often pointed out how tough their early life was and how his mother's hard work took them from very working-class beginnings to a more middle-class lifestyle, Don believed there was collateral damage.

'You can make of that what you will,' he said. 'I think it was much more emotional depravation than it was physical depravation.'

Don's wife Sue recalled an incident when they were visiting Felix in Mustique that highlighted not only Dorothy's sense of standards, but also her parenting style.

'If you'd have got out of the bath and had a shower and washed your hair and put your make-up on fresh, she'd walk in and you'd feel like you'd just scrubbed the kitchen floor,' she said. 'She was absolutely extraordinary, and once in Mustique, I injured my eye. We were driving in the mule and I hit some branch with some acid on it, and it was very painful. And she was staying there at the time, and she said to me, "Susan, sit down here, put your head on my knee," and I thought, "I'm not putting my head on her knee," and she said, "I'm very good at this because I have absolutely no sympathy for people."'

As Don said later, 'That's how she treated Felix.'

Since he managed to impact on the lives of so many people, it is perhaps inevitable that Felix's life would attract debate and opinion, especially about what created the enigma that became Felix Dennis, but, as he knew probably better than anyone else, it isn't medical, psychological or social labels that define a person, it is the way they live their lives.

Few could deny that Felix lived an extraordinary life, and more.

CHAPTER 29

MIDWIFE TO THE MUSE

At the end of the 2007, Felix visited a boat mooring near his home in Dorsington to look at buying an inland waterway cruiser. Thinking back to the many wonderful holidays he had enjoyed on the Norfolk Broads in his late teens, he told the seller that it would be lovely for his friends' children to be able to enjoy trips down the river when they came to stay. Unfortunately, the seller thought the boat was far too good to have children playing on it and refused to sell. As Felix was leaving, he noticed that the whole site was for sale and in a fit of pique he instructed his estate manager to buy the place. A week later, he spent nearly £750,000 on the whole business, which of course included the boat. It proved a sound investment and he later bought a caravan park next door.

Not all investments were such a success, though. A while later, an over-enthusiastic offer for a website that he thought would be a great online fit for *The Week* had his board scrambling to renegotiate, while another heartfelt attempt to help a failing business in Somerset didn't prove to be quite so sound an investment either.

Caroline Rush took some of the flak for mentioning that the printer who had printed *Island of Dreams* was going into administration. Felix was horrified. Since writing poetry and reading books were the pursuits that gave him the most pleasure, he was very unhappy at the prospect of a big player in the British book printing industry becoming a thing of the past. He insisted, against the judgement of many of those around him, that he was going to invest in Butler & Tanner in Frome, Somerset. By investing money and talent, he was sure that he could turn the company around and, with 300 people facing redundancy, he ploughed many millions into the business as well as bringing in Sir Robin Miller to help bolster the management team.

Sadly, despite everybody's efforts the new business, which had been renamed Butler Tanner & Dennis, simply couldn't survive and, although Felix fought to save it, the company went into administration six years after his original intervention. Sir Robin Miller was as much disappointed for Felix as he was for those directly involved.

'I have a real regret that we didn't make it work better for him,' he said afterwards. Sir Robin explained that he felt Felix got into the business on a whim, 'which is not a great basis to go into anything, quite frankly'. He said the forces against them had been quite formidable and with 'printing companies falling like nine pins over the last three years' it had been a battle they simply couldn't win. Even though the company was to go into administration, Felix's own investment still made a difference. He had personally guaranteed employees a certain level of redundancy if things were to go wrong and he honoured that.

One of the first books printed by the new company in 2008 was Felix's *Homeless in My Heart*. After a reading for the Woodland Trust at the Hay Festival in Hay-on-Wye on a particularly wet and stormy day in the spring, he began to prepare for his next poetry tour to promote the new book. It came during an autumn that offered some stunning Indian summer days. The tour started with a preview in a marquee in his Dorsington arboretum and was followed by Felix completing 15 radio and print interviews in one day. It took in a range of venues, from the Shaw Theatre in London to the Jongleurs Comedy Club in Edinburgh, and had the added bonus of a reading at the Merlin Theatre in Frome, where many of the Butler Tanner & Dennis employees turned up. He remembered it as 'a terrific end to the tour'.

Still on a high, the following week Felix won the Mark Boxer Lifetime Achievement award from the British Society of Magazine Editors. After the ceremony he took the award to Miranda's, his club below the flat in Kingly

Street, where those celebrating with him filled it with champagne and toasted the 'Bearded Dwarf', the nickname he had acquired and dedicated a company poem to. He recalled it as a great party but, when the Society requested the award back in order to engrave his name on it, nobody could remember where it was! Safely tucked away behind the bar, it was retrieved the next day.

Felix had already received the Marcus Morris Award in 1991 from the Professional Publishers Association (PPA) and, to make the triple in 2009, he received the Belsky Award bronze medallion from the Society of Portrait Sculpture for his contribution to sculpture.

But when it came to awards and honours, some were more amusing than gratifying. At a party in Kingly Street in 2011, a friend of Marie-France's awarded Felix a Légion d'honneur medal in honour of his contribution to the consumption of French wine. It was truly an incentive to drink even more French wine. In a rare moment of emotion, Felix hugged the Frenchman but by the end of the evening, unsure what to do with the medal, he stuck it onto the chest of an oil painting of Haile Selassie, former emperor of Ethiopia, that hung on a wall of his flat.

However, of all the awards that Felix was involved with, the one that gained legendary status amongst his employees was an in-house award that he presented at a ceremony at London's Park Lane Hotel in November 2003. Having just completed a poetry reading with actors from the Royal Shakespeare Company at the Swan Theatre in Stratford-upon-Avon, he was used to being the star of the show. However, he had agreed to present the award at the company's Computer and Video Games Golden Joystick Awards ceremony and turned up, as planned.

The evening was hosted by comedian Phill Jupitus, and, after a bit of ad-libbing, Jupitus announced that it was time for the serious business of the evening. With a flourish, he then asked the audience to welcome to the stage 'The chairman of Dennis Publishing, Mr Felix Dennis!' The assembled gathering cheered and a slightly rotund Felix did a penguin walk towards the stage, his hair and beard looking as though it was attempting to escape in a dozen different directions. As the applause died down, Jupitus took one look at him, leaned into the microphone and, with precision timing, said, 'Fuck me, Jeremy Beadle's let himself go a bit!'

Through gritted teeth, Felix gave out the award and when he came back to the table hissed to his sales director Ian Westwood, 'Westy, get me out of here and tell Lloyd to get the fucking car!'

There are no recorded memories of Felix offering to present awards after that evening. From then on, he took no chances and shared the stage with only his poems and a glass of wine.

In 2013 he won the British Media Lifetime Achievement award and from Mustique he sent a video message that included what he claimed was a quote from Groucho Marx: 'If you only hang on long enough, sooner or later the next generation will load you up with victories, none of which are true; load you up with medals, none of which you earned and then load you up with free drinks, all of which you will certainly come to need.' He finished with an autobiographical poem called 'Dwellings'.

Sitting in Writer's Cottage in Mustique in January 2014, Felix admitted that in the days when he was making his living playing drums in a rock and roll band he had no idea how hard actors or other performers worked at their craft. Explaining that watching his poetry being read by RSC actors was a revelation, he said, 'I didn't realise there was a craft. I thought it was just like being a musician. The only way I ever became a musician was I just got up on stage and started playing. I remember people saying you're the worst drummer that has ever fucking lived!'

Watching the RSC at work in 2003 helped him to develop a stage presence that he took forward to future tours. His delivery became more polished and his confidence grew as audiences enjoyed the performance aspect of his readings.

As usual, he put himself through the equivalent of his own university course – watching, learning, reading and rehearsing. It was the same with the craft of writing poetry.

'I had to learn it all myself,' he said. 'I had to sit there and figure out how you write a sestina [a complex verse form] and read all the books. Fortunately there are wonderful, wonderful books on poetics, thank God, because without them I would have been completely fucking lost. But I did put myself through university when I started to write poetry. It was brutal.'

He realised how hard a university student had to work to get a first.

'And I could stop any time I wanted, there was no one going to examine me. But it did mean that once I started to meet poets, once they deigned to talk to me after about six or seven or eight years, they instantly relaxed because I obviously knew a fucking hell of a lot about poetry!'

Indeed, as his poetry improved, so too did his poetry readings.

By the beginning of 2009, Felix had finished the second draft of a book of poems that he was producing to support the Tree Council. Entitled *Tales from the Wood*, it was later taken up by Ebury Publishing and Felix decided to do another poetry tour to promote it. This time, however, he was not only going to add a couple of dates in Ireland but he also decided to commission a writer to produce a book about the tour. *Did I Mention the Free Wine?* was to tell its own story, and, although its author and one-time *Maxim* editor Jason Kersten had a vague hope that it might be another *Fear and Loathing in Las Vegas*, it didn't quite live up to that level of mayhem. As he explained, 'We weren't going to have hard drugs and we weren't kids.'

However, he still subtitled it *Madness, Mayhem and The Muse*. Part of his contract with Felix included agreement that he could scatter his grandmother's ashes over Edinburgh from Felix's helicopter.

A resident of Brooklyn, New York, Jason had originally grown up in northern California and, after winning an in-house poetry competition at Dennis Publishing in America, he had ended up having lunch with Felix in the boardroom. What he had envisaged as a smart boardroom lunch with the chairman turned out to be sandwiches and a glass of wine, and when Jason foolishly told Felix what he thought was wrong with the company, Felix invited the other employees in to listen. It took some time before Jason's colleagues forgave him for his outburst.

However, he did get to know Felix and to see him through a highly entertaining poetry tour.

'He's one of the few larger-than-life characters I got to know well,' remembered Jason, 'and certainly the wealthiest person I have ever met.

He definitely breaks the mould in a lot of ways. He walks the decks with the people who work for him. I think he could have had an even bigger company, but if he had gotten too removed from it, he wouldn't have enjoyed it so much. He's very family-oriented. He doesn't have children but he's got paintings or drawings of all the employees at Dennis UK and Dennis US. He thought of it as his family and he was accessible.'

The tour had many moments of amusement and drama that Jason brilliantly recorded in his book, but there were also times when he saw a side of Felix that most people didn't get to see.

'I've seen him sad and I've seen him crying – that was hard,' he explained.

Midway through the tour, Felix attended the funeral of the wife of an old friend and read out his poem 'I Just Stepped Out'. The following day he was informed that another old friend, Sue Miles, had also passed away.

In the previous 12 months, 11 of his friends and colleagues had died, and, as Jason remembered, it had hit him hard. 'He wasn't hiding it, he wasn't being stoic or anything,' said Jason.

One of the big lessons he remembered learning from Felix on that tour was that 'You could be rich as Croesus but, if you're not happy, it doesn't matter. Wealth can provide a certain amount of comfort and privilege but it's not going to make you a happy person.'

While Jason agreed that one of the things often bothering Felix was not being taken seriously by the poetry elite, he also believed he had learned to accept it.

'He's come to grips with that,' said Jason. 'How many poets are recognised while they are alive?'

Despite Felix's belief that his work might get better attention in the years after his death, his fan base was growing and, after he had completed three successful tours, his poems were reaching out to people on many different levels. Although his work was labelled 'populist', that didn't bother him. He was speaking about his life and reaching an incredibly varied audience that both empathised and understood what he was saying.

At a fundraiser for the Marines in Exeter Cathedral in November 2010, Major General Buster Howes read Felix's poem 'On News of a Friend's

Sudden Death' to a congregation of over 3,000 people. His ode to canine friends, 'An Old Dog is the Best Dog', had already found its way onto tea towels, aprons and T-shirts all over the world, and, as he would explain to audiences during his poetry tours, it even had its own pirated video on YouTube.

In 2011, he was invited to join a poetry reading to celebrate the fiftieth anniversary of Amnesty International, having just sold out two nights at the Courtyard Theatre in Stratford-upon-Avon.

One of his favourite stories to tell audiences on tour was about his mother's reaction when he first showed her one of his poems in a Penguin anthology. After looking at it intently, she gently tugged at the page and, on finding it hadn't been stuck in by Felix, said, 'That's very nice, dear, but how much did you pay them to put it in?'

By the end of 2011, Felix was being filmed for a documentary for Sky Arts, *Felix Dennis: Millionaire Poet, Britain's Rich List Bard*. In the middle of filming, however, Felix dropped a bombshell.

A couple of days after a board meeting where Dennis Publishing UK celebrated their best ever year, Felix had undergone root canal work at a Harley Street dental clinic. He then boarded a private jet to head off to Mustique for the Christmas holiday. His guests over the break included Dick Pountain and his partner Marion, Jon Snow with his wife Precious, as well as Eric and Carolyn Shaw, at whose wedding in New York Felix had taken on the role of best man. Having completed 21 poems in one month, he was in buoyant mood, except for a slight irritation in his throat, which he initially put down to the recent dental treatment. He and Marie-France threw a big party at Mandalay, where Felix spent much of the time chatting to Robbie Williams.

The next day, his other close friends, Don and Sue Atyeo, arrived for a two-week stay, only to find that Felix's doctor had decided to order him back to England. He was concerned that the irritation that Felix was experiencing could possibly be caused by cancer of the pharynx. By 4.30pm that day, Felix shakily boarded a Gulfstream jet to Birmingham. After travelling to London the next morning, he underwent tests that confirmed his worst fear: he had cancer.

As many cancer victims have explained, once a diagnosis has been made, things can happen fast. In Felix's case he spent one day holed up in the Old Manor in a state of shock before calling close members of staff together to give them the grave news. He spent the next few days trying to get to grips with a range of differing opinions from specialists, all of whom believed their own suggestion of treatment would be best. Sitting in his Kingly Street office in May 2013, he remembered the bewildering range of opinions and revealed how he believed wealth may have affected his treatment.

'That's another problem with having too much money,' he declared. 'You go and see too many, it's ridiculous!'

He admitted that in some ways he was going from one doctor to another, waiting to get the diagnosis he wanted.

'Everywhere I went, I got different advice,' he explained. 'Then I began to realise that a turf war, a cancer turf war, had erupted in London.'

Felix believed that the number of cancer treatment centres around the city was going to be reduced and that they were all fighting to survive. He got the impression from some that he might have provided a useful public relations coup, if they had saved him. One doctor told him that he was going to undertake a great operation and, in return, Felix would build him a hospital. That particular episode left him more than a little sceptical and he found the whole experience of meeting with some of those who might save his life traumatic, to say the least.

'Meeting all those consultants, specialists, surgeons, radiographers, the whole panoply, was utterly confusing, terrifying, contradictory and very frightening,' he revealed.

In the end he chose the John Radcliffe Oxford University Trust hospital, partly because it was only a little over an hour away from the Old Manor, but also because the surgeon he spoke to offered some hope about what had become one of Felix's most important attributes – his voice. He told him that he was aware of his interest in reciting poetry and said there was no guarantee, but that he was pretty sure he could do the operation without damaging the vocal cords. In every aspect of his life, whether arguing with teachers, singing in a band, shouting at his staff or reading poetry on tours around the world, Felix's voice was a profound expression of his personality.

After receiving news that his stepmother, Pam Allery, had died unexpectedly in Australia, and knowing he would soon undertake major surgery, Felix began writing letters to close friends and business colleagues. On 24 January 2012, he wrote a note to all of his personal staff, senior managers and colleagues, leaving instructions that it wasn't to be opened until after his death.

'This is a letter I hoped you would never read because it means that I am dead and no longer around to shout at you,' he wrote. 'But the company is not dead! My poetry is not dead! My trees in the forest are not dead. And best of all, my dear friends and colleagues, you are not dead.'

He went on to explain that he had had a wonderful life and that he had packed more into it than some could have done with three or four lifetimes. All he asked was that people should remember him with a smile on their face.

Two weeks later, he underwent a successful six-hour neck and mouth operation and those letters were put back in the safe. It appeared that Felix had cheated death once again.

By the end of March, having agreed to undertake a course of radiotherapy, Felix sat in the kitchen at Welshman's Cottage to film an interview with Jon Snow, an additional segment of the *Felix Dennis: Millionaire Poet* documentary. Those present remembered it as one of the most extraordinary interviews they had ever witnessed.

Over the years, Jon and Felix had become close friends and the emotion in the room was palpable. Felix explained that he was enraged to have contracted cancer.

'I'm just a human being,' he said, 'and I'm frightened with what is happening and what's going to happen in the near future. I have been lucky, I was born lucky.'

Reminding him that when they began filming for the documentary Felix had talked casually about death and ageing, Jon then steered the conversation onto love, asking Felix if he had ever been in love.

'I'm too selfish,' he replied. However, he believed there were many people that shunned love, explaining, 'To do so makes you defenceless.'

Felix spoke with honesty and strength and this was a conversation where he seemed to ignore the cameras. There was none of the bluster and dramatics that he had shown himself to be so adept at during previous filming.

'A lot of rot is spoken about passion and love,' he continued. 'I think that a hell of a lot more important than so-called love is respect, companionship and friendship.'

Those were things that he said he had experienced 'abundantly'.

Throughout the following year, that abundant experience of respect and friendship was apparent through the endless trail of messages and well-wishers who wrote to him and visited him. Close friends such as Don Atyeo and his wife Sue, Dick Pountain and his partner Marion and Peter Godfrey spent time with him at the Old Manor as he attempted to recover. The Prime Minister of St Vincent, Ralph Gonsalves, and his wife Eloise visited, as did Basil Charles, Sir Robin Miller, Tony Elliott, Major General 'Buster' Howes and Sir Freddy Ballantyne, past Governor-General of St Vincent and the Grenadines. Marie-France entertained guests and cooked for Felix as he tried to develop an appetite.

Felix's dream of providing a beautiful place for his friends and colleagues to visit and enjoy his hospitality blossomed as those who cared about him came to help him recuperate.

His voice held all of its power but his diet was curtailed to foods that didn't hurt his throat or set his mouth on fire. Most irritating of all, he was unable to drink much from his cellar of fine wine, at least not without sacrilegiously diluting it with water.

Throughout this time his mother suffered a number of falls, illnesses and a stroke, and he and his brother Julian did their best to make her comfortable. However, despite appearing to have beaten throat cancer, other aspects of Felix's health still haunted him. He developed a hernia, suffered from shingles again and even endured a lung cancer scare, which was discounted after a chest X-ray. At times he was utterly despondent and even the delivery of two new cars, a Maybach and a Bentley Mulsanne, didn't ease the pain.

But what galled him most was the fact that he felt his poetry output had waned. He had joked with Jon Snow that the cancer should have been a great opportunity to write masses of hugely profound verse, but later complained this hadn't been the case. The fact is he did write poetry throughout the year of his treatment and recovery but he was furious at the low volume of the output. He had neither the time nor the strength to 'play midwife to the muse', he said. What's more, his brush with death hadn't kick-started inspiration as he thought it should: 'It was galling to discover, too, that the fear of death supplied so little creative juice. I had imagined one would be scribbling away like mad as oblivion neared.'

As Dennis Publishing launched a new magazine, *Cyclist*, named by Felix even though he wasn't entirely convinced of its potential, he battled through his treatment, determined that, as he had been born lucky, he would eventually get through.

On 4 October 2012, two days after writing a poem to Marie-France banning her from his presence so she would have better memories of him, he was given the all clear. Kerin O'Connor, Ian Leggett and Wendy Kasabian were in the room when he put a call from his doctor on speakerphone after a CT scan.

'All clear. No cancer found,' was the result. Felix was to live to fight another day.

CHAPTER 30
I JUST STEPPED OUT

One of the first things Felix decided to do on learning that he had been given a cancer 'all clear' was to instruct Caroline Rush to book a date at the Courtyard Theatre in Stratford-upon-Avon for a poetry reading. It proved to be a huge success.

On 13 December 2012, he played to a packed house and was buoyed by both the support of friends and colleagues, as well as the enthusiasm of the local crowd. Within days he was discussing publishing proposals for 2013 with his long-time friend and publisher Gail Rebuck, now Baroness Rebuck, of Random House. While spending Christmas in Mustique he further developed his plans, which included a new book to be named after a poem he had written on the day he had first been diagnosed. It was to be called *Love, of a Kind* and he would promote it with a 30-city poetry tour. In his excitement, he contemplated another tour of America and even hinted at going further afield. He also planned another two books, as well as a boxed set of songs from the Mustique Blues Festival entitled *Blues in Paradise*. In line with the style of his book *88 The Narrow Road*, Felix had developed a habit of making lists of what he hoped to achieve in each coming year and, practically bubbling with enthusiasm, he added in a plan to celebrate the planting of his millionth tree, as well as organising a David Hockney-style painting plan for a new shepherd's hut for the garden of the Old Manor.

Despite his long association with the computer industry, he had always refused to use an email address but he did take to using Facebook to announce his poetry plans, as well as adopting it as a platform to expound some of his occasionally antagonistic philosophies. He also took the time to write a series of letters giving an insight into what defined his life during what some might have called his middle age. He explained that, although he was still in love with the business of making money, something else had overtaken all other influences on his soul.

'Poetry is it,' he said. 'Poetry is the "Power of One" for me. Like the Delta Blues musician Robert Johnson, I have sold my soul in a Faustian pact to compose at least one or two immortal lines of verse. No matter who mocks such an ambition, no matter how impossible it is. No matter how many thousands of hours are spent trying to write those lines. Destined to fail or to succeed, I shall perish in the trying.'

This turned out to be a poignant and prophetic statement. Delving into the furthest recesses of his heart, he had at last laid himself bare for all to see. He had found love – at least love of a kind. But it wasn't with any one human being, it was with the mysteries of life. His true love was an obsession with distilling those mysteries into easily digestible stanzas, and, if at all possible, sharing those thoughts with as many people as might listen. In some ways he had opened up as the little boy who wanted to tell everybody what he had just discovered on the beach.

After what would be Felix's final performance at the Mustique Blues Festival, when his voice simply couldn't get away with singing any more, the Prime Minister of St Vincent and the Grenadines came to stay at Mandalay in February 2013. Felix threw a cocktail party but was disappointed when Prince William, Duke of Cambridge, called to say that he and his wife Kate would have to decline his invitation because, if the Prince attended a party with a prime minister present, it would have been seen as an official visit.

Kate's sister Pippa was able to attend but she had to remind Felix of their first meeting when he had invited her family to tea on one of their first visits to the island. It had been so many years before that at first he didn't recognise her, and was surprised to be reminded that she and her sister had played in his games room many times. Relating the story a year later, he laughed, 'The future Queen of England was playing in my games room and I didn't even know it!'

Having selected 365 poems from an initial list of 1,150, Felix came up with the idea to illustrate the next book with Eric Gill drawings. Although he admitted that he was an unlikely collector, over the years he had acquired a wide range of art and sculpture and his Gill collection was one of the largest in private hands. Over the coming months, with the help of designer Rebecca Jezzard, he put the finishing touches to the manuscript and began recording poems with composer George Taylor, who had long been collaborating with Felix on recordings and videos for his poetry tours and books. With the book due to be launched in May of that year, Caroline Rush was busy organising the next *Did I Mention the Free Wine?* poetry tour, which they had decided to call *The Cut Throat Tour – 'A Smile from Ear to Ear'*. Billing Felix as an 'international phenomenon', whom poet and author Christopher Rush had called 'the uncrowned Poet Laureate', the tour was structured in two 'slices'. The first, in June and July, would start in London and finish in the Irish city of Cork and the second slice would run from 9 September in Cambridge and finish in Coventry on 17 October.

After raising another £17,000 opening his garden for charity, Felix prepared for what would be his fifth major poetry tour of the UK. Autographing copies of the new book in his Kingly Street office before taking to the stage at London's Bloomsbury Ballroom, he was animated. It had already been more than a year since he had given up smoking, a monumental feat in itself but especially for a man who had publicly berated New York Mayor Rudy Giuliani in a restaurant for banning smoking in public places. However, he looked fitter than he had in some time and joked that perhaps taking on such a long tour so soon after dealing with throat cancer might be a bit mad.

'This is a bit like an old Lothario who's now in his sixties,' he mused, 'trying to prove he can still pick up girls and drink and do all the things he used to do. Possibly he can, but it will take its bloody toll!'

Despite his age and the strain that a lifetime of pushing himself to over-achievement might have taken on his body, he had no intention of shirking when it came to delivering a great performance for those who would come to his gigs.

Like the old Lothario he had alluded to, he also couldn't resist a plug for the sexual excesses that had been a big part of the Felix Dennis brand over his earlier years. Joking about how the actor Michael Douglas had recently blamed cunnilingus for his throat cancer, Felix said, 'And you know what? I think he may be right. How amusing it would be if all the girls had had their revenge on me and it had nothing to do with the cigarettes and Johnnie Walker!'

On an uncharacteristically personal level, he also talked about some of the traits that allowed him to reach beyond what he could naturally comprehend.

'I'm not as immensely empathetic as perhaps my poetry is,' he explained. 'When I'm writing, I'm a totally different person because I'm immensely patient, I'm incredibly empathetic, very empathetic, and I can put myself in a woman's position, in an old person's position, in a dying person's position, in a young child's position. I can do that and I've always been able to do it. Can I do this in real life? ... No!'

He admitted that perhaps his consumption of literature might have had some effect.

'I think I may have read far more than is good for me,' he said, 'and there is a lot of wisdom in poetry and prose and maybe some of it has rubbed off.'

However, he believed the real motivation for his obsession with learning was his impatience. His long-time personal assistant Wendy Kasabian had put it mildly, saying he had 'the patience of a gnat'.

His explanation was: 'Because life is so short and there's so many things to do, so many sights to see, so many things to achieve and try, I'm terribly, terribly impatient. I just cannot bear wasting time.'

His friend Jon Snow had always been struck by how Felix knew so much. Sitting in Felix's Kingly Street kitchen in 2014, he said, 'He had a really encyclopaedic knowledge of life. It is very difficult to encapsulate him because he is a complete one-off. There is nobody else on earth that has lived the life he's lived.'

*

The opening night of the tour proved to be a triumph. Felix's voice gave no clue of what it had been through, and he prowled the stage and turned on the drama for a crowd that showed their appreciation as though they were at a Rolling Stones concert. In poetry terms, perhaps they were. As he signed copies of books for the long queue of well-wishers and fans after the performance, he was jovial and energised. In so many ways it was a comeback tour and, for Felix, it was coming back from an abyss that a little over a year beforehand had seen him writing what he thought were to be last letters to loved ones and colleagues.

He had planned the tour to include a long enough break in the middle to completely rest and then he flew to Mustique, where he worked on a small book of advice for young teenagers. It was called *Do What The Fuck I Say* and he planned to publish it under a pseudonym. Felix also completed the first draft of another book, *This is the Way of the World*, a selection of poems charting life's course from birth through death. Compiled in life stages, it was illustrated by Bill Sanderson.

Sadly, during July, as he was working on it, his old friend Mick Farren collapsed and died onstage at the Borderline in Soho. Felix later arranged to have Mick buried in Dorsington Woods, just below the Old Manor. He remembered the funeral as a raucous, bittersweet affair and Mick was buried with a 'tot of Jack Daniel's and a loaded dice'. Felix wrote a poem for Mick, which was carved into a headstone in the shape of a belt and buckle. He credited him as a 'true friend, a true original and a lynchpin of the sixties'.

The following day, Felix attended a ceremony in a field at his nearby estate of Middle Spernal, near the Old Manor, where, along with 200 guests, he planted the Heart of England Forest's millionth tree. It was an extraordinary achievement at which wine connoisseur Hugh Johnson appeared as one of the many guests of honour, and, in true Felix form, he went from table to table, shaking a bucket full of coins to encourage guests to contribute to the charity fund. In his element, he explained that the million British broadleaf trees that he had planted were just 10 per cent of what he hoped would eventually make up the Heart of England Forest.

He admitted that there was no chance that he would live long enough to see even a fraction of the rest of those saplings go into the ground, but what he didn't know was just how few of those trees he would actually live to see planted.

Ten days later, still in the middle of his poetry tour, Felix was diagnosed with terminal lung cancer. Tests had found tumours in both lungs, and his condition was inoperable.

With the last quarter of the tour still to come, Felix went into shock. Later, he explained that, before the diagnosis, he had actually had a premonition that he had lung cancer. Despite a lifelong reluctance to involve himself in irrational superstition, he related how the day before his tests he had been walking in Ralph's Wood, the first wood he had ever planted, and had stopped to rest his hand on a rowan tree.

'I suddenly became convinced that I had lung cancer,' he recalled. On his return he immediately phoned his doctor, Tim Shackley, who suggested that it was probably just a cold, but when Felix insisted there was something more, Tim had booked him in for a chest X-ray in Stratford-upon-Avon the next morning.

Later, Felix talked about the supposed magical powers of the rowan tree and mentioned how in folklore the tree was said to be able to talk to humans. He admitted that he didn't really believe a tree had spoken to him but, as he had often spoken to his trees as though they were his children, he said he could never be certain that there hadn't been some kind of organic intervention. Later looking at a positive aspect of the event, he said that the episode had allowed him a little extra time to decide what he wanted to do with the rest of his life.

The rest of the tour was a maelstrom of emotional turmoil. Readings were suffused with intensity and public passion, while beneath Felix's attempts at bravado there was private despair. He visited Oxford, London, Norwich, Liverpool, Leeds, Manchester and Coventry and decided to add an extra date at the Bloomsbury Ballroom in London to secretly bid a poignant farewell to friends, colleagues and fans. Along with the free wine, he added free champagne to every table, and, wearing his Légion d'honneur, he read his poems with a passion that surpassed anything audiences had seen before. As the whole crew gathered on the stage for the end-of-tour photographs, only a handful of people realised that the tears Felix had wept backstage were due to more than the emotion brought about by the culmination of the tour.

He had decided to tell only those who needed to know. This was the second time that he had faced a loaded gun but on this occasion there was no way out, and he didn't want to put everyone else through the months of pain and anguish that lay ahead. The agony of telling the truth to those close to him, while lying to those well-wishers who congratulated him on his recovery from throat cancer, had been overwhelming. There were times, as he dealt with the enormous task of organising the life that he would leave behind and appearing to live the life that others expected of him, when he felt everything that was going on around him was like a blurred cinematic dream on an endless loop. Colleagues were shell-shocked, friends were desolate and lovers inconsolable.

Before going to have a last lunch with Michael Heseltine at Thenford Manor, to give him the news and have a walk around Lord Heseltine's arboretum, Felix watched as the daughter of one of his old friends, Maria Lexton, scattered her mother's ashes in his own arboretum across the lane from the Old Manor. Every moment and every act seemed coated with a glaze of poignancy as he tried to combat a growing sense of a destiny beyond his grasp.

He then made a final trip to New York to inform senior staff and spend the night in his apartment there. Surrounded by his books, with the words of Chaucer, Aristotle, Dostoyevsky, Gabriel García Márquez, as well as Frost, Wilde, Keats and Wilbur, he stared past the all-seeing Buddha that was always a powerful presence in his sitting room. With the noise of the traffic from 2nd Avenue seeping through the balcony door, he said an emotional goodbye to his old girlfriend Suzen, and had his driver Alen Chen take him to Candlewood Lake for one last meeting with his long-time partner Peter Godfrey.

As he waited for Peter to arrive, Felix slowly ambled around the house. Every wall in every room called to him. On the mantelpiece he fingered the hunting knife which, inspired by Sherlock Holmes, he had used to pin papers to the wooden surface. A bowler hat stuffed with predictions and wisdom from dozens of fortune cookies sat on a sculpted head by his reading chair. On the outside deck, a tree growing through the timber boards seemed to relax and breathe as the boats that sped across the lake made their way home, and in the basement, alongside his selection of fine wines, Felix pushed his thumb against the flipper lever of one of two pinball machines that brought back memories of evenings spent in London pubs.

He and Peter shared a bottle of Puligny-Montrachet and wept quietly together. Felix later explained that they had explored depths of sensitivity that neither had known existed.

Back in England he spent two days working on his will with Simon Goldberg from Simons, Muirhead & Burton, the firm whose help he had enlisted after his former solicitor Michael Nixon had died many years before. Felix had originally helped fund the firm's pro bono team that looked after the interests of prisoners on Death Row (the department later became known as the 'Death Penalty Project'). Working on his will, Simon recalled that Felix was forensic in his quest to ensure he looked after his friends and colleagues. His efforts came as no surprise to Simon. 'I can't tell you how many clients that we have, where Felix picked up the tab,' he said. 'All kinds of things, matrimonial, property, litigation, educational – sometimes even his private office didn't know he was doing it. He really disliked injustice.'

By the middle of November 2013, Felix had made a major decision: he was going to spend the last days of his life doing what he loved best, working and writing poetry. However, he wasn't going to let anyone see him degenerate, he would do it alone. Before leaving to take a private jet to Mustique, he sat in the conservatory overlooking Highfield and the Old Manor garden, and signed two Christmas cards: one was for his mother and the other for his brother Julian.

Later, he wrote a poem that explained his feeling of needing to 'leave the tribe'. The final two lines were: 'I would not have them see what I became – Far better they remember what I did'.

Arriving in Mustique, not knowing how long or painful the next phase of his life might be, Felix worked on the list of what he wanted to achieve in 2014. It was a shorter list than normal but included efforts to look after those close to him, as well as deal with the business and charity arrangements for Dennis Publishing and the Heart of England Forest. He had always said he would leave his money to the charity and so he set about finalising those plans. He also fought bitterly with his financial advisers to try to ensure his homes around the world could be kept available to his friends and colleagues. After commissioning the final sculptures for his Garden of Heroes & Villains, one of blues musician Robert Johnson and one of himself holding a sapling, he also began work on what he assumed would be his last book of poetry. To be called *I Just Stepped Out*, it would be what he described as a 'verse diary' of poems written in the months leading up to his death. He guessed, quite rightly, that a mind such as his, inspired by the imminence of death, might offer profound insights into the lives that we lead. However, he laughed at the possibility that it might be published while he was still alive, joking that he had better be dead by the time it came out, or people might think he was milking the sympathy.

The final two items on his list of things to achieve were: 'Keep pecker up; break open the good wine; combat despair' and 'Die "a good death" whenever, wherever'.

Like a short remission, Felix's need to avoid visitors didn't come for a few months. Close friends came to stay at Mandalay and for a time he was able to use Facebook as a platform to communicate with the many people who wanted to keep up with him. Having spent a great deal of their friendship debating religion and the existence of God, the Prime Minister of St Vincent and the Grenadines rang from Italy with the news that he had recently seen the Pope and had asked him to pray for Felix. It was an amusing interlude later to be blighted by news of a Christmas Eve storm that caused terrible damage on the nearby island of St Vincent. On Christmas Day he made his traditional journey, dressed up as an elf, to accompany Basil Charles and give out Christmas presents to the local children.

Felix took a childlike pleasure in having drinks around the new fire pit that had been built in the grounds of the main house. He entertained neighbours and visitors and also took the opportunity to discuss his philosophy of life whenever he had the energy. Sitting on the small deck at the edge of Writer's Cottage, with a breathtaking view of the ocean below, he was able to appreciate the life he had lived and those who had played a part in it.

'I've been very lucky,' he said, 'very lucky, with men and women. For whatever reason, I've had bucket-loads of loyalty. I've never married, it's true. I didn't have any children, but in a way, with my companies and my private office and my estate, I have created families. So they are my families.'

However, he admitted that he often preferred to be alone. He remembered the times when he would disappear for days on end and revealed: 'I'm a loner. I've always enjoyed being on my own.' He confided that when he was younger he had often just 'buggered off' to go walking in the woods and would stay in a bed and breakfast. And like anyone living in close proximity to their families, he enjoyed time away from them.

'When you're making decisions all the time and you've got a big personal staff, they do get on your nerves after a while,' he said. 'You just want to get away from them.'

Jon Snow, who was one of his guests during the weeks around Christmas 2013, believed that Felix had taken a conscious decision some time before to avoid the intimacy that came from caring too much for those around him.

'It's as if he sort of resolved that he wouldn't be able to be who he wanted to be, and do what he wanted to do, if he cluttered himself up with this baggage of care,' said Jon, 'which meant that he could spread it around, which he did. He did so many things for so many people.'

Remembering the moment in *Millionaire Poet* when he had asked Felix if he had ever been in love, Jon said: 'And he said, "No, I never have," which is an extraordinary statement when you think there was so much love in his life. He was very loved and he gave a lot of love. Maybe the fact that he didn't have a huge "love target" meant that he could spread it about more.'

Gail Rebuck, chair of Penguin Random House UK, had known Felix from his early days at *Oz* magazine and agreed that he had taken control of his life at an early age. Sitting in her office in Random House in London, she believed that poetry was the expression of Felix's intelligence that had been hidden by his earlier years as a 'crazy non-conformist'. She thought that he was able to access the same emotions as those around him but that he had taken a conscious decision to build a wall about himself, and was unable to knock it down.

'He just made a decision very, very young that his trajectory was going to be forward,' she said. 'He was going to be successful and he wasn't going to listen to anyone and he was going to do it his way.' Remembering that he had brushed off setbacks and taken massive bets in his life, she believed that Felix had elected to 'artificially believe in himself'. So much so that that artificial belief became real and 'he created this persona which became locked. It was concrete, it was there and that's where he remained.'

James Tye explained that Felix was very loved, 'but he would have hated if anyone had said it'. He believed love was something that Felix could never really deal with very well.

'He went through life believing he couldn't love anyone because it was a weakness,' said James, 'but life's not that simple. He did engender a lot of love. People were really affectionate toward him, even if they only met him a few times. It's the complexity of Felix that makes him so intoxicating.'

The tragedy that often emerged in his poetry was the image of a lost child unable to accept the love that was denied him in his youth. Jon Snow believed Felix to be 'profoundly lonely' and, as his close friend Don Atyeo admitted, Felix didn't enjoy his wealth that much either. Even though he owned beautiful houses in Warwickshire, he tended to hide away in a converted barn on the edge of the estate. Felix admitted that he did shy away from people and listed the places that he could go to: 'The Welshman's, The Summerhouse, The Shepherd's cote, The Recording Studio, The Quiet Room, The Old Manor Study... So there's quite a few.' To him all these places were dens to which he could escape, to be alone or just to get away from people in general. If he couldn't get away, he said they would 'drive me crazy'.

Understanding Felix's needs, Don pointed out, 'When he's in Mustique, he has all these houses, but he's down in the Writer's Cottage from dusk to dawn!'

As well as spending his money on creating places in which he could hide in hobbit-like splendour, there were also occasional moments of amusement with Felix's lavish outlay. He often told the story of how he commissioned a watch that was so exclusive that it took nearly a year to have made, and when he stopped wearing it for a while he wondered why it ceased to work. The watchmaker explained that the watch was designed to be worn consistently and if Felix wanted to leave it unused for a period of time then he would have to find a way to ensure it was given a shake every now and then. On hearing that the Duke of Edinburgh used a similar device, he spent £5,000 on an electronic rotating wrist to keep the watch ticking.

On another occasion, when he couldn't decide which of two Rolls-Royces to buy, one of his friends laughed that he had paintings on his living room wall worth more than the two cars put together. Felix promptly bought both cars.

In order to ensure he could listen to the music he liked in each of his homes, he had identical jukeboxes placed in each one, with an identical selection of tracks so he wouldn't have to spend too much time finding what he wanted to listen to.

But as he went to great lengths to explain in his book *How to Get Rich*, Felix's obsession with chasing money hadn't made him happy. What had made him happy, and what had truly defined him, was writing poetry.

For the next six months, when he wasn't sorting out his affairs or helping to re-energise the deal to provide every child in St Vincent with a free computer; or making sure that the other huge legacy of his life, the Heart of England Forest project, would succeed, he wrote poetry. He filled hundreds of yellow lined pages with words he hoped would live long in a world that he was furious to be leaving behind.

By June 2014, Felix had written nearly 200 poems since his lung cancer diagnosis. He selected from those for the new book, *I Just Stepped Out*, and in many ways he saw it as his swan song. He had read the book

When I Die: Lessons From The Death Zone, which had been written by Gail Rebuck's late husband Philip Gould, while he was dying of cancer. There were many parallels to the ways both he and Felix chose to deal with their impending deaths. In Felix's case there were no children to leave behind and his predominant emotion was anger, but, in the same way as Lord Gould, he was determined to chart the journey to its end, in his case through the use of poetry. Lord Gould wrote that having an idea of the likely timescale of your life is a privilege not available to many. It is much better than sudden death with no time to prepare, he said. He believed that the knowledge of one's likely early death also allowed a person to reconfigure time. In his case he began to look at time in terms of what he called 'richer conceptions of progression – relationships, emotional connection and spiritual understanding'.

One of the poems in Felix's book *I Just Stepped Out*, entitled 'Time Dying', was his response to Lord Gould's concept of the reconfiguration of time.

'Expanding or contracting, cursed or blessed, Time dying is infinity compressed,' he wrote.

By the end of May 2014, having long since chosen not to have any further treatment for his cancer, Felix was constantly suffering from breathlessness and was beginning to show outward signs of his deep anger and frustration at his helplessness. He wrote what he said was the most 'reluctant poem' he had ever written, confiding that perhaps it was time to lay aside his pen, worried he had little left to say. In fact, he would write more poems, but, as his close friends Don Atyeo and Dick Pountain came to Mustique to spend time with him, he was desolate and shocked when told by his doctor that his time was running out.

For months he had faced his death and had mined his thoughts and emotions to try to make sense of his life. However, two things conspired to undermine whatever spirit had sustained him since the previous October; one was his worry that he didn't have the energy to write down his thoughts anymore and the other was the fact that his voice was wavering. As Gail Rebuck explained later, Felix's voice was his power source.

'It was the outside manifestation of that self-belief,' she said.

And it was under attack.

On 8 June, Felix wandered from room to room in Mandalay looking at and touching objects that he would never see again. He noted it as a very sad day, knowing that everything he looked at or spoke to was for the last time after 19 years.

After flying by private jet to Coventry, he was collected by his chauffeur Lloyd and brought back to the Old Manor, where he refused to see even his closest friends. Within a week he found that the effort to speak to his colleagues in London was impossible, even by telephone – so he took complete control of his own destiny. Voiceless and helpless, he decided it was time to shut down.

On Sunday, 22 June 2014, Felix curled himself into a foetal position in his bed, and with Marie-France holding his hand, simply stopped breathing. Left to be alone with him while staff went to contact an undertaker, Marie-France climbed into the bed beside him and, finding him still warm, she closed her eyes, silently wept, and slowly went to sleep.

MORE LIVES THAN ONE

For those who live more lives than one,
Who live a life as I have done,
Where 'X' and 'Y' know 'B' and 'C'
But none know 'D' excepting me;
Their life a stone stripped bare of moss,
New ancient mariners of loss,
Cold connoisseurs of solitaire,
Whose laughter barely masks despair;
Whose sum is less than all their parts,
Who wander — homeless in their hearts —
Through others' lives, as in a play,
Who roam to keep the world at bay;
Who comet-like, delight to force
Unwary planets from their course,
Whose speech is consciously deployed
To camouflage an aching void...
With such as these — with all who nurse
This wanton, self-inflicted curse,
Beware their flares — and learn to shun
All those who live more lives than one.

AFTERWORD

In a tranquil corner of the Dorsington Estate, Stephen Coffey, forestry manager for the Heart of England Forest, has planted a small group of elm trees. They are surrounded by a circle of grassland, which itself is then surrounded by more trees. To one side of the circle the grassland zigzags in two sharp bends around more elms, leading to a dead end of woodland.

For a walker the area might appear to be nothing more than a pleasant, though slightly random, oasis of grassland in the midst of a beautiful wood, but from the air or on a map the planting scheme shows something more meaningful. The trees and grassland are in the shape of an 'O' and a 'Z' in tribute to what many people felt was one of the defining periods of Felix Dennis's life – his beginnings at *Oz* magazine.

It is also perfectly designed if any celestial bodies should happen to glance in that direction, and for those who might like to believe that Felix is sitting on a cloud next to the Angel Gabriel, gazing down at the growth of a vision that drove him to carry on making money for the Heart of England charity, the picture of OZ in one corner of the forest is apt.

He wasn't a religious man and had he found himself in Heaven he would probably have spent most of his time arguing for a complete rethink of God's marketing strategy. But he was a man with a vision, and it was an ambition larger than most of those who knew him could really grasp.

He had planted his first wood in Dorsington in 1996. Called Ralph's Wood (named after Felix's first farm forester), it included more than 7,000 trees, which ranged from oak to hazel and rowan to hornbeam. Many more woods followed over the next few years and, as Felix's vision grew, so too did his confidence. Between 2003 and 2004, he planted over 58,000 trees.

By 2009, the figure had risen to over half a million British broadleaf trees. Although he would occasionally snap when naively asked whether he was salving his conscience at using trees to make magazines, more often than not he would patiently explain to journalists that the trees used to make newspapers and magazines were a crop, sustainably produced mostly in Scandinavia and that 'nobody chops down an oak tree to make pulp'.

Felix's motivation to plant what he hoped would one day become a connected series of woods, so extensive that it might form one of the largest forests in England, was to create an environment both wildlife and humans could enjoy – a haven from the commotion of modern life. It was a dream that he knew he would never live to see but one he was passionate enough about to leave the bulk of his fortune to. The Heart of England Forest Trust would receive all profits from his businesses and whatever other income could be gained from the dispersal of his estate. It was to help realise what he had called the 'impossible dream'.

At a small gathering around the spectacular swimming pool in Highfield on 27 June 2014, where Jon Snow remembered his friendship with Felix as an 'intoxicating experience' and described him as 'focused, determined, brilliant, cantankerous, loving, generous' but also 'absurd', he raised a toast to Felix's mother. She was to outlive her son by only 27 days.

With Felix flanked on either side by two life-sized sheep made entirely from spark plugs and a line of girlfriends around the coffin, the first strains of Brian Jones' guitar introducing the Rolling Stones' 'The Last Time' brought the sun out on what had been an otherwise dismal morning. A small troupe then followed Felix through his arboretum for one last journey to Dorsington Wood, where he was buried next to a one-and-a-half-times-size statue of himself holding a sapling.

A couple of weeks earlier, just two days before he had left Mustique, one of the projects that he had been working on had come to fruition – the provision of laptops for every schoolchild in St Vincent and the Grenadines. On 6 June 2014, the local newspaper on St Vincent announced in huge headlines, 'Laptops Here'. Twelve thousand five hundred Acer notebooks had been received at the port by the Prime Minister, Dr Gonsalves. In his address the Prime Minister thanked all those who had helped make this gift a reality, including Felix Dennis and Dennis Publishing. He pointed out that students from St Vincent and the Grenadines would now 'not be left behind' – 'There are not many countries in the world,' he said, 'where the primary and secondary schoolchildren all have laptops.'

The deal to provide them, a combination of efforts from Acer, Microsoft, Trend Micro and Dennis Publishing, along with a grant from the Bolivarian Republic of Venezuela, had given Felix much pride. In a foreword to a Dennis Publishing MagBook, produced to help the students get to grips with their new laptops and written before they had arrived, Felix had pointed out that Dennis Publishing was an entrepreneurial company and that many of the businesses that start today begin with a laptop and an idea.

'Now that your laptop is in your hands,' he wrote, 'the rest is up to you!'

The provision of those laptops was an important part of Felix's final days on Mustique and part of his legacy to St Vincent and the Grenadines, but the question that many people asked was what would Felix Dennis's overall legacy really be?

Would it be the trees, the Heart of England Forest, he had been so passionate about? Would it be the poetry that had touched so many people, the words that he had so brilliantly teased into form? Might it even be the effect of the *Oz* generation? Or would it be Dennis Publishing, the company that he founded more than 40 years before his death? Everyone had an opinion but there was no unequivocal answer. The likelihood is that it will be a combination of all, but two things very quickly became intertwined.

Sitting in a tearoom in Tottenham Street, London at the end of March 2015, James Tye, CEO of Dennis Publishing and the man responsible for the future of Felix's business legacy, was relaxed. 'Felix is in our DNA,' he explained. 'He trained us all very well.' He then stated that the company is as entrepreneurial and opportunistic as ever and in better shape than it has been at any other time. In the previous nine months they had either acquired or launched six new brands. However, there is one enormous and unique difference in its aspiration for the future: everyone working at Dennis now has a goal beyond the normal purpose of a commercial enterprise. Every penny of profit the company makes goes towards the planting of the largest forest in the UK, a forest that Jon Snow referred to as a 'lung' for the heart of England.

It's a goal that has been embraced at every level of Felix's company. New employees who go on tree-planting days grasp the vision immediately and enthusiastically. Steve Fowler, editor-in-chief of *Auto Express*, pointed out that having the largest native broadleaf forest in England 'is something to be really proud of'. Alison Hunter, head of HR at Dennis Publishing and a trustee of the Heart of England charity, says that visiting the forest and seeing the scale of the dream gives staff a 'greater connection' with Felix's ambition. Holden Frith, editor of *The Week* online in the UK, shares the view that there is now a greater purpose to ensuring the future success of the business. 'When we come to work, rather than working to enrich an individual or a group of shareholders,' he says, 'we are instead working to contribute to something that will benefit the landscape and the environment for generations to come.'

James Tye perhaps summed up one of the more surprising benefits. 'For the company it's been an absolute slam dunk,' he observed. 'They actually prefer working for the forest.' Explaining that in many ways there is now a much more substantial objective, he said that most people in the company never saw Felix, nor had a real connection with him. 'They feel very warm about working for the forest,' he said. 'It's an epic legacy and it's tangible.'

With extraordinary foresight, it appears that Felix Dennis managed to weave his impossible dream into his company and, by taking himself out of the picture, left a clear path for his business to grow, both metaphorically and commercially.

At a memorial on 4 October 2014, held in an enormous marquee in a field below his Dorsington home, Felix's old friend Jim Anderson pointed out that, if there was a highway to Hell and a stairway to Heaven, Felix was likely to have taken a Segway to a place of his own creation. He recalled – with no shortage of emotion – the evening when he and Felix had put together the cover of *Oz* magazine that had resulted in thousands of people from their generation standing up for change. As Jim danced his way from the stage to tumultuous applause from those who had survived the era, as well as those who had lived through other parts of Felix's life, another level of his legacy crystallised.

This was a party that Felix would have approved of. In fact, it was one of many that he had requested as part of his last wishes. He had hoped that his friends and colleagues would enjoy his world and the world that he envisioned, even without him in it.

And that, perhaps, represents one of the most enduring legacies of Felix Dennis – the people whose worlds he inhabited, and whose lives he enhanced. James Tye admitted that personally, and for many of his colleagues, there was a huge void.

'I'm surprised at how often I think of him,' he said, 'he was my friend and mentor.'

As his great friend Don Atyeo put it, Felix left a lot of legacies: successful businessman, philanthropist, bon vivant, 'free spirit who didn't take shit from anyone' and much-loved poet.

'But for me,' said Don, 'his legacy was his belief that, more than all the money, fame and power, in the end it's friendship that counts.'

ACKNOWLEDGEMENTS

To attempt to thank everyone who contributed to this book would be a lengthy task and inevitably someone would be omitted. However, I would like to thank all of those that gave their time and their memories of Felix, especially: Marie-France Demolis, Julian Dennis, Jim Anderson, Richard Neville, Dick Pountain, Marion Hills, Don Atyeo, Sue Ready, Peter Godfrey, Bob Bartner, Jon Snow, Brian Alexander, Dana Gillespie, Caroline Rush, Wendy Kasabian, Catherine Law, Sue Bandy, Toby Fisher, Hilary Bliss, David Bliss, Ian Leggett, James Tye, Suzen Murakoshi, Mark Williams, Cathy Galt, Maggie Kayley, Jerina Hardy, George Taylor, Jonathan Noone and Michael Hyman. I would also like to thank my family for accepting my absences and unsociable working hours. Thank you also to all at Ebury, especially Sara Cywinski. And of course a special thank you to Felix Dennis.